ECONOMIC EVOLUTION AND REVOLUTION IN HISTORICAL TIME

ECONOMIC EVOLUTION AND REVOLUTION IN HISTORICAL TIME

Edited by
Paul W. Rhode, Joshua L. Rosenbloom,
and David F. Weiman

STANFORD ECONOMICS AND FINANCE

An Imprint of Stanford University Press

Stanford, California

Stanford University Press
Stanford, California

Printed in the United States of America on acid-free,
archival-quality paper

Library of Congress Cataloging-in-Publication Data

Economic evolution and revolution in historical time / edited by
Paul W. Rhode, Joshua L. Rosenbloom, and David F. Weiman.
p. cm.
Papers originally presented at a conference sponsored by Stanford
University's Institute for Economic Policy Research (SIEPR) and held
Sept. 26–27, 2008.
Includes bibliographical references and index.
ISBN 978-0-8047-7185-6 (cloth : alk. paper)
1. United States—Economic conditions—19th century—
Congresses. 2. United States—Economic conditions—20th century—
Congresses. 3. Economic history—Congresses. I. Rhode,
Paul Webb. II. Rosenbloom, Joshua L. III. Weiman, David F.
IV. Stanford Institute for Economic Policy Research.
HC105.E35 2011
330.9—dc22   2010033458

Designed by Bruce Lundquist
Typeset by Westchester Book Composition in 10/15 Sabon

For Gavin and Cathe for opening their hearts, home, and minds to us.

Contents

Contributors

JEREMY ATACK is Professor of Economics and History at Vanderbilt University, Research Associate of the National Bureau of Economic Research, and former coeditor of the *Journal of Economic History*. His recent publications include *The Origins and Development of Financial Markets and Institutions* (2009, coedited with Larry Neal) and coauthored papers in the *Economic History Review* (2005), *Explorations in Economic History* (2008), and *Social Science History* (2010).

LEONARD A. CARLSON is Associate Professor of Economics at Emory University. His previous publications include "Indian Removal, 'Squatterism,' and Slavery: Economic Interests and the Passage of the Indian Removal Act of 1830," *Explorations in Economic History* (2006) and *Indians, Bureaucrats and Land: The Dawes Act and the Decline of Indian Farming* (1981).

SUSAN B. CARTER is Professor Emeritus at the University of California, Riverside. She is one of the general editors of *Historical Statistics of the United States, Millennial Edition* (2006) and editor of the chapters on labor, immigration, cohorts, and utilities.

KAREN CLAY is Associate Professor of Economics at the Heinz College, Carnegie Mellon University. Her previous (coauthored) work on natural resources includes "Migrating to Riches? Evidence from the California Gold Rush," *Journal of Economic History* (2008) and "Order without Law? Property Rights during the California Gold Rush," *Explorations in Economic History* (2005).

ROBERT K. FLECK is Professor of Economics at Montana State University. His recent publications include work on the New Deal (*Journal of*

Political Economy, 2008), joint work with F. Andrew Hanssen on democracy and women's rights in ancient Greece (*Journal of Law and Economics*, 2006; *Economics of Governance*, 2009), and joint work with Christopher Kilby on foreign aid (*Journal of Development Economics*, 2010).

ROB GILLEZEAU is a doctoral candidate in the Department of Economics at the University of Michigan. He is writing a dissertation on the impact of the Community Action Program on the 1960s race riots and the development of the American labor movement during World War II.

GEORGE GRANTHAM is Professor Emeritus of Economics at McGill University. His recent publications include "Explaining the Industrial Transition: A Non-Malthusian Perspective," *European Review of Economic History* (2008); "The Industrious Revolution and Labour Force Participation of Rural Women: Evidence from Mid-Nineteenth-Century France," in *The Birth of Modern Europe: Culture and Economy 1400–1800*, edited by Laura Cruz (2010); and "What's Space Got to Do with It? Distance and Agricultural Productivity before the Railway Age," *Journal of Economic History* (forthcoming).

MICHAEL HAINES is the Banfi Vintners Professor of Economics at Colgate University. Besides his joint work with Jeremy Atack and Robert A. Margo, his recent publications in the area of historical demography appeared in *Economics and Human Biology* (2008), *Demography* (2008), and *Review of Economics and Statistics* (2007).

STACEY M. JONES is Senior Lecturer in the Albers School of Business and Economics at Seattle University. Her research is on the historical development of the labor force in the United States, focusing on education, gender, and inequality.

FRANK LEVY is a labor economist in the Massachusetts Institute of Technology's Department of Urban Studies and Planning. His recent publications include "How Technology Changes Demands for Human Skills," OECD Directorate for Education Working Paper (2010), and

"Offshoring Professional Services: Institutions and Professional Control," *British Journal of Industrial Relations* (forthcoming).

ROBERT A. MARGO is Professor and Chair in the Department of Economics at Boston University and a Research Associate of the National Bureau of Economic Research. He is the author of *Race and Schooling in the South, 1880–1950: An Economic History* (1990) and *Wages and Labor Markets in the United States, 1820–1860* (2000).

ALAN L. OLMSTEAD is Distinguished Research Professor of Economics and a member of the Giannini Foundation of Agricultural Economics at the University of California, Davis. He is one of the general editors of *Historical Statistics of the United States, Millennial Edition* (2006), and coauthor (with Paul W. Rhode) of *Creating Abundance: Biological Innovation and American Agricultural Development* (2008).

SCOTT A. REDENIUS is Senior Lecturer in the Department of Economics at Brandeis University. His recent publications include "Designing a National Currency: Antebellum Payment Networks and the Structure of the National Banking System," *Financial History Review* (2007) and "New National Bank Loan Rate Estimates, 1887–1975," *Research in Economic History* (2007).

PAUL W. RHODE is Professor of Economics at the University of Michigan and a Research Associate of the National Bureau of Economic Research. He is coauthor (with Alan Olmstead) of *Creating Abundance: Biological Innovation and American Agricultural Development* (2008) and coeditor (with Gianni Toniolo) of *The Global Economy in the 1990s: A Long-Run Perspective* (2006).

JOSHUA L. ROSENBLOOM is Professor of Economics and Associate Vice Provost for Research and Graduate Studies at the University of Kansas, and a Research Associate of the National Bureau of Economic Research. He recently edited *Quantitative Economic History: The Good of Counting* (2008), and he is the author of *Looking for Work, Searching for*

Workers: Labor Markets during American Industrialization (2002) as well as numerous articles on the historical development of U.S. labor markets.

WILLIAM A. SUNDSTROM is Professor of Economics at Santa Clara University. He is the author of numerous articles, including "The Geography of Wage Discrimination in the Pre–Civil Rights South," *Journal of Economic History* (2007), and coeditor (with Timothy Guinnane and Warren Whatley) of *History Matters: Essays on Economic Growth, Technology, and Demographic Change* (2004).

RICHARD SUTCH is Distinguished Professor Emeritus of Economics at the University of California, Riverside and a Research Associate of the National Bureau of Economic Research. He is one of the general editors of *Historical Statistics of the United States, Millennial Edition* (2006), and editor of the chapters on national income, business cycles, savings, slavery, immigration, industrial classification, and the courts and criminal justice.

PETER TEMIN is Gray Professor Emeritus of Economics at the Massachusetts Institute of Technology. His most recent (coauthored) books are *The World Economy between the World Wars* (2008) and *Reasonable RX: Solving the Drug Price Crisis* (2008).

TA-CHEN WANG is Assistant Professor of Economics at California State University, Sacramento. His recent publications include "Paying Back to Borrow More: Reputation and Bank Credit Access in Early America," *Explorations in Economic History* (2008), and "Banks, Credit Markets, and Early American Development—A Case Study of Entry and Competition," *Journal of Economic History* (2008).

DAVID F. WEIMAN is Alena Wels Hirschorn '58 Professor of Economics at Barnard College and an affiliated member of Columbia University's History Department. His recent coauthored publications include "From Drafts to Checks: The Evolution of Correspondent Banking Networks and the Formation of the Modern U.S. Payments System," *Journal of Money, Credit, and Banking* (2010), and "The Political Economy of the U.S. Monetary Union: The Civil War Era as a Watershed," *American Economic Review, Papers and Proceedings* (2007).

WARREN C. WHATLEY is Professor of Economics at the University of Michigan. His recent publications include "The Most Significant Racial Integration in American History," *Labor History* (2007), and *History Matters: Essays on Economic Growth, Technology, and Demographic Change* (coedited with Timothy Guinnane and William Sundstrom, 2004).

SUSAN WOLCOTT is Associate Professor of Economics at Binghamton University. Her most recent publications include "An Examination of the Supply of Financial Credit to Entrepreneurs in Colonial India," in *The Invention of Enterprise*, edited by David S. Landes, Joel Mokyr, and William J. Baumol (2009), and "Strikes in Colonial India, 1921–1938," *Industrial and Labor Relations Review* (2008).

GAVIN WRIGHT is the William Robertson Coe Professor of American Economic History at Stanford University, where he has taught since 1982. His latest publication (with Gary R. Saxonhouse) is "National Leadership and Competing Technological Paradigms: The Globalization of Cotton Spinning, 1878–1933," *Journal of Economic History* (2010). Professor Wright has a long-standing interest in the economy of the American South and has published three books on that subject, most recently *Slavery and American Economic Development* (2006).

Editors' Introduction

THE CONTRIBUTIONS to this volume were first aired at a conference sponsored by Stanford University's Institute for Economic Policy Research (SIEPR). The occasion was a celebration of the luminous career of Gavin Wright, a senior fellow at the institute and a member of the Stanford Economics Department faculty since 1982. The conference assembled Wright's past PhD students and close peers to reflect on his myriad contributions to the political economic history of the United States and to a historically informed practice of economics.

The intent was not simply to recollect Wright's scholarly and pedagogic influences. The organizing committee—Avner Greif, Timothy Guinnane, and William Sundstrom—asked speakers to address the dominant themes of Wright's research and teaching. This research cannot be reduced to a single methodological approach. If anything, Wright has made a virtue of a historically and theoretically informed eclecticism that draws inspiration from economics and other social sciences. Following one of his own mentors William Parker, Wright has insisted that economic history must still be history, not just economics, so that it can fruitfully engage colleagues in adjacent disciplines. He has also advocated a healthy respect for the evidence and its limitations and cautioned against the use of excessively complex analytical and statistical models as a substitute for actual historical research.

Substantively, Wright's research has brought greater clarity to some of the most perplexing issues of U.S. history, economic or otherwise. Through a steadfast skepticism of the conventional wisdom, he has always recognized that the first step to "getting the right answers" is "asking the right questions." The broad scope of Wright's research "questions" and "answers" resists easy classification, but most of his published work can be organized around three broad themes: regional development, slavery and freedom, and the dynamics of historical economic change.[1]

Wright's work on regional economies starts from the conventional premise that natural resource endowments exert a powerful effect on regional development, in delineating the climatic boundaries of the nineteenth-century Cotton South or in laying the raw materials foundation for U.S. industrial hegemony in the twentieth century. He has, however, rejected geographic determinism and instead advanced an alternative conception of the region that hinges on formative institutions, whether plantation slavery in the Cotton South or subsoil property rights in the western United States. In his typical fashion, however, Wright has never seen the problem in dichotomous terms, as resource endowments versus institutions. Instead, his more nuanced approach recognized the complementarities between what some have called a region's *first* and *second* nature and showed how their mutual interactions forged distinctive paths of regional economic development. His explanation of the American export invasion of Europe, for example, regards the country's rich diverse mineral endowments as a *necessary* condition, whose systematic economic exploitation depended on the property rights regime and the cumulative development of capacities in areas ranging from geology and metallurgy to distribution and marketing.

Nowhere is Wright's approach more evident than in his research in understanding the historical specificity of slave and free labor in the Americas and in turn the regional differences between slave and free states. Wright conceives of slave and free labor as complex amalgams of economic and social relationships embedded within families, farms (i.e., units of production), and the larger political economy, and not simply as polar abstractions. At a more micro level, he recognizes the degrees of difference between free and slave labor—the elements of coercion on family farms and in factories in the North and of choice in the incentive systems on southern slave plantations. His most recent book, *Slavery and American Economic Development*, takes a more macro approach, viewing free and slave labor as alternative "property rights" and, ultimately, political regimes that biased economic incentives and wealth accumulation in the North and South but also sparked interregional political competition and conflict akin to cold war rivalries.

For Wright the central methodological question is not whether, but how, history matters. Following the thrust of much "new" economic history, he has embraced an *evolutionary* view of economic development, which emphasizes incremental cumulative changes in population, natural resources, and technology. In *The Political Economy of the Cotton South*, for example, he shows how the rapid growth of world cotton demand before 1860 diffused slavery and the plantation system across the southern frontier and in turn carved out a distinct regional *cotton* economy. He has also revived an older tradition that divides historical development into distinct epochs punctuated by *revolutionary* structural changes. This perspective is elaborated in *Old South, New South*, where he delineates the manifold impacts of the Civil War and emancipation on the southern economy.

The real challenge, of course, is how to reconcile these perspectives. Wright offers a tantalizing synthesis in which history truly matters. Gradual cumulative changes, he suggests, set the stage for, but do not dictate, the nature and direction of revolutionary change. The latter depend on historical agency in the form of collective decisions and actions, whether undertaken by the informal associations of civil society or the various levels and branches of government. In his contribution to *Reckoning with Slavery*, for example, Wright spoke of the "internal contradictions" of the antebellum Cotton South. Its increasing economic dependence on the fleecy staple, he argued, would inexorably lead to relative economic stagnation, but not emancipation, after 1860. Most recently, in work with Paul David, he has analyzed how the gradual diffusion of the electric motor and the cumulative innovations in this and complementary technologies paved the way for a second industrial revolution, whose full fruits awaited the advent of a truly "high wage" economy thanks in part to New Deal policies.

Mirroring Wright's diverse interests and approaches, conference participants tackled a broad array of topics in U.S. and global economic history. Some authors generalized Wright's analyses to comprehend the impacts of the New Deal and civil rights revolutions on national, not just southern, labor markets and politics. Others took his institutional perspectives on regional development to new shores and new sectors. And still others extended the disciplinary scope of the agenda, and in true *Wrightian* fashion challenged received wisdoms, even those of Wright himself, on the paradoxes of slavery and Americans' *mineral mindedness*, to borrow Parker's felicitous phrase.

After two days of stimulating presentations and avid discussion, it became clear to us that this commemoration had taken on a life of its own.[2] Collected into an edited volume, the papers would constitute an independent scholarly contribution to the field of economic history but also to a more historically informed economics. Substantively, the essays naturally fell into three broad thematic areas corresponding to the sections of this volume: (1) evolutionary economic change, (2) regional development, and (3) revolutions in labor markets. As important, they all combine historical and economic perspectives to understand the past as well as the dynamics of change in real, that is, historical, time.

As the introductory chapter by Gavin Wright makes clear, this outcome was not an accident but can be traced to the sometimes obvious and otherwise subtle influences of a Stanford tradition of economic history. The Stanford faculty, Wright asserts, does not have a monopoly over these approaches and substantive issues. But, as he also shows, they have been tackling them for over half a century. Through the training of new generations of economic historians and through their (and their students') myriad interactions with colleagues, their scholarly labors have had a formative impact on the practice and direction of economic historical research.

Coincidentally the Stanford conference took place at the very moment—September 26 and 27, 2008—of the U.S. and global financial meltdown. This crisis was so potentially catastrophic that it invited obvious comparisons to the Great Crash of 1929 and the banking panics of the early 1930s. None of the contributions in this volume directly addresses the specific macroeconomic issues raised by the recent credit crisis and "Great Recession." Nonetheless, they do, we believe, offer valuable lessons on the dynamics of historical economic change that are directly relevant to the current debates among economists and policy makers.

Many in the economics profession have dismissed recent events as mere blips on the radar screen, transitory departures from a stable equilibrium path. Grounded in an *ahistorical* equilibrium way of thinking, their reaction is not too surprising, at least to us. But as historians and historically minded economists, we are disciplinarily inclined to connect the dots and to cogitate upon their implications. In particular, the essays in this volume challenge the more conventional ways of thinking in the economics profession and invite a fresh perspective to view recent events, one that conceives history as a succession of evolutionary but also revolutionary moments. Indeed, as several contributions illustrate, recent economic events bear many of the hallmarks of earlier crises, which precipitated revolutionary economic change in the past. Thus, following in Wright's path, we hope to show the relevance of economic history and historical economics to contemporary issues but at the same time to avoid the pitfalls of a too-alluring presentism.

The Stanford Institute for Economic Policy Research provided generous financial and administrative support in convening the conference. We are indebted to its director, John Shoven, for his warm embrace of our gathering, which made this volume possible. In addition, we thank Deborah Carvalho and Dafna Baldwin at SIEPR, whose attention to the myriad logistical details before and during the conference assured its success. Publication of this volume was facilitated by a generous subvention from SIEPR and the Stanford Department of Economics. In addition to Shoven, we thank Lawrence Goulder, the department chair, for his timely support. Barnard College, the University of Kansas Department of Economics, and the University of Michigan Department of Economics also provided financial support for this project.

While we assumed responsibilities for editing the volume, our task was feasible only because of the intellectual labors by Avner Greif, Timothy Guinnane, and William Sundstrom, who were responsible for the conference program. As editors we were most fortunate to work with an exceptional group of scholars and benefited greatly from the advice and support of our editor at Stanford University Press, Margo Beth Crouppen, and her assistant, Jessica Walsh. We also benefited from the advice and encouragement of the readers selected by the press to review our manuscript.

Finally, we wish to express our gratitude to Gavin Wright, whose scholarly research has set an example for all involved in this project. We are indebted to him not only for the inspiration that his scholarship provides but for his steadfast friendship, support, and encouragement.

NOTES

1. A selected list of Wright's publications is included as an appendix to this volume.

2. Discussion at the conference and so the quality of this volume were enhanced by the contributions of, among others, Ran Abramitzky, Kenneth Arrow, Charles Calomiris, Herrick Chapman, Latika Chaudhary, Gregory Clark, Liz Cohen, Jan De Vreis, Alexander Field, Stephen Haber, Howard Kunreuther, Naomi Lamoreaux, Phillip Mirowski, Joel Mokyr, Chiaki Moriguchi, Petra Moser, John Pencavel, Kerry Pannell, Arlene Saxenhouse, Masao Suzuki, and Richard White.

ECONOMIC EVOLUTION
AND REVOLUTION IN
HISTORICAL TIME

CHAPTER I

The Stanford Tradition in Economic History

GAVIN WRIGHT

STANFORD UNIVERSITY HAS a long and distinguished tradition in economic history, many elements of which are richly on display in the present volume. The purpose of this essay is to offer a brief synopsis of this backstory and to point out some of the linkages between these contributions and the Stanford tradition. It may be hoped that non-Stanford participants and readers will forgive the measure of chauvinistic exaggeration inevitably associated with such an exercise. Certainly Stanford has no monopoly or exclusive claim to any of the ideas discussed here. But identifying intellectual legacies and continuities is part of the historical craft and as such needs no apology. If the effort helps future practitioners to motivate and frame issues pertaining to historical economics, then perhaps it will have some redeeming social value beyond mere nostalgia.

To quote from the letter we send to prospective graduate students: "The hallmark of the Stanford tradition may be summarized in the expression 'History Matters,' which is to say that we think of ourselves as active participants in the discipline of economics, upholding the view that historical events and processes make a difference for economic outcomes."[1] We sometimes trace our heritage back to Thorstein Veblen, who taught at Stanford from 1906 to 1909 and is often identified as the founder of institutional economics. But unlike many earlier institutionalisms, economic history at Stanford has never been "anti-economics." We accept economics as the parent discipline but insist that good practice should consider the historical context within which economic processes occur. In this way, Stanford economic history dissents not just from unhistorical economics but from approaches to historical research that make no such methodological distinction—sometimes referred to as "applied economics with old data." This case was articulated in Veblen's time by Frederick Jackson Turner, in his 1910 presidential address to the American Historical Association:

The economic historian is in danger of making his analysis and his statement on the basis of present conditions and then passing to history for justificatory appendixes to his conclusions. . . . In fact the pathway of history is strewn with the wrecks of the "known and acknowledged truths" of economic law, due not only to defective analysis and imperfect statistics, but also to the lack of critical historical methods, to insufficient historical-mindedness on the part of the economist, to failure to give due attention to the relativity and transiency of the conditions from which his laws were deduced. (Turner 1911, pp. 231–232)

The challenge has been to transmute this largely negative critique into a positive agenda for historical research that meets the standards and informs the understanding of both parent disciplines. It should be evident in what follows that the Stanford tradition in economic history does not offer a standardized methodological recipe. Good research in historical economics may be abstract and theoretical, cliometric, archival, or some combination of these, as appropriate for the question at hand. What counts is the commitment to taking history and historical processes seriously in addressing economic topics. The intellectual underpinnings of the historical approach have been ably expounded and demonstrated by my Stanford colleagues over the years.

INFLUENTIAL ECONOMIC HISTORIANS AT STANFORD

In the 1950s, 1960s, and 1970s economic history was shaped with a distinctive Stanford flavor by Moses Abramovitz, Paul David, and Nathan Rosenberg. Moe Abramovitz became widely known in the 1950s as one of the founders of growth-accounting, when his pioneering work with national income statistics revealed (at about the same time as Robert Solow) that most historical output growth could not be explained by the expansion of labor and capital (Abramovitz 1956). But Moe always insisted that the residual gap between output and inputs should not be identified as "technological change." It was merely, he said, "a measure of our ignorance." Moe's later work in collaboration with Paul David put historical flesh on this skepticism by showing that the "stylized fact" attributing most U.S. growth to the residual held only for the twentieth century, contrasting with the nineteenth century dominated by the expansion of land, labor, and capital. Not, they hastened to say, because there was "no technological progress" in the nineteenth century but because new technologies in that era were *biased* in a labor-saving, capital-using direction. Abramovitz and David (1993) argued that U.S. economic history should be conceptualized as a series of disequilibrium traverses between stable growth paths, the shifts between them driven by deep changes in the underlying technologies. Their position, in other words, was that macroeconomic trends and fluctuations should be interpreted in historical context, using frameworks that allow for the possibility of epochal shifts between eras. The subsequent record of unanticipated shifts in prevailing macroeconomic regularities amply confirms the wisdom of this broad perspective. Moe continued to wrestle with these matters for the rest of his life.[2]

An important aspect of historical economics is technology and, going further, the institutions of a society that generate and direct technological change. Long before coming to Stanford in 1974, Nate Rosenberg was writing economic history from "inside the black box" of technology, well beyond the boundaries most economists impose on themselves. The central theme of Nate's work has been to show that economics can gain from viewing technologies from the perspective of inventors, engineers, and innovating firms. To be sure, most technological change is driven by economic motives. But innovators cannot give equal attention to all possible directions of change, and Nate shows that new opportunities often emerge to technicians as a "sequence of engineering challenges" with an apparent internal logic of their own. The resulting historical trajectories are deeply path dependent, implying, as Nate has always argued, that "the most probable directions for future growth in knowledge can only be understood within the context of the particular sequence of events which constitutes the history of the system."[3] Economic historians feel that we were studying endogenous technological change long before the advent of new growth theory. But to do so in a substantive as opposed to a formalistic manner means taking technology history seriously.[4]

Urging economists to take history seriously has been Paul David's mission throughout his long career. Paul arrived at Stanford in 1962, still working on his dissertation on the economic history of Chicago.

3

Harvard awarded Paul a PhD in 1973, not because he had finished the thesis but on the basis of a collection of already-published articles. Among the many topics on which Paul has worked over the years, perhaps the biggest impact has come from his articulation of the intellectual basis for historical economics in the concept of "path dependence," using the persistence of the QWERTY typewriter keyboard as a metaphorical illustration.[5] Stanford was a hotbed of historical thinking related to technology in the mid-1980s, as Paul, Nate Rosenberg, Brian Arthur, Kenneth Arrow, and numerous visitors and graduate students thrashed out and debated these concepts and their implications.[6]

Out of this milieu came the second of Paul's major impact papers, "The Dynamo and the Computer," which appeared in 1990, in the midst of the productivity slowdown known as the "Solow Paradox": If productivity growth is generated mainly by new technology, why was productivity stagnant in the midst of dramatic advances in computer technology? Paul suggested an analogy between computers and electrification, in which major productivity effects lagged by a full generation behind the breakthroughs in technical feasibility (David 1990 and a fuller version, David 1991). Why the delay? Because diffusion of electric power required complementary investments in infrastructure, and exploiting the productivity potential of electrification required a new capital stock designed with this purpose in mind, plus reconfiguration of work routines on the shop floor. All of these processes took time, and they came to fruition in a discontinuous manner during the U.S. investment boom of the 1920s. The productivity surge after 1995, closely associated with computers and other information technology, has given Paul's paper iconic status.

Path dependence and QWERTY are often mischaracterized as pertaining to narrow issues and anomalies in the history of technology. But Paul has always stressed that the QWERTY keyboard is meant as a broader metaphor for historical economics. Societies feature many other types of persistence in institutions, norms, locational patterns, and other realms of economic life. Not that any of these are permanently "locked in" to a single unchanged status forever. But they tend to change in an incremental, evolutionary manner, constrained by the legacy of the past. As Paul puts it, institutions are the "carriers of history" because they represent solutions to historical coordination problems, often built on complex codes and information channels with many of the properties of highly durable capital goods (David 1994).

I came to Stanford in 1982, in the midst of writing a book on the economic development of the U.S. South since the Civil War. Stanford was an attractive place for an economic historian, largely because of the strength of the faculty (especially after the arrival of Steve Haber in 1985) but also because of the rich harvest of graduate students working on historical topics. This intellectual setting helped me to formulate the thesis of *Old South, New South*, which was that the southern economy was characterized not by the survival of slave-like institutions but by persistent regionalism in the labor market. Low-income southerners were geographically mobile, blacks as well as whites, but prior to World War I their migration routes were east–west rather than south–north. These patterns were of course shaped by culture, geography, and politics, but the labor market in turn accentuated regional distinctiveness along all of these dimensions. In short, the South became locked into a low-wage political-economic equilibrium, vividly illustrating the powerful role of history in spatial economic processes.

In the late 1980s, with Paul David's encouragement, I began to broaden my horizons beyond the South to the larger issue of U.S. development in comparative and international context. At a time when Japanese innovations seemed to be overwhelming American industries, we began a search for the historical origins of U.S. "technological leadership." As often happens in historical research, the quest turned in an unexpected direction when I discovered that the most salient characteristic of U.S. manufacturing exports during the country's surge to world leadership (roughly 1890–1910) was intensity in nonreproducible natural resources. Thus began a preoccupation with minerals that has captivated me ever since. Because the United States was the world's leading producer of virtually every major industrial mineral during this era, at first glance it appeared that industrial leadership was the fortuitous result of generous geological endowment. Over time, however, Paul and I came to the conclusion that the United States was no better endowed with minerals than other large nations. Abundance instead derived from early development of the country's mineral potential, through investments in physical capital, exploration, human capital, and, above all, diverse forms of knowledge (Wright 1990; David and Wright 1997). This insight proved more far-reaching than we could have imagined, implying that so-called natural resources are not really natural but socially constructed as an economic matter, a perspective that mainstream economists find extraordinarily difficult to absorb.

Paul David and I worked together on several projects over the years, but no collaborative effort was more fruitful than recruiting, promoting, and retaining Avner Greif at Stanford. Superficially, Avner's background and methodology—a Northwestern University PhD whose research specialties were game theory and medieval trade—might seem very different from those just described. But it did not take long after his arrival in 1989 for a deep sense of common purpose to emerge, in Avner's insistence on the essentially historical character of the institutions that allowed long-distance medieval trade to flourish in the absence of formal legal enforcement systems. In a series of stunning papers published in the mid-1990s Avner launched an interpretive paradigm known as "historical institutional analysis" that was at once more rigorous and more historical than earlier approaches.[7] The core perspective is that "institutions" should be understood not as exogenously specified constraints on individual behavior but as the outcome of historical processes in which individual responses to a structure also serve to reproduce that structure. Characterizing institutions as equilibria in a game theory setting is a powerful way to encapsulate this view. The real payoff, however, has been to use this framework to generate persuasive historical narratives for understanding fundamental economic phenomena. An example would be Avner's contrast between the "collectivist" Maghribi traders of the eleventh century and the "individualist" Italian city-states—each one a viable institutional "solution" to agency problems in long-distance trade but with very different implications for the subsequent evolution of these societies.[8]

EVOLUTIONARY PROCESSES IN ECONOMICS

All of the essays in Part One highlight the role of historical context in shaping the early development of institutions that became economically significant at a later phase. Although he has never had formal association with Stanford, George Grantham (Chapter 3) fits nicely into the tradition just described. Grantham argues that the "institutionalization" of science in European universities between 1780 and 1850 represented a resolution of emerging problems specific to that era; he suggests that the observed outcome, far from being inevitable, was "historically unlikely." Yet establishment of an institutional apparatus capable of supporting careers in science, verifying scientific claims, assigning credit, and rewarding novel findings was crucial for Western economic progress across the next two centuries and beyond. As Grantham notes, his analysis complements Paul David's (2008) account of the rise of the social network known as "open science" in seventeenth-century Europe. In that story princes competed for the services of renowned scientists for reasons of court prestige but also to advise their patrons on the validity of novel scientific claims advanced by others. The outcome of this process was a transnational system that encouraged rapid public disclosure of new findings, in hopes of validation and consequent recognition (and reward) for priority in discovery. Though modified in innumerable ways across the centuries, these early mechanisms are recognizable in scientific validation and reward systems in our own times.

The idea that knowledge generation depends on institutional arrangements may not surprise economists, but Karen Clay (Chapter 2) extends this thought into what is still unfamiliar territory to nonhistorical economists, in suggesting that the American minerals sector circa 1900 was an integral part of the "knowledge economy" of its day.[9] If this is so, Clay asks, why then have many resource-rich nations performed poorly in modern times? Her answer is that such countries have not developed their resource potential as the United States has, through an indigenous historical process, but have instead experienced mineral production as an exogenous shock from the outside, an enclave with limited linkages to the rest of the economy. This insight is broadly consistent with the findings of Stephen Haber and Victor Menaldo (2010), whose exhaustive quantitative studies show (contrary to widespread "resource curse" theorizing) that political regimes have virtually never been created or destroyed by resource discoveries.[10] Thus historical studies of resource-based development have indeed become a Stanford tradition.

Leonard A. Carlson (Chapter 5) and Warren C. Whatley and Rob Gillezeau (Chapter 4) deal with historical encounters between Europeans and indigenous peoples and demonstrate the enduring impact of early experiences on long-term outcomes. When a set of socioeconomic relationships becomes entrenched ("locked in" by analogy to technologies) for extended periods, it can be difficult to imagine that any historical alternative was possible. Economic historians often face the challenge of persuading readers or students that history really could have gone in a different direction. Carlson's response to this challenge is to draw on comparative history, contrasting the negotiated territorial treaties with American Indians—which often seemed little more than fictitious legal veneers for displacement and expropriation—with the Australian theory that native peoples had no prior claim to land recognized by the law. Because legal evolution is precedent based, it is path dependent virtually by design. As biased as both legal systems undoubtedly were in practice, Carlson shows that their differing starting points did make a difference for the outcomes. History mattered.

Showing the plausibility of an alternative historical path is nowhere more challenging than in the case of African development in relationship to European contact. Generations of Africans and sympathetic scholars have attributed African underdevelopment to the slave trade, but these assertions have generally been dismissed by economists as ideologically driven exercises in special pleading. Indeed, the rhetoric of blame-shifting goes back to the days of the slave trade itself. The chapter by Whatley and Gillezeau is an important contribution to a major reconsideration of this history now under way, as historical economists strive to replace rhetoric with more dispassionate analysis and evidence.[11] Whatley and Gillezeau's central premise is that Africa's condition of weak states, ethnic rivalries, and violence should not be understood as reflections of an autonomous geographic culture ("bad institutions" in the parlance of development economics) but instead were the outcomes of historical interactions between forces internal and external to the continent. Perhaps in response to the historically impoverished state of the development field in recent years, a number of shorthand historical-determinist hypotheses have recently found favor. From the perspective of the Stanford tradition, discovery of dramatic statistical correlations between beginnings and endpoints should be understood as only the beginning of the research agenda. It is encouraging to see scholars undertaking the more challenging task of tracking development across the intervening decades and centuries, in what may be envisioned as a rich new frontier for economic history.[12]

SPATIAL PROCESSES AND REGIONALISM
IN ECONOMIC HISTORY

A key feature of the Whatley-Gillezeau chapter is the analysis of the configuration of villages and states across the landscape of Africa, an exercise in political-economic geography. Spatial processes such as these have long been a source of discomfort for economics. The dominant tradition in the theory of international trade, for example, assumes that factors of production are fully mobile within countries but immobile between countries, effectively treating the nation as a dimensionless point in space. Empirical studies of comparative economic performance rarely move beyond this conceptual framework. Although the inadequacy of these assumptions is often noted, the practice persists, perhaps because when we open the black box of economic geography, both theoretical and empirical analyses quickly become complex. Possibly even more threatening is the realization that spatial models of economic activity are often indeterminate, which is a way of saying that the outcomes depend on history. Citing the work of Paul David and Brian Arthur, Paul Krugman (1991, p. 100) writes: "For at least insofar as the location of economic activity in space is concerned, the idea that an economy's form is largely shaped by historical contingency is not a metaphysical hypothesis; it is simply the obvious truth." To be sure, economic geography has its own venerable traditions, in such heterodox writers as Gunnar Myrdal, Albert Hirschman, and Nicholas Kaldor, and efforts to bring these ideas into the mainstream through formalized models are now in resurgence. But the upshot of these models is that economic geography requires explicit historical contextualization, which is where economic historians come in.[13]

The foremost geographic challenge in American economic history is the regional divergence between North and South, a topic to which I have now devoted three books (Wright 1978, 1986, 2006). One of the encouraging features of this profession is that even after forty years of work on a relatively specialized topic, one can still encounter new evidence and a reformulation that compels us to view the old issues in a new way. The feeling is especially warm when one of the authors is a Stanford man (Paul W. Rhode), writing in collaboration with one of the trailblazers for economic history in California (Alan L. Olmstead). The Olmstead-Rhode essay on the regional dynamics of development in the slave South (Chapter 8) should be read in conjunction with their other recent work bringing out the important but neglected role of biological innovation in American agricultural history (Olmstead and Rhode 2008a, 2008b). Here, they take up the old debate over how much of the apparent growth in the late antebellum slave economy was attributable to the one-time effects of migration onto the rich alluvial soils of the southwest, arriving at what seems to be a definitive answer: east–west shifts were critical for aggregate productivity growth, but their impact was magnified by dramatic improvements in the quality of the cotton plants— innovations particularly suited to western soils, which were better to start with and became "increasingly better" over time. Through all the debates over scale economies, effort levels, and management systems under slavery, this type of geographically biased technological progress was neglected, almost without exception.

Other spatial processes have always been central to economic history, such as the "transportation revolution" of nineteenth-century America. The essay by Jeremy Atack, Michael Haines, and Robert A. Margo (Chapter 7) extends their long-term study of U.S. manufacturing by examining the linkage at the county level between railroads and the rise of factories between 1850 and 1870. Their results suggest that improved access to rail transportation accounted for more than one-third of the expansion of factory production during these decades. In other words, industrialization was not driven exclusively by advances in manufacturing technology, and indeed one may plausibly conjecture that such technological advances were themselves encouraged by progress in transportation. These findings also shed light on the North–South divergence, because they imply that southern antebellum underperformance in manufacturing was attributable at least in part to regional underinvestment in transportation.

North–South regionalism persisted after the abolition of slavery, though its form changed. Scott A. Redenius and David F. Weiman (Chapter 9) explore an important aspect of this topic, underdevelopment of the southern banking system and credit markets. Not content to attribute the regional gap to generalized "backwardness" based on ignorance or lack of sophistication, the authors present a formal microeconomic analysis of the supply and demand for bank credit, a prime feature of which is that southern banks had to cope with extreme seasonality emanating from the cotton crop. High seasonality raised the cost of intermediation in the South, an effect aggravated by rigidities in the national banking system, which was primarily designed to serve the mixed-farming and industrial economies of the North and West. Behind financial dependence on the seasonality of one crop, of course, lay the broader underdevelopment of the regional economy, reflected in its lack of diversification. Nonetheless, these findings extend to the financial sector the broad argument that ostensibly "national" institutions and technologies were not well suited to the distinctive needs of regional economies—a condition giving rise to charges of "colonial" exploitation. This may not have been a satisfactory diagnosis to an economist, but, as the authors note, the lack of regional congruence was sufficient to induce most Cotton South banks to refuse membership in the Federal Reserve.

The fit between banking and economic structure is also the subject of Ta-Chen Wang's comparative study of Boston and Philadelphia in the early nineteenth century (Chapter 6). Modern growth economists routinely list financial development as a key determinant of a country's economic performance, a proposition often supported by economic historians (see Sylla 2002). But Wang shows that at a time in U.S. history when banks were largely governed by state legislation, these two industrializing cities had systems that looked very different from each other. In Massachusetts many banks operated as virtual arms of big textile corporations, a phenomenon dubbed "insider lending" by Naomi Lamoreaux (1994). Philadelphia had fewer and larger banks, which concentrated on short-term commercial loans to merchants. Differences in industrial structure mirrored those of banks, Philadelphia featuring greater industrial diversity, more proprietorships, rental rather than ownership of capital, and so on.

Rather than seeing one-way causal effects of banking on industry or vice versa, it is more natural for an economic historian to characterize these as patterns of mutual adaptation and coevolution, beginning from somewhat different starting points and arriving at distinct regional equilibrium outcomes. In the abstract it would be difficult to rank either system as inherently superior to the other. But the case supports and enhances Philip Scranton's (1983) point that American industrial history has much more diversity than is commonly acknowledged in standard narratives.

From a global or even a national perspective, the gap between Boston and Philadelphia may seem small. In contrast, the distance between colonial India and the postbellum South seems enormous, though both are usually analyzed as examples of economic underachievement. Susan Wolcott (Chapter 10) has fruitfully compared them, different as they no doubt were, using southern merchants as a standard in making her case for the efficiency of Indian moneylenders during the colonial era. According to Wolcott, credit was generally available to impoverished Indian farmers despite their lack of collateral, and default was comparatively rare because the caste system provided a form of collective-liability enforcement. On this view, many highly touted features of modern microfinance programs were already provided by traditional village moneylenders. As a byproduct, Wolcott's analysis enhances appreciation for the high rates of geographic mobility that prevailed in the postbellum South, countervailing the notion of "debt peonage." Thus her research confirms the adage that you can learn a lot about your own society by studying a very different one. This insight is a standard part of the case for including economic history in the core curriculum for students of economics.

LABOR MARKETS AS HISTORICAL INSTITUTIONS

With the advent of the economics of information in the 1970s, many economic historians have drawn upon insights from this approach to analyze historical credit markets as information-processing systems.[14] Many of these considerations apply to labor markets as well, though this similarity is often overlooked. Employers hire workers whose attributes they do not know with certainty, and the same can be said for potential workers choosing among jobs. Because acquiring better information is costly and time consuming, employers typically use particular attributes as criteria for hiring and job assignments, an exercise in signal extraction or statistical discrimination. They also have to make decisions about the balance among recruitment efforts, working conditions, and wages in expanding their workforces. Labor economists conventionally estimate wage functions using such variables as age, experience, education, gender, and race, but to an economic historian, such conventional procedures do not fully substitute for historical studies of the information signals and recruitment systems actually used by real employers in specific historical conditions. Analyzing such systems and their consequences is something of a Stanford tradition, going back at least as far as Melvin Reder's (1955) classic article on occupational wage differentials.[15]

The present volume includes many contributions that reflect and extend this tradition. Drawing a parallel with the constraints facing blacks in the Jim Crow South, Susan B. Carter (Chapter 16) recounts the difficulties faced by Chinese immigrants in moving out of the unskilled labor market into better-paying (but more discriminatory) jobs. An advantage enjoyed by the Chinese was that they could draw upon mutual aid societies known as *huiguans* for employment information, credit, insurance, and other services. This preexisting organizational capital facilitated entry into self-employment, an option whose attractiveness was enhanced by the Chinese Exclusion Act first passed in 1882. An indirect consequence was the dispersion of the Chinese population throughout the country, because the opportunities in personal service (initially laundries, subsequently Chinese restaurants) required close proximity to the customers. Thus the American revolution in ethnic food had its origins in labor-market institutions, a linkage that could be uncovered only by the detailed historical research represented by Carter's essay.

Richard Sutch (Chapter 15) revisits the impact of the federal minimum wage by characterizing it as a disruption of the previously existing relationship between worker attributes and job characteristics. Seen in this way, the essential question to be addressed is not "what was the elasticity of demand for labor" (the subject of countless empirical studies), but "what were the adjustments on both sides of the labor market" to what

Sutch calls an "engineered shortage of low-skill, low-paying jobs." Although his results are preliminary, Sutch's approach underscores the broader point that economic analysis and empirical research often restrict the allowable channels of labor-market adjustment quite arbitrarily. Adjustment channels may in fact be constrained in particular historical settings, as Joshua L. Rosenbloom and William A. Sundstrom (Chapter 11) argue. But these constraints or market conventions in practice may not be the same as the conventions of standard microtheory. Adjustments may also occur along unconventional margins such as school enrollment, emigration, crime, or marriage. The balance among modes of market adjustment thus depends crucially on historically specific aspects of the setting.

Sutch's analysis is complementary to the broader historical synthesis advanced by Frank Levy and Peter Temin (Chapter 14). They focus less on the microfunctioning of labor markets and more on the internally consistent set of U.S. national policies bearing on inequality that prevailed from the New Deal through the 1970s. Using the 1947 labor–management agreement known as the Treaty of Detroit as a suggestive label, Levy and Temin identify the core components of the package as unions, progressive taxes, and a high, rising minimum wage. Since all of these measures served to restrain inequality, Temin and Levy characterize the era as "market outcomes strongly moderated by institutional factors." A more labor-market-oriented version of their analysis might give equal emphasis to the massive expansion of public schooling and higher education during the same historical period, a measure that seemed to underpin the strong positive trends in productivity and real wages between World War II and 1973. Because these annual dividends became built into expectations and behavior on both sides of the labor market, one might say that they were virtually "institutionalized" as features of what Rosenbloom and Sundstrom call a "labor-market regime."

The questions then arise: If labor-market and complementary institutions have such powerful tendencies toward coherence and persistence, why then have they changed so frequently historically, and why have these regime changes so often been sudden and surprising, to participants as well as to the experts? On reflection, these patterns follow logically from the concept of path dependence, the other side of that two-edged sword. With institutions as with technologies, when we say that they have become "locked in" to a given state, we do not mean that they remain unchanged forever, only that they are no longer responsive to incremental changes in incentives. But if structures are unresponsive to incremental changes in underlying conditions, the corollary is that when regime change does occur—as the result of an exogenous shock, an accumulation of small changes that undermine its social or political supports, or most commonly a combination of these—it is likely to be both discontinuous and unexpected. Because the regime's collapse typically sets in motion a host of complementary adjustments in diverse parts of the economy, the events may appear to have been the inevitable results of inexorable historical forces after the fact. But this apparent inevitability is superficial and perhaps illusory. As Rosenbloom and Sundstrom write, "trends in the underlying economic 'fundamentals' that are often given causal primacy [may] themselves [be] partly the endogenous product of institutional regimes."

This perspective is beautifully illustrated by Stacey M. Jones's analysis of the market for teachers in the 1960s (Chapter 13), which should be read in conjunction with her article on the "unexpected transformation of women's higher education" between 1965 and 1975 (Jones 2009). Drawing on a framework developed by Timur Kuran (1995) that is very much in the Stanford tradition, Jones depicts young women as choosing between homemaking and careers, in a setting permeated by peer pressures, social norms, and institutional constraints. Because norms and institutions were responsive only to quantitatively large changes in behavior, the system constituted a multiple-equilibrium structure. As late as 1964, observers (feminists included) saw virtually no hope for change in the rigid norms governing women's roles. Yet within a remarkably short historical span, women in large numbers were enrolling in law school, medical school, and business school—and delaying marriage and motherhood, either as a consequence of or a corollary to their new career choices. Jones's analysis demonstrates the futility of attempting to choose a statistical victor among competing economic, demographic, or cultural interpretations. All three are better viewed as complementary parts of the shift from one equilibrium to another.

The formal structure of Jones's interpretation invites comparison with Chiaki Moriguchi's analysis of an earlier transition in American labor relations, from "welfare capitalism" in the 1920s to contract-based collective bargaining in the 1930s and after. Moriguchi (2003) argues that the reputation-based system of the 1920s constituted a stable, self-reinforcing equilibrium in a game-theoretic context. This equilibrium was upset by the massive shock of the Great Depression, which forced employers to renege on their implicit-contract promises, a breach that in turn impelled workers to lose faith in such arrangements, turning to labor unions and enforceable contracts instead. Because the new system was accompanied by a host of other political, ideological, and institutional changes, it too seemed to be the result of powerful historical forces. Moriguchi, like Jones, faces the challenge of persuading readers that American labor relations really could have evolved differently had they not been disrupted by the Depression. This is no easy task, because standard econometric tools are not generally helpful in tracking a history that did not happen. But Moriguchi is able to evoke the plausibility of her case by drawing on the comparative example of Japan, whose private-order, reputation-based system was actually reinforced by the experience of the Depression. Because the Depression was much milder in Japan than in the United States, Japanese employers were able to keep their implicit promises, reinforcing workers' confidence in their good faith.

An even more intricate path of historical contingencies is advanced by Robert K. Fleck (Chapter 12) in his masterly account of the ultimate impact of the New Deal on social and economic progress in the American South. Because Fleck proposes a synthesis based on two of my own long-standing research interests, I may lack sufficient critical distance to comment objectively. But I will try nonetheless, because the essay so nicely exemplifies qualities that I see as vital to the Stanford tradition, as well as the capacity of former students to reach beyond the limits of their teachers.

Fleck's argument begins with an article that I published in 1974, in which I addressed the apparent paradox that the impoverished South received less federal spending per capita under the New Deal than any other region in the country (Wright 1974). My proposed answer was that the South lacked political priority for the New Deal because the region was already solidly Democratic. Several decades of regression-running have demonstrated that this formulation was only partly correct. New Deal spending was largely allocated according to plausible proxies for economic need as well as to political goals, and the formulas underlying these priorities seem largely to have been pursued in good faith rather than tweaked state-by-state for political advantage.[16] Overall, as Fleck argues, it is difficult to distinguish between political and economic motives in this context, because the two were meant to reinforce each other. Contrary to the impression conveyed by my original article, however, the impact of the New Deal on the South was momentous.

Although per capita federal spending on infrastructure was lower in the South than elsewhere, the effects on economic life were probably greater than in any other region. Roads, cheap power, electric lights, and the radio brought many rural southerners out of isolation, while investments in water and sewage facilities and disease eradication modernized southern cities far in advance of what they could have accomplished on their own. In cotton, federal price supports and subsidies promoted mechanization of preharvest operations and restructuring of the plantation. Similarly, in southern industry, imposition of national wage standards fostered rapid productivity growth through modern labor-saving technologies. Remarkably, however, although African Americans participated in work-relief projects and other New Deal programs, the revolutionary changes in the economy made little dent in the southern racial regime. As Fleck notes, if anything the short-term impact was to intensify segregation. Southern blacks were excluded almost entirely from the benefits of the two most celebrated New Deal programs, the Tennessee Valley Authority and the GI Bill.

This picture seems bleak, but as Fleck goes on to argue, displacement of African Americans in the 1930s also set in motion forces that ultimately led to the demise of the Jim Crow regime. With few opportunities open to them in their native region, blacks left the South in large numbers beginning with World War II and continuing through the 1960s. They were not always welcome in the North and West, but blacks did have voting rights in their destination states. As Fleck recounts, making a long story short, pressure from these new "swing voters in swing states" played a major role in enacting the landmark Civil Rights legislation of the 1960s (see also Gregory 2005, chap. 7). To compound the historical irony, although white southerners would never have voted for these reforms if they had been left to their own devices, in retrospect (as journalist Peter Applebome [1996, p. 17] writes) "the Civil Rights revolution turned out to be the best thing that ever happened to the white South, paving the way for the region's newfound prosperity."

CONCLUSION

Economic history is alive and well in the twenty-first century, not just at Stanford but at intellectual centers across the United States and at many new locations around the world. As always happens, prevailing issues and methods in the field change over time, reflecting new research tools offered by technological progress and new interests and perceptions of the past that inevitably change with the passage of historical time. All of these signs of life are encouraging, but it is especially heartening to see intellectual traditions carried forward by new generations of scholars, increasingly diverse in their individual cultural backgrounds. This is so even when the new research forces one to reopen previously settled issues and revise old positions, as is the case more often than not. The deep continuity in the Stanford tradition in economic history is thus not in particular historical doctrines or interpretations but in the spirit of the historical-economics enterprise. May the circle be unbroken.

NOTES

1. This phrase is the title of an earlier volume (Guinnane, Sundstrom, and Whatley 2004) of essays presented in honor of Paul David.

2. See especially Abramovitz (1993), his presidential address to the Economic History Association.

3. See "Path-Dependent Aspects of Technological Change," in Rosenberg (1994), p. 10.

4. These themes are elaborated in Rosenberg's (2010) most recent collection of essays, *Studies on Science and the Innovation Process.*

5. David (1985); a fuller version of the QWERTY article (David 1986) appeared in a volume edited by Bill Parker, making the case for economic history as an essential part of graduate training in economics.

6. See Arthur (1989). A recent book by a Stanford PhD (Puffert 2009) is recognizably descended from this part of the Stanford tradition.

7. A selected list would include Greif (1993, 1994a, 1994b) and Greif, Milgrom, and Weingast (1994).

8. A consolidated statement of this methodology and historical interpretation may be found in Greif (2006).

9. A similar perspective is implicit in Clay and Wright (2005).

10. Many examples of successful resource-based development in modern times are provided in Wright and Czelusta (2006).

11. Essential citations include Bates (2008) and Nunn (2008).

12. An example showing the importance of tracking developments through historical time, as opposed to endpoint correlations, is Aldo Musacchio's (2009) study of financial institutions in Brazil. This book is one in a distinguished series on Latin American history by students of Stephen Haber, many of whom were jointly advised by economics faculty.

13. A good illustration of the historical significance of spatial processes usually neglected by economists is provided by Field (1992).

14. In addition to Wolcott's essay, contributions in the Stanford tradition include Calomiris and Gorton (1991), Guinnane (2001), Knodell (2006), and Wang (2008).

15. A study inspired by Reder's approach is David (1987).

16. Studies of lasting value include Wallis (1998), Fishback, Kantor, and Wallis (2003), and Fleck (2008).

REFERENCES

Abramovitz, Moses (1956). "Resource and Output Trends in the United States since 1870." *American Economic Review* 46: 5–23.

Abramovitz, Moses (1993). "The Search for the Sources of Growth: Areas of Ignorance, Old and New." *Journal of Economic History* 53: 217–243.

Abramovitz, Moses, and Paul A. David (1973). "Reinterpreting Economic Growth: Parables and Realities." *American Economic Review* 63: 251–272.

Applebome, Peter (1996). *Dixie Rising*. New York: Times Books.

Arthur, W. Brian (1989). "Competing Technologies, Increasing Returns, and Lock-In by Historical Events." *Economic Journal* 99 (March): 116–131.

Bates, Robert (2008). *When Things Fell Apart: State Failure in Late-Century Africa.* Cambridge: Cambridge University Press.

Calomiris, Charles, and Gary Gorton (1991). "The Origins of Banking Panics." In *Financial Markets and Financial Crises*, edited by R. Glenn Hubbard. Chicago: University of Chicago Press, pp. 109–173.

Clay, Karen, and Gavin Wright (2005). "Order without Law? Property Rights during the California Gold Rush." *Explorations in Economic History* 42: 155–183.

David, Paul A. (1985). "Clio and the Economics of QWERTY." *American Economic Review* 75: 332–337.

David, Paul A. (1986). "Understanding the Economics of QWERTY: The Necessity of History." In *Economic History and the Modern Economist*, edited by William N. Parker. New York: Blackwell, pp. 30–49.

David, Paul A. (1987). "Industrial Labor Market Adjustments in a Region of Recent Settlement: Chicago, 1848–1868." In *Quantity and Quiddity: Essays in U.S. Economic History*, edited by Peter Kilby. Middletown, CT: Wesleyan University Press, pp. 47–97.

David, Paul A. (1990). "The Dynamo and the Computer." *American Economic Review* 80: 355–361.

David, Paul A. (1991). "Computer and Dynamo: The Modern Productivity Paradox in a Not-too-Distant Mirror." In *Technology and Productivity: The Challenge for Economic Policy*. Paris: OECD, pp. 315–347.

David, Paul A. (1994). "Why Are Institutions the 'Carriers of History'? Path Dependence and the Evolution of Conventions, Organizations, and Institutions." *Structural Change and Economic Dynamics* 5: 205–220.

David, Paul A. (2008). "The Historical Origins of 'Open Science': An Essay on Patronage, Reputation and Common Agency Contracting in the Scientific Revolution." *Capitalism and Society* 3: 1–103.

David, Paul A., and Gavin Wright (1997). "Increasing Returns and the Genesis of American Resource Abundance." *Industrial and Corporate Change* 6: 203–245.

Field, Alexander (1992). "Uncontrolled Land Development and the Duration of the Depression in the United States." *Journal of Economic History* 52 (December): 785–805.

Fishback, Price V., Shawn Kantor, and John Joseph Wallis (2003). "Can the New Deal's Three Rs Be Rehabilitated? A Program-by-Program, County-by-County Analysis." *Explorations in Economic History* 40: 278–307.

Fleck, Robert K. (2008). "Voter Influence and Big Policy Change: The Positive Political Economy of the New Deal." *Journal of Political Economy* 116: 1–37.

Gregory, James N. (2005). *The Southern Diaspora*. Chapel Hill: University of North Carolina Press.

Greif, Avner (1993). "Contract Enforceability and Economic Institutions in Early Trade: The Maghribi Traders' Coalition." *American Economic Review* 83: 525–548.

Greif, Avner (1994a). "On the Political Foundations of the Late Medieval Commercial Revolution: Genoa during the Twelfth and Thirteenth Centuries." *Journal of Economic History* 54: 271–287.

Greif, Avner (1994b). "Cultural Beliefs and the Organization of Society: A Historical and Theoretical Reflection on Collectivist and Individualist Societies." *Journal of Political Economy* 102: 912–950.

Greif, Avner (2006). *Institutions and the Path to the Modern Economy: Lessons from Medieval Trade*. New York: Cambridge University Press.

Greif, Avner, Paul Milgrom, and Barry Weingast (1994). "Coordination, Commitment and Enforcement: The Case of the Merchant Guild." *Journal of Political Economy* 102: 745–776.

Guinnane, Timothy (2001). "Cooperatives as Information Machines: German Credit Cooperatives, 1883–1914." *Journal of Economic History* 61: 366–389.

Guinnane, Timothy W., William A. Sundstrom, and Warren C. Whatley, eds. (2004). *History Matters: Economic Growth, Technology, and Demographic Change*. Stanford, CA: Stanford University Press.

Haber, Stephen, and Victor Menaldo (2010). "Do Natural Resources Fuel Authoritarianism? A Reappraisal of the Resource Curse." Working Paper, Stanford University.

Jones, Stacey (2009). "Dynamic Social Norms and the Unexpected Transformation of Women's Higher Education, 1965–1975." *Social Science History* 33: 247–291.

Knodell, Jane (2006). "Rethinking the Jacksonian Economy." *Journal of Economic History* 66: 541–574.

Krugman, Paul (1991). *Geography and Trade*. Cambridge, MA: MIT Press.

Kuran, Timur (1995). *Private Truths, Public Lies: The Social Consequences of Preference Falsification*. Cambridge, MA: Harvard University Press.

Lamoreaux, Naomi (1994). *Insider Lending: Banks, Personal Connections, and Economic Development in Industrial New England*. New York: Cambridge University Press.

Moriguchi, Chiaki (2003). "Implicit Contracts, the Great Depression, and Institutional Change: A Comparative Analysis of U.S. and Japanese Employment Relations, 1920–1940." *Journal of Economic History* 63: 625–665.

Musacchio, Aldo (2009). *Experiments in Financial Democracy: Corporate Governance and Financial Development in Brazil, 1882–1950*. New York: Cambridge University Press.

Nunn, Nathan (2008). "The Long-Term Effects of Africa's Slave Trades." *Quarterly Journal of Economics* 123: 139–176.

Olmstead, Alan L., and Paul W. Rhode (2008a). "Biological Innovation and Productivity Growth in the Antebellum Cotton South." *Journal of Economic History* 68: 1123–1171.

Olmstead, Alan L., and Paul W. Rhode (2008b). *Creating Abundance: Biological Innovation and American Agricultural Development*. New York: Cambridge University Press.

Puffert, Douglas J. (2009). *Tracks across Continents, Paths through History: The Economic Dynamics of Standardization in Railway Gauge*. Chicago: University of Chicago Press.

Reder, Melvin (1955). "The Theory of Occupational Wage Differentials." *American Economic Review* 45: 833–852.

Rosenberg, Nathan (1994). *Exploring the Black Box: Technology, Economics, and History*. Cambridge: Cambridge University Press.

Rosenberg, Nathan (2010). *Studies on Science and the Innovation Process*. Hackensack, NJ: World Scientific Publishing.

Scranton, Philip (1983). *Proprietary Capitalism: The Textile Manufacture at Philadelphia, 1800–1885*. Cambridge: Cambridge University Press.

Sylla, Richard (2002). "Financial Systems and Economic Modernization." *Journal of Economic History* 62: 277–292.

Turner, Frederick Jackson (1911). "Social Forces in American History." *American Historical Review* 16: 231–232.

Turner, Sarah, and John Bound (2003). "Closing the Gap or Widening the Divide: The Effects of the GI Bill and World War II on the Educational Outcomes of Black Americans." *Journal of Economic History* 63: 145–177.

Wallis, John J. (1998). "The Political Economy of New Deal Spending Revisited, Again: With and without Nevada." *Explorations in Economic History* 35: 140–170.

Wang, Ta-Chen (2008). "Paying Back to Borrow More: Reputation and Bank Access in Early America." *Explorations in Economic History* 45: 477–488.

Whatley, Warren C. (1983). "Labor for the Picking: The New Deal in the South." *Journal of Economic History* 43: 905–929.

Whatley, Warren C. (1985). "A History of Mechanization in the Cotton South: The Institutional Hypothesis." *Quarterly Journal of Economics* 100: 1191–1215.

Whatley, Warren C. (1987). "Agrarian Labor Contracts as Impediments to Cotton Mechanization." *Journal of Economic History* 47: 45–70.

Wright, Gavin (1974). "The Political Economy of New Deal Spending: An Econometric Analysis." *Review of Economics and Statistics* 56: 30–38.

Wright, Gavin (1978). *The Political Economy of the Cotton South: Households, Markets, and Wealth in the Nineteenth Century*. New York: Norton.

Wright, Gavin (1986). *Old South, New South: Revolutions in the Southern Economy since the Civil War*. New York: Basic Books.

Wright, Gavin (1990). "The Origins of American Industrial Success, 1879–1940." *American Economic Review* 80: 651–668.

Wright, Gavin (2006). *Slavery and American Economic Development.* Baton Rouge: Louisiana State University Press.

Wright, Gavin (2010). "The New Deal and the Modernization of the South." *Federal History*, issue 2: 58–73.

Wright, Gavin, and Jesse Czelusta (2006). "Resource-Based Growth Past and Present." In *Natural Resources: Neither Curse Nor Destiny*, edited by Daniel Lederman and William Maloney. Stanford, CA and Washington, DC: Stanford University Press and the World Bank, pp. 183–211.

Evolutionary Processes in Economics

THE TERM "EVOLUTION" has several distinct connotations. In current economic parlance it has come to mean a "movement or change in position" of any variable, such as the gross domestic product (GDP) or the capital stock. GDP "evolves," in this sense, only because today differs from yesterday and will no doubt be different from tomorrow. It implies a notion of history criticized by Toynbee (or perhaps Truman) as a mere succession of events, "one damn thing after another."

The chapters in Part One conceive of evolution in more biological terms, as a process of development—a succession of incremental changes, perhaps, but ones firmly rooted in and conditioned by their history. In economic parlance we speak of a "path-dependent" process because today's outcome depends critically on prior, "initial" conditions. Regardless of the specific mechanism—scale economies, complementarities, externalities, and so on—these cumulative processes are self-reinforcing, biasing change in one direction and foreclosing others.

Karen Clay (Chapter 2) pursues this line of reasoning in search for the holy grail of economics, the causes of the *Wealth of Nations*. The more recent debate has centered on the question whether abundant resource endowments are a blessing or curse. Her careful critical review of this literature details the limitations of cross-sectional evidence and even panel data covering brief time spans. By dissecting the U.S. case, moreover, she shows how the developmental impact of its diverse natural resource base depended on the timing of discoveries but also on complementary innovations (in transportation, in science and engineering, and in property rights regimes) that diffused and cumulated their economic benefits. Ultimately, she suggests, it comes down to governance: the norms and formal rules that delineate the rights over resources and distribute their returns but also that channel this wealth along complementary lines of development.

George Grantham (Chapter 3) steps back in time to understand a necessary prior condition for the economic exploitation of natural resources that fueled (literally and figuratively) the second industrial revolution. The institutionalization of scientific and engineering research in the university system and research institutes, according to Clay (and David and Wright 1997), accelerated the discovery and processing of mere "natural" resources into strategic industrial inputs. Despite the occasional "revolution," Grantham observes, modern scientific-technological knowledge advances through an evolutionary cumulative process that depends on and elaborates a foundational scaffolding. No matter how "ideal" their products, scientific practitioners could routinely contribute to this collective endeavor only because of complementary developments on the "ground"—of innovations in communication and publication technologies and the growing demands of the captains of the military and of industry for trained technical personnel (or their wares). The latter, in particular, coalesced the critical mass thresholds that made science and engineering an economically viable profession (most often housed in the university), not just an intellectually gratifying occupation.

Chapters 4 and 5 (by Warren C. Whatley and Rob Gillezeau and by Leonard A. Carlson) analyze the evolutionary processes ignited by the "colonial encounters" of indigenous populations in Africa, North America, and Australia with seafaring northwestern Europeans in search of new sources of riches and power. Like all such path-dependent processes, these contributions show, the initial conditions of encounter mattered. They fundamentally reconfigured existing social-political arrangements among indigenous populations and skewed the paths of their demographic-political development, often with debilitating if not deadly consequences. In many ways the impact of the slave trade in Africa can be viewed as a perverse instance of the "resource" curse. By literally valuing human beings, the slave trade decisively shifted the incentives of existing political empires and so their allocation of military power from wars for domestic political-economic ends to slave raiding for purely economic ones. The net result, Whatley and Gillezeau suggest, was greater political and ethnic diversity, which has plagued the continent's economic development ever since (especially after another round of colonial encounters that combined these mini-states into larger polities often under rule by minority factions).

Carlson analyzes the divergent demographic paths of the indigenous populations in the North American mainland and Australia following their encounters with English colonizers. When compared to white settlers and their successors, Native American tribes have fared poorly in terms of standard demographic and socioeconomic measures. Yet, compared to their counterparts in Australia, they managed to secure a modicum of de-mographic stability and political economic power. Carlson traces these differences back to the initial conditions of encounter, whether English settlers did (in the North American case) or did not (in the Australian one) recognize indigenous tribes' prior land claims. While agnostic on settlers' motives in each case, he clearly demonstrates the enduring impact of these fateful decisions in securing Native Americans' claims, albeit admittedly residual, to their land.

P. W. R., J. L. R., and D. F. W.

CHAPTER 2

Natural Resources and Economic Outcomes

KAREN CLAY

WHY DO SOME COUNTRIES grow while others do not? This question is one of the most important in economics. Literally thousands of papers have been published on the topic. And it is of enormous policy significance, because the current understanding of the answer to this question affects the behavior of a variety of organizations including the World Bank, the International Monetary Fund, the Inter-American Development Bank, and the Gates Foundation. Economists have recently begun to recognize that growth may well be path dependent. If it is, then understanding the current state of economic development is not sufficient to make policy. One needs to understand the historical evolution of the economy or economies in question. Only then can appropriate policies be formulated.

During the 1980s the United States experienced declining industrial competitiveness in the world economy. The reasons for the decline were hotly debated. As a means of informing the debate, Wright (1990) sought to understand the basis for American industrial success up to 1940. Economists tended to assume that America's advantage had always been technological. Among economic historians, some of whom had thought more carefully about the issue, the conventional wisdom was slightly more nuanced. Chandler (1959, 1977) argued that the buildout of the transportation network during the nineteenth century in the United States allowed the creation of a single national market and that this market enabled the rise of large-scale manufacturing enterprises. Indeed, Atack, Haines, and Margo (in this volume) show that the building of railroads was not merely associated with the growth in manufacturing from 1850 to 1870—it was causal. Goldin (1998) and Goldin and Katz (2008) show that the expansion of human capital also played an important role in the development of technology and industrial competitiveness more broadly. Technology was important, but it was intimately related to the emergence of national markets and the expansion of human capital.[1]

Wright (1990) showed that the conventional wisdom missed an important part of the story. "The most distinctive characteristic of U.S. manufacturing (from 1879 to 1940) was intensity in nonreproducible natural resources" (p. 651). Technology was certainly important, but it was a technology built on national markets and a specific class of natural resources. Wright addressed a second issue: "whether resource abundance reflected geological endowment or greater exploitation of geological potential" (p. 651). He argued that abundance built primarily on greater exploitation.

Wright's argument that American prewar economic success was built on natural resources would shortly come into apparent conflict with a new literature that grew out of Sachs and Warner (1995). Sachs and Warner demonstrated that during the 1970s and 1980s countries with higher natural resource exports as a percentage of gross domestic product (GDP) experienced slower growth. The negative relationship between resources and growth came to be known as the resource curse. Beginning with Ross (2001), a parallel line of research in political science examined the negative effect of natural resources on political outcomes.

This chapter reviews the state of these divergent and apparently conflicting literatures and then offers an interpretation that reconciles the findings.

AMERICAN INDUSTRIAL GROWTH

American manufacturing exports burst onto the international scene in 1890s. Most American exports were producer goods, which dominated European goods in their quality and technical specifications. Although success was the culmination of a long historical process, American export growth was not particularly visible. That changed in the 1890s, when the United States became the largest producer of world industrial output. Shortly before 1913, the United States became the largest producer of industrial output per capita. Figure 2.1 shows the trajectories of industrial output per capita for three of the major industrial nations—the United States, the United Kingdom, and Germany. The United States' rapid growth

FIGURE 2.1   *Industrial Output per Capita (United Kingdom in 1900 = 100)*

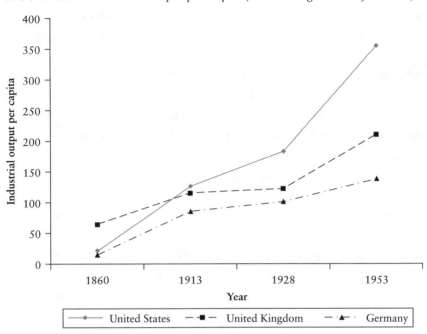

Sources: Data from Bairoch (1982) reprinted in O'Brien (1998), p. 12, table 4.

in industrial output per capita seems to have been attributable to its over-all comparative advantage in manufacturing. Broadberry (1993) docu-mented that American labor productivity levels in manufacturing were roughly twice British levels over the period 1869 to 1989. For much of this time, American labor productivity levels were also twice the German levels. Although much of the American output was consumed domesti-cally, an increasing share was consumed abroad. Using data for 1937 for the United States and Britain, MacDougall (1951) found a positive relation-ship between relative labor productivity and relative exports. The United States exported more goods than Britain in segments in which it had high relative labor productivity.

To evaluate the sources of American success in the export market, Wright (1990) used data for 165 manufacturing industries in six years over the interval from 1879 to 1940. He compared the inputs for indus-tries for which the United States was a net importer with the inputs for industries for which it was a net exporter. Although the United States was exporting relatively more capital-intensive and skill-intensive goods than it was importing, Wright found that the differences were generally modest. At its peak the capital-to-labor ratio for exports relative to imports never exceeded 1.9, and the relative skill intensity as measured by average wages never exceeded 1.2.

For natural resources, the story was quite different. U.S. exports were much more natural resource intensive than its imports and relative resource intensity was generally rising from 1879 to 1914. In 1899 manufacturing exports were 3.5 times more natural resource intensive than imports in direct use and 1.7 times more intensive in direct and indirect use.[2] In 1914 the peak year for resource intensity, the ratios had risen to 7.4 for direct use and 2.4 for direct and indirect use. Further analysis showed that up to 1928, capital and natural resources were complements in net export performance. This finding was consistent with work by Cain and Patterson (1986), James (1983), and James and Skinner (1985) showing complementarities between capital and materials in production more broadly during the nineteenth and early twentieth centuries.

Wright linked the rise in natural resource intensity back to American success in world export markets. "This trend [in natural resource intensity] was growing both absolutely and relatively over *precisely the historical period when the country was moving into a position of world industrial preeminence.*"[3] Despite contemporary concerns regarding resource exhaustion, input prices in the United States were falling—not rising—following the Civil War. Falling prices reflected more intensive and efficient search for new deposits, greater efficiency in extraction of existing deposits, and falling costs of transportation. The United States dominated world production of nearly all economically important minerals.

Cheap steel was increasingly important as an export, both in its own right and as an input into machinery and automobiles. By 1913 steel, machinery, and automobiles accounted for 28 percent of American exports. Adding in petroleum products lifted the total to 38 percent of exports.[4] By 1929 steel, machinery, automobiles, and petroleum products accounted for 51 percent of American exports. Irwin (2003) tied the surge in American exports in iron, steel, machinery, and automobiles to the commercial exploitation of the Mesabi iron ore range. The availability of Mesabi ore caused domestic ore prices to fall by 50 percent. Lower ore prices made American exports increasingly competitive in the world market.

Erosion of the natural-resource-based success came with falling trade barriers after World War II. American industrial success continued as a result of its technological lead. Nelson and Wright (1992) argued that the postwar lead in high-technology industries stemmed from "investments in higher education and in research and development, far surpassing the levels of other countries at that time."[5] Erosion of the technological lead came as other countries made huge investments in higher education and research and development.

SUCCESSFUL EXPLOITATION OF
NATURAL RESOURCES

American industrial success was integrally related to its early and successful exploitation of its geological potential. In one of the only papers to examine how successful exploitation occurred, David and Wright (1997) identified several factors that facilitated rapid discovery and extraction of oil and minerals. These factors included public knowledge as embodied in geological surveys, mining education, an ethos of exploration, and incentives.

Individuals, states, and the federal government began to invest in geological surveys as early as the 1820s. In 1821 Stephen Van Rensselaer commissioned a survey of his vast landholdings, and he commissioned a survey of the route of the Erie Canal three years later. Responding to the discovery of gold in the state, North Carolina authorized a survey in 1823. The next year South Carolina followed suit. A wave of surveys followed. Table 2.1 shows the dates of state geological surveys to 1870 and their costs. North Carolina appropriated $250 per year for four years to defray the travel expenses of Denison Olmstead, a professor of chemistry at the University of North Carolina. South Carolina appropriated $500 for Lardner Vanuxem, a professor at South Carolina College, to make "a geological and mineralogical tour during the recess of the college."[6] The sums appropriated for later surveys appear to have been substantially higher than the amounts appropriated in North Carolina and South

TABLE 2.1 *Dates of State Geological Surveys to 1870*

State	Statehood	Survey	Survey Appropriation
Northeast			
Connecticut	1788	1835	
Maine	1820	1836	$8,000
Massachusetts	1788	1830	$2,030
New Hampshire	1788	1839	
New Jersey	1787	1833	
New York	1788	1836	
Pennsylvania	1787	1836	
Rhode Island	1790	1839	$2,000
Vermont	1791	1845	
South			
Alabama	1819	1848	
Delaware	1787	1837	
Georgia	1788	1836	
Kentucky	1792	1838	
Louisiana	1812	1869	
Maryland	1788	1833	
Mississippi	1817	1850	
North Carolina	1789	1823	$1,000
South Carolina	1788	1824	$500
Tennessee	1796	1831	
Texas	1845	1858	
Virginia (and West Virginia)	1788	1836	
Midwest and West			
California	1850	1853	
Illinois	1818	1851	
Indiana	1816	1837	
Iowa	1846	1855	
Kansas	1861	1864	
Michigan	1837	1837	$29,000
Minnesota	1858	1865	
Missouri	1821	1853	
Ohio	1803	1836	
Wisconsin	1848	1853	

Sources: Merrill (1906); Hendrickson (1961), fn. 18. All dates are the beginning of the first state survey. Survey appropriations could not be determined for most states. Survey appropriations for states with values are from Merrill (1906).

Carolina. In addition to expenses, later appropriations often covered salaries and printing of reports. The printing of reports, and more generally the dissemination of the geological information in the reports, was greatly aided by the fall in the cost of printing.[7]

State geological surveys served multiple purposes. Hendrickson (1961) finds:

In all states a major purpose was to locate, describe, and publicize such natural resources as salt and mineral springs, building stones, shales, clays, slates, coal, and ores. . . . In some states—Maryland, Connecticut, Virginia, Georgia, Indiana, North Carolina, South Carolina and Massachusetts—there was a close tie between the demand for systems of internal improvements and the authorization of geological surveys. [8]

Surveys played important roles in the development of natural-resource-based industries, including the copper and cement industries.[9] The ties between internal improvement and geological surveys are also noteworthy because they link the buildout of the transportation infrastructure, the creation of the national market, and the development of natural resources.

Although bigger in scope, federal surveys tended to serve similar purposes. As Atack, Haines, and Margo (in this volume) discuss, the federal government made 59 surveys of roads, canals, and railroads between 1824 and 1838. Geological information was an ancillary benefit of these surveys. During the 1830s federal surveys examined the mineral lands of Iowa, Wisconsin, and Illinois. After a state survey in Michigan identified rich copper deposits on Chippewa land, the federal government purchased the land. Authorization of federal geological surveys of the Chippewa land and the area around Lake Superior followed shortly thereafter. In 1853 Congress appropriated $150,000 for surveys to determine the best route from the Mississippi to the Pacific Ocean. The Corps of Topographical Engineers examined four potential routes and collected considerable scientific information. Transportation was also the impetus for the Geological Exploration of the Fortieth Parallel (the route of the Pacific railroad).

Oddly, individuals involved in oil exploration tended to dismiss geological surveys as only being relevant for minerals. This changed suddenly in 1911 with the discovery of oil in the Cushing Field in Oklahoma. The Cushing Field vividly demonstrated that oil was associated with anticlines, and in the west, locating the anticlines was a key to discovering new oil. Knowles (1959) writes: "The majority of discoveries during the next fifteen years resulted from the industry's sudden acceptance of petroleum geology as a science. . . . Most of the large companies established permanent geological departments."[10]

American universities quickly saw the utility of establishing mining-related courses. In many universities this built on existing programs in civil and other types of engineering.[11] Civil engineering had long been part of the curriculum in military academies and a variety of other private and public universities. With the increasing importance of bridges, roads, canals, dams, and buildings during the nineteenth century, the value of systematic training in civil engineering became evident. The Morrill Acts of 1862 and 1890 facilitated the expansion of training of engineers by providing federal funding through grants of land to states to support the creation of new colleges and universities. Together the acts aided the establishment of more than 70 land grant colleges. It was explicitly part of the colleges' mandate "to teach such branches of learning as are related to agriculture and the mechanic arts."[12] By 1882–1892 the largest share of graduates and nongraduates (46 and 39 percent) of land grant universities were in engineering. The share had shrunk slightly to 33 and 34 percent by 1919–1922, but engineers were still the largest group.[13]

Universities' actions were prompted by rich donors who had made their money in mining, state legislatures, or demands by business. Columbia University was the leading American university, graduating nearly half of the mining engineers trained prior to 1892. By the end of the nineteenth century many other universities offered coursework in mining-related topics such as geology, mining, or metallurgy. For example, students could take mining-related courses at the Case School of Applied Science, Harvard University, the University of Illinois, Lafayette University, Lehigh University, the Massachusetts Institute of Technology, the University of Michigan, Rensselaer Polytechnic Institute, Stanford University, Vanderbilt University, Washington and Lee University, Washington

University, the University of Wisconsin, and Yale University. Many land grant universities had founded or were in the process of founding full-fledged mining schools. Many were in important mining states including Alabama, Arizona, California, Colorado, Iowa, Michigan, Missouri, Montana, Nevada, New Mexico, North Dakota, Ohio, South Dakota, Tennessee, and Utah.[14]

Because of their emphasis on practical training, American universities came to be preferred over European universities by students interested in studying mining. Before the Civil War, Americans interested in mining traveled to Europe for training. Of the European universities, the Bergakademie in Freiberg, Saxony, and the École Nationale Supérieure des Mines in Paris, France, were the most highly regarded.[15] With the rise of mining coursework in American universities after the Civil War, most Americans stayed home.

The success of the American-style training is evident from the recruitment of American-trained, rather than European-trained, engineers to operate foreign mining operations.[16] A 1917 manpower census found that 28 percent of American mining engineers had worked abroad. Most had worked in Canada or Mexico, but many had worked elsewhere. These numbers are corroborated by evidence from the Colorado School of Mines. In a survey of alumni from 1900 to 1940, 64 percent had worked abroad at some point, 39 percent for several years.

Successful exploitation of mineral resources required more than just courses aimed at getting resources out of the ground. For the resulting oil and minerals to be put to use, they had to be translated into products by relatively skilled workers.[17] Some skills were self-taught or learned on the job, but many skills were developed or refined in universities. American universities—both public and private—offered courses in areas such as accounting, business, chemistry, metallurgy, civil engineering, and mechanical engineering. This relatively sophisticated practical education was suited, by design, for big business. Although the numbers of university-trained students involved were small in absolute terms, their impact was large. Graduates with business backgrounds managed hundreds or even thousands of workers, while graduates with technical backgrounds made critical breakthroughs in products and processes.

David and Wright (1997) attributed the differences in exploration among the United States, Great Britain, and Australia largely to differences in beliefs. Americans believed that minerals were there, while the British, and to a greater extent the Australians, did not believe that minerals were there. The reliance on beliefs is somewhat unsatisfactory because it begs the question of where they came from. If the timing of geological surveys is indicative of beliefs, the United States fared poorly. The United States established a geological survey in 1879. By that point Britain, Canada, India, and Australia all had had geological surveys for at least a decade. Certainly all of these governments expected to benefit from surveys, yet the United States was somehow uniquely successful in leveraging surveys and other information into natural resource development and industrialization. Beliefs may well have been linked to incentives.

Incentives in the United States context arose from two factors—federal ownership of the public domain and the inclusion of mineral rights in the bundle of rights attached to land. The federal government permitted and even encouraged mining on the public domain, which covered much of the land from the Appalachians to the Pacific. Although individuals and corporations paid minimal or even no fees, they obtained relatively secure possessory rights. These conditions encouraged exploration and investment. Unlike some countries, where the central government explicitly reserved mineral rights, American property owners almost always held the mineral rights. Ownership gave them an incentive to develop their mineral holdings.

Clay and Wright (2005) used the California gold rush as a case study to better understand how property rights in mineral-bearing land operated in practice.[18] Many mining camp rules that emerged during the California gold rush were later codified by the federal government in the Mining Laws of 1866 and 1872. Thus understanding the rules and their operation in practice is important for understanding incentives.

One of the key questions was: How secure were property rights? Because investment is related to the security of property rights, security has implications for understanding both the early stage of mining, which focused on placer mining, and later stages of mining, which focused on quartz mining. During the placer mining phase, levels of investment were generally low. Men progressed from panning for gold to more involved methods such as long toms and cradles. Long toms and cradles required some investment, but the investment could be protected by having one of the miners on site most of the time.

Property rights were insecure if miners were absent from their claims for extended periods of time. This often happened if miners left to prospect for gold elsewhere. Claim jumping—seizing a claim that was not currently in production—was a perennial issue. As population rose—and it rose extremely rapidly throughout 1849 and 1850—newly arrived miners wanted to mine these claims. Strikingly, claim jumping was institutionalized in mining district constitutions through requirements on how claims must be marked, how many claims could be held, and how often the claim had to be worked for the use right to be maintained. Exceptions were often made for sickness and lack of water. However, to a first approximation, if the marking and work requirements were not met, others could begin mining the land. Conflict was inevitable, because newcomers often seized a claim first and asked questions later. Previous occupiers, having not met the work requirements, would also sometimes return and try to assert their claim by force. An unattractive variant on this was Americans simply using force to drive Mexican, Chinese, or other foreign-born miners off valuable claims.

Insecurity arose for somewhat different reasons also in riskier, larger-scale projects. Damming and river-turning projects were common because they allowed direct access to placer gold in the river bottom. Here, one set of risks arose from the fact that other groups upstream or downstream would engage in similar projects, rendering the existing project infeasible. There was sometimes collateral damage for nearby placer claims, which either were flooded or lost access to customary sources of water. A second set of risks emerged from weather and engineering. Poor weather, particularly excessive rainfall, could sweep away partially completed projects or prevent their completion. Even under normal weather conditions, dams and other projects could fail due to poor design.

Quartz regions had their own issues. Claim jumping was less of an issue, because much of the work was done by corporations. But the apex rule and the possessory nature of claims still led to conflict. In her discussion of one of the most famous early quartz companies, the Mariposa Mining Company, Maureen Jung notes, "Like so many early mining companies, it was also plagued by lawsuits. Mariposa's legal disputes over mineral and water rights spanned a number of years and a variety of succeeding companies."[19] The conflict was evident more generally in the number of cases reaching the California Supreme Court from 1850 to 1866. Most of these cases were brought by large quartz or water companies. Conflict of this type was not confined to California. According to Goldman (1981) in the Comstock, "Between 1860 and 1865, twelve major mining companies were involved in 245 different lawsuits, generating ten million dollars in litigation fees alone."[20]

The surprise is not that property rights were insecure, but that semi-secure property rights emerged in the midst of the chaos. As Zerbe and Anderson (2001) argued, cultural concepts of fairness led to the establishment of norms that were acceptable to American miners. These norms were often written down in mining district constitutions. The existence of culturally acceptable norms greatly facilitated the operation of the private-order institutions that governed property rights, by guaranteeing that miners would engage in first-party and second-party enforcement of property rights. In this context first-party enforcement meant that many miners would choose to obey the norms. Second-party enforcement meant that miners would resolve disputes among themselves through a combination of reference to norms and threats of punishment (usually violence) for violation of the norms.

However, norms in and of themselves were not sufficient to guarantee the successful operation of an institution. Most private-order institutions, including those that supported property rights in the gold rush, require the threat of third-party enforcement of property rights. That is, individuals who were not directly involved in the conflict (third parties) need to participate in the punishment in order for incentives to be maintained. Diaries, letters, and other historical accounts from the period offer some examples of third-party enforcement. In some instances third-party enforcement was simply neighbors helping neighbors. In more complicated disputes there would be a mining-district meeting or a smaller meeting in which the *alcalde* or some respected person within the mining district heard the two parties' arguments. Once a decision was made, the parties were expected to abide by the decision. If the loser(s) did not, third-party enforcement would, in principle, ensure compliance. In practice the assembled miners or *alcalde* might well side with the stronger party, irrespective of the merits of the other party's claims. Or the decision simply might not be enforced. The question is why miners who were not directly involved in the conflict would take costly actions such as taking time away from mining to attend a camp meeting or risking physical injury by helping force recalcitrant miners off a claim. Information transmission limited the functioning of third-party enforcement.

Taken together, the combination of public knowledge, education, the ethos of exploration, and incentives proved extremely powerful. Key stakeholders saw the value of investing in federal and state geological surveys and the education of mining engineers. Americans believed that minerals were around and so invested in finding them. Incentives were strong in the sense that federal and state governments did little to regulate, tax, or otherwise impede private exploration and development. All of these contributed to the early exploitation of American mineral resources.

NATURAL RESOURCES AND GROWTH

Were natural resources good or bad for economic growth? Wright (1990) argued that they were good for growth in industrial exports, while Sachs and Warner (1995) argued that they were bad for economic growth. Figure 2.2 illustrates Sachs and Warner's basic empirical relationship. Natural resource exports as a share of GDP in 1970 was negatively related to growth over the next two decades in a large sample of countries. This relationship holds in a regression framework across a variety of specifications.

Sachs and Warner (1995) evaluated a number of hypotheses for the negative effect of resources on growth, including rent seeking and corruption, protectionism, the pricing of tradable and non-tradable goods, and shifts in labor demand from learning-by-doing sectors. They found limited evidence of natural resources affecting growth through bureaucratic quality. The evidence was stronger for protectionism. In most economies, resource abundance negatively affects the manufacturing sector, which

FIGURE 2.2   *Natural Resource Exports and Growth*

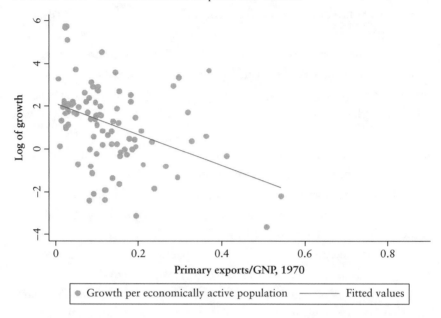

Source: Created from original data for Sachs and Warner (1997a), available at http://www.cid.harvard
.edu/ciddata/ciddata.html.

leads to a protectionist response. In a few oil countries this does not
hold. Overall, they found evidence of a U-shaped effect. Other effects were
small.

One might wonder whether the United States was in some way unique,
but evidence suggests that states have also suffered from resource curses.
Goldberg, Wibbels, and Mvukiyehe (2008) conduct an analysis similar to
that of Sachs and Warner for the American states for the years 1929–
2002. They find negative relationships between natural resources and per
capita income, a measure of very long-run growth, and between natural
resources and growth. Figure 2.3 illustrates the relationship between
natural resources and per capita income.

Why do the two types of analysis yield different answers? Part of the
difference arises because the papers study different numbers of economies, different time periods, and different outcomes. Wright studied the
U.S. (national) economy from 1879 to 1940, and most of the effects he

FIGURE 2.3   *Per Capita Income and Oil and Coal Production as a Share of GDP in U.S. States*

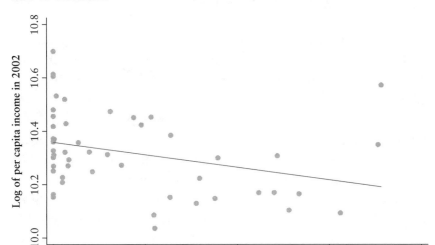

Source: Created from original data for Goldberg, Wibbels, and Mvukiyehe (2008), p. 492. The authors kindly shared their data.

finds were for the period up to 1928. Sachs and Warner studied growth in 97 countries from 1971 to 1989, and Goldberg, Wibbels, and Mvukiyehe studied growth in the American states from 1929 to 2002. Wright investigated differences in inputs into American exports and imports, while Sachs and Warner and Goldberg, Wibbels, and Mvukiyehe examined the effect of natural resources exports on country-level and state-level economic growth. Yet questions remain as to why these papers reach such very different conclusions. I will return to these differences at the end of the chapter.

In light of this conflict and to better understand the resource curse, subsequent studies investigated the mechanisms through which natural resources acted on growth. Mehlum, Moene, and Torvik (2006) studied growth over a longer period (1965–1990) using the sample of 87 countries from Sachs and Warner (1997b). They found that the effect of resources on growth was mediated by institutions. In countries where

resource exports represented more than 10 percent of GDP the resource curse held only for the countries with low-quality institutions.
In countries with low-quality institutions rent seeking and production
were competing activities, while in countries with the high-quality institutions rent seeking and production were complementary activities.
Robinson, Torvik, and Verdier (2006) modeled the interaction of natural resource growth with political policies. Based on the model and
empirical analysis, they found that institutions were important media-
tors of the effects of resource booms. Subsequent work by Yang (2010)
argued that policies and not institutions affected outcomes. Countries
with good institutions could have bad policies and the reverse.

Other papers questioned Sachs and Warner's measure of natural resources. The measure used by Sachs and Warner (1995) and later scholars
was a measure of export dependency and not endowment or production.
New measures of resource endowments from Brunnschweiler (2008) suggest that endowments and growth are positively related. The basic empirical relationships between endowments and growth are illustrated in
Figure 2.4.

The literature has a number of interrelated deficits, including the
short period over which growth is typically measured, the reliance on cross-
sectional identification of effects, and the cursory examination of institutions and policies. Ideally, the period of study would extend back into the
nineteenth century. With a panel data set, time-series and cross-sectional
estimates of the effects could be constructed and compared. One could
also test whether the relationships between natural resources and economic growth have shifted over time. For example, the observed relationships could be examined for the period from 1879 to 1928, the period in which Wright (1990) found strong positive effects of natural
resources on American exports. This chapter is not the first to remark on
the short periods over which growth economists examine outcomes. In
his paper "Why, Indeed, in America?" (1996), Paul Romer noted the lack
of dialogue between the economic history literature and the growth literature and the short horizon that most growth economists consider. More
than ten years later the situation remains the same.

FIGURE 2.4 *Natural Resource Abundance and Growth*

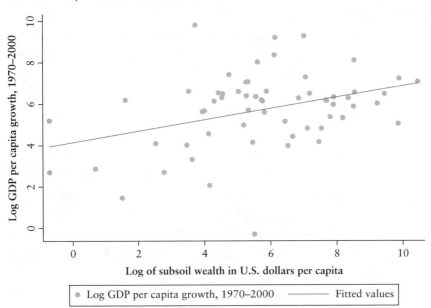

Source: Created from original data for Brunnschweiler (2008), p. 402, figure 1. The author kindly shared her data.

A more detailed examination of political institutions and policies related to public knowledge, education, incentives, and technology can clarify their importance. Drawing on a number of current and historical case studies, Wright and Czelusta (2004) argued that policies are critical determinants of the effects of natural resources on growth. Countries with policies that have focused on exploration, technology, and knowledge-related investments have been successful. Similarly bad policies or institutions can lead to undesirable outcomes such as rent seeking and corruption. "If minerals are conceived as fixed stocks, and mineral abundance as a 'windfall' unconnected to past investment, then the problem becomes one of divvying up the bounty rather than creating more bounty."[21] Subsequent work by Brunnschweiler and Bulte (2008) explored these themes further. They conclude, "Contrary to the paradoxical result that resource abundant countries tend to invite rent seeking and therefore suffer from worse institutions, we find that countries with certain institutional designs may fail to industrialize—and failing to develop significant non-resource sectors may make them dependent on primary sector extraction."[22] This line of work represents a promising start, but there is all too little of it.

NATURAL RESOURCES AND POLITICAL OUTCOMES

Ross (2001) began a line of research on natural resources and economic outcomes that very much parallels the work in economics. Using data for 113 countries over the period from 1971 to 1997, he examined the relationship between oil exports as a percentage of GDP and the polity scores of countries.[23] Polity scores capture the degree to which regimes are authoritarian and democratic, with higher values indicating greater levels of democracy. He found that countries with high levels of natural resource exports were less likely to be democratic.

Goldberg, Wibbels, and Mvukiyehe (2008) took a very similar approach but examined the American states. They showed that natural resource dependence was associated with less competitive state politics. Their work also suggests a mechanism through which resource dependence acts on politics. Because tax revenue is easier to generate in states with high levels of resource dependence, political elites can take actions that preserve their political power at lower cost. Thus natural resources have a conservative influence on the political structure.

Later authors found that the sign of the effect depended on a variety of factors. For example, Jones Luong and Weinthal (2006) found that private ownership of the oil industry was good for democracy and state ownership was bad for democracy. Analysis by Dunning (2008) showed that the effect was dependent on the size of the economic rents from the natural resource and the structure of the economic elite. Herb (2005) used a different measure of natural resources—the percentage of government revenue from resources. This weakened the relationship between resources and democracy. Other plausible measures such as windfall profits from oil or minerals as a fraction of GDP or per capita generate no association at all (Ross 2006). And as Haber (2006) notes, one needs to be concerned about reverse causality. Authoritarian regimes may be bad for GDP, which would account for the negative association in any measure of natural resources that is computed as a share of GDP.

In contrast to the economics literature, the political science literature has recently begun to move beyond cross-sectional identification. Haber and Menaldo (2009) built a data set that allows for time-series identification of the effects of natural resources on political outcomes as measured by the polity score.[24] Using a variety of archival and contemporary sources, they constructed extended series of the percentage of government revenue from oil or minerals for seventeen countries. Like the use of endowments rather than the exports in the growth context, government revenue from natural resources appears to be a more appropriate independent variable than natural resource exports as a share of GDP in the political context. All seventeen countries had average natural resource exports as a share of GDP of at least 6 percent and so were significant exporters. Haber and Menaldo find no relationship between the percentage of government revenue from resources and the polity score. They also reanalyze the conventional data sets using time-series techniques. No effect is found there either. What they do find is that the conventional cross-sectional relationships are sensitive to a variety of factors including how one deals with outliers.

UNDERSTANDING NATURAL RESOURCES, GROWTH, AND POLITICAL OUTCOMES

I want to advance a historical framework within which the empirical patterns for natural resources, growth, and political outcomes can be reconciled. Suppose countries with strong political institutions were the first to develop their natural resources. And for these countries, natural resources facilitated growth. Although some countries may have experienced more success than others for a variety of reasons, natural resources were often a complement to manufacturing. One reason was that high transportation costs and limited functioning of world markets made exporting most natural resources without further processing or value added unattractive. Countries without strong political institutions and some manufacturing or processing capability simply did not develop their natural resource base. Eventually, particularly after World War II, transportation costs fell and world commodity markets expanded. This made it profitable for many more countries to develop their natural resources, often with the aid of large multinational corporations. But most of the countries with large and relatively untapped natural resource bases were precisely those countries with weak political institutions or limited manufacturing or processing capability. To be sure, there were some exceptions. North Sea Oil discoveries in Britain and Norway would certainly be examples. But the vast majority of countries were negatively selected. This did not necessarily doom them. Some countries began to invest in education, technology, and processing. Many other countries experienced turmoil because newfound wealth, volatility in world commodity markets, and weak institutions proved to be an unfortunate combination. Hence we observe a resource curse.

A similar relationship may hold for the American states, although possibly for slightly different reasons. Western states may or may not have had weaker political institutions initially, but they certainly had fewer settlers. Low density and late settlement led to later discovery and development of resources. By the time they were discovered, transportation costs within the United States had already fallen dramatically. As a result, resources were transported to eastern and midwestern states that already had manufacturing capability. Thus resources may have been a curse at the state level yet simultaneously have been a benefit at the national level.

This hypothesis is in principle testable at both the country and state levels. While testing it is beyond the scope of this chapter, the hypothesis suggests that bringing together natural resource, growth, and political data over a long time span would be a fruitful exercise. One would need to define what strong political institutions might mean: security of property rights, a democratic regime, the competitiveness of elections, a lack of corruption, or perhaps all of the above. Measures of some of these variables exist for many countries from 1800 on and most American states beginning around 1870. Similarly, data on growth and natural resources exist or could be constructed for a substantial number of countries back to 1900 or earlier. Analysis of these panels could inform current debates regarding the interrelation among politics, resources, and growth. Given the importance of the issue, such an endeavor seems worthwhile.

NOTES

1. See Davis and Cull (2000), Engerman and Sokoloff (2000), and Lamoreaux (2000) for overviews of the economic history literature on specific parts of this story. Romer (1996) offers a brief synthesis of the literature from a growth perspective.

2. See Wright (1990), table 3.

3. Wright (1990), p. 658 (emphasis in original).

4. See Wright (1990), table 6.

5. Nelson and Wright (1992), p. 1960.

6. Quoted in Hendrickson (1961), p. 359.

7. See Grantham (this volume). The fall in printing costs was also facilitating dissemination of information in farming, including cotton production. See Olmstead and Rhode (this volume). Indeed, there are some interesting parallels between the exploitation of point source resources such as minerals and more diffuse resources such as land capable of growing cash export crops such as cotton. For discussion of the South's exploitation of its comparative advantage in cotton, see Wright (1978).

8. Hendrickson (1961), p. 361.

9. David and Wright (1997); Prentice (2006).

10. Knowles (1978), p. 149.

11. This draws on Reynolds (1992) and Thelin (2004).

12. Morrill Act of 1862, 7 U.S.C. 301 et seq.

13. See Bowman (1962), especially tables 2 and 3.

14. See Read (1941).

15. Scientific research had only recently come to be located in universities. See Grantham (this volume).

16. See David and Wright (1997) for a discussion of changes in technical training and the experience of U.S. mining engineers and chemists abroad.

17. See Goldin and Katz (2008).

18. See Carlson (this volume) for a discussion of the effects of the gold rush on Native Americans in California.

19. Jung (1999), pp. 63–65.

20. Goldman (1981) citing Spence (1970).

21. Wright and Czelusta (2004), p. 36.

22. Brunnschweiler and Bulte (2008), p. 250.

23. Ross's polity score is derived from the Polity98 data set compiled by Gurr and Jaggers (1999), which scores countries on a 0 to 10 scale for autocracy and level of democracy. The autocracy measure is subtracted from the democracy measure and rescaled to 0 to 10.

24. Haber and Menaldo use the Polity IV data set, a later version of the data set used by Ross (2001). They use the combined polity2 score, which "measures the competitiveness of political participation, the openness and competitiveness of executive recruitment, and the constraints on the chief executive." Haber and Menaldo (2009), p. 10.

REFERENCES

Bairoch, Paul (1998). "International Industrialization Levels from 1750 to 1980." In *Industrialisation: Critical Perspectives on the World Economy*, vol. 2, edited by Patrick Karl O'Brien. Berlin: Walter de Gruyter, pp. 3–35.

Bowman, Mary Jean (1962). "The Land-Grant Colleges and Universities in Human-Resource Development." *Journal of Economic History* 22: 523–546.

Broadberry, Stephen (1993). "Manufacturing and the Convergence Hypothesis: What the Long-Run Data Show." *Journal of Economic History* 53: 772–795.

Brunnschweiler, Christa (2008). "Cursing the Blessings? Natural Resource Abundance, Institutions, and Economic Growth." *World Development* 36: 399–419.

Brunnschweiler, Christa, and Erwin Bulte (2008). "The Resource Curve Revisited and Revised: A Tale of Paradoxes and Red Herrings." *Journal of Environmental Economics and Management* 55: 248–264.

Cain, Louis, and Donald Patterson (1986). "Biased Technical Change, Scale, and Factor Substitution in American Industry, 1850–1919." *Journal of Economic History* 46: 153–164.

Chandler, Alfred D. (1959). "The Beginnings of 'Big Business' in American Industry." *Business History Review* 33: 1–31.

Chandler, Alfred D. (1977). *The Visible Hand: The Managerial Revolution in American Business*. Cambridge, MA: The Belknap Press of Harvard University Press.

Clay, Karen, and Gavin Wright (2005). "Order without Law? Property Rights during the California Gold Rush." *Explorations in Economic History* 42: 155–183.

David, Paul A., and Gavin Wright (1997). "Increasing Returns and the Genesis of American Resource Abundance." *Industrial and Corporate Change* 6: 203–245.

Davis, Lance, and Robert Cull (2000). "International Capital Movements, Domestic Capital Markets, and American Economic Growth, 1820–1914." In *Cambridge Economic History of the United States*, edited by Stanley Engerman and Robert E. Gallman. Cambridge: Cambridge University Press, pp. 733–838.

Dunning, Thad (2008). *Crude Democracy: Natural Resource Wealth and Political Regimes*. New York: Cambridge University Press.

Engerman, Stanley, and Kenneth Sokoloff (2000). "Technology and Industrialization, 1790–1914." In *Cambridge Economic History of the United States*, edited by Stanley Engerman and Robert E. Gallman, pp. 367–402. Cambridge: Cambridge University Press.

Goldberg, Ellis, Eric Wibbels, and Eric Mvukiyehe (2008). "Lessons from Strange Cases: Democracy, Development, and the Resource Curse in the U.S. States." *Comparative Political Studies* 41: 477–514.

Goldin, Claudia (1998). "America's Graduation from High School: The Evolution and Spread of Secondary Schooling in the Twentieth Century." *Journal of Economic History* 58: 345–374.

Goldin, Claudia, and Lawrence Katz (2008). *The Race between Education and Technology*. Cambridge, MA: Harvard University Press.

Goldman, Marion (1981). *Gold Diggers and Silver Miners: Prostitution and Social Life on the Comstock Lode*. Ann Arbor: University of Michigan Press.

Gurr, Ted R., and Keith Jaggers (1999). "Polity 98: Regime Characteristics, 1800–1998." Database, University of Maryland.

Haber, Stephen (2006). "Authoritarian Government." In *Oxford Handbook of Political Economy*, edited by Barry Weingast and Donald Wittman. Oxford: Oxford University Press, pp. 693–707.

Haber, Stephen, and Victor Menaldo (2009). "Do Natural Resources Fuel Authoritarianism? A Reappraisal of the Resource Curse." Working Paper, Stanford University.

Hendrickson, Walter B. (1961). "Nineteenth-Century State Geological Surveys: Early Government Support of Science." *Isis* 52: 357–371.

Herb, Michael (2005). "No Representation without Taxation? Rents, Development, and Democracy." *Comparative Politics* 37: 297–317.

Irwin, Douglas (2003). "Explaining America's Surge in Manufactured Exports, 1880–1913." *Review of Economics and Statistics* 85: 364–376.

James, John (1983). "Structural Change in American Manufacturing, 1850–1890." *Journal of Economic History* 43: 433–459.

James, John, and Jonathan Skinner (1985). "The Resolution of the Labor-Scarcity Paradox." *Journal of Economic History* 45: 513–540.

Jones Luong, Pauline, and Erica Weinthal (2006). "Rethinking the Resource Curse: Ownership Structure, Institutional Capacity, and Domestic Constraints." *Annual Review of Political Science* 9: 241–263.

Jung, Maureen A. (1999). "Capitalism Comes to the Diggings: From Gold-Rush Adventure to Corporate Enterprise." In *A Golden State: Mining and Economic Development in Gold Rush California*, edited by James J. Rawls and Richard L. Orsi. Berkeley: University of California Press, pp. 52–77.

Knowles, Ruth Sheldon (1978). *The Greatest Gamblers: The Epic of American Oil Exploration*. Norman: University of Oklahoma Press.

Lamoreaux, Naomi (2000). "Entrepreneurship, Business Organization, and Economic Concentration." In *Cambridge Economic History of the United States*, vol. 2, edited by Stanley Engerman and Robert E. Gallman. Cambridge: Cambridge University Press, pp. 403–434.

MacDougall, G. D. A. (1951). "British and American Exports: A Study Suggested by the Theory of Comparative Costs, Part I." *Economic Journal* 61: 697–724.

Mehlum, Halvor, Karl Moene, and Ragnar Torvik (2006). "Institutions and the Resource Curse." *Economic Journal* 116: 1–20.

Merrill, George Perkins (1906). *Contributions to the History of American Geology*. Washington, DC: Government Printing Office.

Nelson, Richard R., and Gavin Wright (1992). "The Rise and Fall of American Technological Leadership: The Postwar Era in Historical Perspective." *Journal of Economic Literature* 30: 1931–1964.

Prentice, David (2006). "A Re-Examination of the Origins of American Industrial Success." Working Paper, La Trobe University.

Read, Thomas (1941). *The Development of Mining Industry Education in the United States*. New York: American Institute of Mining and Metallurgical Engineers.

Reynolds, Terry (1992). "The Education of Engineers in America before the Morrill Act of 1862." *History of Education Quarterly* 32: 459–482.

Robinson, James, Ragnar Torvik, and Thierry Verdier (2006). "Political Foundations of the Resource Curse." *Journal of Development Economics* 79: 447–468.

Romer, Paul (1996). "Why, Indeed, in America? Theory, History, and the Origins of Modern Economic Growth." *American Economic Review* 86: 202–206.

Ross, Michael (2001). "Does Oil Hinder Democracy?" *World Politics* 53: 325–361.

Ross, Michael (2006). "A Closer Look at Oil, Diamonds, and Civil War." *Annual Review of Political Science* 9: 265–300.

Sachs, Jeffrey, and Andrew Warner (1995). "Natural Resource Abundance and Economic Growth." National Bureau of Economic Research Working Paper No. 5398. Cambridge, MA: National Bureau of Economic Research.

Sachs, Jeffrey, and Andrew Warner (1997a). "Natural Resource Abundance and Economic Growth." Working Paper, Center for International Development and Harvard Institute for International Development.

Sachs, Jeffrey, and Andrew Warner (1997b). "Sources of Slow Growth in African Economies." *Journal of African Economies* 6: 335–376.

Spence, Clark C. (1970). *Mining Engineers and the American West: The Lace Boot Brigade, 1849–1933.* New Haven, Conn.: Yale University Press.

Thelin, John (2004). *A History of American Higher Education.* Baltimore: Johns Hopkins University Press.

Wright, Gavin (1978). *The Political Economy of the Cotton South: Households, Markets, and Wealth in the Nineteenth Century.* New York: Norton.

Wright, Gavin (1990). "The Origins of American Industrial Success, 1879–1940." *American Economic Review* 80: 651–668.

Wright, Gavin, and Jesse Czelusta (2004). "Why Economies Slow: The Myth of the Resource Curse." *Challenge* 47: 6–38.

Yang, Benhua (2010). "Resource Curse: The Role of Institutions versus Policies." *Applied Economics Letters* 17: 61–66.

Zerbe, Richard O., and C. Leigh Anderson (2001). "Culture and Fairness in the Development of Institutions in the California Gold Fields." *Journal of Economic History* 61: 114–143.

CHAPTER 3

The Institutionalization of Science
in Europe, 1650–1850

GEORGE GRANTHAM

GAVIN WRIGHT'S CONTRIBUTIONS to economic history represent a sustained effort to mediate the tension between the timeless logic of economics and the narrative logic of historical contingency. The logic of economics explains outcomes as special cases of a general class describable by abstract reasoning, the logic of historical contingency by the specific contexts that made their history what it was and not something else.[1] This chapter addresses the same issues as they are presented by the emergence of institutionalized science, which became central to Western and world economic development from around the middle of the nineteenth century. The story of the "Rise of Science" is conventionally told as a sequence of discrete intellectual "revolutions" that opened the door to more promising generalizations and lines of inquiry into nature's secrets (Kuhn 1970). While this narrative draws attention to the nature of scientific paradigms as public goods, it sidesteps a fundamental question of how communities of highly trained specialists in scientific problems emerged when and where they did. Between 1660 and 1850 European science experienced a massive expansion in the number persons working at high levels of scientific specialization and communicating their findings with each other through professional journals and professional gatherings. Why did large-scale organized science emerge between the middle of the seventeenth and the early nineteenth centuries, and not earlier or later? Why in Western Europe rather than in one of several other literate civilizations, where as we now know, scientific curiosity and achievement were far from lacking?[2]

Historians tend to explain both the time and the place of the scientific revolution in terms of cultural particularities that emerged with the recovery of the classical inheritance in the fifteenth and early sixteenth centuries that privileged explanations of natural (and spiritual) phenomena based on logic controlled by experience.[3] Yet perhaps the most striking feature of sixteenth-century scientific thought was its hermeneutic interpretation of the natural and spiritual worlds in terms of similarities, analogies, and antipathies revealed by their empirical "signatures." In that science birth defects are the "monstrous signs of secret sins in the parents," black eyes signify a healthy constitution and a mind "free from doubt and fear," gray eyes reveal "a crafty man, ambiguous and inconsistent" (Waite 2002 [1893], pp. 173, 176). Founded in the belief that God marked His world with visible signs to guide men to her useful secrets, sixteenth-century science was logical and empirical, but hardly differed from the styles of thought commonly held to characterize the "pre-rational" civilizations of the East.[4] Another common view holds that the autocratic constitutions and obscurantist religious beliefs in Asian civilizations blocked the emergence of a "scientific world view." Yet early modern Europe was hardly less priest-ridden; indeed, the scientific revolution coincided with the height of the Inquisition, renewed persecution of alleged witches and sorcerers, and a century of murderous religious conflict.[5] Nor does the resurgence of antiscientific fundamentalism in the United States suggest an innate cultural propensity to logical argument and empiricism. In Europe scientific discovery was supported (and rejected) by democracies and autocracies alike.[6] Cultural peculiarities, then, cannot have been the deciding factor that located the emergence of modern science in Europe.

The principles of economic analysis seem to offer little by way of resolving these issues. Nevertheless, for scientific investigation of the material world to have persistent significant effects on productivity, it had to be carried out on a scale large enough to breach the high threshold of tested fact and theory needed to establish reliable generalizations covering phenomena characterized by great complexity that are difficult to isolate and observe. This was especially true of what might be called the "taxonomic" sciences like natural history, mineralogy, and chemistry, where the initial work consisted in identifying and classifying phenomenal types, but except in pure mathematics it was everywhere present.[7] Because the expansion of scientific knowledge rested on secure, accurate observations through controlled experimentation, it required extensive division of labor. Division of labor in science, however, requires institutions capable of overcoming the barriers to coordination posed by the asymmetric status of information produced by individual research. The history of how that institutionalization was achieved was long and its outcome far from inevitable. Economics explains the impediments to it; the history explains how they came to be overcome.

This essay is organized in two parts. The first describes cognitive features of scientific discovery that help to explain why the emergence of large-scale science was improbable. The second part recounts how between 1650 and 1850 the organizational problems posed by information asymmetries arising from those characteristics were surmounted. The outline of the historical argument is as follows: Large-scale science rested on three institutional innovations. The first displaced the hermeneutic tradition of guarding discoveries for personal exploitation as private property by an ethos and institutional framework supporting immediate free exchange of new findings and methods of investigation, or what Paul David (2008) has aptly termed "open science." This seems to have been achieved by the middle of the eighteenth century. The second was the provision of institutions for peer review as a means of warranting and assigning priority of discovery. Initially centralized in scientific academies, the function of critical review passed in the second quarter of the nineteenth century into the hands of academic editors of specialized periodicals. The third was finding a way to recruit and reward scientific talent, a problem finally resolved in the German universities by combining research with teaching.

COGNITIVE PROBLEMS OF SCIENTIFIC ORGANIZATION

Science has been defined as "the activity of investigating problems in the context of an abstract technical discipline," differing from ordinary learning in revealing things not previously known, and from technological invention in that the problems it addresses are less strongly influenced by considerations of practical utility (Ravetz 1971). The two types of invention nevertheless draw on similar creative processes. Usher has characterized that process in terms of a sequence of cognitive stages. The first is the formulation of a problem such that it can potentially be solved; the second is assembling materials relevant to the solution in a way that suggests it; the third is the instant of insight. The final stage is the testing of the insight and working out its details and implications (Usher 1954, chap. 2). While chance enters at all stages, a discovery does not come "out of the blue," but is conditioned by physical and intellectual materials accessible to inventors that restrict the kind of discoveries that are possible at each point in time. For example, the availability of accurate chemical balances was necessary for the eighteenth-century discovery of the law of the conservation of matter, while the recognition that water vapor is a constituent of air created the possibility for conceiving that its condensation in a closed vessel could create a vacuum harnessing the energy in air pressure. Although they originally drew on different bodies of skill and knowledge, the two forms of creation thus did not differ in intrinsic difficulty, and the early academies of science hardly distinguished them.[8]

The primary difference between technological invention and scientific discovery is that whereas an invention is recognized when it solves a practical problem, scientific novelty is recognized when it can be assimilated to a formal frame of reference supporting its propositional description (Hansen 1969). An invention is judged by how it works; a scientific finding by how it fits. That connection between scientific novelty and general systems of thought makes a scientific discovery social: to serve as an input to generalization and further discovery, it must be recognized as valid; to be recognized as valid, it must be shared. The sharing, however, is obstructed by uncertainty. Is that speck in the night sky a new star or an aberration in the lens? How can we tell? Two persons observing the same phenomenon frequently "see" different things.

Tis with our judgments as our watches, none
Go just alike, yet each believes his own.

Pope's quip about literary criticism was just as true of contemporary science. The early history of astronomy and microscopy is littered with disputes occasioned by failure to replicate observations even when replication involved the same instruments.[9] Similar problems occurred when the volume of work required delegation of tasks. Kollreuter's field experiments in plant breeding were ruined by workmen not following his instructions to the letter (Olby 1966, p. 24).

As a psychological event, a new discovery is idiosyncratic; what one perceives is influenced by what one knows, and each person knows something different. In *An Essay Concerning Human Understanding* Locke reported a conjecture by a French correspondent (since experimentally confirmed) that upon recovering vision a person blind from birth would be unable to tell a cube from a sphere by sight alone.[10] Hansen suggests that a person entering a physics laboratory for the first time sees only various objects attached by wires and tubes to other objects. To see them as a physicist, he has to learn enough physics to know what the apparatus is for (Hansen 1969). As he elegantly puts it, "There is more to seeing than meets the eyeball" (Hansen 1958, p. 7). But because different people "see" different things, they often find it hard to see the same thing, which means that scientific discovery originates in informational asymmetry. That asymmetry has critical significance for the organization of science.

In considering why scientific production tends to be underprovided by market mechanisms, economists tend to stress its status as a public good, from which it follows that the main problem is organizing the purchasers (Arrow 1962). The informational asymmetry seems more fundamental. Collective goods can be collectively purchased, but collective purchase of scientific information has no particular implication for the quality of what is purchased. The history of "commissioned" science in the eighteenth and nineteenth centuries shows a systemic failure resulting from the inability of scientific patrons to distinguish reliable work from bad. None of the famous names in eighteenth-century invention appear in the list of winners of prizes awarded by the Royal Society of Arts, which was nevertheless expressly established to encourage invention.[11] Prizes were awarded for false solutions and withheld from inventors offering promising but incomplete contributions to the solution of a problem.

That demand for information provided an insufficient basis for the emergence of large-scale science is well attested by the history of agricultural experimentation. There was obvious and strong demand for scientific findings bearing on agriculture from at least the time Francis Bacon steeped seeds in Malmsey to see if the liquor inhibited smut, but in light of the number and complexity of the factors bearing on growth and fructification of plants, it is hardly surprising that numberless "trials" failed to turn up anything remotely useful, with the possible exception of the principles of Jethro Tull's horse-hoeing husbandry, which had to be reintroduced by Arthur Young from France. For his part, Young's undisciplined enthusiasm for the "system" led him to undertake more than 2,000 field "trials" that because they had no control plots yielded no useful information (Fussell 1935, p. 82). Eighteenth-century sponsors of agricultural research might have hoped science would improve productivity, but they were more interested in assessing the profitability of current best practice than in uncovering biological processes that might explain how it worked. It was in that spirit that the Royal Dublin Society ordered the manager of their experimental farm to discontinue investigations into how row cultivation affected yields of different varieties of wheat, and get on with the job of demonstrating the profitability of "best practices" propagandized by Arthur Young.[12] Reliable field experiments came only in the late 1830s, when the need to test the effect of mineral fertilizers on different crops and soil types led to an influx of trained chemists who understood the need for experimental controls. It was failure of nonprofessional testing that led to the establishment of the first true agricultural research station at Möckern in Germany.[13] The institutional innovation consisted in adapting the institutional form and ethos of organized science to agricultural research (Grantham 1984, pp. 191–214). The form, though not the ethos, was of recent vintage.

The initial difficulties in applying science to agriculture thus illustrate a systemic impediment to "market-driven" science. As Charles Daubeny, himself a distinguished geologist, remarked in his address to the Royal Agricultural Society in 1841, any real addition to agricultural knowledge had to come from men trained in "proper methods of experimenting," not from laymen conducting trials in an "unscientific manner" (Daubeny 1842, pp. 137–138; Crowther 1936, pp. 54–57). That training was necessarily technical, and to outsiders inaccessible and esoteric. The intrinsic ambiguity of "first sightings" discussed above means that their assimilation into the body of tested and accepted scientific knowledge is a task for experts armed with codes devised to facilitate transmission and storage of highly specialized information (Marschak 1968, pp. 1–18; Arrow

1974, pp. 37–43). Conceptual work in science is largely dedicated to developing and refining such codes, which because of the heavy individual investment required to master them and to master the experimental techniques with which they are associated erect significant entry barriers to those unable or unwilling to undertake that investment.[14] While analogous barriers characterize the skilled trades and other learned professions, the organizational problems resulting from ambiguity in the production of scientific novelty are of a higher order of magnitude. The first, as noted above, is the difficulty of defining an effective demand price for scientific knowledge when assessment rests on specialized knowledge that can be acquired only through costly training. The second is the need for material incentives to induce individuals to undertake scientific work and to ensure high standards of scientific performance. The third is how to recruit scientific talent in the face of the risk attached to investment in highly specific human capital for which there exist few alternative employments.[15] As in the skilled trades and learned professions, the institutional solution is autonomous, self-regulating organization. But whereas the trades and professions possessed institutional homes reaching far back into the Middle Ages, and provided services that were sufficiently well-defined to be sold in markets, the practice of science was beset by ill-defined property rights in discovery and by the heterogeneity of products specialized to meet the demands of exceptionally rarefied and specialized clienteles.

A degree of autonomous self-regulation seems to be a necessary condition for the coordination of scientific research. Given the inherent difficulty of communicating and assimilating truly novel findings, an economic explanation of scientific activity on a scale large enough to exploit the advantages of specialization would predict its location in small groups comprised of persons engaged in intense communication with each other. Members of these "invisible colleges" make reciprocal, person-specific investments that provide a basis for judging the quality and reliability of the work of individuals within the community. Much of that person-specific information is tacit knowledge in that it cannot be entirely codified and is therefore inaccessible to outsiders. For individual scientists, however, that investment constitutes scientific reputation. Coagulation of scientific activity into small clots of specialists can thus be interpreted as a means of warranting quality and assigning priority in research through peer review.[16] The same holds for recruiting new talent. An invisible college functions like a caste system in that persons who accept patently "bad" information are tossed out of the club.[17] Sociologists of science report that scientists working outside such established groups are relatively unproductive and that their research tends be unoriginal and repetitive (Crane 1972).

The growth of science, then, required institutions capable of warranting and conferring property rights in discovery, recruiting scientific talent, and maintaining scientific standards of precision and reliability on a scale large enough to permit advances on a broad front. By the third quarter of the nineteenth century the scientific enterprise had acquired the institutional stability and independence from governmental and religious interference that would carry it into the second half of the twentieth century. How did this happen?

INSTITUTIONAL INNOVATION

The above discussion suggests that effective scientific organization required a system of review and rewards controlled by persons capable of assessing scientific performance. The hypothesis advanced below is that institutional forms incorporating these functions, as well as providing a means for talented young researchers to signal their ability, did not emerge full-blown, but were assembled over a long period of time. An economic approach might hold that institutions having the highest net value would be the most likely to be developed first. Yet, before the middle decades of the nineteenth century, by which time the basic institutional form was in place, market demand for scientific output was limited. One must therefore look for explanations of the institutionalization on the supply side, in changes that affected the costs of organizing scientific work.[18] Of the solutions, peer review was the first to be achieved, because it depended on little more than a willingness to reveal reinforced by a natural desire to publish one's discoveries to the world. The critical barrier was the cost of communication. Recruiting scientists from beyond the ranks of the leisured curious was more difficult, because it required finding a way to identify and encourage young scientists without giving them so much security that they ceased to be productive. Most difficult of all was developing pay and employment structures that rewarded scientific achievement. Because the rewards required effective monitoring of the output, a review system had to be in place first, while the reward system had to be present in order to recruit new talent. Once all the pieces were in place, a science capable of expanding and employing large numbers of men and women in specialized pursuits could emerge. There was nothing, however, to ensure that solutions should be found precisely when the social benefit exceeded their cost. That something was socially desirable did not make it inevitable.

Opening Up Science

The first stage, prerequisite for all the others, was institutionalizing the revelation of scientific discovery, so that, in the words of the late Renaissance scientist and polymath Giambattista Della Porta (1658, Preface), "The wonders of Nature are not to be concealed." In the absence of "open science" the incentive to investigate those secrets of nature possessing little or no material value would have been reduced to the anticipated pleasure of satisfying a curiosity. The coming of what David calls "open science" was the consequence of two linked historical changes. The first involved the displacement of a hermeneutic epistemology that identified the hidden connections between things by searching for signs intimating their similitude by an epistemology based on analyzing phenomena into simple constituents to be investigated using the language of measure and order (Foucault 1966). Foucault dates this tectonic change to the early seventeenth century. It was critical to open science because unlike hermeneutical science based on the "signatures" of things, the new epistemology supplied both the means and justification for experimental verification.

The second change was disclosure. David argues that the shift from hermeneutic treatment of discovery as a proprietary good to its status as a public good shared by the community of scientists was precipitated by increasing inaccessibility of scientific findings, particularly in mathematical sciences having practical applications in military and public works. But once science became inaccessible, princes seeking to enhance their prestige by pensioning scientists had to draw on the expertise of scientific peers to determine whether to recruit or retain the services of a particular candidate. For scientists, their situation was summed up by the founder of Europe's first scientific academy: "The Professor of this science must be rich: for if we lack money, we can hardly work in these cases: for it is not Philosophy that can make us rich; we must first be rich, so that we can play the Philosopher" (Della Porta 1658, p. 4).

To secure patronage needed to support their work, scientists needed the recognition of their peers; to secure that recognition, they had to reveal their findings. David argues that by permitting scientists to reward themselves with honors remunerated by outsiders, competition among princes for eminent scientists conferred on the scientific community a significant share of the "informational rents" generated by scientific work.

Positive feedbacks also came into play, because as public recognition became more relevant to acquiring a patron, questions of priority in discovery became more urgent, which increased the incentive to divulge completed work without delay.[19] In turn, the productivity of individual scientists—the likelihood of making an original discovery—was increased by open access to the findings of other scientists.[20] Open science also sharpened incentives to rigorously review new work, as a flawed contribution could contaminate the work of others and bring down the prestige of scientific self-administration. By the second quarter of the eighteenth century a transnational social network based on reciprocal disclosure and collective warranting of discoveries was in place. Apart from the need to secure resources to fund research, the system functioned autonomously, elaborating and administering its rules of demonstration and rewards. That independence, which as late as the middle of the eighteenth century was still far from secure, is perhaps its greatest achievement.[21]

Peer Review

Although peer review emerged in the context of patronage, it also has roots in the psychology of invention. Students of science and invention agree that the instant of discovery is one of intense emotional excitement, when nature seems to speak directly to the discoverer. But the moment is personal. As Adam Smith observes, we do not experience another person's toothache. The desire to publish findings was also motivated by a need to have one's vision validated by approbation of persons competent to judge. Darwin confessed in his *Autobiography* that

I believe that I can say with truth that in after years, though I cared in the highest degree for the approbation of such men as Lyell and Hooker, who were my friends, I did not care much about the general public. I do not mean to say that a favourable review or a large sale of my books did not please me greatly, but the pleasure was a fleeting one, and I am sure that I have never turned one inch out of my course to gain fame. (Cited in Selye 1964, pp. 13–14)

The audience is the peer group. Scientific peer groups emerged as soon as there were men possessed of the means and leisure to investigate nature, and the willingness to publish their findings to others. Their emergence was thus a natural consequence of increasing scale of scientific activity. As the number of persons interested and engaged in science increased, such groups emerged wherever the cost of communicating findings was not prohibitive.[22]

Although validation of the kind Darwin desired was psychologically rewarding, public recognition of priority in discovery still needed a degree of formal warranting. The initial institutional solution was to place the validation of scientific findings in the hands of an authorized company of scientists sitting as judges. That centralization of the review function reflected the view that the accumulation of knowledge is a collective enterprise and that assignment of priority ought to be carried out collectively. In that spirit, seventeenth-century scientific societies published findings under their collective name, on the grounds that after prolonged discussion it was impossible (as it still is) to disentangle individual contributions to a scientific finding. An assembly of persons having broadly similar interests in a subject, however, did not guarantee effective judgment. Samuel Goodenough, an authority on seaweeds, complained of the Society for Promoting Natural History, that

The present Society goes on in the usual way of having a fossil or a plant go round the table; nothing is or can be said about it. It is referred to a committee to reconsider: the committee call it by some name and send it back to the society. The society desires the committee to reconsider it. In the meantime nothing is done; indeed it does not appear to me that any of them can do anything. (Cited in Fletcher 1969, p. 26)

In France the system of academic warranting of research findings broke down when more and more experiments came to be conducted off the premises of the Académie des Sciences. (Hahn 1971, pp. 24–29). Even after anonymous contributions were abandoned, however, members of the Académie were forbidden from attaching their name to new work until it had been cleared by the entire company. Centralization failed because it was physically impossible to conduct experiments in one place. But decentralizing verification of new work required an efficient medium of scientific communication.

From Letters to Scientific Periodicals

Prior to the late eighteenth century, the cost of publishing scientific journals for the small audiences that could effectively use them was too high for them to function as a medium for diffusing and evaluating scientific findings. With minor exceptions, there does not seem to have been any significant decline in publishing costs between 1600 and 1800. Presses and printing technology hardly changed, while the cost of paper, which was the most expensive variable input, remained high.[23] Scientific publication was costly, especially when engraving was involved. The cost of engraving for publications in descriptive sciences like natural history was prohibitive. Printing Nehemiah Grew's *Anatomy of Plants* and Willoughby's *Historia Piscium* so exhausted the Royal Society's funds that it found itself unable to publish Newton's *Principia*, the cost of which was defrayed by a contribution from Halley.[24] In the 1790s the *Annales de Chimie*, subsidized by the French State, cost 12 francs at a time when the daily wage was less than one (Yagello 1968, p. 426). The Royal Horticultural Society spent more than £3,000 in 1817 printing its *Transactions*, which sold at more than twice an English workingman's weekly wage (Fletcher 1969).

Journals were thus not the preferred method of communicating scientific findings too brief to be written up as a book. Instead, scientists relied on personal correspondence, often formally written up.[25] Circulating in manuscript form, scientific letters served to announce and discuss new findings. By the middle of the seventeenth century their volume had grown to a point that clearing houses emerged, a task performed by Père Mersenne and Ismaël Boulliau in Paris and Henry Oldenburg in London.[26] Among the advantages of correspondence was freedom from the pervasive censorship to which printed material was then subject. The disadvantage was its growing volume, which soon became overwhelming, though no one seems to have matched the output of French astronomer and savant Fabri de Pereisc, who is said to have had more than 500 correspondents and once wrote 42 letters in a single day (Hatch 1998). Correspondence networks did not originate in the scientific community, however. Epistolary diffusion of insights and findings to selected correspondents goes back at least to Petrarch. Early scientists thus had no need to invent a new means of communication. They borrowed from the international literary community, and well into the seventeenth century shared its network of correspondence.

The French Académie des Sciences attempted to short-circuit private and uncontrollable networks by centralizing the communication of scientific findings in its transactions, but publication was so slow that findings were dated by the time they appeared in print. The delays continued into the nineteenth century. Fourier's great work on the theory of heat lay buried for fourteen years in the Académie's archives before his revolutionary mathematical analysis was finally published. Fresnel's first memoir on the diffraction of light was read to the Académie in 1818 and received a prize in 1819, but was not printed until 1826, apparently mislaid, allegedly because of the opposition of Laplace. Not surprisingly, personal, semipublic correspondence remained the preferred method for establishing priority in discovery into the early eighteenth century (Hunter 1998).

The first "learned" journals thus played a modest role in sifting and diffusing scientific discoveries, and were used more as digests to be browsed by persons preparing to attend a salon than serious venues for research. As the editor of the *Journal des Sçavans*, the official organ of the Académie des Inscriptions, complained, "Journals have been invented for the relief of those either too indolent or too occupied to read whole books. It is a means of satisfying curiosity and becoming learned with little trouble" (Barnes 1934, p. 258). The same was true of the nonofficial periodicals which first appeared in Germany during the first half of the eighteenth century. Published by booksellers, they aimed at a wide readership and were therefore printed in large runs.[27] Not surprisingly the mortality rate was high. Of the 167 learned German periodicals founded before 1746, 36 percent died in the first year, and only 5 percent survived five years (Kirchner 1928–1931, p. 37). The high mortality persisted through the first two-thirds of the century, despite or perhaps because of the growth in the number of periodicals published. The main reason was unspecialized readership. At a time when the number of competent specialists in individual scientific fields probably did not exceed two or three dozen persons, periodicals published for profit were poor vehicles for disseminating original scientific findings.[28] Unlike "transactions" of officially sponsored scientific societies, contributions to the early scientific journals were not refereed beyond a minimal level needed to avoid censorship. Always short of material, editors accepted or translated what they could get their hands on (Barnes 1936, pp. 167–169). German periodicals are perhaps unique in that the states subsidized publication for the benefit of their educated elite, and circulation was mainly local. Although they served a valuable function in republishing foreign work and popularizing science among educated people, they could not serve as true scientific journals, which demanded editing by scientists (Kirchner 1958–1962, pp. 74–75).

The first professional journals to accept original scientific findings date to the 1770s, with the Abbé Rozier's *Observation sur le physique* (1771) and the series of chemical journals initiated in 1778 by Lorenz von Crell (Thornton and Tully 1971, pp. 273–284). They were nevertheless edited by amateurs, although Crell had studied under Black at Glasgow. The title of one of his journals reveals the audience to whom it was intended: *Chemische annalen für die Freunde der Naturlehre,*

Arzneigelehrheit, Haushaltkunst und Manufacturen (Annals of Chemistry for the Friends of Natural History, Medicine, Household Management and Manufactures) (Kronick 1962). The first scientific journal controlled by professional scientists was the *Annales de Chimie* (Annals of Chemistry, 1790), whose editorial board included Fourcroy, Lavoisier, Guyton de Morveau, and Berthollet (Delepine 1962, p. 1). The *Annales* was a special case precipitated by the French Revolution. Elsewhere, editorship of learned journals tended to stay in the hands of interested amateurs. It was only in the second quarter of the nineteenth century that editorial control passed irrevocably to professional scientists.

The passage was not peaceful. Justus Liebig's transformation of a sleepy north German pharmaceutical periodical into the leading chemical journal of its day was little short of a coup. Periodicals reporting pharmaceutical and medical findings had appeared in the 1780s to keep pharmacists and physicians abreast of the latest developments in chemistry, but they were essentially newsletters featuring items of interest to pharmacists and describing new drugs and methods of preparing them. Liebig, who "for the sake of the money involved" agreed to coedit the *Magazin für Pharmazie und die dahin einschlagenden Wissenschaften*, revolutionized the journal by subjecting chemical findings to criticism and as far as possible to verification. He renamed the journal the *Annalen der Chemie*. The innovation led to disputes with his coeditor, who quit to found his own journal. In the first five years of his editorship Liebig edited the *Annalen* with the help of pharmacists teaching in other universities or academies, who in effect served as referees. In 1837 he acquired total control of the journal and, having secured the services of Dumas and Thomas Graham, made it the most powerfully edited scientific journal of its time (Klooster 1957, pp. 27–30; Kirchner 1958–1962, Bd. 1, pp. 231–237; Bd. 2, pp. 40–41).

Although peer review continued to employ correspondence and manuscripts circulating among scientists, its supreme institutional expression down to the third decade of the nineteenth century was the scientific academy, where material rewards, status, and the opportunity for intense discussion with experts supplied a powerful mechanism for screening and publicizing new findings. The effectiveness of that institutional arrangement depended on the quality of the members, and between the last quarter of the eighteenth and the first two decades of the nineteenth century the French Académie des Sciences assembled a company of scientific geniuses that has rarely if ever been equaled. Writing to Lakanel in the summer of 1793, Lavoisier pleaded with the revolutionary Convention to preserve the Académie des Sciences, despite its connection to the Old Regime. The belles lettres, he wrote, can survive on reading and personal experience. "It is not the same in the sciences, most of which cannot be successfully cultivated by individuals working alone. It requires a united effort." When qualified men assemble to hear and criticize new work, "there results a true judgment without which it would inspire less confidence" (Lavoisier 1862–1868, vol. 4, pp. 616–617, 619). The signature of the Secretary of the First Class of the Institut, which was the successor to the Académie des Sciences, constituted the seal of authentication for major discoveries; on occasion the Institut sat as a court to determine priority of discovery.[29]

Centralization nevertheless had its limits. Just as experiments could not be centralized for verification, so the increasing specialization of scientific research made it impossible for a small group of men to evaluate all of it. By the first decade of the nineteenth century French Academicians were complaining that meetings had ceased to be scientifically useful because members lacked the specialized knowledge needed to judge and criticize topics presented to them, and because "real" work was being conducted and published elsewhere. Fourcroy, LaPlace, Cuvier, Lacépede, and Legendre observed that "today so much of science is so specialized that it cannot enter into a general education, and the most highly educated man does not understand what is said unless he has devoted himself to that particular subject" (Crosland 1967, pp. 159–160). Specialized journals edited by professional scientists offered an alternative, but to do so they had to be widely circulated.

The substitution of scientific periodicals for correspondence networks and scientific academies as the locus of validation of scientific work raised other barriers to the assessment and diffusion of scientific information, however. As late as 1841 Liebig's colleague Robert Bunsen was unaware of the *Annalen* (Klooster 1957, p. 28). Cambridge botanist James Henslow complained to the Royal Agriculture in 1841 that it was impossible to keep up with continental work on diseases in wheat because the University library did not carry the relevant books and journals (Henslow 1841, p. 3). Jacob Schleiden, a cofounder of cell theory, had no knowledge of microscopic work by mycologists on spores, which he supposed to be diseased cells. Liebig thought blights were caused by bad sap (Parris 1968, pp. 34–38). As scientific journals became more specialized and more professional, the quality of the work improved, but the audience narrowed. Increased specialization also entailed the condensation of new findings in current surveys of research, a task eminently suited to professorial teachers of survey courses.

Scientific journalism nevertheless benefited from the decline in the cost of printing in the 1820s following the invention of lithography and the steam press. This was especially important for natural history, where graphical description is crucial to taxonomic identification. Before the fall in cost, such books were so dear they were accessible only to gentleman scholars (Allen 1976, pp. 96–99). Yet on the whole, declining printing cost played a modest role in the emergence of a decentralized system of peer review. The primary driving forces driving behind that development were the increasing numbers of scientists and the proliferation of specialized scientific languages. Once scientists gained control of publishing, simple growth in the numbers of scientists (and the number of sciences) seems to have been sufficient. This condition had been achieved by the 1840s.

Solving the Problem of Recruitment

Although scientific networks reduced the transaction cost of monitoring effort, they did little to encourage individual investment in long-lived and risk-prone human capital. Given the specificity of that capital, prospective scientists needed assurance of a steady and reasonable return on a costly investment. For their part, potential employers of scientific talent required assurance of its productivity. Recruitment thus raised signaling problems on both sides of the market for specialized scientific skill. In the absence of institutions producing reliable signals, individual investment in scientific human capital would have been restricted to well-off or exceptionally dedicated individuals. Darwin is a good example of the former; his codiscoverer of the principle of natural selection, Alfred Wallace, exemplifies the latter (Schermer 2002). For a large scientific community to emerge, it needed a broader base of material support.[30]

The older academies of science were not well suited to that role. As elite institutions to which entry came as an honor, their membership was generally poorly rewarded. The stipends for academicians in eighteenth-century France were at best two-thirds of a comfortable middle-class income (Hahn 1975, p. 131). The Royal Society was notoriously under-funded, its annual income as late as the 1740s being only £240 (Merz 1976 [1907], p. 228). Moreover, scientists entered a major academy only after they had made their reputation. As a means of recruiting and supporting talent, the academies established to promote science were thus a catch-22. For the very few, positions at the top of the scientific hierarchy could be highly remunerative. Gay-Lussac's accumulation of several posts in Paris earned him the truly princely annual income of 55,000 francs, and a full professor at the Institut de France or the Museum of Natural History received 5,000 to 6,000 (Gerbod 1965; Crosland 1978, p. 230). Successes like these, however, were like winning tickets in a lottery that only a handful of scientific fields could support. Faraday's experience was more typical. The receipts from his lecturing on popular science at Rumford's Royal Institute barely kept the establishment alive. In his words, "We were living on the parings of our own skin" (Merz 1976 [1907], p. 246). Until the early nineteenth century, scientific research was overwhelmingly self-financed, a luxury of the great and the relatively wealthy.

In the course of the eighteenth and early nineteenth centuries the pool of scientific talent was deepened in two ways. The first drew on the traditional method of patronage, which reduced the informational asymmetries discussed above through informal methods of acquiring person-specific information. The second was the result of growing demand for skills requiring formal scientific training, which created a derived demand for science teachers and a joint supply of potential scientists. When in the first two decades of the nineteenth century the two processes combined at Paris in the École Polytechnique and the École Normale Supérieure, powerful mechanisms for screening and supporting young scientists were brought into play.

Aristocratic patronage of promising young men goes back to the fifteenth century. Patronage had the advantage of providing the patron with a flow of information about the candidate based on performance, and of providing a candidate a loose expectation of his prospects. It thus lowered the risks of investing in scientific human capital. Its major drawbacks were its dependence on chance encounter and the relatively small numbers of persons whom it could support, and it was spread across the whole range of literary and scientific fields. To the patron, science was but one of many areas in which he could place his funds in the interest of enhancing his prestige. Nevertheless, the growing interest in the potential benefits of science to which Mokyr has recently drawn attention seems to have resulted in a growth in the scale of support that changed the operation of recruitment by patronage in the same way that the competition of patrons for eminent scientists helped to bring about open science (Mokyr 2005, 2010). Just as the increasing difficulty of science led patrons to rely on scientists to warrant the achievements of their potential clients, so in the end, they came increasingly to rely on scientists to identify promising recruits.

Crosland's history of the Society of Arcueil illustrates the changing patterns of patronage in France. When Claude Berthollet arrived in Paris in 1772, he secured an introduction to the Duke of Orléans, who in turn recommended him to Madame de Montesson as her personal physician, which gave him enough income and time to conduct chemical research in his own laboratory. His contemporary and colleague Antoine Fourcroy was the son of an apothecary in the Duke's household who attended medical school on the advice of the inventor of comparative anatomy, Felix Vicq-d'Azyr. Vicq-d'Azyr owed his ascent to prominence to the friendship of Condorcet and Turgot. In the decades preceding the Revolution, however, the source of patronage shifted to prominent scientists. Vauquelin got his entry through a letter of introduction from Fourcroy; Thénard was admitted to Fourcroy's laboratory through the intercession of Fourcroy's sisters. In the 1790s and early 1800s Arago, Poisson, and Gay-Lussac were recruited for minor teaching positions by competition from among the already highly selected students at the École Polytechnique, where they distinguished themselves before their illustrious teachers. Posted to Beauvais to teach mathematics in a lycée, Biot secured Laplace's patronage by offering to correct the proofs of the great man's *Mécanique céleste* (Crosland 1967, pp. 77, 125–127, 254–255). Probably the most prominent patron at the turn of the nineteenth century was Alexander von Humboldt, who identified Justus Liebig and secured his entry to Gay-Lussac's laboratory. He then persuaded the Hessian government to create a post of extraordinary professor for him at the University of Giessen. Ten years later, he met and encouraged the young Boussingault, one of the discoverers of the nitrogen cycle, off to Bogota for ten years to establish a school of engineering and study volcanoes.[31] Sir Joseph Banks, whose spidery web of correspondence touched almost every branch of late eighteenth- and early nineteenth-century natural history, encouraged the timorous Thomas Knight to publish his research on plant physiology.[32]

The ability to control the allocation of scientific positions was critical to the growth in scientific manpower. The creation of subordinate positions in teaching and research establishments in France provided promising young men with material means to finance their research. There were also private subsidies. Berthollet's opening his laboratory facilities at his estate in Arcueil on the outskirts of Paris to promising chemists is perhaps the best example. The crucial feature of these positions was that they remained in the giving of professional scientists who possessed the ability to assess prospective scientific talent. The number of apprenticeships, however, was small, which restricted the number of qualified persons who could be so accommodated (Crosland 1975). The growth of scientific specialization needed a broader institutional foundation. In this respect the highly centralized scientific establishment in Paris, which had done so much to advance the prosecution of physical and natural sciences in the late eighteenth and early nineteenth centuries, was to prove less effective than the diffuse university system that grew up in Germany after the Reformation and the Thirty Years War to supply principalities with civil servants, priests, and medical specialists.[33]

Science and the University

That the scientific enterprise was to lodge in what in the eighteenth century was still an essentially medieval institution dedicated to training civil servants, priests, high school teachers, and medical professionals could not have been predicted in 1750. Such science as was then conducted took place in private libraries and laboratories, and in a handful of specialized institutes like the Jardin du Roi. Scientific analysis of ancient and medieval documents found an institutional home at the Benedictine Abbey of Saint-German-des-Prés and among the Bollandists in Antwerp, but while monastic life supported disinterested study and trained young researchers, its scientific inquiries were confined to the technical work of editing and criticizing ancient manuscripts. Mendel's experiments in the garden of the Augustinian abbey at Brunn are a notable exception, but his revolutionary findings were ignored, possibly because of his isolation from the scientific community.[34] The one institution possessing the capacity to provide advanced technical training was the craft guild, of which the medieval university was a distant cousin. But guilds were protectionist and conservative, guarding their secrets closely, and even had they been more open, their utilitarian focus and limited ability to support apprentices inhibited any tendency to investigate and publish the general principles of their respective crafts.[35] Perhaps the greatest impediment to doing science through the guild, however, was lack of employment opportunities for trained researchers unable to support themselves by scientific research once they graduated.

In the eighteenth century universities were still burdened by a medieval curriculum. In France the straitjacket was circumvented by creating new institutions outside the university, beginning with François I's establishment of the Collège de France in 1530 as an alternative to the Sorbonne. Universities were for teaching, not research. A scientist of no less importance than Thomas Young, author of Young's modulus and co-discoverer of the principle of the wave theory of light, declared in 1810,

It must be remembered that the advancement of learning is by no means the principal object of an academical institution: the diffusion of a respectable share of instruction in literature and in the sciences among those classes which hold the highest situations and have the most extensive influence in the State is an object of more importance to the public than the discovery of new truths. (Cited in Merz 1976 [1907], p. 261)

The same was true elsewhere. By virtue of its political fragmentation Germany had the largest number of universities, all small, with the majority of students in 1800 matriculated in the Faculty of Theology. The lecture courses provided the opportunities for professors to develop new ideas, as the works of Fichte and Hegel amply illustrate, but the university was not a place for learning how to do research.

The origins of university-based science are to be found in the pedagogical seminars established in the third quarter of the eighteenth century at Halle and Göttingen to prepare future masters in the study of biblical and ancient texts. In this respect they continued the work of the Benedictines and Bollandists in a new setting. The work involved exact textual criticism, testing the meaning of words and phrases by collating and comparing texts. Rather than presenting students with finished results, the seminars trained them to conduct a research project by formulating a question, gathering the information bearing on it, analyzing that information, and asserting a conclusion. It was this model that inspired Liebig to establish his teaching laboratory at Giessen (Morrell 1972). It was a spectacular success. Liebig later confessed that he was fortunate to have landed in a small provincial university where his energies would not have been dissipated. At Giessen he and his students could concentrate on chemistry,

and this was a passionate enjoyment. The necessity of an institute where the pupil could instruct himself in the chemical art, by which I understand familiarity with chemical operations of analysis and adroitness in the use of apparatus, was then in the air, and so it came about that on the opening of my laboratory . . . pupils came to me from all sides. . . . The greatest difficulty presented itself, as the numbers increased, in the practical teaching itself. In order to teach many at once, an ordered plan was required and progressive way of working, which had to be thought out and tried. (Cited in Merz 1976 [1907], p. 190)

Liebig's spectacular success was copied in the following decades and became the model for university-based research. That success, however, was not in itself sufficient to produce the expansion of scientific effort that marked the second third of the nineteenth century. For this we need to consider certain peculiarities of the German academic system around the turn of the nineteenth century.

By a custom inherited from medieval times German universities permitted anyone possessing the appropriate degree to teach privately for fees. In mid-nineteenth-century Germany the unpaid position of *privatdozent*, which gave access to the university library and laboratory facilities, played a role similar to that of the assistantships at the Parisian Grandes Écoles. Because fee-rich general courses were monopolized by professors, *dozenten* typically taught the smaller specialized courses. A major difference between *dozenten* and French teaching assistants was that the employment of *dozenten* was not restricted by the institution's funding. Any *dozent* capable of attracting a sufficient number of students could pay his own way, and those with the means could teach without pay. The problem of quality control, however, remained. In the course of the eighteenth century titled professors, concerned that the growing popularity of tutorials given by *dozenten* was eating into their fees, began to impose examinations and the *habilitationschrift* as a condition for acceding to the *dozentur*.[36] Although the initial purpose of the reform was protectionist, an unintended consequence was to transform the *dozentur* from a modest self-employment into a specialized occupation geared to research in expectation of an ultimate appointment to the professoriat (Busch 1959, pp. 7–21). All this lay in the future.

The greatest boost to expanding the basin of potential scientists came from growth in demand for science-based skills. The expansion of scientific education in the first quarter of the nineteenth century reflected growing demand for a few well-defined specialties, such as military engineering, pharmacy, and medicine, which required basic and in some instances advanced instruction normally given in the university. The demand for scientific professionals created a derived demand for more science teachers, which gave a stable means of support for investment in advanced scientific skills. This effect was reinforced by certification examinations imposed by states on physicians, pharmacists, and teachers in state-financed gymnasia. The need to prepare exams covering scientific material further increased the demand for science courses and instructors. This effect was especially marked in Germany, where the exams for prospective teachers covered a sufficiently broad area of science to generate a steady clientele for instructors in the elementary courses (Paulsen 1902; Turner 1971, p. 140). The growth of job opportunities in fields for which the training involved exposure to advanced science and research methods also reduced the risks of specializing for a career in science. The ability to earn a living in pharmacy was an insurance policy for someone investing in advanced training in chemistry and plant physiology.

The growth in outlets for scientifically trained persons thus created a positive feedback loop. By reducing the average cost of instruction and creating new openings, larger classes and greater job opportunities for university graduates expanded the possibilities for pursuing a scientific career to a broadening stratum of the population. A growing proportion of scientists after 1830 came from the lower middle classes, for whom scientific achievement provided one of the few contemporary vehicles for social advancement. These feedbacks help to explain the sequence of institutionalization of the individual sciences. On the basis of observational facility alone, one would expect the science of economic entomology and plant pathology to have developed before agricultural chemistry. Chemistry, however, was a required course of study for aspiring pharmacists and by the nineteenth century its findings were being exploited by manufacturers who in turn encouraged its study. Except in geology, which had economic support in mineral exploration, the sciences of natural history had few commercial outlets. There were few job opportunities for mycologists and entomologists, though the rate of publication accelerated there as elsewhere (Tuxen 1973, pp. 95–117). Entomologists were generally poor men who gained their living from a grab bag of poorly paid employments (Howard 1930, pp. 203–204; Lindroth 1973). Mycology, too, was slighted and relegated to amateurs. Only botany with its intimate link to the preparation of pharmaceutical samples retained a strong base in institutionalized science. The expansion of university-based research was thus tied to particular economic circumstances of the early nineteenth century that favored chemistry and geology, and only later spread into the physical sciences associated with electrical and physical phenomena.

New openings were not in themselves enough to sustain the expansion and proliferation of scientific work, because teaching positions were neither originally nor inherently research positions. Professors published books, but most books were their lecture notes, and although nomination to the highest scientific honors demanded original contributions, a satisfactory academic career could then as now be quietly pursued as long as the teacher stayed on the good side of his colleagues and the authorities. Decentralized science on a large scale required stronger incentives and stronger measures to ensure quality and productivity. One means of encouraging sustained effort was the institution of ranks or grades, advancement through which exposed scientists to repeated screening. The Institut de France was so organized, but once a member was admitted he could also progress by longevity. In Germany the professorial hierarchy was well defined and strictly maintained, with two professorial ranks plus the untenured *privat-dozenten*. Above that local hierarchy stood a hierarchy of institutions, with the major metropolitan universities in Berlin, Munich, and Leipzig attracting better students and more funding for research laboratories and possessing greater prestige than the smaller provincial institutions. By the 1820s Germany, then, with its professorial hierarchy and multiplicity of institutions, possessed the institutional basis for continuous screening and promotion of scientific talent.

The crucial missing element in making appointments and promotions was scientific control and the application of scientific criteria. Although their role as a repository of information and as the place of instruction in advanced studies made educational institutions likely venues for scientific research, university-based science was by no means a sure thing. One can imagine the scientific enterprise supported by sinecures, as had been the case in the seventeenth and eighteenth centuries and remained the case in early nineteenth-century England. The lack of original research in universities before 1800 and its thinness through much of the nineteenth century in local academies and technical schools are a warning against a too-easy identification of higher learning with advanced scientific research (Mc-Clelland 1980). Down to the end of the Napoleonic Wars, German universities were parochial institutions whose internal affairs were managed somewhat like those of a private club. Although excellence did not go unrewarded, what mattered was collegiality and what mattered even more were good connections. Although they were funded by the state, and like other sovereign entities comprising the Holy Roman Empire were legally bound to a superior entity, the universities were in practice quasi-independent. And because the universities, like the states that subsidized them, were divided along religious lines, the main items of contention before the rise of atheism were off the table. Professors could thus engage in research, or spend their time teaching and writing works of scientific popularization. It didn't matter, because success in research yielded no differential reward, and indolence no penalty.

Turner's (1971) account of the rise of university-based science in early nineteenth-century Germany indicates that the critical event permitting the seizure of academic appointments and promotions by scientific peer groups was the Prussian government's decision to remove responsibility for appointments and promotions from local professors and confide it to a larger community of scholars. The event was the Carlsbad Decrees in 1819 made in response to the murder of a conservative journalist by a deranged student. The decrees enjoined the states of the German Confederation to dissolve student associations and impose censorship on university teachers suspected of democratic tendencies. They effectively placed the universities in trusteeship by ordering member states to appoint curators to vet lectures in order to ascertain and encourage the political reliability of the instructors. As the bureaucrats in the ministries of interior extended their reach, however, they found it useful to shield themselves from charges of interfering in purely "academic affairs" by drawing on the expertise of outsiders in questions of academic appointment, thereby removing the power to appoint and promote from local professors who might be swayed by personal and parochial allegiances to hire political undesirables to more reliable outsiders.[37] To give a patina of credibility to this interference in academic affairs, the bureaucrats relied on well-known scientists to do the vetting in the sciences. Subject to a political constraint, it was inevitable that once the system was in place, the scientists would impose original publication as a criterion for appointment and promotion. The vetting process also provided a means of placing students.

With this, the last element of an institutional form capable of supporting rapid expansion of scientific research fell into place. By the middle of the nineteenth century the central elements of scientific organization were all present: employment in universities and research institutions provided incomes independent of results, thus providing insurance in what was otherwise an impossibly risky enterprise, and networks of peer review overcame the moral hazard associated with that insurance while a loose hierarchy of positions allocated by the scientists themselves provided a material incentive to do good science. Much remained to be done. Probably the most important institutional innovation within the university was Justus Liebig's teaching laboratory at Giessen.

That the lodging of science in the universities was far from inevitable can be inferred from what happened in France, where control of the university, which comprised all secondary school teachers licensed by the state, was in the hands of the grand master who controlled their advancement. Jules Simon writes of his experience as a teacher under the autocratic regime of Victor Cousin that the master personally presided over the *aggré-gation* (the competitive examination for teaching positions), determined where the *aggrégés* taught, and managed their careers. Because university regulations guaranteed tenure, Cousin simply left chairs open and had them taught by *chargés de cours,* who performed all the duties of a full professor but received only that part of the salary that Cousin decided to give them. Their position was precarious, as any deviation from Cousin's philosophical party line could result in exile to the provinces.[38] Despite the size and excellence of the French scientific establishment concentrated in Paris and perhaps because of it, the provincial universities in France never achieved the scientific prominence of provincial universities in Germany. Within the narrow confines of the Grandes Écoles and the great Parisian research establishment at Jussieu, the selection of scientists was rigorous and effective. But the system could not expand beyond those limits.

CONCLUSION

By the middle of the nineteenth century a system of decentralized science much like the one we know today was in place. One sign of its robustness was the speed at which agricultural experiment stations transformed themselves into quasi-academic associations with tight links to the universities. The first station was founded in 1850 in Mockern, Saxony. By the early 1860s Germany had more than a dozen of them, and in 1862 they had formed an association supporting two "academic" journals and holding annual meetings at which researchers presented their research, all this in the science of fertilizer analysis and bovine respiration. Successful researchers moved to larger research stations and eventually obtained professorships in universities. The incentive system perhaps played against purely practical demands for farmers for information on optimal feeding formulas for dairy cattle, but it is hard to see what other kind of organization would have sustained the research that produced the discovery that bacteria living in symbiosis with the roots of legumes were the primary source of nitrogen in the soil.

NOTES

1. For examples, see Saxonhouse and Wright (1984); Wright (1990, 2006).

2. Wikipedia entries for Ottoman Science, Persian Science, Arab Science, Indian Science, and Chinese science reveal a vast unknown territory whose coastal regions have only begun to be explored by modern scholarship.

3. The following passage stands for many related views. "The spirit, which, molded to the circumstances, social forms, and human material of the fifteenth, sixteenth, and seventeenth centuries, was called classical or Greek, was a radical individualism resting all salvation, all expression, all attainment on the God or gods men found in themselves, or in their perceptions of and reasoning on nature, or ultimately on no God at all, except man, and among men, upon one's self" (Parker 1984, p. 5). Mokyr's identification of accelerated and sustained technological change in the eighteenth century with the European Enlightenment presents an analogous "values" explanation of economic discontinuity (Mokyr, 2005, 2010).

4. "For whatever God has created for the use of men that He has put in the man's hands as a property, so that it not remain hidden. And although He has created it hidden, yet He has added these particular outward signs leading to investigation" (Waite 2002 [1893], p. 185). On the logic of sixteenth-century epistemology, see Foucault (1966).

5. The Reformation was initially antagonistic to classical letters and destroyed several centers of culture, including the University of Basel (Merz 1976 [1907], p. 163). The Counter-

Reformation was no better. In 1579 Pope Paul V shut down Europe's first scientific academy, significantly named the Accademia dei Segreti, under suspicion of sorcery.

6. Among the major European scientific powers, the British government was least supportive of scientific research outside the practical domain of celestial navigation. During the Revolution and under Napoleon, publications of the Académie des Sciences were closely monitored to excise any generalizations that might have some contact with political controversy.

7. The first major scientific breakthroughs in theoretical physics were in optics and celestial mechanics, where contextual variation is comparatively slight. Harvey's discovery of the circulation of blood would seem to be an exception, but the structural connections between the heart, arteries and veins, and valves are the same across species, making it possible to generalize from comparative anatomy.

8. Vaucanson, who was elected to the Académie des Sciences to prop up its practical side, complained, "The intelligent public will understand that it is much easier to make meteorological observations, or to stage demonstrations with ice, magnets or electricity, than to invent and construct a good machine. In the one case it is only a matter of explaining as one likes certain known effects; in the other one must produce new effects. This is why the great majority direct themselves towards theory rather than practice." Cited in Briggs (1991), p. 84.

9. Astronomers sometimes shipped lenses to other astronomers for confirmation of their discoveries using the same equipment, but it was often difficult to tell whether a reported object was something real or an artifact of imperfection in the glass or an atmospheric convection current. The difficulty occasioned bitter disputes, when the correspondent declared that the initiating astronomer had seen something that was not there, to which the astronomer retorted that his correspondent was acting in bad faith (Daumas 1953, p. 42).

10. Locke (1979 [1690]), "Of Perception," Book II, chap. 9.

11. Wood (1913), pp. 240–243. The French Académie des Sciences and its successor, the Institut de France, were also slow to credit important inventions, usually on the grounds of insufficient originality. Leblanc never received the prize set in 1783 for the method of obtaining salt from soda that is named after him. Philippe de Gérard's claim for the million franc prize offered by Napoleon for a machine to spin flax was rejected because his (successful) design was deemed too simple (Crosland 1967, pp. 27, 31).

12. Young supported the Royal Dublin Society on the grounds that the farm had been set up to demonstrate the new husbandry, not as an occasion for Baker to gain knowledge and scientific reputation at the society's expense (Fussell 1931; White 1955, pp. 13–16).

13. Kuhn (1877), pp. 33, 48–55. Theodor Reuning, who was the Saxon official most directly responsible for the establishment of the first station at Möckern, explicitly defended its scientific vocation on the grounds that only by rigorously adhering to the scientific method of investigation could real results be achieved (Reuning 1856, pp. 40–52).

14. The problem seems initially to have emerged in mathematics, where the development of algebra and the geometry of conic sections made the field increasingly inaccessible to the mathematicians' potential patrons (David 2008, p. 40).

15. The demand by financial institutions for "quants" possessing advanced degrees in mathematical sciences is a spectacular exception. The case of pharmacy as an alternative occupation for trained chemists in the early nineteenth century is reviewed below.

16. The alternative mechanism using algorithms designed to assess scientific work is defeated by heterogeneity. One attempt to "grade" a two-page paper based on "objective" criteria yielded 36 concepts and 6 hypotheses (Lipetz 1965).

17. Akerlof (1976). Caste systems "outcast" persons who break the caste rules. The purchaser of a noncaste good is penalized along its supplier, lowering his income to the point where it is preferable for him to buy the caste product even though the noncaste good might be cheaper. Because the advantage of the caste system over autarky is that it is specialized, it follows that if the number of outcasts becomes large enough to secure the economies of specialized production, the caste can be broken. There are analogies to this phenomenon in the history of scientific revolutions.

18. There are exceptions. The usefulness of geology in locating mineral deposits was recognized by the 1830s and induced significant public support for the training and employment of professional geologists.

19. That it be completed was critical. Newton withheld publication of the *Principia* for 20 years because of the mathematical difficulty of proving that the mass of a sphere like the earth could be modeled as if it were located in a single point at its center. The proof was essential in getting the critical distances in his theory of universal gravitation right.

20. Mokyr (2005) argues the same point in the wider context of the application of science to technology in the eighteenth century. The timing is close enough to suggest a common cause.

21. That it was not complete is demonstrated by the government's banning of Diderot's *Encyclopédie* in response to vigorous protests by the religious authorities. Darwin's self-censorship in delaying publication of his theory of natural selection for much the same reason is another example.

22. The attentive reader will note that this account differs from David's in that the source of peer review is located in Smith's premise that self-expression constituted the psychological motivation to cooperate. The two arguments are complementary because science could not have expanded as rapidly as it did without outside support.

23. For an extensive collection of data on periodical publishing costs in Germany in the eighteenth and early nineteenth centuries, see Krieg (1953); Kirchner (1958–1962), Bd. 2, pp. 430–472.

24. The society reneged on its promise to publish (Merz 1976 [1907], pp. 68, 288).

25. Leibniz is said to have composed a treatise in philosophy in a letter to a German princess (Kronick 1962, pp. 50–55).

26. A list of such letters is inventoried in Hatch (1982).

27. The historian of scientific journalism in Germany claims that the absolute minimum run was 500 volumes, and that owing to high fixed cost of distributing them few runs were under 1,000 (Kirchner 1928–1931, p. 54).

28. Mokyr (2005) argues that they disseminated scientific information to potential inventors and entrepreneurs.

29. On June 21, 1813, the Institut sat in secret session to consider Arago's protest to Biot's claim of priority (Crosland 1967, p. 334).

30. English science is in this respect an exception, and self-financed research remained dominant in that country into the second half of the nineteenth century. The pantheon of major English scientists in this period includes such names as Young, Dalton, Faraday, Lyell, Hamilton, Kelvin, Davy, and Darwin. The lack of support shows up at lower levels of

scientific production requiring a significant amount of rote work, such as in chemistry, where in the second half of the century England had to recruit much of its talent from Germany.

31. Humboldt wrote Boussingault in November 1825, "Avec les talents que la nature vous a donnés, avec une activité dans exemple, vous vous placerez parmi les hommes supérieurs qui ont illustrés votre patrie; il ne s'agit chez vous que d'avoir toujours une forte volonté. C'est comme cela que j'ai deviné d'avance . . . Gay-Lussac et Arago. Je ne me tromperai pas plus sur vous que ne me suis trompé sur eux." Cited in Leouzon (1905), p. 321.

32. Knight was so shy and retiring that it was only through Banks's wheedling that he was persuaded to publish his research. He wrote to Banks in 1799, "If I have become a troublesome scribbler to you, I must claim your pardon on the ground that you have made me such; for without the attention I have been honoured with from you, I am certain that I should never (in print) have scribbled at all" (Fletcher 1969, pp. 63–64). Knight's extremely long and verbose correspondence with Banks can be found in Dawson (1958). See also Banks's life chronicled in O'Brian (1987).

33. The scientific institutions in Paris at the end of the eighteenth century included the Collège de France, the Collège et École de Chirurgie, le Jardin des Plantes, École Royale des Mines, École des Ponts et Chaussées, École Vétérinaire, the Académie des Sciences and the Académie royale de Chirurgie, to which the French Revolution added the École Polytechnique, the École Normale Supérieure, and the Musée d'Histoire Naturelle.

34. There is some evidence that his experiments were deliberately ignored.

35. The instrument makers were a partial exception, as the work combined mathematics and craft skills of the highest level. Their achievement, however, was embodied in physical instruments that were custom built for discerning clientele with the ability and willingness to pay. For an important example, see McConnell (2007).

36. The *habilitationschrift* is a second doctoral thesis undertaken after a candidate has completed his PhD and requires a higher level of independent scholarship.

37. McClelland (1980). The young Marx, who postulated for a post in philosophy at Leipzig, was a victim of that policy.

38. "Au moindre écart, il pouvait être envoyé de Paris à Carpentras" (Prost 1968).

REFERENCES

Akerlof, George (1976). "The Economics of Caste, the Rat Race, and Other Woeful Stories." *Quarterly Journal of Economics* 90: 599–617.

Allen, David E. (1976). *The Naturalist in Britain*. London: A. Lane.

Arrow, Kenneth J. (1962). "Economic Welfare and the Allocation of Resources for Invention." In Universities–National Bureau Committee for Economic Research, *The Rate and Direction of Inventive Activity*. Princeton, NJ: Princeton University Press, pp 609–625.

Arrow, Kenneth J. (1974). *The Limits of Organization*. New York: Norton.

Barnes, Sherman B. (1934). "The Scientific Journal, 1665–1730." *Scientific Monthly* 38: 257–260.

Barnes, Sherman B. (1936). "The Editing of Early Learned Journals." *Osiris* 1: 167–169.

Bourke, P. M. Austin (1962). "The Scientific Investigation of the Potato Blight in 1845–46." *Irish Historical Studies* 13: 26–32.

Briggs, Robin (1991). "The Académie Royale des Sciences and the Pursuit of Utility." *Past & Present* 131: 38–88.

Busch, Alexander (1959). *Die Geschichte des Privatdozenten*. Stuttgart: Ferdinand Eake Verlag.

Crane, Diana (1972). *Invisible Colleges: Diffusion of Knowledge in Scientific Communities*. Chicago: University of Chicago Press.

Crosland, Maurice (1967). *The Society of Arcueil: A View of French Science at the Time of Napoleon I*. Cambridge, MA: Harvard University Press.

Crosland, Maurice (1975). "The Development of a Professional Career in Science." In *The Emergence of Science in Western Europe*, edited by M. P. Crosland. London: Macmillan, pp. 139–159.

Crosland, Maurice (1978). *Gay-Lussac: Scientist and Bourgeois*. Cambridge: Cambridge University Press.

Crowther, E. M. (1936). "The Technique of Modern Farm Experiments." *Journal of the Royal Agricultural Society* 97: 78–88.

Daubeny, Charles (1842). "Lecture on the Application of Science to Agriculture." *Journal of the Royal Agricultural Society* 3: 136–159.

Daumas, Maurice (1953). *Les instruments scientifiques aux xviie et xviiie siècles*. Paris: PUF.

David, Paul A. (2008). "The Historical Origins of 'Open Science': An Essay on Patronage, Reputation and Common Agency Contracting in the Scientific Revolution." *Capitalism and Society* 3: 1–103.

Dawson, W. R., ed. (1958). *The Banks Letters*. London: The British Museum.

Delepine, Marcel (1962). "Les *Annales de Chimie* de leur fondation à la 173e année de parution." *Annales de chimie* 13 série 7: 1–11.

Della Porta, Giambattista (1658). *Natural Magick*. London.

Fletcher, Harold R. (1969). *The Story of the Royal Horticultural Society, 1804–1848*. Oxford: Oxford University Press.

Foucault, Michel (1966). *Les mots et les choses: Une archéologie des sciences humaines*. Paris: Gallimard.

Fussell, George E. (1931). "John Wynn Baker: An 'Improver' in Eighteenth-Century Ireland." *Agricultural History* 5: 151–161.

Fussell, George E. (1935). "The Technique of Early Field Experiments." *Journal of the Royal Agricultural Society of England* 56: 78–88.

Gerbod, Paul (1965). *La condition universitaire en France au xixe siècle*. Paris: PUF.

Grantham, George (1984). "The Shifting Locus of Agricultural Innovation in Nineteenth Century Europe: The Case of the Agricultural Experiment Stations." In *Technique, Spirit and Form in the Making of the Modern Economies: Essays in Honor of William N. Parker*, edited by Gary Saxonhouse and Gavin Wright. Greenwich, CT: JAI Press, pp. 191–214.

Hagstrom, Warren O. (1965). *The Scientific Community*. New York: Basic Books.

Hahn, Roger (1971). *The Anatomy of a Scientific Institution: The Paris Academy of Sciences, 1666–1803*. Berkeley: University of California Press.

Hahn, Roger (1975). "Scientific Careers in Eighteenth-Century France." In *The Emergence of Science in Western Europe*, edited by M. P. Crosland. London: Macmillan, pp. 127–138.

Hansen, Russell Norwood (1958). *Patterns of Discovery*. Cambridge: Cambridge University Press.

Hansen, Russell Norwood (1969). *Perception and Discovery: An Introduction to Scientific Inquiry*. San Francisco: Freeman, Cooper.

Hatch, Robert A., ed. (1982). *The Collection Boulliau (BN FF. 13019–13059): An Inventory*. Philadelphia: American Philosophical Society.

Hatch, Robert A. (1998). "Pereisc as a Correspondent: The Republic of Letters and the Geography of Ideas." In *Science Unbound: Geography, Space, Discipline*, edited by B. Dolan. Umeå, Sweden: Umeå University Publications, pp. 19–58.

Henslow, J. S. (1841). "Report on the Diseases of Wheat." *Journal of the Royal Agricultural Society* 2: 1–26.

Howard, O. (1930). *A History of Applied Entomology*. Washington, DC: Smithsonian Institution.

Hunter, Michael, ed. (1998). *Archives of the Scientific Revolution: The Formation and Exchange of Ideas in Seventeenth-Century Europe*. Woodbridge, UK: Boydell Press.

Kirchner, Joachim (1928–1931). *Die Grundlagen des deutschen Zeitschriftswesen mit einer gesamtbibliographie der deutschen Zeitschriftswesen bis zuer Jahre 1790*. Leipzig: Hiersemann.

Kirchner, Joachim (1958–1962). *Das deutsche Zeitschriftswesen*, Bd. 1 and 2. Weisbaden: O. Harrassowitz.

Klooster, H. S. van (1957). "The Story of Liebig's *Annalen der Chemie*." *Journal of Chemical Education* 34: 27–30.

Krieg, Walter (1953). *Materielen zu einer Entwicklungsgeschicte der Bucherpreise*. Wien: Stubenbach.

Kronick, David A. (1962). *A History of Scientific and Technical Periodicals: The Origins and Development of the Scientific and Technological Press, 1665–1795*. New York: Scarecrow Press.

Kuhn, Gustav (1877). "Geschictliches über die Landwirthschafliche Versuchs-Station Möckern." *Die Landwirtschaftlichen Versuchs-Stationen* 22.

Kuhn, Thomas S. (1970). *The Structure of Scientific Revolutions*. Chicago: University of Chicago Press.

Large, E. C. (1938). *The Advance of the Fungi*. London: J. Cape.

Lavoisier, Antoine (1862–1868). *Oeuvres*. Paris: Imprimerie Impériale.

Leouzon, Louis (1905). *Agronomes et éléveurs*. Paris: J.-B. Baillière et fils.

Lindroth, Carl H. (1973). "Systematics between Fabricius and Darwin, 1800–1859." In *History of Entomology*, edited by Ray Smith, Thomas Mittler, and Carroll N. Smith. Palo Alto, CA: Stanford University Press, pp. 117–154.

Lipetz, Ben-Ami (1965). *The Measurement of Efficiency of Scientific Research*. Carlisle, MA: Intermedia.

Locke, John (1979 [1690]). *An Essay Concerning Human Understanding*. Oxford: Oxford University Press.

Marschak, Jacob (1968). "Economics of Inquiring, Communicating, Deciding." *American Economic Review Papers and Proceedings* 58: 1–18.

McClelland, Charles E. (1980). *State, Society and University in Germany, 1700–1914*. Cambridge: Cambridge University Press.

McConnell, Anita (2007). *Jesse Ramsden (1735–1800): London's Leading Scientific Instrument Maker*. Aldershot, UK: Ashgate.

Merz, John Theodore (1976 [1907]). *A History of European Thought in the Nineteenth Century*, vol. 1. Gloucester, MA: Peter Smith Reprints.

Mokyr, Joel (1980). "The Deadly Fungus: An Econometric Investigation into the Short-Run Demographic Impact of the Irish Famine, 1846–1851." *Research in Population Economics* 2: 237–277.

Mokyr, Joel (2005). "The Intellectual Origins of Modern Economic Growth." *Journal of Economic History* 65: 285–351.

Mokyr, Joel (2010). *The Enlightened Economy: An Economic History of Britain, 1700–1850.* New Haven, CT: Yale University Press.

Morrell, J. B. (1972). "The Chemist Breeders: The Research Schools of Liebig and Thomas Thompson." *Ambix* 19: 1–46.

O'Brian, Patrick (1987). *Joseph Banks: A Life.* London: Collins Harvill.

Olby, Robert C. (1966). *Origins of Mendelism.* London: Constable.

O'Neill, T. A. (1946–1947). "The Scientific Investigation of the Potato Crop in Ireland, 1845–1846." *Irish Historical Studies* 5: 123–138.

Parker, William N. (1984). "What Historians Must Explain." In *Europe, America, and the Wider World: Essays on the Economic History of Western Capitalism,* vol. 1: *Europe and the World Economy,* edited by W. N. Parker. New York: Cambridge University Press, pp. 3–11.

Parris, C. K. (1968). *A Chronicle of Plant Pathology.* Starkville, MO: Johnson and Sons.

Paulsen, Friedrich (1902). *Die deutschen Universitäten und das Universitätsstudium.* Berlin: A. Asher.

Prost, Antoine (1968). *L'enseignement en France, 1800–1967.* Paris: A. Colin.

Ravetz, Jerome R. (1971). *Scientific Knowledge and Its Social Problems.* Oxford: Clarendon Press.

Reuning, Theodor (1856). *Die Entwicklung der Sachsischen Landwirtschaft in den Jahren 1845–1854.* Dresden: G. Schönfeld's Buchhandlung.

Saxonhouse, Gary, and Gavin Wright (1984). "Two Forms of Cheap Labor in Textile History." In *Technique, Spirit, and Form in the Making of the Modern Economies: Essays in Honor of William N. Parker,* edited by Gary Saxonhouse and Gavin Wright. Greenwich, CT: JAI Press, pp. 3–32.

Selye, Hans (1964). *From Dream to Discovery.* New York: McGraw-Hill.

Shermer, Michael (2002). *In Darwin's Shadow: The Life and Science of Alfred Russel Wallace.* Oxford: Oxford University Press.

Thornton, John L., and R. I. J. Tully (1971). *Scientific Books, Libraries and Collectors: A Study of Bibliography and the Book Trade in Relation to Science,* 3rd rev. ed. London: Library Association.

Turner, R. Steven (1971). "The Growth of Professorial Research in Prussia: Causes and Context." *Historical Studies in the Physical Sciences* 3: 137–182.

Tuxen, S. L. (1973). "Entomology Systematizes and Describes." In *History of Entomology,* edited by Ray Smith, Thomas Mittler, and Carroll N. Smith. Palo Alto, CA: Stanford University Press, pp. 95–117.

Usher, Abbot Payson (1954). *A History of Mechanical Invention.* Cambridge, MA: Harvard University Press.

Waite, Edward Arthur (2002 [1893]). *Hermetical and Alchemical Writings of Paracelsus, Part I.* Whitefish, MN: Kessinger Publishing Company.

White, Terence de Vere (1955). *The Story of the Dublin Society.* Tralee: The Kerryman.

Wood, Henry Trueman (1913). *A History of the Royal Society of Arts.* London: Murray.

Wright, Gavin (1990). "The Origins of American Industrial Success, 1879–1940." *American Economic Review* 80: 651–668.

Wright, Gavin (2006). *Slavery and American Economic Development.* Baton Rouge: Louisiana State University Press.

Yagello, Virginia E. (1968). "The Early History of the Chemical Periodical." *Journal of Chemical Education* 45: 426–429.

CHAPTER 4

The Fundamental Impact of the Slave Trade
on African Economies

WARREN C. WHATLEY AND ROB GILLEZEAU

WHAT WAS THE IMPACT of the transatlantic slave trade on African economies and societies? Traditional answers have tended to focus on depopulation. Studies by McEvedy and Jones (1978) and Manning (1990) conclude that the slave trade slowed population growth in Africa and may have even reduced the aggregate population between 1700 and 1850. But the causal impact of population growth on development is difficult to assess.[1] Instead, in this chapter we focus on the impact of slave *production* and its associated externalities on the development process broadly conceived. Patterson (1982) calls the production of slaves the production of "social death." It is a violent process where a person is brought to the brink of death, spared, and then ritualistically put to social death, left to owe the remainder of the person's life to another person. One would think that centuries of producing social death would leave a mark on social outcomes and institutions, some with lasting consequences for development. First of all, slave raiding disrupts production and social life in general. Where slave raiding is frequent, ethnic boundaries and the ability to distinguish insider from outsider might proliferate as people struggle to manage the risk of being caught. Similarly, an increase in the profitability of slave raiding might induce elites to raid for slaves rather than build powerful states, further exacerbating the destabilizing effects of slave production.

How widespread was slave production in Africa? It is impossible to know with any degree of confidence, but we venture a guess. Between the sixteenth and nineteenth centuries more than 13 million slaves were produced in Africa and transported across the Atlantic. Seventy-seven percent of these slaves (10.1 million) were produced along the west and west central coasts of Africa during the 150 years between 1701 and 1850.[2] In

1700 the estimated population in this region was 28 million people (McEvedy and Jones 1978, pp. 241–256). If the average life span was 30 years, then the 10.1 million slaves were produced over five lifetimes. That yields 2.6 million slaves produced per lifetime, or 9.3 percent of the total population. If we take into account collateral damage, the probability of being a victim of slave production increases further. Slave producers killed and injured others to capture their slaves. Captives died during the long trek to the coast, in the holding pens along the coast, and during the Middle Passage. And many captives remained in Africa. The physical and social deaths needed to produce 13 million slave exports could have easily reached twice that number.[3]

In this chapter we trace out the impact of effective demand on the structure of African economies and societies. What do we mean by effective demand? When the international demand for enslaved Africans becomes an effective demand, it has essentially driven the value of people as slaves above their value as producers. The very first impact is the devotion of more African resources to the enslavement and export of people. In other words, there is an increase in the economic returns to slave raiding. We test for, and find evidence for, an effective international demand for enslaved Africans. We then develop a simple model of cooperation and conflict between nations and villages in order to trace out the impact of effective demand on several institutions thought to influence economic development. The model reveals the conditions under which the slave trade reduced the size of states, increased social and ethnic stratification, and created a reign of terror. The model can also roughly trace out the impact of changing slave prices and capture technology on these features of African economies and societies.

THE SLAVE TRADE AND AFRICAN DEVELOPMENT

Our discussion begins with Walter Rodney's book *How Europe Underdeveloped Africa* (1972). Rodney argues that the slave trade fundamentally altered African economies. First, the slave trade discouraged state building and encouraged slave raiding. It encouraged the capture of slaves for sale and discouraged the capture of land and the cultivation of a citizenry for the purposes of taxation. Quoting Rodney:

There have been times in history when social groups have grown stronger by raiding their neighbors for women, cattle, and goods, because they then use the "booty" from the raids for the benefits of their own community. Slaving in Africa did not even have that redeeming value. Captives were shipped outside instead of being utilized within any given African community for creating wealth from nature. . . . If the prisoners were to develop into a true serf class, then those prisoners would have had to be guaranteed the right to remain fixed on the soil and protected from sale. (pp. 100, 118)

There is some empirical support for Rodney's underdevelopment thesis. Looking at the relationship between gross domestic product (GDP) per capita today and participation in the slave trade centuries ago, Nunn (2008) finds that the slave trade had a negative long-term effect on economic performance. He also presents preliminary evidence that suggests the legacy of the slave trade operated through increased ethnic diversity and underdeveloped political structures. Studies of contemporary Africa tend to support the view that ethnic diversity and underdeveloped states have contributed to Africa's poor economic performance in the post–World War II period. Easterly and Levine (1997) argue that a quarter of the difference between the post–World War II growth experiences of African and Asian economies can be explained by the greater ethnic diversity in Africa. Perhaps centuries of slave raiding increased the cultural value of being able to quickly and easily distinguish friend from foe. Similarly, Bates (2008) argues that the predatory nature of the postcolonial state in Africa created political and military challenges to its authority. When the challenges intensified, ethnic stratification also intensified to the point where "things fell apart." Again, it is not difficult to imagine centuries of slave raiding producing predatory political cultures and ethnic stratification. What might at first seem "traditional' " or exogenous about African ethnicity and political culture may actually be endogenous when viewed within the context of centuries of slave raiding.

Curtin (1975) shows how we can begin to assess the impact of the slave trade on Africa by looking at the empirical relationship between slave demand and slave exports. If slave exports were insensitive to the level of demand, then slaves were likely produced by political events unrelated to the international demand for slaves. Curtin calls this the "political model" of slave exports, where slaves were produced in the normal course of political events. This situation is depicted in Figure 4.1 by the perfectly inelastic slave supply curve. Greater demand increases price but not quantity. On the other hand, if the producers of slaves responded to economic incentives, then the quantities exported should increase with demand. This is depicted by the positively sloped slave supply schedule in Figure 4.1. The appendix at the end of this chapter reports an econometric test of these models and finds that African slave exports were responsive to changes in the international demand for slaves. A doubling of real British commodity investments in the slave trade increased African slave exports by 43 percent.

FIGURE 4.1   *Political and Economic Models of Slave Supply*

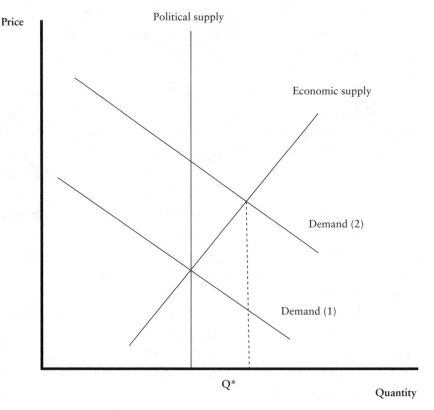

The next question is, "What impact did effective demand have on African economies and societies?" Eltis (1991) and Eltis and Jennings (1988) answer "Not very much" because the slave trade was a small share of Africa's overall economic activity. This may or may not be true. The data on African GDP in the eighteenth century are extremely thin. In either case, the negative externalities of producing slaves may have swamped the private costs. For example, using the heights of Yoruba captives as a measure of Yoruba welfare, Eltis (1990) finds that "for every increase in slave departures (exports) of 1,000, mean heights of the birth cohort declined by more than one fifth of a centimeter" (p. 519). One can interpret this as evidence that slave production had far-reaching and measurable effects on African welfare.

Fage (1969) argues that the slave trade actually encouraged the consolidation of political states and favored economic development in the long run. Our model predicts that effective demand *reduced* the incentive to build states. By implication, we argue that the states that emerged in eighteenth-century Africa would have been larger and less militaristic in the absence of the slave trade. Our model also predicts the conditions under which a "Fage" effect might appear.[4]

At the conclusion of his study of warfare in Africa, Thornton concludes that the production of slaves was primarily a by-product of political struggles, but he differs from the Curtin dichotomy in that he also concludes that the slave trade "changed the way wars were waged at the lowest level" (Thornton 1999, p. 151). Most of the recent scholarship on this issue also concludes that the slave trade changed the way the political game was played. In his study of the Slave Coast, Law concludes that "by the end of the seventeenth century, the European demand for slaves had brought about a profound transformation of African societies of the Slave Coast. Although this was primarily an economic transformation, it had dramatic effects in the political sphere also, in the collapse of political order leading to the rise of the new state of Dahomey" (Law 1991, p. 345).[5] Inikori (1982, 2003) argues that the slave trade encouraged the formation and spread of banditry and militarized states. One finds similar conclusions in Barry's (1998) study of the Senegambia region and Daaku's (1970) study of the Gold Coast.

This literature suggests that the impact of the slave trade on Africa is more complex than Curtin's (1975) formulation would lead us to believe. First, the slave trade may have shifted the political supply function, with indigenous conflict producing a greater number of slaves than otherwise would have been the case. An example is the ex post practice of "eating the countryside," or selling the population of the vanquished as a way to weaken one's enemy.[6] The slave trade increased the frequency of this kind of "politically" motivated slave supply. In this sense the supply elasticity we report in the appendix is a minimum estimate of the impact of effective demand on slave exports.

Similarly, some of the supply elasticity picked up by our estimating procedure might come from changes in institutions and not simply a reallocation of resources. Examples include the proliferation of banditry and marauding bands of slave raiders as the demand for slaves increases; or the expansion of militarized slave-raiding states at the expense of nation building and the cultivation of a citizenry; or a reduction in the probability of a peaceful settlement of conflicts; or turning walled cities, once havens for refugees, into garrisons for slave raiders.[7] The model we develop in the next section is our effort to capture the impact of effective demand on these types of institutional changes. One can think of these as externalities of the slave trade.

THE IMPACT OF EFFECTIVE DEMAND: A MODEL OF WAR AND RAIDING

In this section we develop a model showing how an effective international demand for enslaved Africans can impact the institutional structure and cultural practices of African societies. The model is simple, but it generates powerful results and insights. The players are the rulers of nations and villages who interact over an infinite time horizon in sequential play. We make this assumption because the slave trade lasted for centuries. Nations have the ability to attack villages to either conquer them or raid for slaves, but nations are unable to attack other nations. We define war as aggression for the purpose of acquiring people and territory (state building). We define raiding as aggression for the purpose of acquiring people only (for the slave trade). Nations may decide to go to war, to raid, or to do nothing.

We assume that villages and nations are absolutist in the sense that the community leaders (elders, chiefs, or kings) have the absolute authority to make decisions for the people when it comes to war or raiding and that this authority derives from the elite's claim to land, be it legitimized by oral history, lineage, or religion.[8] The assumption of absolutism has several important implications. First, decisions are made to maximize the elites' utility, not the people's utility. These are not democracies. Second, if the land of a village is captured in a war, then the victor claims his right to the land by deposing of the elite (meaning a utility of zero for the village chief). In other words, the chief is beheaded. While raiding a chief's people results in a utility penalty (R), war is for the chief's head.

Finally, we assume diminishing returns to war and constant returns to slave raiding, but the results hold so long as the returns to raiding decline slower than the returns to war. This is a reasonable assumption because territory accumulated in war must be protected from outside aggressors. It must be policed and administered internally. Taxes must be collected. Communications networks and roads must be built and maintained. Rebellions in the outer provinces must be put down. The marginal cost of maintaining state territory obviously increases with the size of the territory.[9]

Raiding, on the other hand, is hit-and-run. There is no need to deploy an occupying force or construct infrastructure. Diminishing returns may set in as populations migrate to avoid raiders or as victims adopt other defensive strategies.[10] However, it is unlikely that traveling 50 miles inland to raid for slaves will add more to the cost of acquiring surplus than does defending, integrating, and administering a political outpost that is 50 miles farther inland.

In the following three subsections we present the predictions generated by the model under different scenarios in the presence and absence of effective demand for slaves. The first scenario is the simplest and includes a single nation and a single village. In the second scenario, we extend the first scenario to a single nation and many villages. The third scenario includes a single nation and several villages and allows for alliance formation.

Scenario One: One Nation, One Village

In our first scenario we consider the most basic possible situation in which the presence of effective demand influences the behavior of an African state. In this scenario there is a single nation and a single village that share a common border. We define the nation's labor force as L_n and the village's labor force as L_1. We also define the nation's labor productivity as b_n and the village's labor productivity as b_1. We have defined the ruler's utility function to be logarithmic in produced goods (where the value of produced goods in each region is labor productivity times the regional labor force) minus a fixed cost if aggressive action is undertaken (X is the cost of war, which is greater than R, the cost of slave raiding) plus an additional term paL_i if slaves are captured, which is revenue from slaves captured. Thus the lifetime utility function if a nation does nothing in all periods, raids in all periods, or goes to war in the first period (and then does nothing) is as follows:

$$U(Nothing) = \frac{\log(b_n L_n)}{1 - \delta}$$

$$U(Raiding) = \frac{\log(b_n L_n) - R + paL_1}{1 - \delta}$$

$$U(Conquest) = \frac{\log(b_n L_n + b_1 L_1)}{1 - \delta} - X$$

In the absence of effective demand, which we represent as a slave price equal to zero ($p = 0$),[11] there exist two possible outcomes in equilibrium: the nation may either conquer the village in the first period or choose to take no aggressive action and simply produce goods. The nation will never choose to conquer the village after the first period because it faces the same payoff decision in each period. To determine whether the nation will choose to conquer the village or simply produce, we compare the lifetime utility derived by the rulers of the nation in the two situations (conquering the village versus producing). The nation will choose to conquer the village if the lifetime utility obtained by conquest is greater than that obtained through production:

$$U(Conquest) \geq U(Production)$$

$$\frac{\log(b_n L_n + b_1 L_1)}{1 - \delta} - X \geq \frac{\log(b_n L_n)}{1 - \delta}$$

Thus the nation will conquer the village if the one-time cost of conquest, which we define as X, is less than the discounted lifetime utility added through conquest (meaning that there is a net benefit to war):

$$X \leq \frac{\log(b_n L_n + b_1 L_1)}{1 - \delta} - \frac{\log(b_n L_n)}{1 - \delta}$$

As long as there is a net benefit to war, the nation will choose to conquer the village in the first period. This results in an increase in the size of the nation, as it incorporates the village. If the inequality does not hold (meaning that there is not a net benefit to war), the nation will do nothing and a peaceful equilibrium will be maintained.

If we introduce effective demand into the above scenario, the equilibrium may be altered if there is a net benefit to slave raiding ($paL_1 \geq R$). If we start from a peaceful equilibrium, any positive net benefit to slave raiding will generate a new slave-raiding equilibrium. What does this change relative to the situation in the absence of effective demand? First, it results in increased slave capture and the associated culture of terror. Second, it results in a permanent reallocation of labor from production to slave raiding.

If we start from the conquest equilibrium, effective demand will alter the equilibrium if the lifetime utility for the ruler is greater under slave raiding than under conquest, meaning that

$$U(Raiding) \geq U(Conquest)$$

$$\frac{\log(b_n L_n) - R + paL_1}{1 - \delta} \geq \frac{\log(b_n L_n + b_1 L_1)}{1 - \delta} - X$$

If this inequality holds, the equilibrium will be altered such that the nation will choose to raid the village in each period.

Thus, for a sufficiently large value of paL_1 (the return to slave raiding) or sufficiently small values of R (the cost of slave raiding) the war equilibrium will be disrupted and replaced with a raiding equilibrium.

What are the consequences? In addition to the effects previously noted in the perturbation of the peaceful equilibrium (labor reallocation and more slaves captured) there are implications for ethnicity and state size. The village and the nation both survive in equilibrium with the nation being smaller than it was in the absence of effective demand. Because the village persists, this may be viewed as an increase in ethnic diversity in the long run.

Scenario Two: One Nation, Many Villages

The second scenario generalizes the first scenario to a situation with a large number of villages and a single nation placed along an ordered line. We assume that there are a total of N villages and a single nation. Additionally, we assume that the size of the labor force for both villages and the nation is equal to L and that regional labor productivity is equal to b.

In the absence of effective demand, the nation will choose to conquer at least one village if the ruler's lifetime utility associated with the conquest of a village is greater than his utility when no villages are conquered. The nation, however, may conquer more than a single village, although we assume that it is able to conquer only one village each period. The nation will continue conquering villages until the marginal lifetime benefit of conquering another village is less than the one-time penalty associated with war (X). We may use this condition to define the total number of villages that are conquered (n) in equilibrium. The nation will conquer villages as long as the marginal benefit of conquest is greater than the marginal cost. The nation will continue conquering villages as long as the below inequality holds, where X is the marginal cost of conquering a village and the right term is the marginal benefit of conquering one more village (the benefit of conquering n villages minus the benefit of conquering $n - 1$ villages):

$$X \leq \frac{\log(nbL)}{1 - \delta} - \frac{\log((n - 1)bL)}{1 - \delta}$$

Thus the nation conquers n villages, where n is the largest value such that the above inequality holds. Under optimizing behavior, the nation achieves a size of nL while the number of independent villages in equilibrium is reduced to $N - n$.

If we introduce effective demand into the scenario, the equilibrium condition will be altered. Assuming that N is a very large number (meaning that it is implausible for the nation to conquer all villages), the marginal condition now includes the opportunity cost of not raiding for the period in which the final village is conquered (meaning that, had the nation chosen to not go to war, it would have had the option to raid for slaves). Thus the nation will now conquer villages as long as the marginal cost of war is less than the marginal benefit (this inequality closely mirrors the previous inequality):

$$X - R + paL \leq \frac{\log(nbL)}{1 - \delta} - \frac{\log((n - 1)bL)}{1 - \delta}$$

As before, the above condition determines the number of villages that are conquered in equilibrium, n. If there is a net benefit to raiding, it is necessarily the case that the size of the nation will be smaller than in the absence of effective demand: the left-hand term is greater than it was before the slave trade arrived. This is depicted in Figure 4.2 for the general case as an increase in the marginal net economic return to slave raiding. The effects are similar to those presented in the first scenario. As the economic return to slave raiding increases, nations will generally be smaller in equilibrium and greater ethnic diversity will persist. Again, there is a permanent reallocation of labor rather than a temporary one, as war occurs over a finite number of periods while raiding occurs indefinitely. Furthermore, if we imagine a continuum of nations playing this game, an increase in the price of slaves will produce more raiding. Thus this simple model can generate a positively sloping supply curve.

As an extension, we may imagine this scenario with the villages and the nation located spatially along a line that runs from the African coast toward the interior. We may then contrast cases in which the nation is located either adjacent to the coast or deep within the interior. When a nation that is located along the coast conquers villages, it will be expanding

FIGURE 4.2   *The Fundamental Impact of Effective Demand*

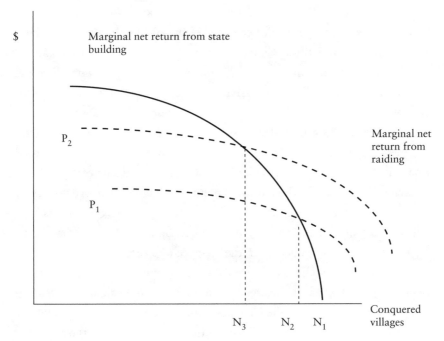

toward the interior. When an interior nation conquers villages it pushes toward the coast. This scenario is interesting if we assume that prices vary by village according to their proximity to the coast. Net slave prices are higher the closer a village is to the coast because transport costs to the coast are smaller. For example, if in equilibrium the nation raids a village near to the coast, the return is higher than if it raids a village deep in the interior. For a nation in the interior, this pricing situation translates into a lower opportunity cost of war for any value of n (where n is the number of villages conquered) relative to a nation on the coast. Additionally, the nation in the interior has an incentive to push toward the coast, as it will result in a higher slave price when it decides to halt conquest and begin slave raiding. The coastal nation has the exact opposite incentives. Thus the introduction of a price gradient discourages expansion for coastal nations and encourages expansion toward the coast for interior nations.

Scenario Three: One Nation, Three Villages and Alliance

In our third and final scenario we suppose that we are in a situation with a single nation and three villages with identical endowments arranged along a line with the nation at one end. Additionally, we introduce the ability of villages to form defensive alliances against aggressive nations or offensive alliances; however, there is a penalty (ε) for doing so. It reflects either the loss of independence or the cost of cooperating with outsiders. Alliance formation provides villages with all the benefits granted a nation: they may not be attacked and are able to raid or conquer independent villages. Given the empowerment of villages in this scenario, it is important to specify the order of play. The preexisting nation moves first, followed by the villages, moving from left to right along the ordered line.

We start by assuming that, in the absence of effective demand, the parameters of the model are such that the nation will conquer all three villages. In other words, the utility increase from conquering the third village must be greater than the conquest penalty. Thus all three villages are conquered if the marginal benefit of conquest is greater than the marginal cost:

$$X \leq \frac{\log(4bL)}{1-\delta} - \frac{\log(3bL)}{1-\delta}$$

As long as this inequality holds, the nation will conquer all three villages. However, it is possible that the villages may choose to voluntarily form an alliance. In order to determine whether this occurs, we must compare the utility of the village rulers if they are conquered with their utility if they form a defensive alliance. If no villages form an alliance and they are all conquered, the rulers of the villages will have utility as follows, where village 1 is the village next to the nation and village 2 is next on the line, followed by village 3:

$$U_1 = 0$$
$$U_2 = \log (bL)$$
$$U_3 = \log (bL) + \delta \log (bL) = (1 + \delta)\, \delta \log (bL)$$

Because the nation is only able to conquer a single village in each period, the third village is in the "best" situation of the three. The only possibility for alliance formation is a joining of villages 2 and 3, as we assume that the nation gets to play first in the sequential game. Because village 3 has a higher utility if no alliance is formed, the binding constraint for alliance formation falls on village 3.

Village 3 will voluntarily enter into an alliance with village 2 if the utility from the alliance is greater than remaining independent and being conquered. Thus villages 2 and 3 will form an alliance if the discounted continuous utility stream provided by survival is greater than the utility from independence and being conquered:

$$\frac{\log(bL) - \varepsilon}{1 - \delta} \geq (1 + \delta)\log(bL)$$

If the alliance penalty is greater than $\delta^2\log(bL)$, village 3 will not enter into an alliance with village 2, resulting in an equilibrium in which the nation conquers all three villages.

If we assume that the alliance penalty is indeed large enough to prevent alliance formation, the introduction of effective demand will alter the equilibrium outcome in a particular manner. With a positive slave price, the nation desires to conquer all three villages only if the persistent value of conquering the first and the second villages is greater than the opportunity cost (not raiding for slaves in each period) of war and the value to conquering the third village is greater than the value of raiding the third village for all remaining periods. This reduces to the second scenario in which there is less conquest, greater ethnic diversity, a permanent reallocation of labor, and more slaves produced.

If the penalty for alliance formation is sufficiently low, villages 2 and 3 may choose to form an alliance in the presence of effective demand. If we assume that the parameters of the model are such that the nation conquers village 1 (in the event that villages 2 and 3 ally), then villages 2 and 3 will form an alliance if the utility to allying for village 3 is greater than remaining independent (but being raided forever). This may be expressed as the following inequality:

$$\frac{\log(bL) - S}{1 - \delta} \leq \frac{\log(bL) - \varepsilon}{1 - \delta}$$

Thus it is apparent that our equilibrium condition for alliance formation is different than it was in the absence of effective demand. If we imagine a certain distribution over values of S, it is now more likely that village 3 will not make an offer of alliance to village 2. This is a result of our assumption of an absolutist state governed in the sole interests of the nation's (or village's) ruler. The logic is that the ruling elite in village 3 will maintain their status while their village is raided but would lose that status (and perhaps their lives) if conquered. Thus in this scenario the introduction of effective demand decreases state size, as village 3 is not conquered and results in a long-term reallocation of labor from productive purposes toward raiding. Ethnic diversity is also greater and persists.

Finally, in a permutation of the third scenario, we may consider another possible equilibrium in which villages 2 and 3 form an alliance (and the nation does not conquer village 1) in order to raid the remaining village. This occurs if the value of conquest (of village 1) for the nation is less than the value of raiding that village forever:

$$\frac{\log(bL) + paL - R}{1 - \delta} \geq \frac{\log(2bL)}{1 - \delta} - X$$

The necessary constraint on villages 2 and 3 to form an alliance is altered such that they will form an alliance only if the benefit to allying (and then subsequently raiding village 1) is greater than remaining independent:

$$\frac{\log(bL) - \varepsilon - R + paL}{1 - \delta} \geq \frac{\log(bL)}{1 - \delta}$$

Additionally, it must be the case that they do not wish to conquer village 1. They do not conquer village 1 if the utility provided by raiding village 1 forever is greater than conquering the village and then doing nothing for all future periods:

$$\frac{\log(bL) - \varepsilon - R + paL}{1 - \delta} \geq \frac{\log(1.5bL) - \varepsilon}{1 - \delta} - X$$

If these inequalities hold, then we have an equilibrium in which the nation raids village 1, and villages 2 and 3 form an alliance which in turn raids village 1. This outcome is more likely to occur for larger values of p and, as such, helps generate an upward-sloping supply curve. In addition, it generates greater ethnic diversity and smaller states. Again, there is a significant reallocation of labor from productive purposes.

All three scenarios suggest several stylized facts. Effective demand (or an increase in slave prices) should produce smaller states with more slave raiding, greater ethnic diversity, and more alliances for the purpose of raiding. Effective demand (or price increases) should also result in fewer defensive alliances and decreased production. Increases in the productivity of labor should increase state building (and as such, decrease raiding and ethnic diversity).[12]

HISTORICAL INTERPRETATION: THE CASE OF ASANTE

Our simple models reveal the conditions under which increases in the international demand for enslaved Africans constrained the growth of states, increased ethnic and social stratification, and produced a reign of terror. In the spirit of future research we wish to take a first pass at using this model to interpret the political and economic developments along the Gold Coast of West Africa during the eighteenth century, the height of the slave trade. We believe our model helps explain the origins and evolution of the Asante Empire.

Asante was a large militarized and bureaucratic state that emerged behind the Gold Coast of Africa (present-day Ghana) at the beginning of the eighteenth century. Eventually all roads led to Kumasi, the capital city located some 200 miles inland and encircled by an efficient farming sector that supported the military and bureaucratic classes that resided in the city. The Asante were powerful enough to defend against British invasion for over half a century. They were the largest and most powerful state in West Africa.[13]

Our model predicts that the slave trade discouraged state building. How, then, could Asante have grown and developed into such an impressive state during the height of the slave trade? Wilks refers to this as the enigma of Asante: "The importance of Asante is most apparent from its sheer geographic extent. At the height of its power in the early nineteenth century, Asante's empire . . . extended not only over all of present-day Ghana with the exception of the far northwest, but also over large parts of what is now Ivory Coast and smaller parts of what is now Togo" (1996, p. 27). What were the incentives to conquer so much territory in the era of the slave trade?

Part of the answer has to do with the common Akan ancestry of the Asante. In our model this would reduce the penalty for alliance, making alliance formation more likely. And Asante did emerge out of an alliance of chieftaincies brought together to defeat Denkyira, the dominant power of the region in the late seventeenth and early eighteenth centuries. According to Wilks, "Asante was not, then, a creation of an Asante tribe. . . . There was no Asante tribe. Asante was a creation of the Kumasis, Dwabens, Nsutas, and so forth, all of whom became Asantes under the new dispensation" (Wilks 1996, p. 28). In our model the alliance penalty was low enough to allow the formation of the Asante alliance for the purpose of conquest and slaving. Our model also predicts the timing of the Asante alliance. It predicts that such an alliance was more likely to be successful if it was attempted before the rise in slave prices that began in the mid-eighteenth century. Common Akan ancestry could overcome the centrifugal political forces before the slave trade, but after the profitability of slave raiding increases small differences (any differences) could serve as a pretext for attack.

But what explains the geographic expanse of Asante? We believe the key factor is the high value of labor on Asante land. Asante was interested in territorial expansion because there was gold in the land (a high value of b). All of the early military Asante campaigns followed the gold.[14] The northern expansions beyond the gold fields resulted not in annexation of territory but in tributaries, where local elites retained semiautonomy if they made annual tribute payment to Asante, most often in captives.[15]

Common heritage may explain the alliance, and gold may explain the impulse to conquer land, but our model also predicts that Asante, while large, would have been larger in the absence of the slave trade. Our model predicts that increases in the price of slaves should forestall political expansion and encourage slave raiding. This appears to be precisely what happened in the case of Asante. According to Wilks (1975, p. 18), "the campaign which destroyed the independent power of Asante's neighbors to the north, south, east and west occurred for the most part in the half-century 1700–1750." We believe that Asante expansion halted after 1750 because the price of slaves started a sharp upward trend such that by the end of the eighteenth century the price had increased by 500 percent.[16]

Finally, our model predicts that Asante, an inland nation, would expand toward the coast to raid for slaves in the villages along the coast, but that the coastal nations would not expand inland but would instead focus on defending their territories. This is because low transportation costs near the coast effectively increase the net revenue from slave production along the coast. In Asante history this is called the "southern problem," where peace was elusive and where rebellion and reconquest were the recurrent pattern (Wilks 1975, pp. 26–28). In the 1750s, for example, Dutch and English merchants interested in attaining peaceful trade to the coast tried to initiate a peace treaty between Asante and the coastal nations of Wassa, Twifo, Denkyira, and Akyem. The negotiations fell apart. The Asante conquered the coastal city of Accra from the Akyem, but the Akyem continued to revolt (p. 28). Wilks argues that the case of Akyem was not unique. He argues that the southern coastal nations were able to resist Asante aggression because the gold they possessed gave them the resources they needed to resist and because the forest offered them military cover against Asante forces (p. 28). Our model predicts that the rising price of slaves after 1750 provided an incentive for the coastal nations to resist Asante and for Asante to attempt to conquer them. The coastal states rebelled, but their posture was always defensive. Why? They had gold like the Asante and so had the resources to stage an attack. They also had a better position in the trade with Europeans by virtue of their coastal location. Our model predicts their defensive posture: the marginal return to slave raiding declines faster when expanding inland than it does when expanding toward the coast. Asante wanted to get to the coast and the coastal nations wanted to defend the coast. It appears that this was the pattern along the entire Guinea Coast from the Gold Coast (Ghana) to the Bight of Biafra (southeast Nigeria).[17]

CONCLUSION

Our model suggests that the slave trade reallocated labor away from agricultural and industrial work and toward the slave trade.[18] Second-order effects, however, may have been even more important. We show the conditions under which the African response discouraged political development and encouraged violence, social hierarchy, and ethnic diversity. As was mentioned at the outset, when placed within the context of the slave trade, many features of today's Africa once thought to be exogenous or "African" in nature (like political culture and ethnic diversity) turn out to be more endogenous than previously thought. We can think of no better reason why the era of the slave trade deserves its place in the periodization of African history. Precolonial, colonial, and postcolonial is just too colonial.

APPENDIX: A TEST FOR EFFECTIVE DEMAND

We test for a positively sloped supply function, or effective demand. The idea is to see if increases in the British demand for slaves increase the African supply of slaves. We start with a simple supply-and-demand system:

$$P = S(Q, X_s)$$
$$P = D(Q, X_d)$$

P is the price that British slave merchants pay for African slaves on the coast of Africa. Q is the quantity of African slaves boarding British ships on the coast of Africa. X_d is a set of exogenous demand shifters and X_s is a set of exogenous supply shifters.

We set $D(Q, X_d) = S(Q, X_s)$ and solve for the reduced-form relationship between equilibrium Q^* and the exogenous variables, $Q^* = H(X_d, X_s)$. We then totally differentiate the reduced form quantity equation to express changes in the equilibrium quantities as a weighted function of changes in the exogenous variables:

$$dQ = \sum_i \frac{\partial H}{\partial X_i} dX_i$$

The weights are the partial derivatives. They capture the marginal impact of changes in the exogenous variables on changes in the number of slaves boarding British ships. If demand affects the numbers supplied, then the partial on the demand covariates should be positive.

We have the data to estimate the following partial derivatives:

$$dSLAVES = \alpha_1 d(INVEST) + \alpha_2 d(SugarQ) + \alpha_3 d(SugarP)$$
$$+ \alpha_4 d(WAR) + \alpha_5 d(GUNS) + \varepsilon$$

SLAVES measures the annual number of enslaved Africans leaving Africa on British ships. These are constructed from *Voyages: The Trans-Atlantic Slave Trade Database* (2009). The year assigned to each ship is the year the ship left Britain.

INVEST is the real value of British commodity investment in the slave trade and is taken from Johnson, Lindblad, and Ross, *The Anglo-African Trade Statistics* (1990). Anglo-African trade was valued at 1699 commodity prices—what the Customs Office called "official prices." INVEST is the real value of British commodities exported to Africa minus the real value of African *nonslave* commodities exported to Britain. What remains is the real value of British commodities used to buy slaves on the coast of Africa.

GUNS measures the annual pounds of gunpowder shipped to Africa on British ships. Annual real values of gunpowder are found in Johnson, Lindblad, and Ross (1990). These are converted into physical pounds of gunpowder by dividing through by the 1699 price for gunpowder, 0.03375 pounds sterling per pound.

SugarQ measures the scale of sugar production. It is the annual pounds of sugar imported into Britain from her sugar-producing slave colonies in the Americas. The data come from Schumpeter (1960) and Deerr (1950).

SugarP is the annual retail price paid for sugar in London or Amsterdam, taken from Deerr (1950, pp. 530, 531). It is converted into real prices using a price deflator for London.

WAR controls for the effect of European wars on the demand for African captives. We construct dummy variables for the Seven Years War (1756–1763), the American Revolution (1775–1783) and the Napoleonic Wars (1792–1815). We also construct a dummy variable to capture the effects of British access to the Asiento (the Spanish slave trade). Between 1713 and 1733 Britain had a monopoly on the Spanish slave trade. After 1789 the Asiento was thrown open to all takers.

TABLE 4.1   *Test for Effective Demand*

	Dependent Variable = dSLAVES	
	Linear	Log-Log
d(INVEST)	0.02**	0.4318**
	(5.93)	(7.09)
d(GUNS)	0.006**	0.1279**
	(2.09)	(2.19)
d(SugarP)	410.40	0.0592
	(0.29)	(0.51)
d(SugarQ)	0.00	−0.0064
	(0.81)	(−0.06)
d(War_7yrs)	1079.77	0.0597
	(0.32)	(0.44)
d(War_AmRev)	−3633.34	−0.1579
	(−1.05)	(−1.14)
d(War_Napoleon)	−4585.99	−0.1225
	(−0.79)	(−0.59)
Constant	−194.91	−0.0076
	(−0.41)	(−0.39)
Adjusted R²	0.646	0.633
N	102	102
F stat	27.34	25.89

Notes: Estimated using ordinary least squares. Student t-statistics are in parentheses. ** means significant at 99% confidence level.

Sources: Based on data compiled from Deerr (1950); Schumpter (1960); Johnson, Lindblad, and Ross (1990); and *Voyages: The Trans-Atlantic Slave Trade Database* (2009). For a full discussion, see the appendix at the end of this chapter.

Results are reported in Table 4.1. They show that a doubling of British commodity investment in the slave trade increased the number of slaves leaving Africa on British ships by 43 percent. The impact was large and statistically significant.

NOTES

We want to thank seminar participants at the University of Michigan, Stanford University, the University of Utah, the University of Vermont, and the University of California, Irvine, and participants at the 2008 conferences of the Economic History Association, the African Studies Association, the All-UC Conference in Economic History, the American Economics Association, and the NBER summer workshop on the Development of the American Economy.

1. For an early effort in this direction, see Inikori (1982), pp. 27–59.

2. All slave trade quantities are calculated from *Voyages: The Trans-Atlantic Slave Trade Database* (2009) at www.slavevoyages.org.

3. The experiences and observations of Olaudah Equiano (1995, pp. 37–48) are instructive. Equiano was born and raised in Igboland behind the Bight of Biafra (southeast Nigeria). He was captured sometime in the 1760s, later became a leading figure in the British abolition movement, and wrote the narrative of his life. In it, he recounts two attempts to capture him. The second attempt was successful. He also remembers frequent battles in the fields, where neighboring villages would fight and capture each other on a regular basis.

4. In our model, the Fage effect comes through when the cost of forming alliances is small.

5. Dahomey was the slave-raiding state par excellence.

6. This is the ex post source of slaves often described by African kings. Ose Bonsu, king of Asante, proclaimed: "I cannot make war to catch slaves in the Bush, like a thief. My ancestors never did so. But if I fight a king, and kill him when he is insolent, then certainly I must have his gold, and his slaves, and the people are mine too" (quoted in Dupuis 1824, p. 163).

7. See Thornton (1999) for similar examples in many parts of Africa in a variety of ecological, political, and cultural environments.

8. A description of what we mean by "absolute" is offered by Equiano: "When a trader wants slaves, he applies to a chief for them, and tempts him with his wares. It is not extraordinary, if on this occasion he yields to the temptation with a little firmness, and accepts the price of his fellow creatures' liberty, with as little reluctance as the enlightened merchant. Accordingly he falls on his neighbour, and a desperate battle ensues" (Equiano 1995, p. 40).

9. See Wilks (1975, chaps. 1–4) for a discussion of the enormous effort it took to build and maintain the Great Roads of Asante, and the administrative and communication cost of ruling the Asante Empire.

10. See the collection of articles in Diouf (2003) for examples of defensive strategies, including relocating in swamps, abandoning villages, changing crops, changing architecture, building walls around cities, and organizing local militia and defensive alliances among villages.

11. In other words, there is no external market for slaves. Thus it may be appropriate to think of this model as before and after the beginning of the international slave trade. Instead of a starting slave price of zero, the results are identical if, in the absence of effective demand, $paL_1 \leq R$ and in its presence $paL_1 \geq R$.

12. A priori, the impact of guns and other capture technologies in this model is ambiguous. If nations are strong enough to control access to guns, then guns reduce the cost of war and raiding. The result is more aggression, but we cannot predict more or less raiding. It is an empirical question, but the strong prior is that state and raiders have the resources, credit, and contacts with Europeans to get all the guns they need to stay ahead of villagers. To the extent that guns and weapons reach the villages, they will be used for defensive purposes, increasing the cost of raiding and war, and producing fewer captives. Asante, for example, prohibited the sale of firearms to the northern provinces for fear that they would be used against them (Wilks 1975, p. 20). In the Bight of Biafra (southeast Nigeria), everyone had access to weapons and a kind of "arms race" ensued. The Aro traders who organized the slave trade in this region also organized the gun trade. They carried guns at all times. Villagers had access to all kinds of weapons. In Equiano's village, "We have fire-arms, bows and arrows, broad two-edge swords and javelins. We have shields also which cover a man from head to foot. All are taught to use these weapons; even our women are warriors. . . . Our whole district is a kind of militia" (Equiano 1995, p. 40). Major A. Leonard, an adventurous British military officer who had penetrated the Ngwa region by the late nineteenth century, reports: "Although the people [Ngwa] who en route turned out in thousands to look at us appeared to be very friendly and peacefully disposed, not a man apparently moved a step without carrying a naked sword in one hand and a rifle at full lock in the other. Even the boys, some of them not higher than an ordinary man's knee . . . walked out armed with bows and pointed arrows" (quoted in Oriji 2003, pp. 128–129).

13. Ivor Wilks is the leading authority on Asante history and we rely heavily on his work.

14. Compare the map of Asante military campaigns found in Wilks (1975, p. 39) with the late nineteenth-century geological map of the gold fields found in Dumett (1998, p. 30).

15. In eastern Gonga, the tribute was 1,000 slaves annually. The same arrangement was achieved with Dagomba and Gyaman (Wilks 1975, pp. 20–23).

16. See Richardson (1991) for the annual British prices paid on the coast of Africa in the eighteenth century and Miller (1986) for the prices paid by Brazilian slavers operating in Angola in the eighteenth century. Both price series show a striking increase of some 400 to 500 percent in the second half of the eighteenth century.

17. We do not want to argue that all such zones were frontiers between interior and coastal states, but many of them were. They were sources of captives between Asante and the coastal states along the Gold Coast, between Dahomey and the coastal states along the Slave Coast (Lovejoy 1983; Law 1991), and between the Aro network and the coastal trading towns in the Bight of Biafra (Oriji 2003). The relentless conflict in this area just behind the coast interrupted the trade to and from the coast and was the subject of frequent comments by Europeans.

18. Similar results are found in Darity (1982) and Nunn (2007).

REFERENCES

Barry, Boubacar (1998). *Senegambia and the Atlantic Slave Trade*. Translated by A. K. Armah. Cambridge: Cambridge University Press.

Bates, Robert H. (2008). *When Things Fell Apart: State Failure in Late-Century Africa*. New York: Cambridge University Press.

Curtin, Philip D. (1975). *Economic Change in Precolonial Africa: Senegambia in the Era of the Slave Trade*. Madison: University of Wisconsin Press.

Daaku, Kwame Y. (1970). *Trade and Politics on the Gold Coast, 1600–1720: A Study of the African Reaction to European Trade*. London: Clarendon.

Darity, William, Jr. (1982). "A General Equilibrium Model of the Eighteenth Century Atlantic Slave Trade." *Research in Economic History* 7: 287–326.

Deerr, Noel (1950). *The History of Sugar*, vol. 2. London: Chapman and Hall.

Diouf, Sylviane A. (2003). *Fighting the Slave Trade: West African Strategies*. Athens: Ohio University Press.

Dumett, Raymond E. (1998). *El Dorado in West Africa: The Gold-Mining Frontier, African Labor, and Colonial Capitalism in the Gold Coast, 1875–1900*. Athens: Ohio University Press.

Dupuis, Joseph (1824). *Journal of a Residence in Ashantee*. London: Cass.

Easterly, William, and Ross Levine (1997). "Africa's Growth Tragedy: Policies and Ethnic Divisions." *The Quarterly Journal of Economics* 112: 1203–1250.

Eltis, David (1990). "Welfare Trends among the Yoruba in the Early Nineteenth Century: The Anthropometric Evidence." *Journal of Economic History* 50: 521–540.

Eltis, David (1991). "Precolonial Western Africa and the Atlantic Slave Trade." In *Slavery and the Rise of the Atlantic System*, edited by B. L. Solow. Cambridge: Cambridge University Press, pp. 97–119.

Eltis, David, and Lawrence C. Jennings (1988). "Trade between Western Africa and the Atlantic World in the Pre-colonial Era." *American Historical Review* 93: 936–959.

Equiano, Olaudah (1995). *The Interesting Narrative of the Life of Olaudah Equiano*. Boston: Bedford Books.

Fage, John (1969). *A History of West Africa*. Cambridge: Cambridge University Press.

Inikori, Joseph, ed. (1982). *Forced Migration: The Impact of the Export Slave Trade on African Societies*. New York: Africana Publishing Company.

Inikori, Joseph (2003). "The Struggle against the Atlantic Slave Trade: The Role of the State." In *Fighting the Slave Trade: West African Strategies*, edited by S. A. Diouf. Athens: Ohio University Press, pp. 170–198.

Johnson, Marion, J. Thomas Lindblad, and Robert Ross (1990). *Anglo-African Trade in the Eighteenth Century: English Statistics on African Trade 1699–1808*. Leiden: Centre for the History of European Expansion.

Law, Robin (1991). *The Slave Coast of West Africa, 1550–1750: The Impact of the Atlantic Slave Trade on an African Society*. Oxford: Oxford University Press.

Lovejoy, Paul E. (1983). *Transformations in Slavery: A History of Slavery in Africa*. Cambridge: Cambridge University Press.

Manning, Patrick (1990). *Slavery and African Life*. Cambridge: Cambridge University Press.

McEvedy, Colin, and Richard Jones (1978). *Atlas of World Population History*. London: Penguin Books.

Miller, Joseph C. (1986). "Slave Prices in the Portugues Southern Atlantic, 1600–1830." In *Africans in Bondage: Studies in Slavery and the Slave Trade*, edited by P. Lovejoy. Madison: University of Wisconsin Press, pp. 43–77.

Nunn, Nathan (2007). "Historical Legacies: A Model Linking Africa's Past to Its Current Underdevelopment." *Journal of Development Economics* 83: 157–175.

Nunn, Nathan (2008). "The Long Term Effects of Africa's Slave Trades." *Quarterly Journal of Economics* 123: 139–176.

Oriji, John N. (2003). "Igboland, Slavery, and the Drums of War and Heroism." In *Fighting the Slave Trade: West African Strategies*, edited by S. A. Diouf. Athens: Ohio University Press, pp. 121–131.

Patterson, Orlando (1982). *Slavery and Social Death: A Comparative Study*. Cambridge, MA: Harvard University Press.

Richardson, David (1991). "Prices of Slaves in West and West Central Africa: Towards an Annual Series, 1698–1807." *Bulletin of Economic Research* 43: 21–56.

Rodney, Walter (1972). *How Europe Underdeveloped Africa*. London: Bogle-L'Ouverture Publications.

Schumpeter, Elizabeth (1960). *English Overseas Trade Statistics, 1697–1808*. London: Oxford University Press.

Thornton, John (1999). *Warfare in Atlantic Africa, 1500–1800*. London: UCL Press.

Voyages: The Trans-Atlantic Slave Trade Database (2009). Available at http://www.slave voyages.org.

Wilks, Ivor (1975). *Asante in the Nineteenth Century: The Structure and Evolution of a Political Order*. London: Cambridge University Press.

Wilks, Ivor (1996). *One Nation, Many Histories: Ghana Past and Present*. Accra: Ghana Universities Press.

CHAPTER 5

Similar Societies, Different Solutions: U.S. Indian Policy in Light of Australian Policy toward Aboriginal Peoples

LEONARD A. CARLSON

THE UNITED STATES and Australia are similar in many ways. Both are developed settler societies with high output per capita, large territories, democratic governments, and a legal system that is derived from the British common law. Both countries also had a substantial native population that was displaced by European settlement. Yet each country treated the property rights of native peoples in very different ways, and these differences have had important implications for the native peoples. In order to fit the native population into English law and policy, new institutions and new legal concepts developed in both countries. Colonial authorities and settlers in Australia created a new legal concept: "terra nullius." According to this legal principle, land in Australia belonged to no one prior to the coming of the English settlers in 1788 and all subsequent private title to land was treated in law as originating with a grant from the English crown (see Connor 2005). By contrast, British colonial authorities in North America and later in New Zealand treated native peoples as having "aboriginal rights" to land that they occupied before the coming of English settlers (Lester and Parker 1973, p. 189). In the United States, this came to mean that Indian title had to be cleared (extinguished) before it could be owned by anyone else. Later in the United States the federal government created special laws for "Indian country" and regulations for negotiating with native peoples. The legal rights of aborigines to land in Australia based on the fact that they lived there prior to English settlement were belatedly recognized in 1992 by the High Court of Australia in *Mabo v. Queensland,* thereby voiding the concept of terra nullius. Since that time Australians have struggled to come to terms with past treatment of the Aborigines by first English and then Australian authorities.

The argument made here is that differences arose (1) because of different initial conditions in Australia and the United States and (2) because of subsequent interactions with native peoples and the settlers. In the United States, English settlers encountered native peoples who farmed land and lived in settled communities. Indian tribes were also a formidable military threat which made them either valuable allies or dangerous foes in the battle between Britain, France, and Spain for control of North America. As a consequence, Indian land claims were treated with respect by colonial governments. In some cases private individuals purchased land from Indians both in colonial times and later, although this practice was not recognized by colonial courts and colonial authorities tried to stop the practice. Indian land was treated as territory controlled by "domestic dependent nations."

By contrast, aboriginal peoples in Australia were not farmers, and they did not engage in land management as recognized by the British. Further, the initial colony in Australia was a penal colony administered by the British military. Poorly armed aborigines were not a major military threat, and they had no European allies.

As settlers spread out from the east coast of the United States, they continued to encounter organized tribes that impeded settlement. First the British and then the Americans tried to minimize conflict with Indians by recognizing tribal territories and enacting formal treaties with tribes. By the 1850s this evolved into a system of tribally controlled territories "reserved" for Indians—reservations. Once in place this system took on a life of its own. Indians knew what land was theirs, and the federal courts, often pressured by white allies of the Indians, treated these rights seriously. Over time court decisions, laws, and executive actions have created institutions that have proven useful to Indians.

In Australia most settlers remained close to the coast. Interior lands were first settled by sheep herders moving into crown lands, often without permission. Some of these "squatters" who used crown lands (ironically cleared of trees by the land use practices of the aborigines) to establish large sheep stations became quite wealthy. Any land "reserved" for aborigines from crown lands were under the control of the state governments or owned by private charitable or religious groups, not the aboriginal people who lived there.

Did the fact that Indians had legal rights to land really matter? Or were these merely "trinket treaties," as some non-U.S. observers claim (Weaver 1996, p. 989; Macintyre 1999, p. 68)? It is clear, in light of later events, that these treaties did matter and were far more than mere formalities. California and Texas, settled by Americans under Mexican laws that did not recognize territorial rights of Indian tribes, provide a "natural experiment" as to what might have happened in the rest of the country had Indian land and treaty rights not existed. The consequences for Indians, especially in California, were tragic.

NATIVE PEOPLES AND THE FEDERAL GOVERNMENT

Both the United States and Australia are federal systems, but the relation of native peoples to the federal governments of the two countries is defined differently in their constitutions. In Australia aboriginal peoples are explicitly mentioned in the Constitution twice. The Commonwealth of Australia Constitution Act of 1900 states: "*In reckoning the numbers of the people of the Commonwealth, or of a State or other part of the Commonwealth, aboriginal natives shall not be counted.*" Further, the Commonwealth Constitution gives the federal government the right to make laws for "people of any race, *other than the aboriginal race in any State*, for whom it is deemed necessary to make special laws."[1]

The italicized clauses were dropped in 1967, but it is clear that aboriginals were considered outsiders who were not citizens and whose welfare was left to the states to decide, except in federal territory.

Like the Australian Commonwealth Constitution, the U.S. Constitution (1789) also refers to native peoples twice. The first time is in Article I, in reference to citizenship to determine representation in the House of Representatives:

Article I, Section 2, Clause 3: Representatives and direct Taxes shall be apportioned among the several States which may be included within this Union, according to their respective Numbers, which shall be determined by adding to the whole Number of free Persons, including those bound to Service for a Term of Years, and *excluding Indians not taxed*, three fifths of all other Persons. (Emphasis added)

Indians who did not live in tribes were taxed and counted in the census, like other people. But Indians who still lived in tribes (Indians not taxed) are not citizens of the United States, but rather members of tribes. By act of Congress in 1924 all Indians in the United States who had not already become citizens were made citizens of the United States (Prucha 1984, vol. 2, p. 973).[2] The second time Indians are mentioned is in the commerce clause, Article I, Section 8, "The Congress shall have the power. . . . To regulate Commerce with foreign Nations, and among the several States, and *with the Indian Tribes*" (emphasis added). Relations with Indian tribes, like those with foreign governments, are reserved for the Congress, not the states, and tribes have a direct relationship with the federal government.

INITIAL CONDITIONS IN NORTH AMERICA AND AUSTRALIA

As already noted, in the Australian legal system all land was originally "terra nullius." This meant that no private title to land before 1788 was legally recognized and all private title to land was ultimately derived from grants to individuals by the English crown after that date. By contrast, British colonial authorities in North America and in New Zealand treated native peoples as having "aboriginal rights" to land that they occupied before the coming of English settlers (Lester and Parker 1973, p. 189). The British in Australia, however, were not alone in failing to recognize the land rights of hunter-gatherers. The Spanish, for example, recognized that Indians in the Americas had a claim to land they used for farming or pasturage, but generally did not recognize claims to territory used by hunter-gatherers (Royce 1896, p. 541).

Australia was initially settled by the "first fleet" that arrived in Botany Bay in New South Wales, Australia, in 1788. The eleven ships brought soldiers and administrators along with prisoners to establish a penal colony on the presumably thinly populated continent. The military had the task of setting up and operating the penal colony and controlling the activities of the prisoners. The native peoples they encountered seemed few in number and technologically backward to them. The easiest course of action was to treat the whole continent as owned by the crown and to try to keep settlers off crown lands unless they received permission to settle from the government. There was a large military presence with vastly superior weapons relative to the aborigines and the military is paid to fight. Thus the incentive to keep peace with the native population by signing treaties or buying land was reduced compared to North America or New Zealand. The fact that the aborigines were hunter-gatherers was also important. Stuart Banner argues, "The absence of aboriginal farms was crucial, because the British were heirs to a long tradition of thought associating the development of property rights with a society's passage through specific stages of civilization" (Banner 2005a, p. 101).

Reformers in the 1830s and 1840s challenged the legal doctrine that native people had no legal claim to the land, but without success. According to Banner (2005b, p. 129), by the 1830s "every landowner in Australia had a vested interest in *terra nullius*. To overturn the doctrine would be to upset every white person's title to his or her land." For example, in 1835 a group of Australians led by John Batman claimed a territory of 200,000 hectares acquired from the Kulin people for goods and the promise of payment of an annual rent. The minister for the colonies dismissed it on the grounds that "such a concession would subvert the foundation upon which all property rights in New South Wales at present rest" (Macintyre 1999, p. 68).

Why didn't English settlers in North America similarly just take possession of Indian land? It would be logical, given self-interest and the feudal tradition that is the basis of the common law. According to one popular textbook on American Economic History, "In theory, all English land belonged to the king. . . . According to English feudalism, all land ownership was a grant for services from the king" (Hughes and Cain 2003, p. 11).

But in North America this theory ran into obvious contradictions. Indians were already farming the land when English settlers arrived. Natural law philosophers such as John Locke saw farmers as having property rights that needed to be respected. Further, there was also the practical issue that Indians were a serious military threat. The first North American

English colonies were settled by small private ventures authorized by the crown. European weapons in the seventeenth century were crude and not that superior to Indian weapons, which meant that the natives could be a serious military threat. Moreover, Indians quickly learned that there was competition for their support in wars between European powers, just as Indians sought allies against enemy tribes.

Indians were also often willing to sell land. European diseases arrived before English settlement, leading to a massive loss of population that left idle improved land that Indians did not need. Once a system of buying land from Indians was in place, however, Banner argues it was hard to abolish. In the 1680s the imperial government argued that "'from the Indians noe title cann be Derived.' The result was uproar, led by some of the most prominent people in New England. If a purchase from the Indians could not serve as the root of a valid land title, declared a group of Boston merchants, then 'no *Man was owner of a Foot of Land in all the Colony.*' The imperial government had to back down" (Banner 2005a, p. 131).

Banner's view is not accepted by many other scholars. Juricek (1989), for example, argues instead that these private transactions were tolerated but never really recognized as part of the law. He concludes that "in the official English view Indian land rights were neither sovereign rights nor civil rights, but were mere 'natural' rights . . . since Indians did not 'own' the land in a sense recognized by English law, no Englishman—not even the king—could 'buy' it from them. . . . Indian rights were not transferred to the English but eliminated—hence the later expression, 'extinguishment of Indian title'" (Juricek 1989, p. xxiv). In either view, however, aboriginal people in North America had a claim to land that British could not ignore.

THE ESTABLISHMENT OF "INDIAN TERRITORY" AND INDIAN PROPERTY RIGHTS IN BRITISH NORTH AMERICA

Another institution that developed in North America, but not in Australia, was formal negotiations with tribal governments. According to Francis Prucha, the leading historian of Indian-white relations,

The eighteenth-century treaties with the Iroquois, for example, were dramatic documents indicating a shrewdness and eloquence on the part of the Indians that were often a match for the self-interest of the whites. . . . *It is in the treaties that one sees best the acceptance by Europeans of the nationhood of the Indian groups that became a fixed principle in the national policy of the United States.* (Prucha 1984, vol. 1, p. 17; emphasis added)

The British treated tribes in other colonies in much the same way.

But treaties did not eliminate costly friction on the frontier. "Conferences between the Indians and the Albany Congress in 1754 emphasized the point. . . . 'We told you a little while ago,' said one speaker for the Mohawks, 'that we had an uneasiness on our minds, and we shall now tell you what it is; it is concerning our land'" (Prucha 1984, vol. 1, pp. 17–18). These frictions and many others led to conflict on the frontier.

To reduce the problem of warfare on the frontier, the British government began to take Indian affairs out of the "incompetent" hands of the colonials in 1755 (Prucha 1984, vol. 1, p. 21). The end of the war with France in 1763 was accompanied by a rebellion on the frontier led by Chief Pontiac. After the costly suppression of the rebellion, the imperial government issued the Proclamation of 1763. The proclamation reserved for Indian nations "all the Lands and Territories lying to the Westward of the Sources of the Rivers that fall into the Sea from the West and North West" (cited in Prucha 1984, vol. 1, p. 24).

The Proclamation of 1763 was a direct statement by the king (not just the Privy Council) and affirmed two important principles. The first was that Indians had a claim to territory, not just land that they farmed, based on aboriginal occupancy. Secondly, only the crown had the right to acquire land from the tribes, not colonists or groups of them. It also established the borders of Indian country. The seriousness with which the British and Indians took these agreements is illustrated by the many treaties and laws negotiated by the British. A recent edited collection of laws and treaties comes to 20 volumes (Vaughan 1979–2003).

Why is there no equivalent of the Proclamation of 1763 in Australian history? One reason is that the British had no European rivals in Australia.

This meant that there was no outside power to provide the aborigines with guns and no competition for alliances with native peoples. Nor did the aborigines acquire horses in large numbers, as the plains tribes did with deadly effectiveness. This was critical. Equestrianism was embraced by Indian tribes in the plains after roughly 1780. Indian tribes on the plains acquired horses from the Spanish by raiding and trade, and feral herds began to roam the Great Plains. This totally transformed the balance of power in the western United States (Hämäläinen 2004). Horses allowed plains tribes, especially the Lakota, to dominate other tribes and to engage in effective guerrilla warfare against white settlers. Aborigines engaged in pedestrian warfare against mounted settlers were far less effective.

From the point of view of British officials, a greater problem for British authority in Australia would have been to anger British settlers by preventing the profitable expansion of the production of wool. The example of the American Revolution, where the Proclamation of 1763 that stopped settlers from moving west was a major grievance of the colonists against the British crown, would have been clearly in the minds of British authorities. Interactions with the native peoples by Europeans in Australia were dominated by sheep herders pushing into aboriginal territory and establishing vast estates controlled by "squatters." The colonial government tried to limit settlement, but this was largely unsuccessful (see Weaver 1996; Attard 2006). The wool that these stations produced became the leading export of the Australian economy and the driving force for the economic growth of much of Australia from 1820 to 1850—described as Australia's "pastoral age" (Jackson 1977, p. 4). Overly aggressive actions to hinder the expansion of the sheep industry onto crown lands could have led to disruptions in output and conflict on the frontier between settlers and the crown.

THE COEVOLUTION OF U.S. INDIAN POLICY AND INDIAN TRIBAL RESPONSES TO EUROPEAN SETTLEMENT

Following the American Revolution, there was temptation in the United States to move toward a system closer to what was evolving in Australia at the same time. Under the Articles of Confederation, states had considerable independent authority, and some states treated western tribes as defeated enemies who had lost the war along with their British allies, thereby forfeiting their claim to territory (Perdue and Green 1995, pp. 7–8). Unlike Australia, the states recognized Indian rights to land but argued these rights had been forfeited during the Revolutionary War. This led to warfare along the frontier as settlers pushed into lands occupied by Indians. This policy proved costly and unworkable and led to a return to the British practice of negotiating treaties with tribes to cede their claims to western lands.

After the passage of the Land Ordinance of 1785, much of the fighting was in federally controlled territory, and, as noted above, the U.S. Constitution of 1789 placed relations with Indian tribes in the hands of the federal government. Henry Knox, the first secretary of war after the adoption of the Constitution and the man in charge of President George Washington's Indian policy,

was convinced that the encroachment of settlers and others onto their (Indian) lands was the primary cause of war on the frontier and that . . . the federal government had a moral obligation to preserve and protect Native Americans from the extinction he believed was otherwise inevitable when "uncivilized" people came into contact with "civilized" ones. Knox's policy and those that followed have been called "expansion with honor." (Perdue and Green 1995, p. 10)

THE CREATION OF AN INDIAN FRONTIER
BEFORE 1840

The attempt to pursue a peaceful and honorable solution in dealing with Indians was confronted with the eager desire of many white settlers to acquire Indian land in fertile farming areas. Serious Indian wars continued east of the Mississippi until after the end of the war of 1812 with Great Britain and its aftermath. By 1820 most tribes north of the Ohio River had been defeated and the policy was to move many of these tribes to new territory west of the Mississippi River. Indians who were willing to give up "the hunt" and agree to hold title under state law could remain. The result was an Indian frontier where Indian tribes had the land west of the Mississippi and whites land to the east. Each tribe had it own relationship with the federal government and its own territory and there were frequent conflicts between groups of Indians in the west.

In general, proponents of removal argued that moving Indians away from whites was a practical and a humanitarian solution. A humanitarian argument for removal was made by Lewis Cass, the leading scholar of Indian languages of his day. Anthony Wallace concludes that, in Cass's view,

> "they" (i.e., the [Indian] men) were ill adapted to sedentary civilized life and languished in indolence and vice when unable any longer to hunt and fight. The only solution was to remove Indians to the forests and plains west of the Mississippi, where they could either choose to return to their former way of life in the untrammeled hunter state or to gradually embrace civilization. (Wallace 1993, p. 48)

Wallace is critical of the factual basis of Cass's views, but he notes, "Many of the smaller [Indian] communities, particularly in the North, were slums in the wilderness." Wallace also points out that other communities in the southeast had made impressive progress as farmers and had established settled communities which those who pushed for the removal of tribes to the west tended to ignore.

Removal was not without its critics in the 1830s. Opposition to removal of the "Five Civilized Tribes" from the southeast was centered in the northeast among opponents of President Andrew Jackson. The most notorious example of forced removal is that of the Cherokee Indians in the southeast. The crisis came to a head in Georgia. Georgia had a unique history. It was one of the original thirteen states and its original territory stretched all the way to the Mississippi River. In 1802 Georgia was the last state to cede its western lands to the federal government. Under the terms of the 1802 agreement with the state of Georgia, the federal government agreed to move Indians from the new boundaries of the state as soon as it could reach agreements with the tribes. Settlement in Georgia was originally confined to the coast and the land along its border with South Carolina. Over time, the Creeks ceded lands in Georgia and moved west.

But the Cherokee Nation successfully put off removal for years in close alliance with members of Congress from the Northeast. The Cherokee invited religious groups in the Northeast to set up schools in their territory in return for being allowed to preach the Christian religion. They also established a written constitution, modeled on that of the United States, and had an elected legislature. By 1828 the cause of the Cherokee and other southern tribes was taken up by opponents of Andrew Jackson, who were in the process of coalescing into the new Whig party. Jackson made removal of the tribes from the southeast a key goal of his administration. The vote to authorize removal passed in the House of Representatives by a five-vote margin out of 199 cast (Carlson 2006). When the state of Georgia and President Jackson pressed to move the tribe, the Cherokee appealed to the Supreme Court. They were represented by William Wirt, a former attorney general of the United States. With the president and the state of Georgia both determined to have the Cherokee leave, the Supreme Court was faced with a constitutional crisis. The Court did not block removal, but made two landmark rulings defining the rights of tribes in the cases of the *Cherokee Nation v. Georgia* (1831) and *Worchester v. Georgia* (1832). In the first of these cases Chief Justice Marshall defined Indian tribes as "Domestic Dependent Nations," and both cases established legal principles relied upon and expanded by lawyers representing Indian tribes ever since.

But even as it authorized removal, Congress clearly recognized that Cherokee and other tribes had a right to their lands in the Southeast and that the tribes had to be compensated for land taken from them. The final treaty with the Cherokees was signed by a minority faction in the tribe that saw removal as inevitable. Once in Oklahoma, the Cherokee and the other "Civilized Tribes" created self-governing republics which existed until the 1890s. Throughout the debate over the removal of tribes to the West, members of Congress took pains to deny that Indian tribes had sovereignty over their territory, but their ownership of the land, especially land that was cultivated, was never in doubt.

Did it matter that Indians had rights to land, given the ability of the federal government to pressure them to move west of the Mississippi River? The answer is yes. This is not a defense of the forced removal of the Cherokee in 1839, but simply an argument that if they were going to be forced to move, it was good to get a legal right to the new territory in return. By contrast, under Australian law at that time, there would have been no need to do such a quid pro quo with native peoples, because they legally did not own the land they occupied. If the lands became valuable, the land could simply be taken for other purposes and the inhabitants moved elsewhere (see Lester and Parker 1973, p. 190).

THE CREATION OF THE RESERVATION SYSTEM

The next major institutional development was Indian reservations, an institution that has persisted to this day. The removal policy as it existed in the years after 1820 theoretically created a permanent "Indian frontier." Indians who lived to the west of that line were to receive goods and be provided with education and protected from the "vices" of white civilization. But the population growth of the United States and the acquisition of vast territory after the Mexican-American War in 1848 made that solution unworkable. Settlers pushed west across the Mississippi River into lands once reserved for Indians. This created pressure to open lands to white settlers while continuing the idea of protecting Indians on lands reserved for their use until they were ready for assimilation.

After 1846 the Office of Indian Affairs began a policy of negotiating with western tribes to establish reservations. After the movement of the Office of Indian Affairs from the War Department to the Department of the Interior in 1849, this movement became more pronounced. Earlier settlements with tribes who had agreed to live in peace with their white neighbors, such as the Iroquois, had resulted in pockets of peaceful Indians owning land under state jurisdiction. These are referred to as reservations as well, but they were not part of a general policy of creating federally recognized reservations.

The reservations were designed to keep the peace between aggressive tribes on the one side and white settlers and peaceful tribes on the other. The treaties creating reservations called for Indians to surrender some of their territory in return for fixed borders and treaty goods and supplies as well as education. Of course much land was opened to white settlement, but substantial amounts remained in Indian hands. The treaties were seen as both practical and humane. For example, the commissioner of Indian affairs in 1856 saw the reservation system as a way to prevent "these poor denizens of the forest [from being] blotted out of existence" (cited in

Prucha 1984, vol. 1, p. 317). This reflected a view also expressed earlier by Thomas Jefferson that Indians should be helped to become settled agriculturalists. Interestingly, initially reservations were seen as only a temporary solution. Once a tribe had agreed to live on a reservation, the federal government appointed an agent to interact with the tribe and distribute promised food ("rations") and provide education, including education in farming. Many treaties contained clauses calling for the future privatization of the reservations by dividing land among individual members of the tribe (allotment), giving them title (in fee simple) to the land, and ending federal supervision. After the American Civil War (1861–1865), President Grant in 1869 launched a so-called Peace Policy which elaborated this policy. His policy was to push for treaties with western tribes to establish reservation boundaries. On the reservations Indians were to be assisted by agents appointed from members of Protestant religious denominations. If Indians "left the reservation" without permission, they were under the army's authority and could be rounded up and brought back (Prucha 1984, vol. 1, pp. 501–533).

The reservation system was a practical solution forged in the context of the movement of settlement west of the Mississippi River. Many settlers were attempting to pass through the plains on their way to land on the West Coast in what is today Oregon and Washington. But to do so they had to pass through territory controlled by aggressive Plains Indian tribes. After 1780 the horse, first acquired from the Spanish by raiding or trading, and guns, acquired by trade, led to dramatic changes in the West as equestrian tribes such as the Cheyenne and later the Lakota came to rely on hunting buffalo and fighting while mounted. Plains tribes fought with sedentary tribes and each other and formed new alliances. Their mobility made them a formidable military force in the West, even though whites greatly outnumbered Indians (see Prucha 1984, vol. 1, p. 493; Hämäläinen 2004). Confining both warlike and more peaceful tribes to reservations came to be the dominant tool for trying to bring peace to the West.

The tribes themselves gradually recognized boundaries of reservations. Legally, white settlers could only acquire land outside the boundaries of these reservations. Indians in the West at times fought against being confined to reservations (Utley 2003), but as the title of an important work on the subject says, reservations were an "alternative to extinction" (Trennert 1975; Prucha 1984, vol. 1, p. 317). As the history of California Indians discussed below illustrates, the alternative to reservations could be extinction.

The reservation system was far from perfect, of course. Substantial amounts of land were removed from Indian control over the years and the failure to deliver all the promised goods because of fraud, theft, and outright reneging was a persistent problem. But in the treaty system and on the reservations, Indian tribes developed institutions to negotiate with the federal government and promote their interests. Once created, Indian reservations proved to be a resilient institution that still exists and is important to Indians today. Reservations persist despite the announced intention of federal policy makers from 1887 to 1934 and again from 1946 to 1960 to abolish reservations (see Carlson 1981; Fixico 1986; Prucha 1984, vol. 2). They are governed by elected officials and subject to tribal and federal laws unique to reservations.

In 1871 the practice of having treaties approved only by the Senate was replaced by a system where laws regarding Indians were passed by both houses of Congress. This came about because members of the House of Representatives had objected to being excluded from legislation affecting Indians in their states (Prucha 1984, vol. 1, p. 530). The end of treaties, however, did not mean that Indian tribes no longer could have land added to their reservations. After the 1870s, land from the public domain was transferred to tribes in cases where there was undeveloped land and a tribe lacked sufficient resources to subsist. These transfers were the result of congressional action or executive orders of the president transferring federal land to a tribe. These have been called "treaty substitutes" (Banner 2005b, p. 252). The amount of land transferred was at times extensive.

Indian tribal lands were something of a legal anomaly within the U.S. legal system, but tribal land was still a property right. Indians had the support of reform groups in the Northeast, and that gave them leverage on Congress and the courts. Congress was reluctant to recognize tribes as being sovereign, but at the same time judges and courts tended to be

FIGURE 5.1   *Indian Reservations in the United States in 1880*

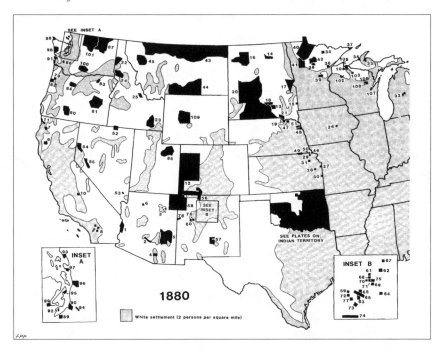

Source: Reprinted from Prucha (1990a), p. 38, with permission.

conservative on issues related to property. Courts did not recognize as legal the taking of Indian land without compensation or some kind of an agreement.[3] Any act that arbitrarily took land from Indians was a threat to property rights in general.[4] Further, there were active and influential supporters of Indian rights in the eastern states trying to influence members of Congress and the courts to support Indian welfare.[5] Some of these groups grew out of the earlier antislavery movement. There were a total of 155 million acres of Indian land under federal supervision in 1881 (Carlson 1981, p. 183). Figure 5.1 shows Indian reservations in 1880.

DID RESERVATIONS MATTER? CALIFORNIA AS A U.S. VERSION OF "TERRA NULLIUS"

Suppose, as in Australia, the United States had not recognized tribes as owning land and that all land was open to settlement. What if there were no reservations? What might have happened? What difference would it have made? As already noted, some scholars have seen the reservation system as an "alternative to extinction." California provides a "natural experiment" to see what might have occurred had American settlement occurred without recognizing Indian land rights. As noted earlier, under Spanish and later Mexican law, Indian land was not recognized unless it was tilled or used as pasture.

The comparison to Australia is apt for several reasons. First, the native peoples in California and Australia were not farmers at the time of European contact. Most were hunter-gatherers who had complex patterns of using plants and animals to survive. Second, Indians in California were divided into several language groups and typically lacked a centralized tribal organization. This is similar to the aboriginal groups settlers found in Australia. Third, until 1848 the legal systems in both Australia and Mexican California did not legally recognize aboriginal claims to territory used for a hunter-gatherer economy. Fourth, California and Australia both experienced gold rushes which brought settlers into native controlled lands; and fifth, in both California and Australia settlers moved into areas with weak control by the central government.

California had the highest population density of any Indian culture area in North America north of Mexico (Ubelaker 1988, p. 290), but "the cultural pattern was a complex mosaic of small territories. These cells, which were particularly small in northern California, were filled by about five hundred culturally diverse independent communities speaking nearly fifty languages belonging to at least six families" (Snow 1966, pp. 176–177). Technically the tribes were hunter-gatherers who gathered resources such as acorns from their territory in complex substance systems. "Each village and, in less settled areas, each wandering band managed its own affairs without regard to the others" (Underhill 1971 [1953], p. 255). The description of Indians in California is somewhat similar to the types of economic activity found among the aboriginal peoples of Australia. The Indians in the California cultural area should not be confused with the Northwest Coast Indians farther up the Pacific coast, who harvested salmon and who, by comparison with California Indians, had a relative surplus of food and a more complex material culture (see Underhill 1971 [1953], chaps. 12 and 13).

The southern half of what is today California was settled relatively late by the Spanish. In part to spread the gospel and in part to defend their territory from the British and the Russians, the Spanish friars entered California to establish a series of missions. Beginning with San Diego in 1769, Franciscan friars led by Father Junípero Serra established missions along the coast, ending in San Francisco Solano, twenty miles north of San Francisco in 1823. Indians near the missions were gathered on mission lands to be Christianized and taught to be farmers, sometimes by force. According to Underhill, "Though they existed in full power for only about sixty years, they (the missions) changed the life of the Indians forever." When the mission system ended, it proved impossible for Indians to go back to their previous way of life. The missions were secularized in 1834 and the stated Mexican policy was to give land to Mission Indians, but this did not happen. Instead, the Mission Indians became peons working on the land of Mexican landlords (Underhill 1971 [1953], p. 84).

East and north of the modern city of San Francisco, first Spain and then Mexico exerted little control. Tribes outside Mexican control continued to hunt and gather as before. According to Ubelaker, as late as 1850, the Indian population of California was 82,980, down from about 200,000 in 1800. But the end of the Mexican-American War and the discovery of gold proved disastrous for California's Indians. By the Treaty of Guadelupe Hidalgo, the 1848 treaty that ended the war, Mexico ceded California to the United States.

Gold was discovered in California a few months before that treaty was signed, but the news had not reached the treaty negotiators (Clay and Wright 2005). The discovery of gold in central California led to a rapid influx of miners into California. Mining law in California was in a state of limbo because Mexican law with respect to mining had been suspended in the gold country by U.S. officials. There is a lively literature discussing how a new system of property rights was created in gold country (see Umbeck 1977; Clay and Wright 2005; Clay, this volume). The fate of Indians in California, however, is usually not mentioned in these accounts, probably because Indians had already been driven out of the area where gold was being mined. Neither Spain nor Mexico recognized California Indians as controlling any territory, and American settlers did not either. The result was the near annihilation of these small bands as they clashed with the new settlers.

An initial attempt to create Indian reservations in California failed. In 1851 the federal government authorized three commissioners to travel throughout California and negotiate treaties with tribes. The commissioners had an immense task and lacked the language skills to fully communicate with the people with whom they were negotiating. The reservations they proposed are shown in Figure 5.2. These treaties were never ratified by the Senate, in part because of the opposition of California's senators who did not want territory closed to them and who had little respect for California's Indians (Prucha 1984, vol. 1, pp. 386–67l; Lamar and Truett 1996, p. 98).

Thus Indians in California were left to the mercy of a state government dominated by settlers who often saw Indians as thieves who raided their farms and ranches. The settlers in the 1850s and 1860s organized militia and attacked Indians to stop these raids (Lamar and Pruett 1996, p. 99). According to Prucha (1984, vol. 1, p. 381), "The relations of the States and Indians in California were particularly disastrous, for the attempt of the federal government to protect them through the treaty machinery was abortive, and the Indians themselves were no match for the aggressive and often lawless gold seekers who flooded the region in 1849 and after." Lamar and Truett (1996, p. 98) conclude that "through the combined effects of disease, starvation, malnutrition and simple homicide, the Indian population plummeted from 150,000 in 1845 to 35,000 in 1860." Similarly, Thornton (1987, p. 109) concludes that "primarily because of killings, the California Indian population . . . decreased almost by two-thirds in a little more than a single decade from 100,000 in 1849 to 35,000 in 1860."[6]

Ultimately a few reservations were established in the north outside the gold country. Beginning in 1870, Mission Indians were granted small reservations known as rancherias. In general, however, "the California experience was outside the main course of reservation history. Indians

FIGURE 5.2   *Proposed Indian Reservations in California*

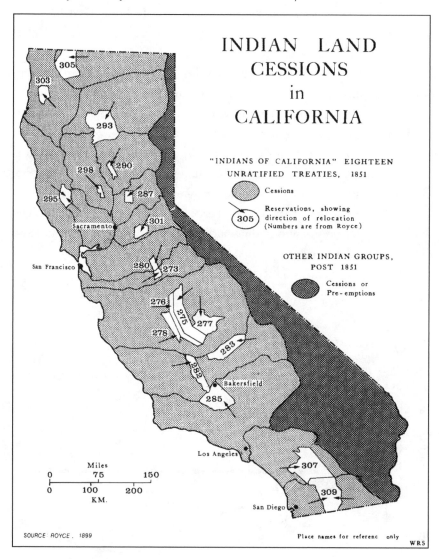

INDIAN LAND
CESSIONS
in
CALIFORNIA

"INDIANS OF CALIFORNIA" EIGHTEEN
UNRATIFIED TREATIES, 1851

Cessions

305   Reservations, showing
direction of relocation
(Numbers are from Royce)

OTHER INDIAN GROUPS,
POST 1851

Cessions or
Pre-emptions

SOURCE: ROYCE, 1899

Place names for referenc only
WRS

Source: Reprinted from Beals (1985), p. 145, with permission.

were allowed no clear title to land and ... presented quite a different situation from examples such as the Sioux reserve in Dakota" (Prucha 1984, vol. 1, p. 392).

The population decline in California was by far the steepest of any Indian group in North America, "even though they [the California Indians] were among the last populations to sustain major disease impact" (Ubelaker 1988, p. 291). There were only 14,825 living members of California tribes in 1900, 7.4 percent of the population at first contact with Europeans. To be clear, this estimate is of the entire population of this cultural group. By 1940, the total estimated population was only 10,000, or less than 5 percent of the population in 1500. By contrast, the population of Plains tribes in 1900 was 52 percent of that of its 1800 level. The Indian population in 1900 in the Southwest was 73.3 percent of its 1800 level and had returned to the 1800 level by 1950 (calculated from Ubelaker 1988, p. 291). This can be seen in Figure 5.3.

FIGURE 5.3   *North American Indian Population as Percent of 1800 Level: Total and Selected Cultural Groups*

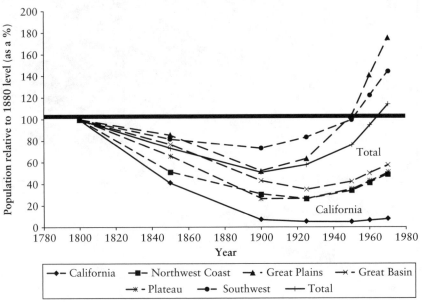

Source: Ubelaker (1988), p. 292.

Texas is an additional example of what happened when there was no recognition of Indian claims to land. American settlers had moved into the Mexican territory and fought a successful war of secession from Mexico in 1836. From that date until its admission as a state in the United States in 1845, Texas waged an aggressive policy of driving the Comanche and Kiowa Indians out of the state. The goal was largely achieved, and except for some small bands, there is very little federally controlled Indian land in the state.

Could California have turned out differently if recognized reservations had been in place before the gold rush? Counterfactual histories are tricky, of course, but suppose gold was not discovered in California in 1848, but ten years later. In that situation perhaps a system of reservations like that proposed in 1851 might already have been in place at the time gold was discovered and settlers flooded into the state. If so, perhaps Indians in California might have fared better. This is not to say that the outcome would have been just by modern standards, but it simply might have been better than what actually occurred.

The other territories in the far west settled under U.S. law, rather than Spanish law, provide evidence of what might have occurred if reservations had been created for Indians in California. An especially interesting example is the history of Indians belonging to the Great Basin cultural group, such as the Indians in Oregon, Utah, and Idaho. These peoples, like those in California, lacked a tradition of centralized authority and lived in small bands. In these states tribes were gathered onto reservations created by treaty, and later, by statutes or executive orders. In some cases tribes who were traditional enemies were placed on the same reservation. But even where groups with little in common were brought together, Indians often proved to be agents of their own destiny and formed new communities based on a fusing of different traditions and acted in their own interests (Underhill 1971 [1953]). These tribes survived and retained their territory into the twentieth century.

CONCLUSION

It seems obvious that, because native peoples in the United States and Australia were there before European settlers arrived, they in some sense "owned the land." But Indians and Australian Aborigines had different economic and political systems than British settlers, and in practice it proved difficult to fit native territorial rights within the framework of European legal systems. One reason is that legal systems, like other economic institutions, evolved over time in a way that is path dependent and often inelegant (David 1994). As a result the way that native rights have been treated has often been awkward and inefficient. In each country native rights were treated differently. These differences mattered. At times small differences in institutions can have important consequences for future development. Gavin Wright (2006, pp. 44–45), for example, concludes that the fact that Illinois was closed to slavery by the Northwest Ordinance of 1787 ensured that it became a free state and not a border state like nearby Kentucky, with vast implications for the course of U.S. history.

In the United States institutions evolved that allowed Indians to maintain a degree of autonomy within the federal U.S. structure that Indians value highly. The example of Australia shows that these institutions might have been developed differently. Institutions in the United States were shaped by initial conditions *and* the history of how Euro-Americans and the Indians responded to each other. Of critical importance was the initial existence of agriculture among American Indians and their formidable strength militarily. Once in place, however, more co-evolution took place, so that the reservation system that emerged in the middle decades of the nineteenth century was shaped by both the federal government and the response of Indian tribes and their allies. Once in place, these institutions— the relationship of Indians to the federal government including the recognition by the courts of Indian property rights and the evolution of tribal leadership among Indians—influenced how Indians interacted with white settlers and the army, even when the Indians did not pose a significant military threat. The fate of Indians in California is used as a natural experiment to show what might have happened if Indians lacked such institutions. Left without legal property rights or reservations, Indians in central California were nearly exterminated during and after the gold rush of 1849.

Although conceived of as a temporary solution, the system of reservations has persisted and become entrenched in the United States. Since 1934 most Indian land in trust status has remained under tribal or federal supervision, and some has been added to Indian control. Roughly 56.2 million acres of Indian land are under federal supervision and there are 326 Indian land areas recognized as reservations.[7] Major reservations as of 1987 are shown in Figure 5.4. Much of this is administered by tribal governments which operate independently of state governments. Indeed, crimes committed on Indian reservations are federal crimes and handled by tribal or federal authorities, not state law enforcement agencies. This is not to say that there are not serious social and economic problems on many reservations. There are. But Indians are committed to maintain these rights. An attempt by Congress to abolish reservations in the late 1940s and 1950s, known as the "termination policy," was fiercely resisted by Indians and their political allies. Indeed one scholar of Indian ancestry concluded, "In everything it represented, termination threatened the very core of

FIGURE 5.4 *Indian Reservations in the United States in 1987*

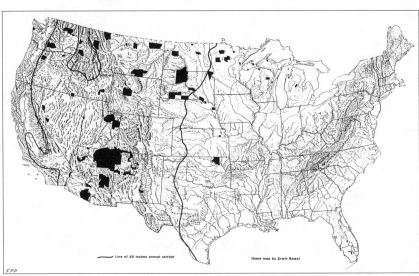

Source: Reprinted from Prucha (1990a), p. 42, with permission.

American Indian existence—its culture" (Fixico 1986, p. 183). President Nixon, in a message to Congress in July 1970, stated that the federal government would never again implement such a unilateral policy. This came to be called "self-determination without termination" (Prucha 1984, vol. 2, p. 112). It was a clear repudiation of the termination policy, and it is hard to imagine another attempt to eliminate tribal governments.

Since 1992 the courts in Australia have recognized that the aboriginal peoples there had a right to the land that they occupied prior to the coming of settlers. Australians have grappled in recent years with how to come to terms with that decision and other aspects of government policies toward aboriginal peoples. I am not suggesting, however, that Australia simply model its policies on those of the United States. An implication of this chapter is that useful institutions suitable to Australia would need to reflect the common history of aborigines and white Australians.

NOTES

I thank participants at the XIV International Economic History Congress, Helsinki, Finland, August 25, 2006; the Social Science History Association Meeting, November 2007; and the conference in honor of Gavin Wright, Palo Alto, California, October 2008 for comments on an earlier draft of this chapter. I also thank John Juricek, Barbara Wilkinson, Christina Carlson, Lauren Rule, Steven Kohlhagen, Claude Chauvigne, Matt Gregg, Jim Oberly, and David Weiman for helpful comments.

1. My source is http://www.austlii.edu.au/au/legis/cth/consol_act/coaca430/ (accessed May 9, 2009).

2. Prior to 1924, many individual Indians were granted citizenship when their reservations were allotted (privatized) by special treaties (Carlson 1981).

3. The Supreme Court decision in *Lone Wolf v. Hancock* (1904) allowed the federal government to divide a reservation into private allotments given to members of the tribe with surplus lands sold to whites. But even then there was no doubt that Indians owned the land—the rationale was that the federal government was acting as a guardian for Indian property (Prucha, 1984, vol. 2, pp. 775–776).

4. This is still true. In 2009 the federal government agreed to pay Indians $1.4 billion for mismanaging Indian lands held in trust (Fahrenthold 2009).

5. Unfortunately, at times these reformers supported well-intentioned policies that in fact harmed Indians. Most notable was the General Allotment Act of 1887 (see Carlson 1981).

6. Thornton's estimate of the population of the Indian population in 1850 is higher than that of Ubelaker (1988, p. 292), who gives an estimate of 82,980.

7. See www.bia.gov/FAQs/index.htm (accessed December 30, 2009).

REFERENCES

Attard, Bernard (2006). "The Economic History of Australia from 1788: An Introduction." In *EH.Net Encyclopedia*, edited by Robert Whaples. Available at: http://eh.net/encyclo pedia/article/attard.australia.

Axtell, James (1987). "Colonial America without the Indians: Counterfactual Reflections." *Journal of American History* 73: 981–996.

Banner, Stuart (2005a). "Why *Terra Nullius*? Anthropology and Property Law in Early Australia." *Law and History Review* 23: 93–131.

Banner, Stuart (2005b). *How the Indians Lost Their Land*. Cambridge, MA: Harvard University Press.

Beals, Ralph L. (1985). "The Anthropologist as Expert Witness: Illustrations from the California Indians Land Claims Case." In *Irredeemable America: The Indians' Estate and Land Claims*, edited by Imre Sutton. Albuquerque: University of New Mexico Press, pp. 139–155.

Carlson, Leonard A. (1981). *Indians, Bureaucrats, and Land: The Dawes Act and the Decline of Indian Farming*. Westport, CT: Greenwood Press.

Carlson, Leonard A., and Mark A. Roberts (2006). "Indian Removal, 'Squatterism,' and Slavery: Economic Interests and the Passage of the Indian Removal Act of 1830." *Explorations in Economic History* 43: 486–504.

Clay, Karen, and Gavin Wright (2005). "Order without Law? Property Rights during the California Gold Rush." *Explorations in Economic History* 42: 155–183.

Connor, Michael (2005). *The Invention of Terra Nullius: Historical and Legal Fictions on the Foundation of Australia*. Sydney: Macleay Press.

David, Paul A. (1994). "Why Are Institutions the 'Carriers of History'? Path Dependence and Evolution of Conventions, Organizations and Institutions." *Structural Change and Economic Dynamics* 5: 205–220.

Fahrenthold, David A. (2009). "Government to Settle Suit over Indian Land Trusts." *Washington Post*, December 9, p. A03.

Fixico, Donald (1986). *Termination and Relocation: Federal Indian Policy, 1945–1960*. Albuquerque: University of New Mexico Press.

Hämäläinen, Pekka (2004). "The Rise and Fall of Plains Indian Horse Cultures." *Journal of American History* 90: 833–862.

Hughes, Jonathan, and Louis P. Cain (2003). *American Economic History*, 6th ed. Boston: Addison-Wesley.

Jackson, R. V. (1977). *Australian Economic Development in the Nineteenth Century*. Canberra: Australian National University Press.

Juricek, John T., ed. (1989). *Georgia Treaties, 1733–1763*. Vol. 11 of Alden T. Vaughan, ed., *Early American Indian Documents: Treaties and Laws, 1607–1789*. Washington, DC: University Press of America.

Lamar, Howard, with Sam Truett (1996). "Greater Southwest and California from the Beginning of European Settlement to the 1880s." In *The Cambridge History of the Native Peoples of the Americas*, vol. 1: *North America, Part 2*, edited by Bruce G. Trigger and Washburn Wilcomb. New York: Cambridge University Press, pp. 57–116.

Lester, Geoffrey, and Graham Parker (1973). "Land Rights: The Australian Aborigines Have Lost a Legal Battle, But . . ." *Alberta Law Review* 11: 189–237.

Macintyre, Stuart (1999). *A Concise History of Australia*. Cambridge: Cambridge University Press.

Perdue, Theda, and Michael D. Green, eds. (1995). *The Cherokee Removal*. Boston: Bedford Books.

Prucha, Francis P. (1984). *The Great Father*. 2 vols. Lincoln: University of Nebraska Press.

Prucha, Francis P. (1990a). *Atlas of American Indian Affairs*. Lincoln: University of Nebraska Press.

Prucha, Francis P., ed. (1990b). *Documents of United State Indians Policy, Second Edition, Expanded*. Lincoln: University of Nebraska Press.

Royce, Charles (1896). "Indian Land Cessions in the United States." In *Eighteenth Annual Report of the Bureau of American Ethnology, 1896–1897*. House of Representatives, 56th Cong., 1st sess., Document 736, pp. 521–997.

Snow, Dean R. (1996). "The First Americans and the Differentiation of Hunter-Gatherer Cultures." In *The Cambridge History of the Native Peoples of the Americas*, vol. 1: *North America, Part 1*, edited by Bruce G. Triggerand and Washburn Wilcomb. New York: Cambridge University Press, pp. 125–200.

Thornton, Russell (1987). *American Indian Holocaust and Survival: A Population History since 1492*. Norman: University of Oklahoma Press.

Trennert, Robert (1975). *Alternative to Extinction: Federal Policy and the Beginnings of the Reservation System, 1846–51*. Philadelphia: Temple University Press.

Ubelaker, Douglas (1988). "North American Indian Populations Size, A.D. 1500 to 1985." *American Journal of Physical Anthropology* 77: 289–294.

Umbeck, John (1977). "The California Gold Rush: A Study of Emerging Property Rights." *Explorations in Economic History* 14: 197–226.

Underhill, Ruth (1971 [1953]). *Red Man's America*. Chicago: University of Chicago Press.

Utley, Robert M. (2003). *The Indian Frontier, 1846–1890*, rev. ed. Albuquerque: University of New Mexico Press.

Vaughan, Alden T., ed. (1979–2003). *Early American Indian Documents: Treaties and Laws, 1607–1789*. Washington, DC: University Press of America.

Wallace, Anthony F. C. (1993). *The Long Bitter Trail: Andrew Jackson and the Indians*. New York: Hill and Wang.

Weaver, John C. (1996). "Beyond the Fatal Shore." *American Historical Review* 101: 981–1007.

Wright, Gavin (2006). *Slavery and American Economic Development*. Baton Rouge: Louisiana State University Press.

PART TWO

Spatial Processes and Comparative Development

FOR ALL OF THE RECENT TALK about overthrowing the tyrannies of distance and making the globe "flat," the processes of evolution and revolution continue to work themselves out in economic space. This space is often characterized by small gradations of difference, yet economic regions are often characterized by large differences. Taking regions as the units of analysis, one sees concretely how multiple equilibria emerge and persist, how different ways of doing things can evolve and coexist in otherwise similar places. Divergence can be a source of pride or of envy. Collective choices are often interdependent and mutually reinforcing. And convergence between regions often does not begin without large, episodic shocks, of the sort Part Three on revolutions helps us understand. The chapters in Part Two explore processes of spatial growth and regional differentiation.

Adopting the tools of comparative regional analysis, Ta-Chen Wang (Chapter 6) studies the interactions between banks and manufacturing firms in New England and the Middle Atlantic states during the American industrial revolution. The contrasts are sharp. Massachusetts hosted a thriving textile sector of vertically integrated firms, which adopted the corporate form and maintained close links to Boston banks. The Philadelphia region was home to a more diverse industrial base of smaller firms with weaker links to the city's handful of very large merchant-oriented banks. This base included textile firms, but these tended to be small proprietors specializing in high-quality products, employing more skilled workers and less fixed capital. The regions present two alternative models for matching the organization and orientation of industrial enterprises with those of the local financial sector. While some scholars may debate which alternative was superior, what is clear is that the models differed and each evolved according to the logic of its own region.

Taking a spatially oriented approach, Jeremy Atack, Michael Haines, and Robert A. Margo (Chapter 7) investigate the impact of the arrival of the railroad on the rise of the factory in mid-nineteenth-century America. To study this long-standing question, the authors adopt a fresh line of attack, applying the techniques of the treatment-effects approach to a rich new county-level data set mapping the spread of the railroad. Their method demands that issues of endogeneity, that is, of two-way causation, be addressed squarely. The authors' identification strategy exploits an important feature of the new transportation technology: it is a network. Places connected to the network enjoy benefits that those outside do not, and more importantly, places located between two existing nodes are more likely to become connected than those located off the beaten track. Using these insights to generate the means to estimate causal effects, Atack, Haines, and Margo attribute about one-third in the growth of the share of manufacturing establishments that were organized as factories to the spread of the railroad.

Alan L. Olmstead and Paul W. Rhode (Chapter 8) tackle another long-standing question in nineteenth-century U.S. history, the rapid geographic expansion of the cotton cultivation. They argue that the movement of population and economic activity into the New South was driven not simply by the availability of cheap land but also by the innovative development in that region of new cotton varieties with higher productivity there. It is a common feature of technical knowledge, in agriculture among other fields, that innovations may be better suited to certain environmental conditions than to others. Despite the traditional depiction of the American South as lacking indigenous innovators, Olmstead and Rhode argue the region, and especially the New South, developed technologies allowing for large increases in output per worker between 1810 and 1860. The differentially rapid growth in productivity in the newer areas propelled the exceptionally rapid rate of western expansion.

Scott A. Redenius and David F. Weiman (Chapter 9) use the lens of finance and its interplay with real economic activity to explore how the development of a regional economy is shaped and constrained by its place within a larger national economy. They examine how the National Banking System (1863–1913) perpetuated the status of the U.S. South as a peripheral economy dependent on cotton monoculture. Moving the cotton crop created large seasonal demands for credit, leading southern banks to draw on correspondents in money centers, principally New York, to finance at high interest rates. At other times of the year, the southern banks had excess reserves, which could only yield low returns when invested in short-term assets. Some may argue these large swings in southern credit demands were caused by the inherent nature of cotton production, its seasonal cycles. Redenius and Weiman reject this crude geographic determinism, showing that the harvest rush was more intense for the North's wheat and corn than for the South's fleecy staple. Instead the peak credit demands arose from the pressures on cotton growers to market their crop immediately and from the "colonial-style" dependence of the entire region on a single crop. The National Banking System, designed to fit conditions in the North, also placed the South in a monetary straitjacket. But the South had its revenge by contributing to the instability of national financial markets in the era before the establishment of the Federal Reserve.

Broadening our geographic perspective, Susan Wolcott (Chapter 10) offers a valuable international comparison. She examines the operation of rural credit markets in the postbellum American South in the mirror of pre-Independence India. Providing credit to small-scale agricultural producers with limited collateral is challenging everywhere. The high interest rates charged to American sharecroppers with only a crop in the field and with mouths to feed until harvest season are well-known. But what Wolcott's comparative perspective reveals is that in rural India, credit was more readily available, even for consumption expenditures. More sharply limited geographic mobility and the pressure of a caste-based enforcement mechanism reduced default rates to levels that would make the micro-lenders of today or the southern country store-keepers of the postbellum period green with envy. But all was not well. Indeed, the situation has the feel of a low-level equilibrium. Many of the loans were for large-scale consumption events, expenses for the very ceremonies that glued family and caste together, rather than for productivity-enhancing investments. As such, the equilibrium appears only locally stable; large transitory shocks inducing higher mobility could undermine all that now appears permanent.

P. W. R., J. L. R., and D. F. W.

CHAPTER 6

Financial Market and Industry Structure: A Comparison of the Banking and Textile Industries in Boston and Philadelphia in the Early Nineteenth Century

TA-CHEN WANG

MODERN LITERATURE in development economics views advanced financial markets as the driving force behind economic development (Schumpeter 1934 [1912]; Gurley and Shaw 1955; McKinnon 1973). Empirical literature shows that differential economic growth rates among countries can be explained by the aggregate size of their respective financial sectors (King and Levine 1993; Levine and Zervos 1998). Both theoretical and empirical literatures conclude a positive relationship between finance and growth (Levine 2005). Economic historians have long stressed the importance of financial markets in fostering the American economy (Sylla 1998, 2002; Rousseau and Sylla 2005). While empirical evidence confirms the influence of a country's financial market on its rate of economic growth, precisely how the financial market affects the course of industrial development is not as well understood. Studying the influence of the financial market on the course of economic development furthers our knowledge of how economic growth takes place and allows us to assess the broader impact of institutions on economic performance. Specifically, this chapter investigates the variations in state banking systems and their impact on the path to industrial development. In contrast, Redenius and Weiman (this volume) examine the effect of the banking and monetary reform on the early twentieth-century Cotton South.

Early nineteenth-century America provides a compelling example of how different financial markets may influence the path of economic growth. The first half of the nineteenth century in America saw the creation of a financial system as well as burgeoning industrial growth. However, developments in financial markets and industry varied significantly across states. As most banks received charters at the state level before the passage of the National Banking Act of 1863, banks in different regions were subject to diverse regulations and entry policies. Since the early nineteenth century these institutional elements have evolved further: some states moved toward free entry while others maintained tighter control over the number of banks throughout the antebellum period. The state banking landscape was forged by both the dynamic interaction between banks and government policies and differences in competitive environment and entry policy.

As a result, different lending practices began to emerge at the state level. In New England the practice of "insider lending" was prevalent. Entrepreneurs often founded their own banks with the purpose of lending to themselves. These individuals, in turn, used the funds from banks to invest in a variety of ventures. The private information and existing monitoring mechanism of kinship networks allowed the extension of long-term credit. In contrast, banks in the Mid-Atlantic region focused on relatively impersonal and short-term credit. Bank ownership was less concentrated with diverse groups of stockholders; the borrower profiles also reflected such diversity (Wright 1999).

Around the same time, different regions in the United States also began the course of industrialization, albeit along different trajectories. Economic historians often view the New England textile mills as the leader in American industrialization (Temin 2000). These mills engaged in large-scale production, often employing a great amount of physical capital and an unskilled workforce. They also tended to specialize in lower-quality cotton goods. However, the New England model was by no means the only course to industrialization. The Philadelphia textile industry provided an alternative path. The majority of textile manufacturers were small proprietors who focused on high-quality, specialized products, employing skilled workers and accumulating capital at a slow rate (Scranton 1983). The small, artisanal production in Philadelphia stood in stark contrast to the large and corporate mills in New England.

Although divergences in the path to industrialization for the two major American textile centers were likely to be the result of many contributing factors, this chapter underscores the distinct financial markets in these two regions as an important determinant. The major differences between the Boston and Philadelphia models lie in the scale and method of production, which in turn relied on accessibility and security of financing sources. In New England banks and insurance companies were often an integral part of the textile industry, but such institutions were noticeably absent in Philadelphia. As a result, New England became the leader in the transformation from agriculture to large-scale, capital-intensive industry.[1] The availability and the terms of bank credit may have thereby influenced the trajectory of industrialization. This chapter proposes that the bifurcation in banking and credit markets was a contributing factor in explaining the different modes of production.

The rest of the chapter is organized as follows: the second section compares the industrial growth in Boston and Philadelphia using the textile sector as an example. The third section describes the parallel development in the banking system and bank lending practices in these two regions. The fourth section attempts to associate the divergent path of industrialization in these regions with differences in banking systems. The fifth section concludes with discussions and proposes a future research agenda.

THE TEXTILE INDUSTRY IN PHILADELPHIA AND BOSTON

In the midst of dramatic progress in organizational and technological capabilities within the New England textile industry, the Boston Associates stood out as the leader in the production of cotton goods. Their Waltham-Lowell system established large-scale, vertically integrated firms. The Associates controlled every aspect of textile manufacturing, from the machine shops to the marketing of final product. This specific business model fostered rapid growth in their production capacity. As of 1845, the members of the Boston Associates were involved in 31 textile companies, making up about 20 percent of the total capacity of the industry in America (Dalzell 1987, p. 79).

In addition to their innovation in production methods, the organizational form of the Boston Manufacturing Company was also distinctive, consisting entirely of incorporated, limited-liability companies. The Boston Associates tightly controlled the operation and ownership of the mills.

In addition, they strengthened their business relationships through kin-ship ties and marriages, ensuring that the business relationship, albeit personal in nature, would not terminate with the death of a specific part-ner. Like their incorporated companies, the underlying business network of the Associates extended beyond the natural life span of individuals. The impact of the Boston Associates extended beyond textile industry. They integrated railroad, banking, and insurance into their business con-glomerate. The Associates controlled seven banks in Boston and com-manded 40 percent of the total authorized banking capital in the city by 1848 (Dalzell 1987, p. 79). They brought similar business patterns into other industries as they did in textiles: heavy capitalization and conserva-tive operations. In this regard, their banks followed the same principles in their daily operations.

How did banks contribute to the industrial success in New England? The Boston Associates would first charter a bank and subscribe enough shares to control the bank. The required paid-in capital was obtained by borrowing from another bank under their control. Then they would de-posit the loan in the new bank and subsequently borrow out the money to pay for a new mill. To replenish funds in the new bank, they either sold the remainder of the stock, usually to their own insurance companies or charitable organizations, or issued bank notes (Lamoreaux 1985). The so-called alchemy of the banks is indeed a way to practice insider lend-ing, and the success and stability rest on the careful selection and moni-toring of borrowers. Without appropriate incentives, this could have easily fallen into the trap of crony capitalism. However, when practiced judi-ciously, insider lending offers a mechanism to affiliate more existing busi-ness partners to the specific investment, with kinship ties providing the information advantage to prevent moral hazard. Mutual interest further strengthens the monitoring incentive among the Associates.

Despite their influence on the financial system of Massachusetts, the Boston Associates did not really view banks as profit-making investments in their own rights. Rather, banks served as the financial arms of their textile empire (Dalzell 1987, p. 82). Although many of the members in the Associates owned bank stocks at some point, they did not own these shares on a large scale (Dalzell 1987, p. 93). Nevertheless, the Associates participated actively in banking operations by chartering banks and maintaining control over lending decisions. In other words, the major purpose of their banks was not so much for generating profit as for guaranteeing access to credit for their own mills. Outside investors were drawn to the investment opportunities that arose from holding bank shares, namely, ownership of a piece of the Boston Associates' business conglomerate.

Because of the contribution of banks to the success of New England textile manufacturers, banks in New England were the engines of economic development (Lamoreaux 1994). However, this observation cannot necessarily be generalized to other locations in the same fashion, even within the industrial Northeast. This is not to say that banks were irrelevant in the economic development outside New England; rather, banks may have contributed to industrial growth in other regions, albeit through distinct channels.

Throughout the first 60 years of the nineteenth century, Philadelphia also emerged as a regional manufacturing center. As the market became more integrated at a regional level, subregions began to specialize in different economic activities (Lindstrom 1978). In the case of the textile industry, the hinterland outside Philadelphia gradually abandoned locally produced textiles and turned to Philadelphia for such goods. While both Boston and Philadelphia experienced rapid growth in textile industry, the path to development taken by the textile industry in Philadelphia provides a sharp contrast to that of New England. In the Quaker City the typical textile firm organization was a proprietor or partnership rather than a modern corporation. Sole proprietorship was common, even for large firms.[2] Each establishment usually specialized in a certain link of the production chain. The production was completed through a series of intermediate good transactions. Skilled, artisanal workers complemented the relatively small amount of capital. The result was a larger variety of products but smaller scale of production.

A coexisting element complementing organizational forms of New England textile firms is financing sources. The Boston Associates maintained control over their factories through familial ties and marriages of heirs. The interlocking network of kinships further allowed the continuation of not just the ownership but the management as well. Such networks of relationships extended beyond the textile firms into the realm of banking. The close familial ties in the business world of the Boston Associates provided an easy way to access the information on creditworthiness. The insider lending practices and tight control over banks enabled advantageous access to private information. Such close relationships also provided easy monitoring of borrower behavior after the loan was made. The ex ante information advantage and the ex post monitoring mechanism alleviated two major problems in credit relationships: hidden information and moral hazard. The practice has strong implications for the rest of the credit demanders. In an era of strong credit needs, once-large firms like the Boston Associates exhausted significant sources of loanable funds, little was left for outsiders. The only way for new entrepreneurs to access bank credit was to establish their own insider lending banks.

In contrast, little evidence indicated that banks in Philadelphia participated in the accumulation of industrial capital. Proprietors, large or small, tended to rely on retained earnings to expand their operation. The prevalence of proprietorships also meant that physical capital often outlasted the natural life span of the artisans. After the demise of its owner, physical capital was often sold to a different proprietor or partnership. In addition to the secondary market for equipment, an active market for rental capital or mill space was also in place (Scranton 1983, p. 94). Thus little initial investment was required to begin textile production. To be sure, the lack of a direct linkage between banks and textile firms does not suggest the former had no impact. It does imply that the channel of such influence must have been different.

Although the discussion uses the textile industry as an example to illustrate the relationship between banks and industry, the rise of Philadelphia as an industrial center was by no means singularly driven by the textile industry. Other industries, such as precious metal, machinery, and pharmaceuticals, also thrived in Philadelphia.[3] Taken as a whole, the diversity of industries within the confines of Philadelphia County once again stood in sharp contrast with the specialized mill towns in Massachusetts. While New England textile firms formed mill towns in the vicinity of Boston, Philadelphia artisans concentrated in the main urban area.

DEVELOPMENT OF EARLY BANKING SYSTEMS
IN MASSACHUSETTS AND PENNSYLVANIA

To analyze the different roles played by banks in regional industrialization, it is crucial to understand the history of banks in the United States. The first commercial bank, the Bank of North America, was established in 1781. Hamilton's financial revolution granted states the right to charter banks. Since then, the number of commercial banks grew over the years, and by 1790 all four major cities (Philadelphia, New York, Boston, and Baltimore) had their own banks. However, the number of banks grew unevenly across locations over the antebellum period. State charter policies and economic growth, interspersed with financial crises, collectively determined the path of banking development before the Civil War. Public finance concerns and incentives dominated the chartering policies for states, which in turn shaped their respective patterns of bank expansion (Sylla, Legler, and Wallis 1987). New England states, such as Rhode Island and Massachusetts, levied taxes on bank capital. The revenue for the state thus depended on the amount of bank capital. In tandem with the incentive of state finance, these states adopted a de facto free-entry policy (Wallis 2007). At the other end of the spectrum, Pennsylvania relied on charter fees and a taxon bank profits. The state revenue thus hinged upon the profitability of banks, and limited entry ensured the extraction of rent. Figure 6.1 demonstrates the impact of differences in charter policies on the growth of banks in Massachusetts and Pennsylvania. With the exception of the 1810s, the number of banks in Massachusetts far exceeded that in Pennsylvania before the national banking era. It is clear that policy responses to incentives in state finance shaped the banking landscape in antebellum America.

Early banks were usually founded by merchants to meet their demand for credit. While the banks did more than simply discount short-term commercial paper, their activities invariably favored merchants. To protect credit access to other groups, states would also charter banks that specifically focused on loans to groups other than merchants, such as farmers, mechanics, and artisans. One example would be the Farmers and Mechanics Bank in Philadelphia. Chartering banks specializing in loans to specific occupational groups was not the only way to extend the reach of bank

FIGURE 6.1   *Number of Banks for Massachusetts and Pennsylvania, 1783–1861*

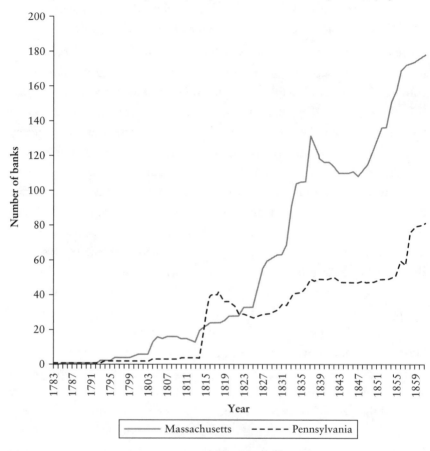

Source: Weber (2005).

credit; some states, like Massachusetts, stipulated that banks allocate a certain percentage of loans to farmers. These legal protections for farmers clearly indicate the dominance of loans to merchants in banks' portfolios. The following section provides more detailed evidence on how banks behaved in the two regions under examination.

Philadelphia

For most of the antebellum period, Pennsylvania had a relatively limited number of banks for a state of its size. Until 1814 only fourteen banks ever existed in Pennsylvania, and two of them (Pennsylvania Bank and Bank of the United States) had closed. Among the remaining twelve banks, only four were officially chartered: The Bank of North America, the Bank of Pennsylvania, the Philadelphia Bank, and the Farmers and Mechanics Bank. In addition to these four banks, there were seven other banks formed under the Articles of Association. Some were organized by local businessmen to meet the needs of finance outside Philadelphia, while others focused on serving specific professions, specifically, farmers, millers, and mechanics. These early banks were allowed to open branches outside their home locations. As early as 1803 the state-chartered Bank of Pennsylvania had opened branches in Lancaster, Pittsburgh, and Easton. This pattern basically followed the one established by the Bank of the United States. Its rival, the Philadelphia Bank, also began to establish branches after gaining a supplement to the charter from the state, though the branches proved unprofitable. Lastly, some banks did not seek state charters and operated as private banks. For example, Stephen Girard formed his own private bank in 1812, which took over the building used by the Bank of the United States after its charter expired. However, these unincorporated banks were prohibited by state law from issuing bank notes.

The Omnibus Act of 1814 dramatically changed the landscape of banking in Pennsylvania: the state chartered 41 banks at once, and 37 of the newly chartered banks opened for business. This drastic change in policy reflected an underlying political struggle that could be traced back to the feud between the Bank of Pennsylvania and the upstart Philadelphia Bank. The Philadelphia Bank made an offer to the state in stock holdings; the Bank of Pennsylvania tried to block the charter of the Philadelphia Bank by giving a gift to the state (Daniels 1976, pp. 64–65). Similar political tensions arose in the passing of the Omnibus Act; the bill was first vetoed by the governor and finally overruled by the state legislature again. The passage of the act reflects the politicians' desires to organize their own banks.

Immediately after the Omnibus Act, Pennsylvania boasted a large number of banks relative to other states. However, its leader status in bank capital was short lived. Seventeen banks failed in wake of the Crisis of

1819. Poor accounting practices, mistakes, and inexperience in the banking business depressed bank profit. The problems were intensified by the Crisis of 1837, leading to more bank failures. The Pennsylvania government's demands for loans further compromised the position of the banks because of the state's high risk of default. As a result, the financial system of Pennsylvania was severely weakened; the number of banks in the state stagnated and eventually fell behind those in Massachusetts and New York. In sum, the one-time aggressive policy in the expansion of banks, followed by contraction, mismanagement, and failed government policy, forestalled the development of a sound financial system in Pennsylvania (Bodenhorn 2000, pp. 35–38).

Massachusetts

Over time, the banking system in Massachusetts diverged increasingly from that of Pennsylvania. The first chartered bank was the Bank of Massachusetts in 1784. Throughout the years of 1790–1860 the number of chartered banks in Massachusetts increased rapidly. Between 1795 and 1803 nine new banks were established. Prior to 1814, at least 41 banks received charters, including re-charters; due to Massachusetts' de facto free entry policy, the number continued to grow up to the Crisis of 1837. Such gradual growth reflected a chartering policy different from Pennsylvania's Omnibus Act. Another feature of antebellum Massachusetts banks was their relatively modest capital stock.[4] Even for some of the unchartered banks in Pennsylvania, the amount of capital was much greater than that of state-chartered banks in Massachusetts in the same period. As shown in Figure 6.2, the average capital stock of Pennsylvania banks exceeded that of banks in Massachusetts for most of the antebellum period.

Despite smaller average capital stock per bank, the aggregate bank capital in Massachusetts was far greater than in Pennsylvania. This was particularly prominent in the late antebellum period, when both the number of and size of Massachusetts banks grew consistently. The liberal charter policy of Massachusetts and the missteps of Pennsylvania banks contributed to the difference. The total bank loans between the two states also diverged since the early 1820s, as shown in Figure 6.3. The side-by-side comparison between bank capital and bank loans reveals that the

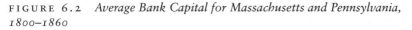

FIGURE 6.2   *Average Bank Capital for Massachusetts and Pennsylvania,*
1800–1860

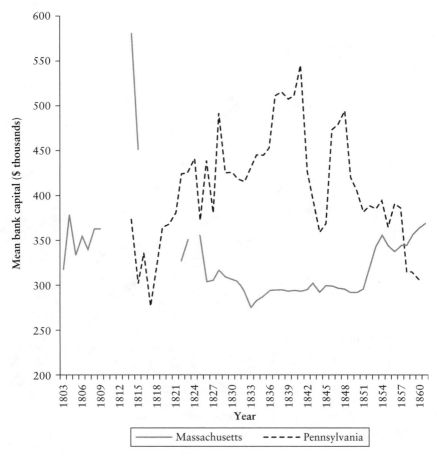

Source: Weber (2005).

divergence in bank capital was the driving force behind this phenomenon. Such contrast is even more striking in per capita terms. Table 6.1
shows the per capita bank capital and loans in these two states. In terms of
both capital and loans, the gaps between the two states widened between
1820 and 1860. The difference between these two measures is even greater
when we compare Suffolk County (Boston) and Philadelphia County.
While bank capital and loans per person declined in Philadelphia, these
figures continued to rise in the Boston area. Thus the availability of bank

FIGURE 6.3   *Total Bank Loans and Capital for Massachusetts and Pennsylvania, 1800–1860*

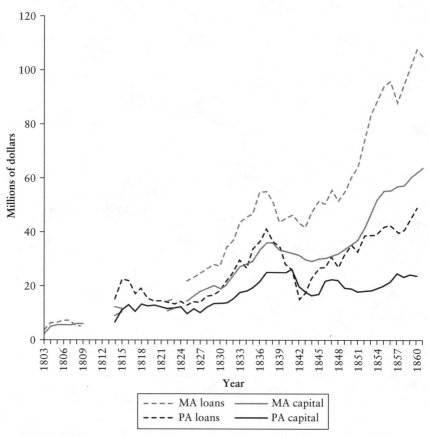

Source: Weber (2005).

credit was dramatically different between Pennsylvania and Massachusetts, at least by this measure.

In addition to the number and relative size of banks in each location, lending practices also diverged in Boston and Philadelphia. In New England, kinship groups maintained tight control over the banks' lending practices. As the banks relied heavily on outside capital, securing stable credit sources was crucial. This is especially important as New England banks often acted as the financial arm for the bank directors' other ventures. In contrast, banks in the mid-Atlantic region (including those in

TABLE 6.1   *Per Capita Bank Capital and Loans, Massachusetts and Pennsylvania, 1820–1860*

	1820	1830	1840	1850	1860
Bank Capital					
State level					
Massachusetts	20.04	31.08	44.28	35.50	50.19
Pennsylvania	12.29	10.09	14.50	8.22	8.22
County level					
Suffolk (Boston)	167.27	204.30	197.86	150.31	203.57
Philadelphia	59.74	52.28	63.32	26.56	18.19
Bank Loans					
State level					
Massachusetts	25.70	44.95	61.16	60.89	87.29
Pennsylvania	13.87	13.69	16.29	15.19	16.80
County level					
Suffolk (Boston)	211.86	299.80	277.01	255.55	350.80
Philadelphia	66.69	69.63	67.53	53.27	40.50

Sources: Historical Census Browser (2004); Weber (2005).

Philadelphia) tended to have a diverse group of shareholders; few of them could dominate banks' loan decision. As a result, banks lent to diverse groups of borrowers (Wright 1999). While insider lending was sometimes observed, the extent of such practice was never as extreme as in New England.

In addition to bank directors' incentives, information advantage played a crucial role in the prevalence of insider lending. Because the recipients of loans were often known to bank directors, through either business dealings or family ties, banks were likely to possess private information on their borrowers. The information advantage served as a useful device to screen out untrustworthy borrowers. After loans were made, the close-knit personal relationship further facilitated monitoring and reduced the possibility of moral hazard. The result was extremely low default rates of bank loans.

From a broader perspective, the practice of insider banking was self-reinforcing. Once the practice became popular with a bank's directors, the borrowing from insiders quickly absorbed all of its available funds.

In an era of thriving business and strong credit demand, it became more difficult for other businesses to borrow from existing banks. The relative ease of forming a bank meant that the best way for new ventures to secure credit was to establish their own banks, which in turn employed insider lending practices. Thus the pervasiveness of insider lending, combined with de facto free entry of banks, spawned many new banks that served as the financial arm of various New England business groups and perpetuated the practice of insider lending throughout this region.

BANK LENDING PRACTICES: EVIDENCE FROM MICRO-LEVEL STUDIES

The previous section highlights the banking landscapes in industrial New England and Pennsylvania. While informative, aggregate banking data do not provide information on the lending practices of banks. Recent developments in banking history have uncovered detailed information that is useful in this regard. As usual, there exists a trade-off between depth and breadth. While bank-level studies carefully document a bank's behavior, it may not be representative of all banks in the region. Despite this caveat, existing literature sheds considerable light on differential bank lending practices in these two regions. Such detailed studies provide, at least for the banks under analysis, a precise characterization of loan sizes, duration, borrower information, and interest rates. The following analysis focuses on the comparison of the terms of bank loans between banks in these two regions.

A major distinction between the lending practices of banks in Boston and Philadelphia was the duration of loans. Banks in the Boston area frequently renewed loans time and again. Such renewals were so common that loans could be viewed as de facto long-term (Lamoreaux 1994). For example, 82 percent of loans in the Meldon Bank were renewals of previous loans. Similar patterns are found in the records of Plymouth Bank; between 1803 and 1832, the average duration of loans was 664 days, a situation that was possible only through repeated renewals of 60-day loans. Even for merchants, who often discounted short-term commercial paper, the mean duration was 562 days (Wang 2008).

In contrast, only 16 percent of loans lasted for more than 6 months for the private bank of Stephen Girard in Philadelphia (Adams 1972).

Without studies on state banks in Philadelphia, it is difficult to ascertain if this observation is representative. However, Adams argues that the lending policy of Stephen Girard intentionally followed state banks in the region closely. This suggests that the short-term loans were the norm in Philadelphia. Other studies also confirm the relatively short loan terms outside of New England (Bodenhorn 1999; Bodenhorn 2003, pp. 54–56). Using data from Black River Bank in New York between 1846 and 1856, Bodenhorn finds that fewer than 10 percent of the loans lasted for more than 120 days. From existing records outside New England, the mean loan duration often fell between 55 to 120 days (Bodenhorn 2003, p. 55). The renewal of loans also occurred less frequently, implying that these banks tended to extend short-term credit. Moreover, there was little difference in loan duration for borrowers of different occupations, consistent with the observation that no specific group was able to dominate banks' loan decision.

The difference in bank loan duration relates to the debate on the role of banks in the provision of fixed capital vis-à-vis working capital. To be sure, the functions of a mercantile, real-bills bank and a Schumpeterian bank may not be incompatible; a bank could focus mainly on mercantile credit while still extending long-term loans to support capital formation (Bodenhorn 1999). Meanwhile, the financing sources of early industries were not restricted to bank credit; major New England textile mills borrowed extensively from both institutional and noninstitutional sources (Davis 1960). While it is difficult to identify the use of funds from bank records alone, the multiple loan renewals in Massachusetts seem to suggest that banks played a crucial role in capital formation. Upon closer examination, multiple renewals of short-term loans may have simply provided long-term working capital. Such demand for working capital was by no means trivial. Even for the largest New England manufacturing establishments, the demand for working capital was far greater than that for fixed capital investment (Sokoloff 1984).[5] Regardless of its use, external finance was crucial for the continuation of large-scale production. Even if bank loans only provided liquidity, their existence has strong implication for capital accumulation. A secure source of liquidity allowed firms to more easily tap into their retained earnings for long-term capital formation. While banks in the Philadelphia region could potentially have played important roles in the expansion of specific textile firms, the relatively small aggregate bank credit limited the scope of their impact.

Thus developments in banking literature suggest that not only the banking landscape but also the banking practices were different in Massachusetts and Pennsylvania. Massachusetts developed a financial system consisting of many small banks, which extended long-term credit to their directors. While insider lending could have denied credit access to outsiders, the liberal chartering policy complemented the conservative lending practices. The large aggregate amount of bank capital enabled relatively easy credit access. Insider lending secured stable long-term credit sources for large, vertically integrated textile manufacturers. On the other hand, Pennsylvania had a limited number of large banks, which focused more on short-term credit to diverse groups (Wright 1999). The relatively scarce capital, as reflected in bank loans per person, is consistent with small proprietors accumulating earnings to expand. Financial sources, expansion pattern, product specialization, and corporate structure complement one another in both regions. The divergent paths of financial markets and industry structure thus can be viewed as multiple equilibria.

Several outstanding questions remain to be answered. First, although existing literature explores possible explanations, a complete economic analysis of the causal relationship between financial development and industrialization is still absent. As with other regions, merchants in Philadelphia heavily invested in banks. If merchants were able to invest in the textile industry, the information advantage may have allowed them to channel funds through banks, as the New Englanders did. However, they never exploited such an advantage (Shumate 2004). Without the network of the merchants, proprietors could not secure long-term credit through banks. In any case, the proprietary textile industry thrived in Philadelphia throughout most of the nineteenth century.

Perhaps more importantly, the comparison also demonstrates the intricacy of the potential causal relationship between finance and industrial growth. Although the unique banking policy and practice in Massachusetts were certainly contributing factors in the formation of early large-scale manufacturers, other factors likely played important roles as well.

Undeniably, the difference between these two cities was not limited to the methods of production and financial markets. The distinction extended to culture and social mobility (Baltzell 1979; Doerflinger 1986; Dalzell 1987). External factors such as social mobility and norms invariably influence the cost-benefit decisions of banks and entrepreneurs alike. It may have been less costly to borrow from existing networks that were reliable and stable. Both industry structure and banking practices could have been the outcome of cost-benefit calculations, subject to underlying institutions. Social mobility, labor forces, and immigration may all have played a role.

CONCLUSION

The comparison between Boston and Philadelphia demonstrates the relationship between financial development and economic development. Facing different incentives, Massachusetts and Pennsylvania took decidedly different paths to the chartering of banks. As a result, the banking practices evolved along different lines in these two regions. The New England model successfully fostered large industrial firms by integrating both formal (banks) and informal (kinship networks) institutions, while the Philadelphian failed to do so. Taken at face value, this seems to suggest that the freer entry policy of New England had a stronger impact on industrial growth. However, closer examination reveals that while the Philadelphia textile industry did not follow the New England model of capital-intensive, large-scale production, it was still able to develop a niche that differentiated itself from its northern competitors over time. The artisanal proprietors compensated for the lack of access to bank credit by accumulating retained earnings, relatively low capital intensity, and a skilled workforce. These features shaped a textile industry that specialized in the production of higher-quality goods. In terms of economic development their achievement cannot be ignored.

The success of the Philadelphia textile industry suggests that the impact of the financial system on economic development does not necessarily lie in the rate of economic growth, but the path of development. Under distinct sets of financial regulations and environments, different regions took distinct paths to growth. From a theoretical perspective, if one views the ideals of Schumpeterian banking as the orthodoxy in economic development, then Pennsylvania financial system did not seem to be as successful as that of New England. Nevertheless, proprietors in Philadelphia apparently were able to overcome such setbacks. They thrived despite limited bank credit access.

The evolution of the banking market structure of Boston and Philadelphia also provides an interesting comparison for bank regulation. While both regions at one time experienced the liberal charter policy of banks, the results in providing long-term credit sources were different. Pennsylvania passed the Omnibus Act in 1814 and chartered a large number of banks with one stroke. However, industrial growth did not follow right away. On the contrary, the success story of New England suggested that, at least in this context, the relatively passive de facto free entry was more successful in fostering industrial growth. Moreover, the underlying causes of the relative scarcity of bank capital in Philadelphia could simply be unfortunate timing, when the region was hit relatively hard by the 1819 crisis, as well as underlying social and cultural institutions. At the heart of the New England institution was a group of entrepreneurs closely tied by marriages and their efforts to maintain the longevity of such networks. This was not seen in Philadelphia's textile industry. While a further exploration of this issue is beyond the scope of this chapter, current evidence does suggest that the relationship between finance and growth may rely on the underlying social networks. From a broader view, financial market development and industrialization may both be endogenous variables.

While this chapter does not argue that the financial system was the only determinant in shaping the development in Boston and Philadelphia, the comparison between these two cities does highlight the interaction between institutions and economic development. The success stories of both cities suggest that financial market regulations do not necessarily deter or promote the outcome of economic development. However, as a supporting institution, the banking sector has strong implications for the trajectory of industrialization. Over the course of the nineteenth century, financial markets evolved to complement the features of textile industries, thereby serving as a key determinant of the course of economic development and growth.

NOTES

The earlier draft of this chapter benefited greatly from discussions with Gavin Wright. Charles Calomiris, Naomi Lamoreaux, Paul Rhode, Joshua Rosenbloom, and David Weiman; all provided generous and insightful comments. All errors are mine.

1. Temin (2000), p.1.

2. Scranton used Joseph Ripka to illustrate this point. Ripka started his business with a single handloom in 1816. His business started to expand rapidly in the 1820s. It soon became the closest counterpart of the Lowell mills in terms of the size. However, the mills remained a proprietorship throughout his life. See Scranton (1983), pp. 144–147.

3. Paskoff (1983) documents the rise of the Pennsylvania iron industry. Unlike for the textile industry, Philadelphia was the market for the iron industry and production scattered outside the city.

4. See van Fenstermaker (1965), pp. 139–141, 169.

5. In the Waltham-Lowell system, such capital sometimes would be tied up in inventories. If the revenues from selling houses did not arrive in time, the company would need cash to finance their daily operations. As business grew, the amount needed for short-term credit capital exceeded the willingness of the selling houses to invest more. The large inventory of raw material they kept and the short-run credits of selling houses generated strong demand for bank credit.

REFERENCES

Adams, Donald R., Jr. (1972). "The Bank of Stephen Girard, 1812–1831." *Journal of Economic History* 32: 841–868.

Baltzell, E. Digby (1979). *Puritan Boston and Quaker Philadelphia: Two Protestant Ethics and the Spirit of Class Authority and Leadership*. New York: The Free Press.

Bodenhorn, Howard (1999). "An Engine of Growth: Real Bills Doctrine and Schumpeterian Banking in Antebellum New York." *Explorations in Economic History* 36: 278–302.

Bodenhorn, Howard (2000). *A History of Banking in Antebellum America*. Cambridge: Cambridge University Press.

Bodenhorn, Howard (2003). *State Banking in Early America: A New Economic History*. New York: Oxford University Press.

Dalzell, Robert E. (1987). *Enterprising Elite: The Boston Associates and the World They Made*. New York: Norton.

Daniels, Belden L. (1976). *Pennsylvania: Birthplace of Banking in America*. Harrisburg, PA: Pennsylvania Bankers' Association.

Davis, Lance E. (1960). "The New England Textile Mills and the Capital Markets: A Study of Industrial Borrowing 1840–1860." *Journal of Economic History* 20: 1–30.

Doerflinger, Thomas M. (1986). *A Vigorous Spirit of Enterprise: Merchants and Economic Development in Revolutionary Philadelphia*. New York: Norton.

Gurley, John G., and Edward S. Shaw (1955). "Financial Aspects of Economic Development." *American Economic Review* 45: 515–538.

King, Robert G., and Ross Levine (1993). "Finance and Growth: Schumpeter Might Be Right." *Quarterly Journal of Economics* 108: 717–738.

Lamoreaux, Naomi (1985). "Banks, Kinship, and Economic Development: The New England Case." *Journal of Economic History* 46: 647–667.

Lamoreaux, Naomi (1994). *Insider Lending: Banks' Personal Connections and Economic Development in Industrial New England*. New York: Cambridge University Press.

Levine, Ross (2005). "Finance and Growth." In *Handbook of Economic Growth*, vol. 1, edited by Philippe Aghion and Steven N. Durlauf. Amsterdam: North-Holland, pp. 865–934.

Levine, Ross, and Sarah Zervos (1998). "Stock Markets, Banks, and Economic Growth." *American Economic Review* 88: 537–558.

Lindstrom, Diane (1978). *Economic Development in the Philadelphia Region, 1810–1850*. New York: Columbia University Press.

McKinnon, Ronald I. (1973). *Money and Capital in Economic Development*. Washington, DC: Brookings Institution.

Paskoff, Paul F. (1983). *Industrial Evolution: Organization, Structure, and Growth of the Pennsylvania Iron Industry, 1750–1860*. Baltimore: Johns Hopkins University Press.

Rousseau, Peter L., and Richard Sylla (2005). "Emerging Financial Markets and Early US Growth." *Explorations in Economic History* 42: 1–26.

Schumpeter, Joseph A. (1934 [1912]). *The Theory of Economic Development: An Inquiry into Profit, Capital, Credit, Interest, and the Business Cycle*. Translated by Redvers Opie. Cambridge, MA: Harvard University Press.

Scranton, Philip (1983). *Proprietary Capitalism: The Textile Manufacture at Philadelphia, 1800–1885*. Cambridge: Cambridge University Press.

Shumate, Teri L. (2004). "The Origins of the Industrial Manufacturing Class: Boston Merchants and Philadelphia Artisans." PhD diss., University of California, Los Angeles.

Sokoloff, Kenneth L. (1984). "Investment in Fixed and Working Capital during Early Industrialization: Evidence from U.S. Manufacturing Firms." *Journal of Economic History* 44: 545–556.

Sylla, Richard (1998). "US Securities Markets and the Banking System, 1790–1840." *Federal Reserve Bank of St. Louis Review* 80: 83–98.

Sylla, Richard (2002). "Financial Systems and Economic Modernization." *Journal of Economic History* 62: 277–292.

Sylla, Richard, John B. Legler, and John J. Wallis (1987). "Banks and State Public Finance in the New Republic: The United States, 1790–1860." *Journal of Economic History* 47: 391–403.

Temin, Peter (2000). "Introduction." In *Engines of Enterprise: An Economic History of New England*, edited by Peter Temin. Cambridge, MA: Harvard University Press, pp. 1–10.

van Fenstermaker, J. (1965). *The Development of American Commercial Banking: 1782–1837*. Kent, OH: Kent State University.

Wallis, John J. (2007). "Answering Mary Shirley's Question or: What Can the World Bank Learn from American History?" In *Political Institutions and Financial Development*, edited by Stephen Haber, Douglass C. North, and Barry Weingast. Stanford, CA: Stanford University Press, pp. 92–124.

Wang, Ta-Chen (2008). "Paying Back to Borrow More: Reputation and Bank Credit Access in Early America." *Explorations in Economic History* 45: 477–488.

Weber, Warren E. (2005). "Balance Sheets for U.S. Antebellum State Banks." Research Department, Federal Reserve Bank of Minneapolis. http://research.mpls.frb.fed.us/research/economists/wewproj.html.

Wright, Robert E. (1999). "Bank Ownership and Lending Patterns in New York and Pennsylvania, 1781–1831." *Business History Review* 73: 40–60.

CHAPTER 7

Railroads and the Rise of the Factory: Evidence for the United States, 1850–1870

JEREMY ATACK, MICHAEL HAINES,
AND ROBERT A. MARGO

IN THE EARLY YEARS of the nineteenth century, manufacturing production in the United States took place in artisan shops where a highly skilled worker—the artisan—crafted a good from start to finish, perhaps with the help of an assistant or two. Artisans used comparatively little in the way of physical capital—a building, a few general purpose hand tools, and not much else—and their operations were to be found throughout the country. By midcentury, while artisan shops still constituted the majority of manufacturing establishments, a new organizational form—the factory—had emerged. Compared with the artisan shop the typical factory employed a larger number of lower-skilled workers who performed separate tasks, often with the aid of machinery driven by inanimate sources of power such as water or steam (Atack, Bateman, and Margo 2008). A fundamental consequence of these differences in organization and technology is that factories had higher labor productivity than artisan shops (Sokoloff 1984), and for the rest of the nineteenth century, manufacturing production continued to shift toward the factory and away from the artisan shop. Overall, the manufacturing sector grew rapidly and the country became the dominant player in many industries worldwide by the end of the century (Wright 1990; Broadberry and Irwin 2006).

What were the causes of the shift toward factory production? One classic answer invokes the role played by the "transportation revolution" (Clark 1916; Taylor 1951). Before the transportation revolution, the market for manufactured goods was limited to the immediate area surrounding the establishment because transport costs were very high relative to the value of the good at the point of production. Falling transport costs expanded the size of markets, eroding monopoly power and compelling firms to raise productivity through division of labor-cum-mechanization.

In addition, improved transportation reduced the cost of raw materials, and if these were complementary to capital goods that raised the productivity of unskilled labor, optimal firm size would increase. Improved transportation also lowered the likelihood of production downtime caused by input supply disruptions. This allowed firms to shift capital invested in inventories (of raw materials) toward capital (for example, steam power) that was complementary to division of labor (Atack, Bateman, and Margo 2008). Less downtime also meant that the firm could expand employment because workers would accept a lower wage as their unemployment risk was reduced (Atack, Bateman, and Margo 2002).

Although the transportation revolution is a plausible causal factor in the rise of the factory, it is far from being the only plausible cause. Improvement in steam technology is another. Recent work, for example, has shown that steam power was adopted more quickly by larger-scale enterprises arguably because the positive impact of steam on labor productivity (relative to water or hand power) was increasing in establishment size (see Atack, Bateman, and Margo 2008). All else equal, factories would be more profitable if the wage of unskilled labor was low relative to that of skilled labor. Early factories in the Northeast, for example, made extensive use of the labor of young women and children, whose productivity in agriculture relative to that of the adult males was low because of the region's crop mix (Goldin and Sokoloff 1982). As the century progressed, waves of immigration from Europe expanded the relative supply of unskilled labor, arguably fueling the growth of factories (Rosenbloom 2002).[1]

Assessing the relative importance of the transportation revolution as a causal factor in the diffusion of the factory has been hampered by a lack of suitable data connecting the two along with a defensible identification strategy for establishing causality. In this chapter we report on our preliminary efforts to bridge this gap using repeated cross-sections of establishments drawn from the 1850, 1860, and 1870 federal censuses of manufacturing that have been linked to county-level information on transportation access derived from maps from the period. Both the timing and nature of the linked sample cause us to focus attention in this chapter on the diffusion of the railroad rather than other forms of man-made transportation such as canals, which was largely complete by 1850.

Following previous work (Craig, Palmquist, and Weiss 1998; Haines and Margo 2008), we measure rail access as a dummy variable indicating whether a railroad passed through the boundaries of a particular county in a given census year. Some counties already had rail access in this sense in 1850 while others did not. Among the counties that did not have access in 1850, a subset gained access in the 1850s or in the 1860s. We adopt two identification strategies to assess causality. Our first strategy is to use a difference-in-differences (DD) estimator. This estimator measures whether factory status increased on average in counties that gained rail access over the course of the 1850s or 1860s—the "treatment" sample—as compared with a control sample (counties that did not gain access or already had access at the start of the decade). By design, the DD estimator eliminates any fixed factors at the county level that, in a cross-section, would have been correlated with rail access. However, the legitimacy of DD rests on the presumption that gaining access occurred through the equivalent of random assignment, conditional on any observed correlates of gaining rail access.

Consequently, as a check on these results we implement a second estimation strategy using instrumental variables for rail access applied to a cross-section of establishments in 1850. We have used two different instruments in our analysis. One instrumental variable derives from "straight lines" drawn between urban areas as of 1820 and the closest major coastal port; this instrument is used for counties located in the South and the Northeast. The second instrument is also derived from straight lines but uses information on the starting and endpoints of a series of railroad engineering surveys authorized by Congress from the mid-1820s to the late 1830s. This instrument is used for counties in the Midwest. The presumption is that a county would have been more likely to gain rail access by 1850 if it lay along one of the straight lines than if it did not. Judging by our first-stage regressions, this logic is correct: both instruments do a good job of predicting 1850 rail access in their respective subsamples.

Our empirical findings suggest that the coming of the railroad was a causal factor in the rise of factories. Our more precise DD estimate implies, for example, that the diffusion of the railroad after 1850 can account for about a third of the increase in the proportion of establishments that were factories between 1850 and 1870 in our sample.

DATA

Our empirical analysis uses repeated cross-sections of individual manufacturing establishments drawn from the census manuscripts for the 1850–1870 census years. These have been linked to a newly created database of the transportation infrastructure for the nineteenth-century United States. Our data description here is very brief; for further details, readers are directed to the working paper version of this chapter (Atack, Haines, and Margo 2008; see also Atack and Bateman 1999; Atack, Bateman, Haines, and Margo 2010).

To create our transportation database we used digitized images of nineteenth-century maps. These contain information on transportation infrastructure and have been electronically superimposed upon geographic information system (GIS) files showing county boundaries. GIS software is then used to create various measures of transportation access essentially by tracing the historical transportation infrastructure onto the historical county boundary files. In particular, the database records water transportation access as of 1850 by four variables: CANAL (= 1 if there was a canal within or passing through the county); RIVER (= 1 if there was a navigable river passing through or forming a border of the county); GREAT LAKES (= 1 if the county bordered on a Great Lake); and OCEAN (= 1 if the county bordered on the Atlantic or Pacific ocean or the Gulf of Mexico). The database also contains a similar measure of rail access (RAIL = 1 if one or more railroads passed through the county) in a particular census year (1850, 1860, or 1870). Thus, by construction, while our water transportation access variables do not change over time for any given county, our rail access variables will change if the county gained rail access at some point from 1850 to 1870.

We have linked the transportation database to the so-called national samples of manufacturing establishments that were drawn from the 1850–1870 manuscript censuses of manufacturing by Bateman and Weiss as modified and extended by Atack and Bateman.[2] Along with inputs, outputs, and other firm-level characteristics, the Atack-Bateman samples record the location of the establishment, including the county. For additional details on the manufacturing data, see Atack and Bateman (1999).

Linkage between the transportation and manufacturing databases is accomplished through a variable common to both, namely, the county. However, the Atack-Bateman samples are not stratified random samples by county; rather they are, by intention, nationally representative. As such, there are many counties in the transportation database for which no establishment-level observations exist in the Atack-Bateman samples for one or more of the relevant census years. Consequently, we have required that for any specific county in the transportation database to be included in the linked sample, there had to be observations in the Atack-Bateman samples in all three census years. This ensures that the linked sample is balanced—that is, there are $3 \times N$ county-level observations, where N is number of counties. Moreover, because geographic units are the key to record linkage and matching, we require that the counties have fixed boundaries over the sample period (1850–1870).[3] For example, in Illinois in 1850, Will County to the south of Chicago included that part of Kankakee County which lay north of the Kankakee River, but by 1860 the two counties had taken the boundaries they have to this day. Such changes, however, were not exclusively the domain of the newer states. In Pennsylvania, for example, Union County was divided into Union and Snyder counties in 1855, while part of Venango County was split off in the 1860s to be joined to Forest County in the east and more than doubling the size of Forest (Thorndale and Dollarhide 1987). We have also imposed a number of other screens on the manufacturing sample that are similar to those used in other studies using the Atack-Bateman samples (see the notes to Table 7.1), such as a report of each firm's invested capital.

Our final sample contains 8,597 establishments located in 368 counties. Panel A of Table 7.1 shows the distribution of the sample establishments by region. Reflecting the regional distribution of early industrial development in the United States, the overwhelming majority of establishments were located in the Northeast or Midwestern states. Panel B

TABLE 7.1 *Sample Statistics*

Panel A: Distribution of Establishments by Region: Linked Manufacturing-Transportation Database, 1850–1870

State	Number of Establishments	Percent of Total Sample (Establishments)
Northeast	6,123	71.2
Midwest	1,874	21.8
South	600	7.0
Total	8,597	100.0

Notes: Sample is a repeated cross-section of manufacturing establishments from 1850–1870 manuscript censuses of manufacturing linked to county-level data on transportation infrastructure. Counties included are those that existed in the census years 1850–1870 and that had no or very minimal changes in county boundaries over the period, and that were not in the far West. To be included in the sample, establishments had to have positive values of employment, capital invested, raw materials, value of output, and value added (value of outputs – value of raw materials) > $500.00 and total employment ≤ 1,000, and be located in one of the sample counties (N = 368 counties).

Panel B: Sample Establishment Means, Factory Status and Railroad Access

	1850		1860		1870	
Weight	Equal	Workers	Equal	Workers	Equal	Workers
Factory = 1	0.124	0.675	0.142	0.727	0.145	0.772
Rail access = 1	0.781	0.883	0.925	0.948	0.978	0.992
N (establishments)	2,874	31,446	2,897	37,602	2,826	40,018

Notes: Unit of observation is the manufacturing establishment. Factory = 1 if number of employees ≥ 16. Rail access = 1 if railroad passed through county boundary as of year shown. Equal: each establishment counts equally. Workers: establishments are weighted by reported employment. In 1850 and 1860 reported employment is the sum of male and female employees; in 1870 reported employment is the sum of children, female, and adult male employees.

Sources: Atack and Bateman (1999); Atack, Haines, and Margo (2008).

shows the sample means of one indicator for factory status and our rail access variable. The unit of observation is the establishment.

For the purposes of this chapter we have chosen to follow the existing literature (especially Sokoloff 1984) and have defined a "factory" as an establishment with 16 or more workers.[4] However, small variations around the factory cutoff (for example, 15 or 17 workers as opposed to 16) do not affect our substantive findings. We do not separately identify mechanized establishments because mechanization was a complement to the division of labor (Atack, Bateman, and Margo 2008).

Panel B reveals that, although factories were not very common in any of the census years, a majority of workers, even as early as 1850, were employed in factories. The proportion of factories rose between 1850 and 1870 by 2.1 percentage points, whereas the proportion of workers employed in factories also increased from 68 to 77 percent. The panel also shows that over three-quarters of the sample establishments and 88 percent of the workers employed in them were located in counties that already had rail access by 1850. Even so, rail access increased over the sample period by 20 percentage points, weighting establishments equally, a substantial rise.

ESTIMATION

We use our linked database to assess whether the coming of the railroad had an impact on mean factory status in manufacturing. To this end, we adopt as our base specification a standard DD specification:

$$F_{ijt} = \alpha_j + \delta_t + \gamma \text{RAIL}_{jt} + X_{ijt}\beta + \varepsilon_{ijt}$$

Here, $F = 1$ if the establishment was a factory according to our definition; i indexes the establishment, j the county, and t the year; α is the county fixed effect; the δ's are year effects; and the X's are establishment-level variables (for example, industry or urban location). By including the county fixed effect, our specification differences away all (fixed) factors that are associated with the presence of a railroad.[5] Hence we are identifying γ from changes in rail access, that is, counties that gained rail access over time (the "treatment") compared with counties that did not or else had access as of 1850 (the "control").

The hypothesis of interest is $\gamma > 0$, that is, that rail access was positively and significantly associated with the likelihood of an establishment being structured as a factory. There are two economic channels through which a transportation improvement might generate an increase in factories. The first channel occurs on the demand side. To understand the demand-side channel, imagine that firms have access to a technology that increases division of labor as more workers are hired up to some level of output. The division of labor raises productivity ("practice makes perfect") and reduces average costs up to this level of minimum average cost.

If the market were local, it is likely that the number of firms serving the market would be small. Under these circumstances, each firm may have some market power, meaning that the demand curve facing the firm is downward sloping with respect to price. Because demand slopes downward, the optimal size of the firm will be smaller than the size implied by the minimum average cost of production. If the firm is "too small" in this sense, the extent of division of labor will be limited. However, as transport costs fall, the market no longer is local, and the number of firms that compete with each other effectively increases. Because there will be greater competition than in the initial equilibrium, the demand curve facing each firm flattens, causing the firm to produce more output. Given a standard U-shaped average cost curve, this will be achieved through an increase in division of labor and, therefore, by an increase in firm size.[6]

The second channel operates on the supply side. We think the primary mechanism here is the impact of falling transport costs on the geographic extent of the market for raw materials. Certain raw materials are complementary to the growth of the factory system in the sense that a fall in their price makes it more likely that firms will adopt production methods that increase division of labor. In our context, possibly the best example of a raw material that was complementary to capital and unskilled labor was coal. Expensive coal limited the diffusion of steam engines, whereas cheap coal made steam more economical relative to water or hand power. Atack, Bateman, and Margo (2008) show that the productivity effects of steam were increasing in establishment size, most likely because firms that utilized steam could employ a more intricate division of labor.[7] The most plausible explanation of this relative decline is improvement in internal transportation that made it cheaper to transport coal from comparatively remote mines to urban areas where manufacturing production took place.

A reduction in the delivered price of inputs is not the only supply-side way in which a transportation revolution may have promoted factory growth. Improved transportation not only lowers the delivered price of raw materials but also smoothes fluctuations in raw materials prices.[8] A corollary of input price smoothing is that firms are less likely to experience disruptions in input supply. If such disruptions were common, then firms would shut down from time to time. If so, then production will be "part-year" as opposed to "full-year." To the extent that improvements in transportation lessened the likelihood of plant shutdowns, this would also make year-round production more likely and lead to larger firm sizes. Atack, Bateman, and Margo (2002) show that full-year operation in American manufacturing increased over the course of the nineteenth century and that larger establishments were, as hypothesized, more likely to engage in year-round production than smaller establishments.

The coincidence of the increases in factory status and rail access that is evident in Table 7.1 suggests a temporal link between the two, but time series correlation is not evidence of a causal relationship. Table 7.2 shows the DD estimates of γ for various specifications of the regression equation and over different sample periods. The unit of observation is the establishment and the establishments are equally weighted, except in the last column where observations are weighted by employment.

In general, we find a positive effect of rail access on factory status. The effect, however, is not statistically significant unless we include controls for urban status and industry, and year interactions between the water transportation dummies and the state in which the establishment was located. There are good reasons why this should be the case. As pointed out originally by Fishlow (1965), railroads did not arrive "randomly" on the landscape; rather, their location was influenced by prior economic development and transport routes among many other factors (for example, topography) in a cumulative evolutionary process.[9] Broadly speaking, the collection of factors that influence the timing of rail access, and thus when (if ever) a county entered the "treatment" group, is correlated with the year-interactions with the water transportation and state dummy variables. Because these factors may have independently influenced the size distribution of manufacturing firms, it is necessary to control for them to obtain a reliable DD estimate of the treatment effect from gaining rail access.[10]

When the regression covers all three census years as in the full specification just alluded to, rail access adds 3.8 percentage points to the probability that an establishment was a factory, or about 28 percent

TABLE 7.2 *Differences-in-Differences Regression Estimates of the Effect of Rail Access on Factory Status*

Sample	(1) Dependent Variable = 1	(2) County and Year Fixed Effects	(3) Add Establishment Urban Status and Industry	(4) Add State and Water Transportation Year Interactions	(5) Column (4) Weighted by Employment
1850, 1860	Factory	0.021 (0.018)	0.015 (0.018)	0.046* (0.021)	0.092** (0.053)
1860, 1870	Factory	0.020 (0.027)	0.024 (0.025)	0.039 (0.027)	
1850, 1870	Factory	0.023 (0.020)	0.017 (0.019)	0.035 (0.021)	
1850, 1860, 1870	Factory	0.022 (0.015)	0.019 (0.014)	0.038* (0.015)	0.087* (0.041)
1850, 1860, 1870	Artisan	−0.028 (0.024)	−0.024 (0.022)	−0.048* (0.021)	−0.095* (0.032)

Notes: Figures outside parentheses shown in rows 1–4 are coefficients of rail access dummy variable (=1 if railroad line passes through county boundary, 0 otherwise) on factory status (=1 if number of workers ≥ 16). Figures outside parentheses in row 5 are coefficients of rail access dummy variable on artisan shop status (=1 if number of workers ≤ 5). Standard errors, shown in parentheses, are clustered by county. Industry: dummy variables for 3-digit SIC codes. Urban = 1 if establishment located in incorporated village, town, or city of population 2,500 or more. State: dummy variables for state; West Virginia observations are recoded as Virginia for consistent classification over time. Water transportation dummies: Great Lakes = 1 if county bordered on one of the Great Lakes. Canal = 1 if a canal passed through the county as of 1850. River = 1 if a navigable river passed through the county boundary as of 1850. Ocean = 1 if county bordered on ocean as of 1850. All regressions include year dummies. In columns 4 and 5, state and water transportation dummies interacted with row-appropriate time dummies are included. Standard errors are clustered by county. *: significant at the 5 percent level. **: significant at the 10 percent level.

Sources: Atack and Bateman (1999); Atack, Haines, and Margo (2008).

(= 0.038/0.137) of the average of the sample means (1850–1870) shown in Panel A of Table 7.1. If the data are weighted by employment, the effect is larger in absolute terms (0.087, using all three years), but smaller (12 percent = 0.087/0.725) expressed relative to the average of sample means (1850–1870) of the shares of workers employed in factories.

Although our use of a "factory" cutoff at 16 or more workers is well established in the literature (Sokoloff 1984), there is little doubt that division of labor occurred at smaller establishment sizes. As a robustness check we estimated the DD regressions shown in row 6 of Table 7.2 with a different independent variable, ARTISAN (for artisan shops). This variable takes the value 1 if the firm had five or fewer workers; our expectation is that gaining rail access should reduce the proportion of artisan shops, so the treatment effect of rail access should be negative. As can be seen in Table 7.2, this was indeed the case, but once again only after we control for state-year and water transport-year interactions.

As a second robustness check, we perform an estimation using instrumental variables (IVs). For this purpose, we focus on the 1850 cross-section because there was more variation in rail access in this year. The idea behind the IV approach is to find a variable that predicts rail access in 1850 but that otherwise does not have a direct effect on the probability that an establishment was a factory.

Taking note of the links between centers of commerce and trade, our first instrument is a "Port" variable. To construct this instrument we identified all towns and cities of population 2,500 or more in the 1820 census. Next we identified nine "major" ports in 1820 from customs information. These ports were Baltimore, Boston, Charleston, New Orleans, New York, Norfolk, Philadelphia, Portland (Maine), and Savannah. We then drew straight lines between each interior city or town and the nearest port. If a county lay along one of those straight lines connecting cities to their nearest port, our instrument takes the value of one and zero otherwise.

Our second instrument is a "Congressional Survey" variable. Beginning in 1824 with the passage of the General Survey Bill, the President was granted authority to survey routes for "such roads and canals as he may deem of national importance, in a commercial or military point of view, or necessary for the transportation of the public mail" (U.S. Congress 1823–1824). Although the act contains no mention of railroads, beginning in 1825 with a survey to "ascertain the practicability of uniting the headwaters of the Kenawha [sic] with the James river and Roanoke river, by Canals or Railways" (Haney 1908, p. 277), railroads quickly came to the fore. This law remained in effect until it was repealed by the Jackson administration effective as of 1838. According to Haney (1908, p. 283), information on 59 surveys was reported in official congressional documents.

We construct our "Congressional Survey" instrumental variable (IV) as follows. First, we identified the pair of counties that constitute the starting point and endpoint of all railroad surveys listed in American State Papers over the period 1824 to 1838. We then drew a straight line between the geographic centers of the "start" and "end" counties. As with the "Ports" IV, counties that lay along this straight line received a value of one, while those that did not were coded as zero.

The idea behind both of these instruments is that costs mattered in the construction of a railroad. Specifically, all other factors held constant, (1) a lower-cost rail network is preferable to a higher-cost network, (2) a shorter line is less costly to build than a longer line, and (3) the shortest distance between two points is a straight line. Connecting interior places that had already established some level of economic activity in 1820 to the wider world (via ports in existence in 1820) clearly would make economic sense—if the transportation infrastructure were economically feasible. In the case of the congressional surveys, the idea is that existence of such a survey raised the likelihood that a railroad would eventually be built because these surveys provided valuable information about topography and other factors that clearly affected potential construction costs. Indeed, as Taylor (1951, p. 95) notes, "as trained engineers were still very scarce . . . the government rendered a uniquely valuable service by making its experts available for such surveys."[11] In sum, counties that happened to be on the straight lines as described would be at greater risk of gaining rail access earlier rather than later.

Given the location of urban areas in 1820, our "port" IV is capable of predicting rail access in the Northeast and the South but not the Midwest where settlement and development had barely yet begun. Similarly, given where the bulk of the surveys were taken—the Midwest as the region then developing—the survey IV has potential for predicting rail access in the Midwest (but not the other regions). Accordingly we split the sample into two groups—midwestern counties, and counties in the Northeast and South—while deleting observations in the West for which we have no instrument. As in our DD estimates, in addition to rail access, we also control for industry (3-digit SIC code), urban status, the water transportation dummies, and the state in which the establishment was located.

Table 7.3 shows the IV results. The first-stage coefficients are positive and highly significant indicating that the IVs do, in fact, predict rail access in 1850.[12] The second-stage or two-stage least-squares (2SLS) coefficients

TABLE 7.3   *Instrumental Variables Estimation of the Effects of Rail Access on Factory Status in 1850*

Sample	Congressional Survey IV Midwest	Port IV Northeast and South
First stage	0.472* (0.092)	0.248* (0.072)
2SLS	0.076 (0.064)	0.158 (0.124)
Significance level, 2SLS – DD ($\beta = 0.038$)	0.541	0.334
Number of establishments	427	2,435

Notes: Congressional Survey IV = 1 if county lies on a straight line connecting beginning and endpoints (counties) of a congressional railroad survey; Port IV = 1 if county lies on a straight line between urban area of population 2,500 or more in 1820 and nearest major port. The Congressional Survey IV estimation is restricted to sample counties located in the Midwest. The Port IV estimation is restricted to sample counties located in the Northeast and South. First stage: coefficient of rail access in 1850 on instrument. 2SLS: coefficient of factory status on predicted rail access using first-stage regression. Column 1 (Midwest) specification includes dummies for urban status, three-digit SIC industry code, canal, river, Great Lakes, and state. Column 2 (Northeast, South) specification includes the same dummies plus a dummy for ocean counties. Significance level: significance level of test of the difference between the 2SLS coefficient and DD coefficient ($\beta = 0.038$) from Table 7.2, row 4, column 4.

Source: Atack, Haines, and Margo (2008).

are also positive, but while the magnitudes of the 2SLS coefficients exceed the DD coefficient (0.038) in the full specification, standard errors are also fairly large. Consequently, we cannot reject the hypothesis that the IV and DD coefficients are (statistically speaking) the same.

Finally, in Table 7.4, we use the DD coefficient from the full specification (columns 4 and 5, row 5, Table 7.2) to predict the change in factory status from 1850 to 1870 given the observed change in rail access. If the data observations are equally weighted, the change in predicted factory status can account for a third of the actual change in factory status. If the data are weighted by employment counts, the percent explained is still positive (9 percent) but much smaller. Our results suggest, therefore, that the diffusion of the railroad after 1850 was certainly a factor in the rise of the factory system. It is plausible, therefore, that other components of the transportation revolution (such as canals and harbor improvements) also contributed to the rise of the factory, but measuring the treatment effects will require extending our analysis prior to 1850, when many of the relevant improvements occurred. Such an analysis will be complicated and possibly compromised by the absence of relevant data at most earlier censuses.

TABLE 7.4 *Explaining the Change in Factory Status, 1850–1870: The Role of Rail Access*

Weights	Equal	Workers
Actual change in rail access, 1850–70	0.197	0.109
Predicted change in factory status, 1850–70	0.007	0.009
Actual change in factory status	0.021	0.097
Percent explained $(1-\text{row } 2/\text{row } 3) \times 100\%$	33.3	9.3

Notes: Actual change in rail access: see Table 7.1, panel B. Predicted change in factory status: Actual change in rail access × regression coefficient, Table 7.2, column 4 or 5, row 4. Actual change in factory status: see Table 7.1, panel B. Equal: establishments weighted equally. Workers: establishments weighted by number of employees.

CONCLUSION

In the nineteenth century the United States experienced both a transportation revolution and an industrial revolution. In this chapter we report on a preliminary investigation of a particular link between these two revolutions, whether improved access to transportation networks increased the proportion of manufacturing establishments that were organized and structured as factories. The idea here, a very old one in economics, is that establishments that operated in larger markets were more likely to employ a more extensive and complete division of labor.

Our empirical analysis derives from a newly created and linked sample of county-level data on transportation access and establishment-level data from the 1850–1870 censuses of manufacturing. The transportation database has been created from digitized nineteenth-century transportation maps that have been overlaid on maps showing county boundaries, enabling us to measure whether or not, in particular, a railroad operated in a county in a given census year.

Using two separate identification strategies, we have shown that rail access was positively and significantly associated with the probability that an establishment was a factory, which we identify to be establishments with sixteen or more workers. The first identification strategy is a DD analysis applied to repeated cross-sections of establishments, while the second is an IV estimation applied to the 1850 sample of firms. The DD estimate suggests that gaining rail access did increase the proportion of establishments that met our definition of factory status, as well as the proportion of workers employed in factories. The IV estimation, a robustness check, also finds a positive impact of gaining rail access on factory status, and we cannot reject the hypothesis that the two types of coefficients are statistically indistinguishable.

It is important not to overstate the significance of the results. Our current measure of rail access is crude and it would be worthwhile to refine it, for example, by measuring the actual number of rail miles in each county. It would also be a worthwhile extension to develop additional instrumental variables, which would enable us to compute an overidentification test. That said, however, our results do provide a prima facie case that a central feature of the American transportation revolution—the diffusion of the railroad—was a causal factor behind the rise of the factory.

NOTES

This is a revised and shortened version of a paper that was written for the Conference in Honor of Gavin Wright held at Stanford University in September 2008. Comments from the editors of this volume, Latika Chaudhury, Michael Edelstein, and workshop participants at the National Bureau of Economic Research, Stanford University, Case Western University, and Columbia University are gratefully acknowledged.

1. Other factors include the development of financial markets (Rousseau and Sylla 2005) and legal changes in business organization (Lamoreaux 2006; Hilt 2008).

2. Although sample data for 1880 are also available, these are not used here because by 1880 rail coverage was essentially perfect in the counties included in the 1880 sample.

3. Restricting the sample to counties with fixed boundaries ensures that the county fixed effects that are estimated as a by-product of the DD estimation are not compromised by changes in the geographic size of counties. A county whose size was cut in half through political division might experience a change in the size distribution of manufacturing firms depending on how the new county boundary was drawn. This would violate the assumption inherent in the analysis that the county fixed effect was constant over time.

4. In 1850 and 1860 the number of workers is the sum of male and female employees. In 1870 the number of workers is the sum of adult males, adult females, and child employees. We have experimented with the adjustment of entrepreneurial labor suggested by Sokoloff (1984), which involves adding one person to the count of workers, but as our substantive findings were not affected, we only report results using the unmodified census counts. Similarly, no adjustment has been made to render the number of employees comparable across establishments in terms of adult-male equivalents because at least some of the process of division of labor involved the substitution of women and children for adult men (Goldin and Sokoloff 1982).

5. Among the fixed factors differenced away are the level effects of the water access dummies. However, interaction effects between the water access dummies and time are identified (see the text).

6. See Bresnahan and Reiss (1991) for a formal argument similar to the text.

7. Atack, Bateman, and Margo (2003) estimate output and capital good price indices for manufacturing over the period 1850 to 1880. Using these as the base, the price of coal in Northeastern cities clearly fell over the same period, and in all likelihood this relative decline began before 1850. According to our indices, capital goods prices in manufacturing declined by 24 percent relative to output prices between 1850 and 1880; the corresponding decline in the relative price of coal was 31 percent. In this case the coal price pertains to prices in Philadelphia (computed from series Cc237 in Carter et al. 2006, vol. 3, pp. 213–214). Using the same source, coal prices in Philadelphia declined by 35 percent on average from 1836–1840 to 1846–1850. This strongly suggests that the post-1850 trend in the relative price of coal began before 1850.

8. If firms are capital constrained, a reduction in transport costs may also free up capital held in inventories of raw materials that can be used, for example, to purchase capital goods (a steam engine) that is complementary to division of labor. The extent to which firms were capital constrained is likely to have varied with financial development; see Wang (this volume).

9. In particular Fishlow argued that railroads were not "built ahead of demand," as evidenced by changes in population density in the Midwest in the 1840s; railroads were built where population was already relatively dense and growing. However, Fishlow did not estimate per se the treatment effect of gaining railroad access on population density; see Atack, Bateman, Haines, and Margo (2010).

10. Further results available on request from Robert A. Margo suggest that the state–year interactions are more important in the sense discussed in the text than the water transportation–year interactions. In certain regions—the Midwest in the 1850s, for example—there appear to be underlying trends in factory status that were negatively correlated with gaining rail access. Failure to control for such trends would clearly bias the coefficient of rail access toward zero. Because we do not have size distribution data for manufacturing firms for, say, 1840 for our sample counties, we cannot determine if the trends are preexisting (that is, if they predate 1850), nor with so few time series observations can we investigate the underlying sources of the trends. It could be, for example, that growing per capita incomes in the Midwest in the 1850s caused by improvements in the agricultural terms of trade led to an increase in demand for locally produced manufactured goods which, given the relatively low population density at the time, were produced in artisan shops. Atack, Bateman, Haines, and Margo (2010) attribute some of the growth in urbanization in the Midwest in the 1850s from increased rail access to this demand-side phenomenon.

11. See also Haney (1908, p. 284), who remarks, "It is of some significance that in most cases the routes of these government surveys were early taken by railways. . . . In the great majority of cases these early surveys have been closely followed."

12. We also conducted a placebo test of the congressional survey instrument. Specifically we randomly drew 30 pairs of counties using the full universe of U.S. counties in 1840. We then drew straight lines between the pairs; if a county was on such a straight line, it received a value of one, zero otherwise. We estimate a regression of 1850 rail access in our Midwest sample on the placebo IV; the first-stage coefficient is slightly negative and statistically insignificant. The results of our placebo test suggest that the strong first stage with our Congressional Survey IV is not accidental.

REFERENCES

Atack, Jeremy, and Fred Bateman (1999). "U.S. Historical Statistics: Nineteenth Century U.S. Industrial Development through the Eyes of the Census of Manufactures." *Historical Methods* 32: 177–188.

Atack, Jeremy, Fred Bateman, Michael Haines, and Robert A. Margo (2010). "Did Railroads Induce or Follow Economic Growth? Urbanization and Population Growth in the American Midwest, 1850–60." *Social Science History* 34: 171–197.

Atack, Jeremy, Fred Bateman, and Robert A. Margo (2002). "Part-Year Operation in Nineteenth Century American Manufacturing: Evidence from the 1870 and 1880 Censuses." *Journal of Economic History* 62: 792–809.

Atack, Jeremy, Fred Bateman, and Robert A. Margo (2003). "Capital Deepening in American Manufacturing, 1850–1880." National Bureau of Economic Research Working Paper No. 9923. Cambridge, MA: National Bureau of Economic Research.

Atack, Jeremy, Fred Bateman, and Robert A. Margo (2008). "Steam Power, Establishment Size,and Labor Productivity Growth in Nineteenth Century American Manufacturing."*Explorations in Economic History* 45: 185–197.

Atack, Jeremy, Michael Haines, and Robert A. Margo (2008). "Railroads and the Rise of the Factory: Evidence for the United States." National Bureau of Economic Research Working Paper No. 14410. Cambridge, MA: National Bureau of Economic Research.

Bresnahan, Timothy F., and Peter C. Reiss (1991). "Entry and Competition in Concentrated Markets." *Journal of Political Economy* 99: 977–1009.

Broadberry, Steven, and Douglas A. Irwin (2006). "Labor Productivity in the United States and the United Kingdom during the Nineteenth Century." *Explorations in Economic History* 43: 257–279.

Carter, Susan B., Scott Sigmund Gartner, Michael R. Haines, Alan L. Olmstead, Richard Sutch, and Gavin Wright, eds. (2006). *Historical Statistics of the United States: Earliest Times to the Present, Millennial Edition*, vol. 3, part C: *Economic Structure and Performance*. New York: Cambridge University Press.

Clark, Victor S. (1916). *History of Manufactures in the United States 1607–1860*. Washington, DC: Carnegie Institution.

Craig, Lee, Raymond Palmquist, and Thomas Weiss (1998). "Transportation Improvements and Land Values in the Antebellum United States: A Hedonic Approach." *Journal of Real Estate Finance and Economics* 16: 173–190.

Fishlow, Albert (1965). *American Railroads and the Transformation of the Antebellum Economy*. Cambridge, MA: Harvard University Press.

Goldin, Claudia, and Kenneth Sokoloff (1982). "Women, Children, and Industrialization in the Early Republic: Evidence from the Manufacturing Censuses." *Journal of Economic History* 42: 741–774.

Haines, Michael, and Robert A. Margo (2008). "Railroads and Local Economic Development: The United States in the 1850s." In *Quantitative Economic History: The Good of Counting*, edited by J. Rosenbloom. New York: Routledge, pp. 78–99.

Haney, L. H. (1908). *A Congressional History of Railways in the United States*. Madison, WI: Democrat Printing Company.

Hilt, Eric (2008). "When Did Ownership Separate from Control? Corporate Governance in the Early Nineteenth Century." *Journal of Economic History* 68: 645–685.

Lamoreaux, Naomi (2006). "Business Organization." In *Historical Statistics of the United States: Earliest Times to thePresent, Millennial Edition*, vol. 3, part C, *Economic Structure and Performance*, edited by Susan B. Carter et al. New York: Cambridge University Press, pp. 477–494.

Rosenbloom, Joshua (2002). *Looking for Work, Searching for Workers: Labor Markets during American Industrialization*. New York: Cambridge University Press.

Rousseau, Peter, and Richard Sylla (2005). "Emerging Financial Markets and Early U.S. Growth." *Explorations in Economic History* 42: 1–26.

Sokoloff, Kenneth (1984). "Was the Transition from the Artisanal Shop to the Non-Mechanized Factory Associated with Gains in Efficiency? Evidence from the U.S. Manufacturing Censuses of 1820 and 1850." *Explorations in Economic History* 21: 351–382.

Taylor, George R. (1951). *The Transportation Revolution, 1815–1860*. New York: Holt, Rhinehart, and Winston.

Thorndale, William, and William Dollarhide (1987). *Map Guide to the U.S. Federal Censuses, 1790–1920*. Baltimore: Genealogical Publishing Company.

U.S. Congress (1823–1824). *Laws of the U.S. VII, 239. Acts of 1823–24*, Ch. 276.

Wright, Gavin (1990). "The Origins of American Industrial Success, 1879–1940." *American Economic Review* 80: 651–668.

CHAPTER 8

Productivity Growth and the Regional Dynamics of Antebellum Southern Development

ALAN L. OLMSTEAD AND PAUL W. RHODE

AFTER A LONG ABSENCE, slavery has recently reclaimed a place in the limelight of American economic history research. Gavin Wright's *Slavery and American Economic Development* (2006), Stanley Engerman's *Slavery, Emancipation, and Freedom* (2007), Robert Fogel's *The Slavery Debates* (2003), and several contributions in *Slavery in the Development of the Americas* (Eltis, Lewis, and Sokoloff 2004) have all enriched our understanding of the "Peculiar Institution." Many of these works focus on the efficiency of slave plantation agriculture.

Much of this recent literature synthesizes and reinterprets existing evidence with the aim of providing perspective and even closing long-standing debates. Such thoughts of closure are premature. We present new data that provide a fresh perspective on plantation efficiency and the dynamics of southern agriculture. These findings complement our previous research, which showed that the creation and diffusion of easier-to-pick, higher-yielding, and superior-quality cotton varieties changed the face of southern farming by significantly increasing labor productivity and improving the South's position in world markets (Olmstead and Rhode 2008a, pp. 107–114; Olmstead and Rhode 2008b).

Here we focus on understanding how the productivity revolution affected the western movement of cotton production and how western movement in turn affected plantation productivity in the antebellum years. We first review the evidence for a biological revolution in cotton production beginning around 1806. We next offer a critical analysis of how the cliometrics mainstream explained the growth in cotton output and treated the issues of plantation and slave productivity. This literature simply missed the importance of technological change even though many traditional historians and pioneering cliometricians had pointed the way. To provide a fresh insight, we present new data on the bales of cotton produced per worker, by region for the decades between 1800 and 1860, and by county for the census years 1839, 1849, and 1859. This evidence reinforces our previously published findings on the growth of picking efficiency suggesting that, while output per worker advanced everywhere, the improvements were most rapid in the New South. Allowing for regionally biased technological innovation enhances the importance of western settlement in explaining the increase in cotton output and revises the understanding of the distributional impact of settlement on planters in the Old South.

THE BIOLOGICAL REVOLUTION
IN COTTON PRODUCTION

The improvement of cotton varieties had great significance for the geographical expansion of cotton production and on southern economic development more generally. Biological innovation is a key to understanding the growth in southern productivity and the region's growing preeminence in the world cotton market. Many have decried the lack of indigenous technological advances in the antebellum South, but the region was the undisputed world leader in the creation and diffusion of new, superior cotton varieties. Leaders in Britain and elsewhere clearly recognized the importance of the new technologies and repeatedly, but unsuccessfully, tried to adopt American seeds and methods in other producing areas. Most of the technologies were developed in the Mississippi Valley and were better suited for the geoclimatic conditions found there than for the conditions common to much of Georgia and the Carolinas, let alone conditions in India and Africa. These findings help explain interregional differences in production and productivity growth, the extent of the interregional slave trade, and the traditional static comparisons of plantation and nonplantation efficiency.

Southern farmers developed a progression of improved cotton varieties. Around 1800, new green seed cotton varieties boosted southern productivity. But the most important break occurred in 1806 when a Mississippi planter and diplomat, Walter Burling, returned from Mexico City with seeds from some unusually appealing cotton plants. This set in motion a chain of events that would revolutionize southern history and profoundly affect the lives of American slaves. Burling shared his discovery with neighboring planters who over the next several decades perfected the Mexican-style cottons to thrive in the Mississippi Valley. This often involved out-crossing the Mexican imports with local cottons and many generations of careful selection to obtain desirable traits. Breeders marketed dozens of brand names over the antebellum years. Agronomists regard many of these early creations as the founding stock of several of the major cotton types, which would become popular in the South over the next century. One of the earliest and most widely adopted varieties was Petit Gulf, which gained prominence by the mid-1830s. Most of the breeding innovations occurred on large southwestern plantations, and the varieties developed were most productive in the soils and climates where they were bred. This had an enormous implication for southern development. From the mid-1820s through at least the mid-1830s there was a distinct difference between the types of cotton grown in the lower Mississippi Valley and the Southeast. The new western cottons produced higher yields, were of superior quality, were more pest resistant, offered higher lint-to-seed ratios, fetched higher prices, and were significantly easier to pick (Watkins 1908, p. 13; Ware 1950, p. 659). The spread of the new varieties widened the yield and picking efficiency differences that separated the black prairie, brown loam, and alluvial soils of the New South from the poorer lands in the Old South.

In our previous research we employed a sample of over 700,000 individual cotton-picking entries on 142 plantations over 509 plantation years to track the average amount of cotton picked per slave per day in the 60 years preceding the Civil War. Figure 8.1 graphs the picking indices (based on a specification utilizing quadratic time trends) for the total sample, for the Old South, and for the New South. In addition, it presents a new weighted index combining the Old and New South indices using output shares for each region.[1] The All South index based on the total sample shows a quadrupling of the daily picking rates between 1800 and 1862, with a growth rate of 2.3 percent per annum. The weighted index shows a somewhat smaller overall increase, with a still-robust growth rate of 2.0 percent per annum. The weighted index also suggests the change was more evenly spread across the antebellum era.

FIGURE 8.1 *Picking Rate Indexes, 1801–1862*

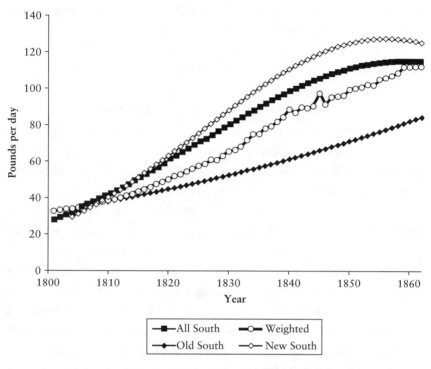

Sources: Compiled from data in Watkins (1908) and Olmstead and Rhode (2008b).

Figure 8.1 also highlights the important regional differences in pick-ing rates. In 1811, when data for both regions first become available, estimated picking rates were 39 pounds per day in the Old South and 42 pounds per day in the New South. The gap was about 9 percent. Over the antebellum era, the gap widened substantially. By 1861 pickers in the New South on average harvested 126 pounds in a day compared to 83 pounds for their counterparts in the Old South, implying a gap of about 51 percent. The growth in picking rates in the Old South was roughly linear in time, whereas growth in the New South was rapid in the 1820s and 1830s and then slowed. As a result, the regional picking rate gap in 1840 reached 81 percent, with the average slave in the New South gath-ering about 111 pounds per day compared to just 61 pounds in the Old South. Contemporaries credited the overall increase in picking rates to the diffusion of new cotton varieties and saw the regional differences in picking efficiency as a product of the differences in diffusion rates. The higher picking rates allowed planters to plant more cotton per slave, leading to an increased specialization in cotton production and to an increase in the annual average number of bales harvested per worker.

THE CLIOMETRIC MAINSTREAM

The evidence on picking rates offers a far more dynamic picture of southern agricultural development than that depicted in the existing cliometric literature. Attention to southern agricultural productivity has mostly focused on static issues such as the differences in total factor productivity of free farms and slave cotton plantations of various sizes. Changes over time have received short shrift. An abbreviated list of participants in the slavery debates includes Fogel and Engerman (1974) for *Time on the Cross*, and Fogel and the many other contributors to the four volumes of *Without Consent or Contract* (Fogel 1989; Fogel and Engerman 1992a, 1992b; Fogel, Galantine, and Manning 1992). Gavin Wright, Peter Temin, Paul David, Roger Ransom, Richard Sutch, William Parker, Robert Gallman, Richard Steckel, Robert Margo, Chris Hanes, Claudia Goldin, Lee Craig, Tom Weiss, Fred Bateman, James Foust, David Weiman, and well over a score of other prominent scholars have made substantive contributions. Parker and Gallman (with their students) played a key role in shaping the contours of the debate by providing their much-cited sample of over 5,000 farms drawn from the 1859 manuscript census.

In *The Slavery Debates* (2003) Fogel offered his view on the current state of knowledge of slave and plantation efficiency. Notwithstanding all of the fireworks concerning *Time on the Cross*, Fogel asserted that its major findings remain intact. In particular, he maintained that slave plantations were highly profitable, efficient, and fully capable of out-competing free farms. The greater efficiency of plantations stemmed from their ability to exploit the gang system. Slaves "who toiled in the gangs of the intermediate and large plantations were on average over 70 per cent more productive than either free farmers [northern and southern] or slaves on small plantations" (Fogel 2003, pp. 28–39). Finally, Fogel asserted that under the gang system slaves worked more intensely but for fewer hours than free workers. The "greater intensity of labor per hour, rather than more hours of labor per day or more days of labor per year, is the reason the index of total factor productivity is 39 percent higher for the gang-system plantations than for free farms."[2]

Fogel and Engerman's productivity findings remain contested. Wright (1978, 1979, 2006) and Schaefer (1983) argued the results are unrepresentative because the analysis focused on a single crop year, 1859, that they claimed was exceptionally favorable for cotton. Relying on cross-sectional data also presents difficulties in controlling for unobserved heterogeneity across plantations that cause endogeneity problems. Differences in managerial ability, soil type, or location could have accounted for the correlation between size and measured productivity, and confounded the cross-sectional relationship pointing to the importance of plantation scale.

In response to this critique, Fogel and Engerman (1977, 1980) questioned Wright's evidence on crop conditions in 1859.[3] They then posed this question: "What then explains the big increase in the output of cotton between 1850 and 1860?" They estimated that the westward shift in cotton production explained only about 8 percent of the increase in output between 1850 and 1860 and that the increase in improved land within each state explained 41 percent of the growth in output. They then deduced that 42 percent of the increase in cotton output resulted from a substitution of land within states from other crops to cotton. "These estimates leave a residual of 9 percent to be explained by all other factors including increases in the use of fertilizers, increases in the labor-to-land ratio, and random fluctuations in yields" (Fogel and Engerman 1977, p. 282). The subsequent debate on the sources of the increase in cotton output carried on in this tradition by offering various technical refinements but little new data.

We take issue with this approach in which movements in cotton production are largely deduced from state-level changes in improved acreage (IA) and corn production.[4] The relationship between improved acreage and the production of cotton and corn appears too loose to warrant closing the debate. The decomposition exercise of Fogel and Engerman may be analyzed using the following equation:

$$\log(\text{Cotton}1859/1849) = \beta_0 + \beta_1 \log(\text{IA}1859/1849) + \beta_2 \log(\text{Corn}1859/1849)$$

In the 10-state region of the Cotton South during the 1850s, cotton production grew at an annualized rate of 7.7 percent, improved land grew at a rate of 3.4 percent, and corn production grew at a rate of 1.8 percent. Fogel and Engerman argue, under the maintained hypothesis of constant yields, that cotton output may be expected to grow directly with the growth of improved acreage. This represents the acreage expansion effect that they posit accounts for 41 percent of the increase. They further argue the corn output might be expected grow at the same rate as improved acreage and any difference between those rates was due to a shift toward cotton. This represents the cropland substitution effect that they posit accounts for 42 percent of the increase. Thus their argument may be captured with the model's parameters specified as $\beta_1 = 1 + \alpha > 1$ and $\beta_2 = -\alpha < 0$:

$$\log(\text{Cotton}1859/1849) = \beta_0 + \log(\text{IA}1859/1849) - \alpha[\log(\text{Corn}1859/1849) - \log(\text{IA}1859/1849)]$$

where α is the ratio of the corn land share to the cotton land share.[5]

In accessing how well Fogel and Engerman's decomposition reflects the realities of southern development, one should ask how tight was the relationship between the growth of cotton production and improved acreage and corn production. It is important to note that improved acreage is a much broader concept than arable or tilled land. Adequate data on the share of improved acreage devoted to specific crops do not become available until the postbellum period. The 1880 census was the first to enumerate crop acreage and yields. The improved-land-to-rural-population ratio was higher in the South in 1880 than in 1850 or 1860, so it is likely that in the antebellum period the share of improved acreage used for crops was lower and that the relationship linking improved land to cotton production was looser. We can calculate the ratio of the sum of acreage in major crops to improved acreage by county in the South in 1880 (excluding the handful of counties where the sum of reported crop acreage exceeded improved land). The land devoted to the 13 major crops—barley, buckwheat, corn, cotton, oats, rye, wheat, hay, tobacco, Irish potatoes, sweet potatoes, rice, and hops—composed 62 percent of improved acreage with a standard deviation of about 21 percent. The coefficient of variation is roughly one-third. Cotton made up 16 percent of acreage with a standard deviation of 17 percent. Corn made up 31 percent with a standard deviation of 14 percent. The bottom line is the cotton acreage is not tightly related to improved acreage in this 1880 cross-section.

Turning back to the antebellum period, we can use the more limited census data to examine the relationship between the growth of cotton production and of improved acreage and crop production at the county level. We focus on 423 cotton-producing counties which have consistently defined boundaries over the 1850 to 1860 censuses.[6] Regressing the growth of the county's cotton output between 1859 and 1849 on the growth of its improved acreage and corn output yields the following results (with the standard errors in the parentheses):

$$\log(\text{Cotton}1859/1849)$$
$$= 0.470 + 0.0447 \log(\text{IA}1859/1849) + 1.175 \log(\text{Corn}1859/1849)$$
$$(0.065)\ (0.124) \qquad\qquad\qquad (0.136)$$
$$N = 423,\ R^2 = 0.371$$

Thus we find that (1) the relationship of improved acreage with cotton was positive but much less than one-for-one; (2) the relationship of corn production with cotton production was strong and *positive*, contrary to the negative sign that Fogel and Engerman posited in their crop substitution argument; and (3) the R^2 is sufficiently low to leave great room for other factors to affect the growth of cotton output. The upshot is that there is little reason to give credence to Fogel and Engerman's widely cited decomposition of the sources of cotton output growth for the 1850s. Placing aside their estimates means that there is significant scope for productivity growth to account for the increase in cotton output over the 1850s specifically and the whole antebellum period more generally.

We want to emphasize that Fogel and Engerman were not alone in overlooking productivity advances. In his earlier work, Wright also downplayed the role of productivity advance in the cotton sector. For example, in *Reckoning with Slavery*, Wright (1976, pp. 326–327) argued "there is very little evidence of substantial productivity growth under slavery other than that associated with the increase in the quantity and quality of cotton land." According to Wright the relocation of cotton production to more fertile soils as well as transportation improvements such as the steamboat and railroad explained the slow secular decline in the real price of cotton. But in *Slavery and American Economic Development*, Wright (2006, pp. 89–91) acknowledges a greater role for biological learning to increase productivity and encourage the western expansion of the cotton frontier. Other scholars have equated productivity growth with mechanization. As an example, Eugene Genovese (1967, pp. 48–51, 54–61) concluded from the absence of mechanical innovations on par with the grain reaper that the South was stagnating.[7]

THE GROWTH OF COTTON BALES PER WORKER

A few economic historians have recognized the significance of productivity growth in the cotton sector, but their work hardly caused a ripple in the mainstream literature. Conrad and Meyer (1964, p. 77) compared the growth of cotton output to the adult slave population over the 1800–1860 period and interpreted the wide difference as a sign of productivity advance. But this exercise raised obvious objections. Wright (2006, p. 88) among others has been skeptical of measuring productivity growth in this way, arguing, "This practice is misleading. The *composition* of southern agricultural output was in flux between 1790 and the 1820s, as cotton replaced tobacco, wheat, and lesser crops in Virginia and the Carolinas." We agree with Wright's (2006, p. 88) assessment that "it makes little sense to define a productivity measure in terms of only one part of the whole. If that part happens to be rising rapidly, such a ratio exaggerates the growth of what economists normally regard as productivity." Fogel and Engerman (1971, pp. 315–316, esp. fn. 9) expressed similar concerns. In addition to considering the shifting composition of agricultural output, one should account for the fraction of slaves who did not work in cotton as well as for the fraction of cotton produced by free workers.

Relying on more disaggregated data than Conrad and Meyer (1964), Whartenby (1977, pp. 54, 104–105) estimated that between 1800 and 1840 cotton yields per acre increased by 46 to 78 percent and that the amount of cotton a slave picked a day more than doubled.[8] For all tasks, Whartenby estimated that the number of bales produced per worker increased 1.9 to 2.3 times over these four decades. The diffusion of new cotton varieties played a leading role in her story. However, given the small size of her sample, Whartenby resisted extending her conclusion to the entire South. Even after Lebergott (1984) added more evidence of productivity gains, cliometricians ignored this path of research. The only other references to biological innovation in antebellum cotton production that we have found in the economic history literature are Scheiber, Vatter, and Faulkner (1976, p. 131) and Campbell (1988).

Why mainstream cliometricians failed to see the cotton variety revolution is even more puzzling because many of the giants of southern history including James L. Watkins (1908), Lewis Cecil Gray (1933), and John Hebron Moore (1956, p. 96; 1958, pp. 13–36; 1988) all touted the essential importance of biological innovation in increasing cotton yields, quality, and picking efficiency. So did many widely read nineteenth-century observers such as Mississippi planter and historian B. C. L. Wailes (1854). Watkins was so impressed with the improved attributes of the Mexican cotton that he proclaimed, "From an economic point of view the introduction of this seed was second in importance to the invention of the saw gin." Cliometricians repeatedly cited these traditional historians and contemporary sources on myriad issues but simply ignored their emphasis on new cotton varieties.

Plantation owners often commented on the number of bales of cotton slaves were expected to produce, could produce, or did produce in a year. As examples, an 1810 advertisement in the Charleston *City Gazette* touted the land tract for sale as capable of producing 3 to 4 bales per hand, whereas another ad for land in the 1857 Macon *Weekly Telegraph* promised 4 to 8 bales.[9] Historians of the era have followed suit. For instance, John Hebron Moore notes, "Farmers, who in 1800 had hoped to average two 400-pound bales to each field hand, by 1837 were trying to produce crops of six to eight bales to the hand" (Moore 1958, p. 46). Moore further observed that "in the years 1833 and 1836 Richard Nutt, son of Dr. Rush Nutt, averaged nine bales of cotton to the hand, a record almost equaled by his brother" (Moore 1958, p. 215, fn. 26).

Although there are many similar claims ascribing 5 to 10 bales per slave, Foust and Swan (1970) suggest that such anecdotal accounts painted an excessively rosy picture of average conditions. Foust and Swan examined the labor-input and cotton-output data in 1849 and 1859 for a sample of farms in 74 cotton-producing counties. Both the 1849 and 1859 samples contained well over 500 cotton farms. They did not rely on direct individual observations of picking rates as we do above, but rather they calculated the output per slave using farm-level cotton output in bales divided by one-half of the number of slaves on a given plantation to arrive at a rough approximation of the number of full field hands (also see Sutch 1965). This represents a vast improvement over Conrad and Meyer's procedure of comparing U.S. cotton production to the entire slave population aged 10 to 54 years old. Foust and Swan found that bales per working slave increased from 1.59 in 1849 to 2.11 in 1859. On "Alluvial" lands the increase was from 2.07 to 2.78, for their "Other New South" region bales per slave went from 1.49 to 2.64, and for their "Old South" region it only went from 1.47 to 1.48. One might question how sensitive these results are to the underlying assumptions and to the weather and other conditions in the two years studied, but there is no denying that something very important was going on. For the South as a whole, the bales per worker went up by an average of 2.8 percent per year; for the "Other New South," the increase was 5.7 percent per year. By contrast there was no change the "Old South."[10]

The Foust and Swan 1859 ratios are means derived from the Parker-Gallman sample. It is informative to explore in greater detail the distributions of the ratio of bales per slave worker in this benchmark sample. We will focus on cotton operations with one or more slaves (age 10 years and over). Such operations account for 91.1 percent of cotton in the overall sample, 92.0 percent in the Old South, and 90.8 percent in the New South. The top panel of Figure 8.2 graphs the cumulative distribution of

FIGURE 8.2 *Distribution of 1859 Parker-Gallman Sample by 400-Pound Bales per Slave*

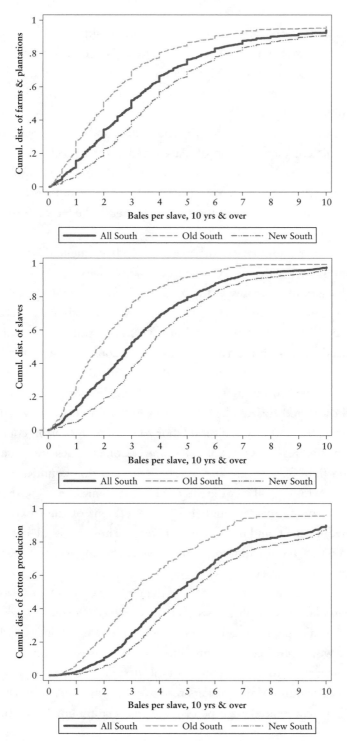

Source: Compiled from data in Parker and Gallman (1991).

farms and plantations by bales per slave. In the Old South, 51 percent of units in the sample had a bale-to-slave ratio of two or less, whereas in the New South 23 percent did. More than 86 percent of the Old South units had a bale-to-slave ratio of five or less, while only 69 percent of New South units did. By this measure the median ratio was 2 bales in the Old South and 3.69 in the New South. The middle and bottom panels graph the cumulative distributions of slaves and cotton production, respectively. The median ratio of bales per working slave was 1.86 in the Old South and 3.67 in the New South, almost twice as high. By each measure the bales-to-slave ratio was substantially higher in the New South than in the Old South.

Employing a data set recently constructed by Craig and Weiss (1998), we can push estimates of bales-per-hand back to 1800. Craig and Weiss created separate estimates of the urban and rural labor force by county in the United States and then for the South assumed about 75 percent of the rural slaves worked in agriculture. This ratio was based on detailed statistics drawn from the 1840 census and is consistent with the finding that a substantial fraction of rural slaves worked in domestic or craft trades.[11] They report numbers of male and female agricultural slaves (age 10 and over) and free workers (10 to 15 and 16 and over). We summed their estimates of the agricultural labor force over the cotton counties in each state and region. For 1800–1830 the cotton counties are those designated on the USDA maps. For 1840–1860 the cotton counties are those with production equal to or greater than 1,000 bales. In 1859 the designated cotton counties accounted for 98.6 percent of the total crop, in 1849 97.3 percent, and in 1839 97.3 percent. Thus almost all cotton production is covered. In addition, most tobacco, hemp, rice, and sugar cane production is excluded.

Table 8.1 shows two estimates of the ratio of cotton bales produced to the number of agricultural workers from 1800 to 1860. The top panel shows the bales per slave worker and the bottom panel includes both slave and free workers.[12] Figure 8.3 provides a visual representation of the same data.[13] According to the top panel in Table 8.1, the national ratio of cotton bales to agricultural slave workers rose over 4.1 times between 1800 and 1860. This represented a 2.4 percent increase per annum. The ratio grew

TABLE 8.1   *Cotton Bales per Worker (Age 10 and over) in the Agricultural Labor Force in Cotton Counties, by Region, 1800–1860*

Panel A: 400-Pound Cotton Bales per Slave (Age 10 and over)

| | | | | | New South Share | |
| | | | | New/Old | | |
	Old South	New South	All South	Ratio	Ag LF	Output
1800	1.00		1.04			
1810	1.15	2.17	1.19	1.89	0.04	0.08
1820	1.25	2.40	1.52	1.92	0.23	0.37
1830	1.66	3.14	2.14	1.89	0.32	0.47
1840	1.95	4.02	2.94	2.07	0.48	0.65
1850	2.65	3.89	3.34	1.47	0.56	0.65
1860	2.56	5.36	4.26	2.09	0.61	0.76

Panel B: 400-Pound Cotton Bales per Free Worker and Slave (Age 10 and over)

| | | | | | New South Share | |
| | | | | New/Old | | |
	Old South	New South	All South	Ratio	Ag LF	Output
1800	0.61		0.63			
1810	0.76	1.28	0.79	1.67	0.05	0.08
1820	0.83	1.37	0.98	1.64	0.26	0.37
1830	1.12	1.87	1.38	1.67	0.35	0.47
1840	1.27	2.67	1.93	2.10	0.47	0.65
1850	1.80	2.55	2.22	1.42	0.57	0.65
1860	1.78	3.49	2.84	1.96	0.62	0.76

Sources: Output based on three-year averages computed from the cotton production series from Carter et al. (2006) and the regional commercial production shares from Watkins (1908), adjusting to constant 400-pound bales.

in both the Old South and New South. The rise in bales per worker in the Old South calls into question interpretations stressing declining soils and falling productivity in the Southeast.[14] Though often depicted as a backwater in antebellum development, the Old South experienced annual growth rates of 4.2 percent in cotton production and 1.6 percent in bales per worker. Cotton production in the New South, of course, expanded even more rapidly because of the availability of new land and higher productivity. The ratio of cotton bales to agricultural slaves in the New South was 89 percent higher than in the Old South in 1810 and 109 percent higher in 1860. Herein was a great incentive to send slaves west. The

FIGURE 8.3   *Cotton Bales per Worker (Age 10 and over) in the Agricultural Labor Force, 1800–1860*

Panel A: 400-Pound Bales per Slave in Agricultural Labor Force

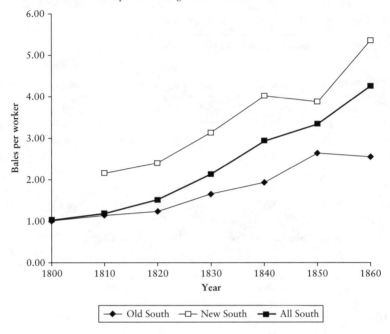

Panel B: 400-Pound Bales per Free Worker and Slave in Agricultural Labor Force

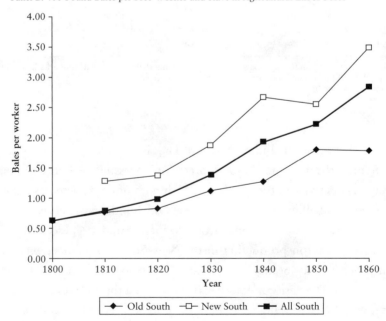

Sources: Compiled from data in Watkins (1908); Craig and Weiss (1998); and Carter et al. (2006).

rapid growth in the bales per worker for the entire South reflects the significant shift in the composition of output from the Old to the New South. In 1810 the Old South produced 95 percent of America's upland cotton; by 1860 this region only produced less than 24 percent. A standard decomposition calculation using data for these two regions over the 1800 to 1860 period reveals about one-half of the increase in the national bales-per-slave ratio was caused by the shift between the two regions and the other half by increases within each region.

A similar picture appears in the bottom panels of Table 8.1 and Figure 8.3. The ratios are obviously lower (because the denominator is larger), but the growth rates are somewhat more rapid because the free labor force grew more slowly than the slave labor force in the cotton areas. It is not obvious which labor force estimate is most appropriate. Indeed, we suggest that for the early years the bottom panel (with slave and free labor) deserves more attention, and for the later years the top panel (with only slave labor) should gain the spotlight. Early in the nineteenth century free whites played a larger role in cotton production. Mendenhall (1940) asserted that cotton was initially (in the 1790s) a small farmer's crop in the Southeast and was only gradually adopted by the larger slaveholders. Based on Hammond and other antebellum observers, Whartenby (1977, pp. 67–70) placed the number of free whites producing cotton in the 1800–1830 period at one-sixth the number of slaves engaged. By the 1850s cotton was overwhelmingly a slave crop. Foust's research indicates that free white farms account for only 5 to 10 percent of the crop—a share that is only slightly above what Campbell (1988, p. 167) estimated enslaved African Americans produced on their own time for sale to their masters. If the composition of the cotton labor force in fact shifted dramatically away from free workers, the ratio of bales to cotton worker rose more rapidly than either panel alone suggests.

Figure 8.4 provides a visual sense of the variation across space and changes over time based on county-level data for 1840, 1850, and 1860. The panels map the number of the 400-pound bales produced per slave worker and per worker, slave and free, constructed from the census output data and Craig-Weiss labor force estimates. The dramatically higher levels of production per worker in specific areas of the Southwest jump out.

FIGURE 8.4   *Output of 400-Pound Cotton Bales per Worker*

Slaves, 1840

Slaves, 1850

Slaves, 1860

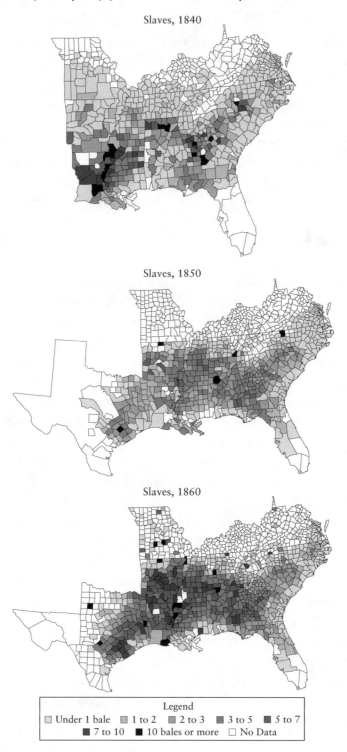

Legend
☐ Under 1 bale   ▨ 1 to 2   ▨ 2 to 3   ▨ 3 to 5   ▨ 5 to 7
■ 7 to 10   ■ 10 bales or more   ☐ No Data

Sources: Compiled from data in Craig and Weiss (1998) and Craig, Haines, and Weiss (2000).

FIGURE 8.4 *(Continued)*

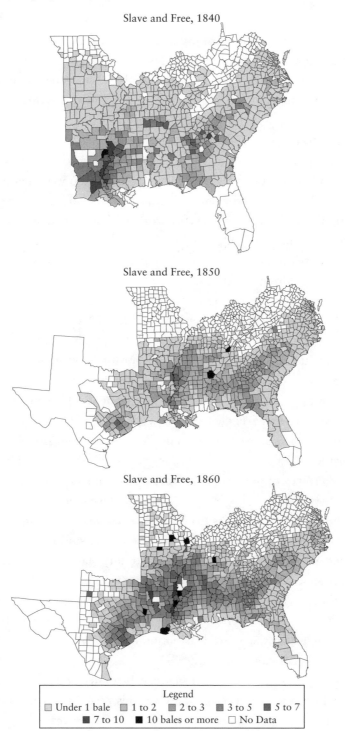

Slave and Free, 1840

Slave and Free, 1850

Slave and Free, 1860

Legend
Under 1 bale 1 to 2 2 to 3 3 to 5 5 to 7
7 to 10 10 bales or more No Data

Both our aggregate and county-level census data on bales per cotton worker are consistent with Foust and Swan's findings that bales per hand remained stagnant in the Old South during the 1850s. Lacking the longer view provided here, Foust and Swan were not able to see this decade as an exception to otherwise vibrant growth in the Southeast. The census data are also consistent with Wright's claim that the South's rapid growth in income between 1850 and 1860 was due, in part, to crop-year effects in 1849 and 1859. Surveying the county-level data shows that large areas of the South, and in particular a swath of prime land along the lower Mississippi, recorded fewer bales per worker in 1849 than in either 1839 or 1859. The Southeast did not suffer noticeable declines in 1849 relative to the other two years. This likely accounts for the Southeast's relatively poor showing during the 1850s.

The next step is to obtain a more detailed sense of the importance of the changes in bales per worker shown in Table 8.2 and Figure 8.4 relative to other factors, including the regional shifts in the labor force. To do this we conduct a decomposition exercise for total cotton output and average bales per worker using county-level data for 1840 to 1860. The results are presented in Table 8.2.[15] It asks what would happen to total output (panel A) and average bales per worker (panel B) if the labor force in the initial year achieved the bales per worker prevailing in a later year.

Panel A in Table 8.2 examines changes in total output, combining the effects of growth of the slave labor force, shifts in its regional allocation, and changes in bales per worker. It varies the slave labor force by county along the rows and the bales per worker by county across the columns. As an example, the entry "1,969" represents the sum of 1840 county bales per worker weighted by the 1840 county slave labor force numbers; it is a factual level of production. By way of contrast, "1,733" represents the sum of 1850 county bales per worker weighted by the 1840 county slave force numbers; it is the *counterfactual* estimate of production assuming that the 1840 distribution of laborers somehow attained the 1850 levels of bales per worker.

Total output increased from 1,969,000 bales in 1840 to 5,360,000 in 1860, or by 5.0 percent per annum. Over this period the aggregate slave labor force working in agriculture in these counties increased 2.1 percent

TABLE 8.2 *County-Level Decomposition of Total Output and Output per Worker, 1840–1860 (Counties Producing 1,000 Bales)*

Panel A: Total 400-Pound Bales (in thousands)

		Varying Bales per Worker			Slave Labor Force (in thousands)
		1840	1850	1860	
Varying	1840	1,969	*1,733*	*2,683*	960
Slave labor	1850		2,469	*3,924*	1,152
Force numbers	1860			5,360	1,460

Panel B: Average Bales per Worker

		Varying Bales per Worker		
		1840	1850	1860
Varying	1840	2.05	*·1.80*	*2.79*
Slave labor	1850		2.14	*3.41*
Force shares	1860			3.67

Notes: The figures in plain text are actual estimates; those in *italicized* text are *counterfactual* estimates; see text. Panel A varies the slave labor force by county along the rows and the bales per worker by county across the columns. Panel B varies the county slave labor force shares along the rows, controlling for overall size of the labor force.

Sources: Compiled based on county-level labor force numbers from Craig and Weiss (1998) and cotton production data from Craig, Haines, and Weiss (2000)

per annum, whereas the average bales per worker increased by 79 percent, or 2.9 percent per annum. Table 8.2 indicates that if the only change that happened was that the 1840 labor force in each county attained its 1860 levels of bales per worker, total production would have summed to just 2,683,000 bales. Growth would have been only 21 percent of what actually occurred between 1840 and 1860. To offer a different perspective, we perform a new calculation showing that if the cotton labor force grew from 960,000 slaves in 1840 to 1,460,000 (the 1860 number) but bales per worker remained at the 1840 level of 2.05, the total counterfactual level of cotton output would have risen by 1,025,000 bales. Thus the change in the size of the labor force holding bales per worker constant accounted for 30 percent of the increase in output that actually occurred between 1840 and 1860. Adding this to the 21 percent attributed to the changes in county-level bales per worker suggests that regional shifts together with interaction effects account for the remaining 49 percent of the change in output.[16] This is a far different story than that found in the cliometrics literature.

Panel B examines changes in average bales per worker. This is more relevant for an analysis of productivity, although of course the bales-per-worker measure embraces both specialization in cotton and efficiency in its production. Average bales per worker grew substantially between 1840 and 1860, with most of the change occurring in the 1850–1860 period. Over the 1840–1860 period, within-county changes in cotton per worker account for 46 percent of the total increase (that is, [2.79 − 2.05]/[3.67 − 2.05]). Over the 1850 to 1860 period, within-county changes account for 80 percent of the total change. In each comparison, the remainder may be interpreted as the effect of regional shifts (together with any interaction terms).[17] The summary view from this decomposition exercise is that, over the whole 1840 to 1860 period, within-county changes and regional shifts made roughly equal contributions to the large increase in average bales per worker. This result on the importance of regional shifts in explaining the increase in bales per worker in the Cotton South is many times larger than Easterlin (1975) and Weiss (1987) found for total agricultural output per worker nationally over the same period. For example, Weiss (1987, pp. 18–19) attributed about 10 percent of the increase in agricultural output per worker to shifts in the regional composition of the labor force.

One must be cautious in interpreting these results because the data clearly indicate that there were crop year effects. Although estimate of the actual bales per worker in 1850 was higher than in 1840, the counterfactual number (holding the 1840 labor force distribution constant) is about 12 percent below the actual 1840 number. Such crop year effects highlight an important advantage of using archival plantation records spanning many years (Olmstead and Rhode 2008a, 2008b). As another caveat, the analysis starts in 1840, and as we have seen above there are signs that productivity rose more rapidly in earlier decades.[18] It is notable that the patterns over time and across regions for the bales-per-worker series displayed in Table 8.1 are in remarkably close accord with independent evidence on daily cotton picking rates from our sample drawn from archival plantation documents discussed above. Our findings of sustained increases in picking efficiency and of substantial regional differences in the growth of picking efficiency lead to a new view of the broader contours of southern development such as the territorial expansion of the cotton-slave frontier.

TERRITORIAL EXPANSION

In the early 1790s, production of cotton was concentrated along the coast of Georgia and South Carolina. By 1839 the geographic center of the production of upland cotton was near Greensboro in west-central Alabama, and by 1859 it was across the Mississippi-Alabama border. The speed of westward expansion of cotton production in the antebellum period is all the more impressive when one realizes that over the next 60 years, the geographic center of production remained within the boundaries of the state of Mississippi. Annual series of commercial cotton output in Watkins (1908) show the movement away from the Atlantic Seaboard states (Virginia, North Carolina, South Carolina, Georgia, and Florida) began in earnest in the early 1810s. Their share of production fell from over 95 percent in 1810 to less than one-half by 1833 and to less than one-quarter by 1859.

There have been numerous claims and counterclaims about the effects of westward expansion on southern political and economic fortunes. In his classic *Slave Power*, Cairnes (1862) argued the slave system needed to expand to new lands to retain viability because slave production of cotton exhausted the fertility of existing soils. Ramsdell (1929) countered that the natural environmental limits to the system were being reached by the late 1850s, and continued expansion (for example, with the railroad allowing the spread into Texas) would herald slavery's doom by leading to "over production" and lower cotton and slave prices. Gray (1930) asserted that the availability of new highly productive lands on the frontier increased slave prices, which in turn drove down land prices in the older area. In addition, it made production in the older areas "unprofitable" but only in the relative sense that the opportunity costs of producing outside the Southwest were so high. According to Gray, the differentials in regional productivity and profitability led observers to mistakenly conclude "that slavery can thrive only on the basis of geographical expansion and a migratory economy, that slavery is adapted only to extensive agriculture, that it inevitably results in soil exhaustion, and that it cannot be profitable in general farming" (1930, p. 46). Genovese (1967, p. 247) posited that outmigration to the Southwest had a negative impact on productivity in the Southeast by retarding much-needed agricultural reforms and drawing away workers who could have been employed rebuilding depleted fields. Even Conrad and Meyer (1958, p. 115) were concerned with regional interactions, arguing that the success of the Old South was due to its "function as the slave-breeding area for the cotton-raising West." Throughout many traditional accounts, the expansion of slavery is intertwined with claims about profitability and viability and with broader strategic issues such as the maintenance of the South's power in the U.S. Senate.

In the 1960s and 1970s, most economic historians concluded that slavery was both profitable and viable, but many issues dealing with western settlement remained unresolved. There were three major lines of inquiry. The first debated how to interpret the estimates of regional per capita income growth displayed in Table 8.3. These statistics, developed by Easterlin (1961) and refined by Engerman (1967, pp. 85–87, 94–95), show the South as a whole grew faster than the national average between 1840 and 1860, but each of the South's three subregions grew as a slower pace. The high overall performance was due to a reallocation of population from the low-income Southeast to the higher-income Southwest, leading to the interpretation that the region's growth hinged crucially on territorial expansion as opposed to internal development. Antebellum southern growth, in the view of many scholars, was largely based on the exploitation of a natural resource that once settled could not be a source of future growth (Parker 1970a, p. 119; Wright 1976, p. 324; Weiman 1990, pp. 128, 131, and 147–148). By contrast, in the North the transfer of resources from the agricultural to the nonagricultural sectors rested on the growing productivity in the later sector. This view clearly needs to be refined. We do not dispute that there was relatively little industrialization in the South or that southerners were moving resources to more productive lands in the West. But technological changes were also at work in the South; specifically, biological innovations significantly increased cotton productivity, especially in the West. These rapid advances acted to keep

TABLE 8.3   *Per Capita Income before the Civil War in 1860 Prices*

	Total Population			Free Population		
	1840	1860	Growth Rate	1840	1860	Growth Rate
National Average	$96	128	1.44%	109	144	1.39%
North	109	141	1.29%	110	142	1.28%
Northeast	129	181	1.69%	130	183	1.71%
North Central	65	89	1.57%	66	90	1.55%
South	74	103	1.65%	105	150	1.78%
South Atlantic	66	84	1.21%	96	124	1.28%
East South Central	69	89	1.27%	92	124	1.49%
West South Central	151	184	0.99%	238	274	0.70%

Note: Free Population estimates treat slaves as intermediate goods with a maintenance cost of $20 per head per year.
Source: Engerman (1967), p. 87.

southern resources in agriculture and thus did not create a more diversified economic base as occurred in the North.

The second line of inquiry examined how the institution of slavery conditioned regional migration. Researchers estimated the interregional flows of the free and slave populations, focusing on ascertaining the fraction of slaves that went west with slave traders versus with their masters (Fogel and Engerman 1974, vol. 1, p. 48; McClelland and Zeckhauser 1983; Tadman 1989, p. 45; Pritchett 2001). A related literature has explored how property rights in slaves sped the expansion of slavery to the more productive Southwest. Attachment to family and place received far lower weight for a slave than for a free person in the migration calculus. In addition, the ability of large planters to capitalize (and borrow against) the enhanced value of their slaves' labor helped to finance migration and the purchase of large tracts of the most fertile western lands (Wright 1986, pp. 24–26; Weiman 1990, pp. 135–140; Weiman 1991, pp. 836–837; Wright 2006, pp. 66–70).

The third line of inquiry used general equilibrium models to analyze the impacts of adding land endowments on the prices of cotton and slaves, on the allocation of labor, and on the financial welfare of different southern interest groups. These exercises reached two novel conclusions that arose from (1) the South's position as the dominant supplier of a product with imperfectly elastic demand and (2) the role of the Old South as a seller of slaves to the New South. Given the assumption of an inelastic demand for southern cotton, Passell (1971) noted that westward expansion likely reduced southern income. Passell and Wright (1972) concluded that for each 10 percent addition of land, the *value* of the marginal product of slaves would fall by 1.2 to 1.8 percent and the average price of slaves by 1.3 to 1.9 percent. Lee (1977, 1978) found that the effect on the price of land in existing cotton areas was even greater. Based on their two-region general equilibrium model, Kotlikoff and Pinera (1977) similarly argued that producers in the Old South had good reason to fear adverse effects from westward expansion. If the elasticity of demand for the South's agricultural output were infinite, a doubling of land in the Southwest would have increased wealth in the Southeast by about 2 percent. Were the elasticity minus unity (meaning that the output price would have moved inversely in exact proportion to the level of southern output), a doubling of land in the Southwest would have decreased wealth in the Southeast by about 20 percent. These results supported the intuitions of Ramsdell rather than those of Cairnes.[19] This line of investigation has generally viewed westward expansion as a process of static reallocation of labor to inherently better soils rather than as a response to the increasing comparative advantage of the New South due to technological progress.

However, acknowledging the technological changes underway in the South casts a new light on this general equilibrium debate. The first important cotton variety innovations came from western plantations, and throughout the antebellum period southeastern planters relied on the Southwest for most breeding improvements. As history transpired, the South's ability to produce high-quality, easy-to-pick cotton was a key ingredient allowing the United States to capture international markets. The technological advances underlying this process depended on westward movement at least up to roughly 1850. Without the new southern cotton varieties, India and other areas would have produced closer substitutes and competed more effectively, thereby slowing the growth in demand for the U.S. product. This would have made the demand for U.S. cotton far more elastic and changed the general equilibrium calculations. Southeastern planters would have faced more price competition from foreigners and would have seen the value of their slaves fall without the compensating growth in the western demand for their chattel. The new seeds also created an additional channel, beyond the expansion of cultivated acreage facilitated by public land sales, to increase cotton output in the South. Thus allowing for biological innovation dramatically affects the general equilibrium story.

CONCLUSION

The antebellum southern development literature has long maintained that the southwestern cotton producers enjoyed a productivity advantage because they had inherently better land than southeastern producers. Moreover, the virgin land in the West had not yet been mined of its nutrients as had occurred in the East. The long-standing explanations of east-west productivity differences are seriously deficient. The rapid shift in production in the years before 1840 occurred precisely when southwestern cotton producers enjoyed a significant varietal advantage over southeastern producers. This is evident in two independent time series—data on daily picking per slave and data on annual bales produced per worker. The new biological technologies represented an improvement on a wide spectrum of soil types, but the new seeds were particularly suited to the fertile lands and climates where they originated. The large plantation regions of the Southwest had better soils to start with, but in a sense a stream of biological innovations made these soils increasingly better. Western movement did not just involve adding more acres of higher-quality land as assumed in the general equilibrium debate; the western shift was associated with moving to higher and higher production possibility frontiers.

It is well understood that in recent decades scientists have made spectacular advances in breeding higher-yielding plants, which laid the foundations of the green and genetic revolutions. But it is not common to think of early nineteenth-century farmers and scientists molding and remolding their plants to enhance performance. The cliometricians who pondered the data showing an increase in cotton bales per hand drew all sorts of inferences: this was evidence of an increase in nonlabor inputs, of the improved management skills of plantation owners and drivers (especially in utilizing the gang system), of the transfer of production to better land, or of differential weather between two data points or perhaps reflected the changing composition of output and a resulting miscalculation of the true size of the workforce in cotton. The recent cliometrics debate never seriously considered whether technological change and improved productivity, the stuff of modern economic growth, led to increased output per worker in the Cotton South. Yet, this is precisely what happened. The development of improved seeds represented a form of endogenous technological change in response to emerging economic opportunities in the region. The spatial pattern of the productivity advances help explain why regional shifts in the location of production were far more important than previously thought in explaining the overall growth in southern cotton production, the increase in cotton per worker, and the dynamics of plantation efficiency. Finally, allowing for technological change cast an entirely new light on the general equilibrium literature, suggesting that western movement was less adverse to southeastern interests as previous estimates suggest.

NOTES

We have benefited from data graciously provided by Lee Craig, Michael Haines, and Thomas Weiss and the helpful comments of Stanley Engerman, Price Fishback, Joshua Rosenbloom, David Weiman, Thomas Weiss, and Gavin Wright. This research has been supported by NSF SES-0550913, SES-0551130.

1. We follow the convention of defining the Old South as including the members of the original 13 colonies (Georgia, North Carolina, South Carolina, and Virginia) and the New South as those states entering the Union after independence (Alabama, Arkansas, Louisiana, Mississippi, Tennessee, and Texas). The one exception is that Florida is treated as a part of the Old South.

The weighted index is calculated as $W_t = 1/[\theta_t/OS_t + (1 - \theta_t)/NS_t]$, where θt is the Old South output weight in year t calculated from state-level cotton output from Watkins (1908), OSt is our Old South index, and NSt is our New South index. The weighted index differs from the All South index because our plantation sample contains disproportionately more observations in the New South. We have tried higher-order polynomials in time with essentially the same results.

2. Fogel argues that small slaveholders (those with 1 to 15 slaves) could not effectively capture the benefits of the gang system, so plantations with more than 15 slaves account for nearly all of the productivity advantage. Large plantations were only slightly more efficient than intermediate size units. See also Toman (2005).

3. Fogel and Engerman (1977) argue their main findings for 1859 would hold even if cotton productivity were substantially lower in that crop year. Wright (2006) finds significant differences in the production relationships between the 1859 Parker-Gallman sample and the 1849 Foust sample.

4. The approach seems at odds with the finding in Fogel, Galantine, and Manning (1992, p. 200) that "land was not a major constraint on cotton production." Fogel (1989, p. 71) notes that just 6 percent of the improved acreage in the Cotton South was planted in the crop and that "the surging demand for cotton during the 1850s put far more pressure on the South's labor supply than on its supply of land."

5. Fogel and Engerman also include an estimate of the effect of western settlement calculated based on combining state-level output shares and data on average antebellum cotton yields from the U.S. Commissioner of Agriculture (1867, p. 415).

6. In this sample, the coefficient of variation of the ratio of cotton to improved land is greater than one in both 1850 and 1860, indicating wide variation in the cross-section.

7. David Weiman (1990, p. 147) also writes of "stagnant agricultural technology" in antebellum southern staples production. Post (2003, p. 296) recounts the bare outlines of the importance of Petit Gulf and of mechanization, but then claims (p. 300): "There is no evidence of systematic and widespread introduction of labour-saving technology in cotton production."

8. Many factors might combine to explain her findings, but improved seeds took center stage. Parker (1979, pp. 228–244, esp. p. 235) also pondered the possibility of technological changes in southern agriculture but did not pursue this notion. Metzer (1975, pp. 123–150) did examine daily picking rates on the Leak plantation in Tippah, Mississippi, over the 1841–1860 period in order to investigate the treatment of pregnant women. In the spirit of our work on wheat, the calculations of increased output per worker do not fully capture the effects of biological innovations because they do not account for the Red Queen effect. In addition to maintenance problems, Whartenby's estimates do not account for the difficulties growers would have faced pushing out the frontiers of the Cotton Belt without varieties tailored for the new geoclimatic conditions (Olmstead and Rhode 2002; Olmstead and Rhode 2008a, pp. 98–154).

9. Charleston, South Carolina, *City Gazette* and *Daily Advertiser*. August 27, 1810; "Southwestern Georgia," *Macon Weekly Telegraph*, January 27, 1857. Among the prominent antebellum estimates of bales-per-hand ratios are Woodbury (1836, p. 14) and DeBow (1854, vol. 1, p. 175). The emphasis on bales per worker as opposed to bales per acre is fairly common and in line with Wright's depiction of planters as first and foremost "labor lords." There exists a problem in comparing bale-per-worker quotes over time; bale weights generally increased over the antebellum period. Watkins (1895) reports their net weight averaged about 225 pounds in 1800, 339 in 1830, and 461 in 1860.

10. Fogel and Engerman (1971, pp. 315–316) argue the soaring cotton output per worker between 1850 and 1860 "strongly suggests that other inputs required for cotton production increased more rapidly than labor."

11. Weiss (1987) and Craig and Weiss (1998) created state and county estimates of the number of agricultural slaves in the labor force, whereas Lebergott (1966) and David (1967) worked only with national figures. Lebergott and David assumed that 95 percent of slaves (age 10 years and over) lived in rural areas and that 87 to 90 percent of these slaves worked in agriculture. As a check against the conventional approach, the Craig-Weiss numbers imply for 1860 that 48.5 percent of *all* slaves in the ten-state Cotton South worked in agriculture.

12. We constructed the regional cotton production data by multiplying total cotton output found in the *Historical Statistics of the United States* by three-year-moving averages of state production shares drawn from Watkins (1908, passim). Our methodology assumes that, for each year, Watkins reported bales of the same weight for each state (Fogel et al. 1992, p. 193 implicitly treats the Watkins data in the same way). If bale weights are not standardized over space and if bales from the Gulf ports were initially heavier than those of the Atlantic ports and if the weights converged (as data from the Liverpool trade suggest), then the actual interregional cotton-pounds-per-worker gaps in the early period would have been even greater than our series indicates. In addition, the actual growth of total output and output per worker in the Old South would be greater than what is indicated.

13. The bales-per-worker statistics reported here are based on more highly aggregated data than those of Foust and Swan (1970). Nonetheless, in the comparison of similar regions, the correlation coefficient between the Foust and Swan numbers and our census bales-per-slave ratios is 0.66 over the combined 1850 and 1860 samples. Comparing our national aggregate numbers with those presented by Whartenby (1977, p. 54) for 1800 to 1840 reveals her numbers start higher in 1800 but reach roughly the same range as ours by 1840.

14. This result supports Fogel's (1989, p. 71) conclusion: "Analysis of census data reveals no evidence of the decline in labor productivity on farms of the Old South that would have been caused by a decline in the quantity or quality of land per worker." Part of the increase in bales per worker in the Old South may have been caused by movement to better lands in western Georgia and elsewhere within the region.

15. Our analysis concentrates on those counties producing 1,000 bales or more. The exercise accounts for changes in county borders over time by forming separate panels for 1840, 1850, and 1860 of consistently defined counties and summing the production and labor force numbers within these entities over the sample years. These panels are unbalanced because the process of western settlement created numerous new counties over time. The absence of bales-per-worker data until a county was settled and began to produce cotton necessitates conducting the analysis forward, not backward. That is, it is not meaningful to consider the cells in Table 8.2 below the diagonal.

16. Note that this (and all other) decomposition exercise mechanically shifts some values while holding constant others, which may not reflect their true underlying relationships. For example, average output per worker in a county might fall as the local labor force increased.

17. There is some evidence of an interaction effect (specifically of greater changes in cotton per worker in the new areas with increasing labor force shares) in the more rapid growth between 1850 and 1860 using the 1850 weights than using the 1840 weights.

18. The lower estimate of the relative importance of regional shifts in the 1850s suggests that literature's focus on the 1850s has generated conclusions not representative of longer-run development patterns.

19. For a counterview, see Schmitz and Schaefer (1981). The cliometrics literature has the relationship between territorial expansion and market power backward in important cases such as the annexation of Texas. The pursuit of continued dominance in the cotton trade stimulated rather than deterred expansion. Advocates for annexation argued adding Texas was necessary to maintain the country's "cotton monopoly," especially in the face of British efforts to develop alternative sources of supply, including those relying on free labor. Cotton production in Texas was likely to expand rapidly after 1840 regardless of whether it joined the United States. Controlling the world's "most favored" cotton lands enhanced

the South's commercial and strategic positions in line with what was later known as "King Cotton thinking." See Walker (1844, pp. 15–17) and Crapol (2006, pp. 65–69).

REFERENCES

Anderson, Ralph V. (1974). "Labor Utilization and Productivity, Diversification and Self-Sufficiency, Southern Plantations, 1800–1840." PhD diss., University of North Carolina.

Anderson, Ralph V., and Robert E. Gallman (1977). "Slaves as Fixed Capital: Slave Labor and Southern Economic Development." *Journal of American History* 64: 24–46.

Cairnes, John E. (1862). *Slave Power: Its Character, Career and Probable Designs, Being an Attempt to Explain the American Contest.* London: J. Chapman.

Campbell, John Douglas (1988). "The Gender Division of Labor, Slave Reproduction, and the Slave Family Economy on Southern Cotton Plantations, 1800–1864." PhD diss., University of Minnesota.

Carter, Susan B., Scott Sigmund Gartner, Michael R. Haines, Alan L. Olmstead, Richard Sutch, and Gavin Wright, eds. (2006). *Historical Statistics of the United States: Earliest Times to the Present, Millennial Edition.* New York: Cambridge University Press.

Conrad, Alfred H., and John R. Meyer (1958). "The Economics of Slavery in the Ante-Bellum South." *Journal of Political Economy* 66: 95–122.

Conrad, Alfred H., and John R. Meyer (1964). *The Economics of Slavery and Other Studies in Econometric History.* Chicago: Aldine.

Craig, Lee A., Michael R. Haines, and Thomas Weiss (2000). "U.S. Censuses of Agriculture, by County, 1840–1880" [Computer file]. Raleigh: Unpublished files provided by the authors, Department of Economics, North Carolina State University.

Craig, Lee A., and Thomas Weiss (1998). "Rural Agricultural Workforce by County, 1800 to 1900" [Computer file]. Available at http://eh.net/databases/agriculture/.

Crapol, Edward P. (2006). *John Tyler, the Accidental President.* Chapel Hill: University of North Carolina Press.

David, Paul (1967). "The Growth of Real Product in the United States before 1840: New Evidence, Controlled Conjectures." *Journal of Economic History* 27: 151–197.

DeBow, J. D. B. (1854). "Cotton and Its Prospects." In *Industrial Resources, Statistics, etc. of the United States*, vol. 1. New York: Appleton, pp. 174–178.

Easterlin, Richard A. (1961). "Regional Income Trends, 1840–1950." In *American Economic History*, edited by Seymour Harris. New York: McGraw-Hill, pp. 525–547.

Easterlin, Richard A. (1975). "Farm Production and Income in Old and New Areas at Mid-Century." In *Essays in Nineteenth Century Economic History: The Old Northwest*, edited by David C. Klingaman and Richard K. Vedder. Athens: Ohio University Press, pp. 77–117.

Eltis, David, Frank D. Lewis, and Kenneth L. Sokoloff (2004). *Slavery in the Development of the Americas.* New York: Cambridge University Press.

Engerman, Stanley L. (1967). "The Effects of Slavery upon the Southern Economy: A Review of the Recent Debate." *Explorations in Entrepreneurial History* 4: 71–97.

Engerman, Stanley L. (2000). "Slavery and Its Consequences for the South in the Nineteenth Century." In *Cambridge Economic History of the United States*, edited by Stanley Engerman and Robert E. Gallman. Cambridge: Cambridge University Press, pp. 329–366.

Engerman, Stanley L. (2007). *Slavery, Emancipation, and Freedom: Comparative Perspectives.* Baton Rouge: Louisiana State University Press.

Fogel, Robert W. (1989). *Without Consent or Contract: The Rise and Fall of American Slavery*. New York: Norton.

Fogel, Robert W. (2003). *The Slavery Debates, 1952–1990: A Memoir*. Baton Rouge: Louisiana State University Press.

Fogel, Robert W., and Stanley L. Engerman (1971). "The Economics of Slavery." In *Re-Interpretation of American Economic History*, edited by Robert W. Fogel and Stanley L. Engerman. New York: Harper and Row, pp. 331–341.

Fogel, Robert W., and Stanley L. Engerman (1974). *Time on the Cross: The Economics of American Negro Slavery*. 2 vols. Boston: Little, Brown.

Fogel, Robert W., and Stanley L. Engerman (1977). "Explaining the Relative Efficiency of Slave Agriculture in the Antebellum South." *American Economic Review* 67: 275–296.

Fogel, Robert W., and Stanley L. Engerman (1980). "Explaining the Relative Efficiency of Slave Agriculture in the Antebellum South: Reply." *American Economic Review* 70: 672–690.

Fogel, Robert W., and Stanley L. Engerman, eds. (1992a). *Without Consent or Contract: The Rise and Fall of American Slavery*, vol. 3: *Technical Papers*, vol. 1:, *Markets and Production*. New York: Norton.

Fogel, Robert W., and Stanley L. Engerman, eds. (1992b). *Without Consent or Contract: The Rise and Fall of American Slavery*, vol. 4: *Technical Papers*, vol. 2: *Conditions of Slave Life and the Transition to Freedom*. New York: Norton.

Fogel, Robert W., Ralph A. Galantine, and Richard L. Manning, eds. (1992). *Without Consent or Contract: The Rise and Fall of American Slavery*, vol. 2: *Evidence and Methods*. New York: Norton.

Foust, James D. (1967). "The Yeoman Farmer and Westward Expansion of U.S. Cotton Production." *Journal of Economic History* 27: 611–614.

Foust, James D. (1975). *The Yeoman Farmer and Westward Expansion of U. S. Cotton Production*. New York: Arno Press.

Foust, James D., and Dale E. Swan (1970). "Productivity and Profitability of Antebellum Slave Labor: A Micro-Approach." *Agricultural History* 44: 39–62.

Gallman, Robert E. (1970). "Self-Sufficiency in the Cotton Economy of the Antebellum South." *Agricultural History* 46: 5–24.

Genovese, Eugene D. (1967). *The Political Economy of Slavery: Studies in the Economy and Society of the Slave South*. New York: Vintage.

Gray, Lewis C. (1930). "Economic Efficiency and Competitive Advantages of Slavery under the Plantation System." *Agricultural History* 4: 31–47.

Gray, Lewis C. (1933). *History of Agriculture in the Southern United States to 1860*, vol. 2. Washington, DC: Carnegie Institution.

Hietala, Thomas R. (1985). *Manifest Design: Anxious Aggrandizement in Late Jacksonian America*. Ithaca, NY: Cornell University Press.

Kotlikoff, Laurence, and Sebastian Pinera (1977). "The Old South's Stake in the Inter-regional Movement of Slaves, 1850–1860." *Journal of Economic History* 37: 434–450.

Lebergott, Stanley (1966). "Labor Force and Employment, 1800–1960." In *Output, Employment, and Productivity in the United States after 1800: Studies in Income and Wealth*, vol. 30, edited by Dorothy S. Brady. New York: Columbia University Press, pp. 117–204.

Lebergott, Stanley (1984). *The Americans: An Economic Record.* New York: Norton.

Lee, Susan P. (1977). *The Westward Movement of the Cotton Economy, 1840–1860: Perceived Interests and Economic Reality.* New York: Arno Press.

Lee, Susan P. (1978). "Antebellum Land Expansion: Another View." *Agricultural History* 52: 488–502.

Lewis, Frank, and Kenneth Sokoloff, eds. (2005). *Factor Endowments, Labor and Economic Growth in the Americas.* Cambridge: Cambridge University Press.

McClelland, Peter D., and Richard Zeckhauser (1983). *Demographic Dimensions of the New Republic: American Interregional Migration, Vital Statistics, and Manumissions, 1800–1860.* New York: Cambridge University Press.

Mendenhall, Marjorie S. (1940). "A History of Agriculture in South Carolina, 1790 to 1860." PhD diss., University of North Carolina at Chapel Hill.

Metzer, Jacob (1975). "Rational Management, Modern Business Practices, and Economies of Scale in Antebellum Southern Plantation." *Explorations in Economic History* 12: 123–150.

Moore, John Hebron (1956). "Cotton Breeding in the Old South." *Agricultural History* 30: 95–104.

Moore, John Hebron (1958). *Agriculture in Ante-Bellum Mississippi.* New York: Bookman Associates.

Moore, John Hebron (1988). *The Emergence of the Cotton Kingdom in the Old Southwest: Mississippi, 1770–1860.* Baton Rouge: Louisiana State University Press.

Olmstead, Alan L., and Paul W. Rhode (2002). "The Red Queen and the Hard Reds." *Journal of Economic History* 62: 929–966.

Olmstead, Alan L., and Paul W. Rhode (2008a). *Creating Abundance: Biological Innovation and American Agricultural Development.* New York: Cambridge University Press.

Olmstead, Alan L., and Paul W. Rhode (2008b). "Biological Innovation and Productivity Growth in the Antebellum Cotton Economy." *Journal of Economic History* 68: 1123–1171.

Parker, William N. (1970a). "Slavery and Southern Economic Development: An Hypothesis and Some Evidence." In *The Structure of the Cotton Economy of the Antebellum South*, edited by William N. Parker. Washington, DC: Agricultural History Society, pp. 115–126.

Parker, William N., ed. (1970b). *The Structure of the Cotton Economy of the Antebellum South.* Washington, DC: Agricultural History Society.

Parker, William N. (1979). "Labor Productivity in Cotton Farming: The History of a Research." *Agricultural History* 53: 228–244.

Parker, William N., and Robert E. Gallman (1991). "Southern Farms Study, 1860" [Computer file]. ICPSR07419-v1. Ann Arbor, MI: Inter-university Consortium for Political and Social Research [distributor]. doi:10.3886/ICPSR07419.

Passell, Peter (1971). "The Impact of Cotton Land Distribution on the Antebellum Economy." *Journal of Economic History* 31: 917–937.

Passell, Peter, and Gavin Wright (1972). "The Effects of Pre–Civil War Territorial Expansion on the Price of Slaves." *Journal of Political Economy* 80: 1188–1202.

Post, Charles (2003). "Plantation Slavery and Economic Development in the Antebellum Southern United States." *Journal of Agrarian Change* 3: 289–332.

Pritchett, Jonathan B. (2001). "Quantitative Estimates of the United States Interregional Slave Trade, 1820–1860." *Journal of Economic History* 61: 467–475.

Ramsdell, Charles W. (1929). "The Natural Limits of Slavery Expansion." *Mississippi Valley Historical Review* 16: 151–171.

Schaefer, Donald (1983). "The Effect of the 1859 Crop Year upon Relative Productivity in the Antebellum Cotton South." *Journal of Economic History* 43: 851–865.

Scheiber, Harry N., Harold G. Vatter, and Harold U. Faulkner (1976). *American Economic History*. New York: Harper and Row.

Schmitz, Mark, and Donald Schaefer (1981). "Paradox Lost: Westward Expansion and Slave Prices before the Civil War." *Journal of Economic History* 41: 402–407.

Sutch, Richard (1965). "The Profitability of Ante Bellum Slavery—Revisited." *Southern Economic Journal* 31: 365–383.

Tadman, Michael (1989). *Speculators and Slaves: Masters, Traders, and Slaves in the Old South*. Madison: University of Wisconsin Press.

Toman, J. T. (2005). "The Gang System and Comparative Advantage." *Explorations in Economic History* 42: 310–323.

U.S. Commissioner of Agriculture (1867). *1867 Annual Report*. Washington, DC: Government Printing Office.

Wailes, B. C. L. (1854). *Report of the Agriculture and Geology of Mississippi, Embracing a Sketch of the Social and Natural History of the State*. Jackson, MS: E. Barksdale.

Walker, Robert J. (1844). *Letter of Mr. Walker of Mississippi, Relative to the Reannexation of Texas*. Philadelphia: Mifflin and Perry. Available at http://www.tsl.state.tx.us/exhibits/annexation/part4/walker_letter_1844_14-15.html.

Ware, Jacob Osborn (1950). "Origin, Rise and Development of American Upland Cotton Varieties and Their Status at Present." Mimeo, University of Arkansas College of Agriculture, Agricultural Experiment Station.

Watkins, James L. (1895). *Production and Price of Cotton for One Hundred Years*. U.S. Department of Agriculture, Division of Statistics, Miscellaneous Series Bulletin No. 9. Washington, DC: Government Printing Office.

Watkins, James L. (1969 [1908]). *King Cotton*. New York: Negro Universities Press.

Weiman, David E. (1990). "Staple Crops and Slave Plantations: Alternative Perspectives on Regional Development in the Antebellum Cotton South." In *Agriculture and National Development: Views on the Nineteenth Century*, edited by Lou Ferleger. Ames: Iowa State University Press, pp. 119–161.

Weiman, David E. (1991). "Peopling the Land by Lottery? The Market in Public Lands and the Regional Differentiation of Territory on the Georgia Frontier." *Journal of Economic History* 51: 835–860.

Weiss, Thomas (1987). "The Farm Labor Force by Region, 1820–1860: Revised Estimates and Implications for Growth." National Bureau of Economic Research Working Paper No. 2438. Cambridge, MA: National Bureau of Economic Research.

Whartenby, Franklee Gilbert (1977). *Land and Labor Productivity in United States Cotton Production, 1800–1840*. New York: Arno Press.

Woodbury, Levi J. (1836). "Tables and Notes on the Cultivation, Manufacture, and Foreign Trade of Cotton." *Executive Documents*, 4, no. 146 (March 4), 24th Cong., 1st sess.

Wright, Gavin (1976). "Prosperity, Progress, and American Slavery." In *Reckoning with Slavery: A Critical Study in the Quantitative History of American Negro Slavery*, by Paul A. David, Herbert G. Gutman, Richard Sutch, Peter Temin, and Gavin Wright. New York: Oxford University Press, pp. 302–336.

Wright, Gavin (1978). *The Political Economy of the Cotton South: Households, Markets, and Wealth in the Nineteenth Century*. New York: Norton.

Wright, Gavin (1979). "The Efficiency of Slavery: Another Interpretation." *American Economic Review* 69: 219–226.

Wright, Gavin (1986). *Old South, New South: Revolutions in the Southern Economy since the Civil War*. New York: Basic Books.

Wright, Gavin (2006). *Slavery and American Economic Development*. Baton Rouge: Louisiana State University Press.

CHAPTER 9

Banking on the Periphery: The Cotton South, Systemic Seasonality, and the Limits of National Banking Reform

SCOTT A. REDENIUS AND DAVID F. WEIMAN

UNDER THE NATIONAL BANKING SYSTEM from 1863 to 1913, the United States experienced a serious banking panic roughly every decade (Sprague 1910; Miron 1986). Yet despite this anomalous record of financial and economic turbulence, the federal government did not take the decisive step toward comprehensive reform until the panic of 1907. Less than a year later Congress adopted the Aldrich-Vreeland Act. Establishing the National Monetary Commission, the act mobilized leading policy makers, bankers, and economists to propose "what changes are necessary or desirable in the monetary system" (White 1911, app. A; Wicker 2005).

Through a parallel private organization representing "the general business public," J. Laurence Laughlin weighed in on the policy debate.[1] In his influential edited volume *Banking Reform* (1912), Laughlin elaborated the consensus view on the defects of the National Banking System and emphasized its negative impact on Main, not just Wall, Street. Its artificial note-issue and reserve regulations, he argued, diminished the elasticity of currency but more importantly banks' short-term credit supplies. The latter constraint was particularly evident during the harvest and crop-moving seasons in the fall and early winter months. Faced with peak demands for credit, banks in agricultural regions turned to their money center correspondents for accommodation but paid a premium for increasingly scarce bank reserves, which they passed on to their farm customers. And, he noted, the resulting financial strains on correspondents increased their vulnerability to runs and panics.[2]

The excess seasonal demands for credit, Laughlin (1912, esp. chap. 19) observed, were especially acute in the cotton-growing states. Like other field crops, the cotton culture was subject to wide seasonal variations in labor and other input requirements with the peak period occurring at harvest time. What distinguished the Cotton South from other agricultural regions, however, was its "colonial-style" dependence on the production of the fleecy staple for domestic and international markets (Fox-Genovese and Genovese 1983, p. 50; Wright 1986, pp. 22–23). The cotton culture, although "not [even] the totality of southern agriculture," was nonetheless the largest sector of the regional economy. Moreover, as Wright notes, it "defined the opportunities and pace of [Southern] *economic* life" (Wright 1986, p. 59; emphasis added). In other words, cotton's impact including its seasonal rhythms was systemic, afflicting related segments of the cotton economy and its pivotal financial intermediaries.

In the spirit of Wright's regional perspective, we explain this systemic seasonality by institutional failure, not simply a "lack of banking capital" (Laughlin 1912, p. 106; Ransom and Sutch 1972; James 1981). We emphasize the dilemmas of collective choice in determining industry standards in the Cotton South. In the case of the cotton industry itself, the region lacked a centralized marketing organization like the Chicago Board of Trade that could galvanize the collective interests of its members and affiliates to develop, diffuse, and ultimately institutionalize through state policy uniform quality standards for grading commercial crops (Rothstein 1966; Cronon 1991, pp. 114–119). By enhancing the information and so economic value of local warehouse receipts, this innovation would have decoupled the link between financial flows into and actual cotton shipments out of the region and so lessened banks' financial burdens during the marketing season.

In the banking industry, local intermediaries confronted the opposite problem of uniform national standards poorly adapted to regional conditions. During the era of Republican rule the federal government enacted national banking policies designed to integrate monetarily the increasingly interdependent regions of the Northeast and Midwest— not surprisingly the base of the Republican Party (Sylla 1969; Redenius 2007b; Egnal 2009). The federal standard for bank formation and note issues bolstered by Republicans' increasing commitment to the gold standard put peripheral agricultural regions like the Cotton South in a monetary straitjacket.[3] These institutional failures "conspired," to paraphrase

Kuznets (1933, p. 9), to transmit the seasonality of the cotton culture to the marketing-shipment stage of the cotton cycle, and amplified local banks' seasonal cash and credit demands and the seasonal premium on short-term interest rates.

We develop our institutional thesis in three sections. In the first section we elaborate our institutional perspective on systemic seasonality in the Cotton South, and through a simple model we show how this systemic seasonality interacted with a rigid national banking policy to increase the liquidity costs of financial intermediation in the region. The second and third sections document the greater systemic seasonality in the Cotton South as compared to a mixed-farming region in the North and its negative impacts on the banking system. Because of the seasonal rhythms of the dominant cotton culture, banks were burdened with excess and insufficient reserves at different times of the year and so incurred greater actual and opportunity costs in accommodating their customers' short-term credit demands.

In the conclusion we return to Laughlin's diagnosis of the mutual problems afflicting the national and southern banking systems but find only mixed support for his policy prescription. Our evidence affirms the disproportionate impact of Cotton South banks on the seasonal liquidity strains in the New York and national money markets prior to the founding of the Federal Reserve System (FRS). Moreover, the design of the FRS along the lines proposed by Laughlin effectively relaxed the macro constraint on seasonal supplies of currency and reserves and in turn smoothed the seasonal variation in interest rates in the New York and national money markets. Yet, the FRS could not remedy the structural constraints on southern banks, which were firmly rooted in the region's historic economic dependence on the cotton culture.

SYSTEMIC SEASONAL CONSTRAINTS ON "COUNTRY" BANKS

Despite their ambivalence, postbellum farmers relied on commercial banks for the most vital economic services. Besides supplying farmers with the very means of payment to conduct their daily transactions, banks were the principal source of short-term credit to finance current production, either directly or through other intermediaries like the local country store.[4] Commercial banks also provided "intermediate" credit for longer-term investments, but in this realm they faced greater competition from other sources: wealthier neighbors, local savings banks and trust companies, and distant life insurance and land companies.

Banks' short-term credit instruments ranged from unsecured promissory notes (with or without an endorsement) to collateralized loans backed by maturing crops, chattel, and land. Despite these differences, they functioned like a line of credit with a fixed maturity or repayment date. Once banks approved the loan, farmers could make payments against their accounts until they reached the borrowing ceiling or end of the term (although they could renegotiate both). From a bank's perspective, then, these short-term credit instruments functioned like a demand deposit, effectively increasing borrowers' current account balances against which they could write checks or purchase bank drafts on demand.

This parallel underlies the potential synergy or complementarity between banks' deposit and short-term credit services, as both draw on the same pool of liquid reserve assets and so share a fixed implicit or opportunity cost. Banks could realize this benefit or economies of scope, only if their customers' deposit withdrawals and short-term borrowing were weakly (better yet, negatively) correlated.[5] Under these theoretical conditions, banks could effectively fund customers' liquidity demands, whether deposit withdrawals or short-term borrowing, with the influx of funds from new deposits and loan repayments. In turn, they could economize on their reserve assets by holding fewer reserves against their outstanding loans and even offering longer terms to their customers (see also Morrison 1966; Baltensperger 1974, 1980).

Writing in the interwar period, agricultural economists grasped these necessary conditions for a more efficient rural banking sector but expressed them concretely in terms of the "type of agriculture" or "agricultural system" (Garlock 1932). Banks' reserve assets, Garlock (1932, p. 2) observed, would constitute a stable "revolving fund," but only under ideal conditions such as in the diversified crop and livestock regions of Iowa. By combining hog, cattle, and dairy production with more seasonal crop cultures, farmers evened out their labor demands over the year but also their receipts and expenses. Consequently they generated the precise pattern of mutually offsetting flows of funds into and out of local banks, and in turn relatively stable levels of outstanding deposits, loans, and hence reserves.[6]

These "banking methods" were "poorly adapted" to other agricultural regions like the Cotton South, where producers depended on a single staple crop—a monoculture for short (Garlock 1932; Wall 1932). In this case deposit withdrawals and short-term borrowing were highly correlated, as farmers' expenditures but especially their incomes were more "periodic," that is, seasonally concentrated. The experience of Texas banks in 1925, depicted in Figure 9.1, vividly illustrates the point. Drawing on their credit lines, farmers steadily accumulated short-term debts from February through June (as shown by the "total borrowed" series). They could only discharge their mounting obligations "periodically," after the cotton harvest in late August through early November (as shown by the sudden increase in the "total repaid"). On net, then, banks' total outstanding loans series followed a pronounced inverted U-shape pattern, peaking in July and August.

To fill this seasonal funding gap, banks turned to correspondents in distant money centers, mainly New York, for accommodation. By contrast, after the marketing but before the next spring planting season, banks were flush with deposits but faced diminished demands for short-term production credit. To meet future seasonal excess demands for liquidity, however, they could not commit these funds to longer-term agricultural loans but instead held them in "quick" assets, initially excess bankers' balances and later in the period call loans and commercial paper.

Banks in monocultural regions, in other words, functioned more like brokers, bundling their customers' loans and deposits for ultimate placement with or by their correspondents. Moreover, they paid a premium for this long-distance financial intermediation, which they passed on to their customers in the form of higher rates and shorter maturities. To secure a credit line, New York correspondents required banks to hold compensating balances, equal to 20 to 25 percent of their seasonal borrowing levels. And they charged an average of 6 percent interest on seasonal

FIGURE 9.1   *Cumulative Monthly Percentage of Amounts Borrowed and Repaid by Texas Cotton Farmers in 1925*

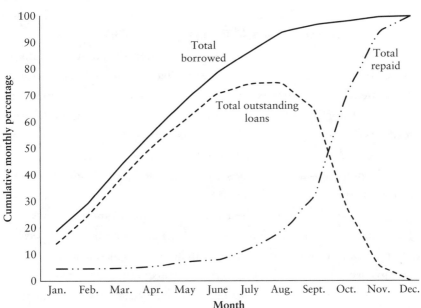

Source: Moulton (1931), p. 5.

loans, as compared to the standard 2 percent interest paid on excess bankers' balances.[7]

It is tempting to explain the seasonal constraints on Cotton South banks by the peak labor and other demands at harvest time. Yet, along this dimension, the cotton crop was no more seasonal than other commercially important crops like wheat and corn (see the next section). We do, however, find clear evidence of a more *systemic* seasonality that permeated subsequent stages of cotton's economic cycle. Numerous studies of rural banking in the early twentieth-century Cotton South remarked on the rapid turnover of the cotton crop right after it was picked (Copeland 1912, p. 180; Macklin 1922, p. 150; U.S. Department of Agriculture 1922, p. 387; Carson 1923, pp. 169, 321). Often under pressure from creditors whether country stores or local banks, growers immediately delivered their crops to primary market centers, where the crops were ginned, pressed, and sold to local buyers.

The seasonality of local marketing accelerated loan repayments by farmers and country stores but did little to replenish the liquid reserve assets of country banks. Despite the increasing centralization of cotton marketing among specialized dealers in distant commercial centers, many local buyers operated independently and relied on country banks to finance their purchases via credit lines or demand notes.[8] When cleared and settled by local banks, these transactions only transformed one kind of cotton-related loan into another on their balance sheets. In other words, they effectively extended the maturity on banks' outstanding cotton-related loans until late December or early January, and so their liquidity pressures and demands for accommodation from New York correspondents.[9]

Of the several reasons suggested for this "hand-to-mouth" marketing of cotton, these studies all fault local, independent warehouses.[10] Because of their humble origins, independent warehouses supplied inadequate storage capacity, which could not effectively protect crops from the elements and theft and increased the risks and insurance costs of storing them locally. As important, they lacked the environmental conditions and expertise to grade crops according to industry standards (Olmstead and Rhode 2003; see also Moulton 1931, p. 187). Backed by crops of uncertain quality and value, their warehouse receipts conveyed limited economic information and so were heavily discounted outside their immediate market area. Consequently the burden of financing cotton inventories fell on local banks, which could inspect and approve the receipts as collateral for loans to local merchants and other intermediaries. In the Midwest, by contrast, standardized receipts issued by licensed and regulated local warehouses were the foundation of a complex chain of financing that extended to regional commercial centers and funded the more "orderly" delivery of crops to final markets (Harris 1911; Cronon 1991, esp. chap. 3).

Perhaps more symptom than cause, the region's sparse fragmented network of warehouses can be traced back to the pre–Civil War period and the region's formative institution, the slave plantation.[11] Because of their scale, plantations bypassed local intermediaries and transacted directly with cotton factors in interior and coastal port cities. They favored these more personalized marketing arrangements to capitalize on fine differences in crop qualities and expected factors to represent their interests in negotiating sales. Despite the "decline of cotton factorage" after the Civil War, postbellum planters continued to rely on this more decentralized marketing system, in which cotton factors functioned primarily as commission merchants and peddled actual samples of stored bales to meet the more refined demands of textile manufacturers.[12] Unlike in the Midwest, then, there were no dominant marketing institutions and intermediaries that could coordinate the development, diffusion, and enforcement of uniform standards for grading crops, often under the auspices of state governments.[13]

After Reconstruction Cotton South banks faced a second institutional constraint, which reinforced the economic burden of their more chronic problem of systemic seasonality. The Republican "revolution from above" not only wiped out the region's main type of collateral but integrated it into a common currency union even though it was not an ideal candidate for membership.[14] Regulated by uniform National Banking Acts after 1865 as well as a tighter gold standard constraint after 1873, banks in the region operated in a more confined monetary environment, characterized by highly inelastic supplies of currency and reserves.

Combined with this "macro" money constraint, the region's acute seasonal demands for cash and credit reinforced the seasonal swings in New York call loan and interbank borrowing and lending rates.[15] We illustrate this point through a simple sorting model in which banks in core (New York City) and peripheral (Cotton South) regions compete for a relatively fixed supply of bank reserves (given by the length of the horizontal axis in Figure 9.2). Each point on the horizontal axis represents an allocation of reserves between New York banks (read from left to right) and Cotton South banks (read from right to left). Reflecting the vast demand for call or overnight loans in metropolitan financial markets, the demand for additional reserves by New York banks is highly elastic. In the peripheral (Cotton South) region, by contrast, systemic seasonality resulted in banks' polar demands for reserves—large and inelastic during the peak season and vice versa during nonpeak times.

FIGURE 9.2   *A Model of the Seasonal Variation in the Cost of Bank Reserves in Postbellum America*

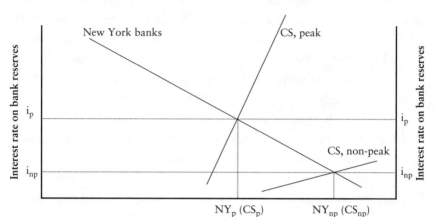

At the equilibrium allocation the two demand curves intersect; that is, banks in both sectors place an equal value on additional funds. They therefore have no economic incentive to bid away reserves from each other, as the marginal value of acquiring more reserves for (say) southern banks would fall short of their marginal cost, equal to the value of these funds to banks in New York. In the peak season peripheral banks are willing to pay a premium for additional reserves to meet their customers' large, inelastic harvest and crop-moving loan demands. Consequently New York call loan rates soar, as reserves are drained from large correspondent banks, either through direct cash shipments or seasonal loans to country banks in the Cotton South. In the nonpeak season country banks face fewer, more marginal local lending opportunities and so take advantage of the relatively higher rates offered by New York correspondents which can channel these funds into the call loan and commercial paper markets. With this influx of excess reserves into New York banks, money market rates plummet.

SYSTEMIC SEASONALITY IN THE COTTON SOUTH

Our empirical analysis of systemic seasonal liquidity risk draws on the obvious analogy to a more commonly cited item affecting the costs of banking in monocultural regions, loan default risk (James 1976; Bodenhorn 1995). The latter depends on the composition of the bank's loan portfolio and the variance of and correlation between the returns on each loan (or type). Banks can reap the benefits of pooling only when the returns on each loan (type) are weakly or negatively correlated, in other words, when their customers derive their incomes from diverse, independent sources. By contrast, they face greater undiversifiable or systemic default risk when their customers are prone to large, correlated negative income shocks.

The same logic applies to the liquidity side of the bank's business, its portfolio of current accounts.[16] In this case, however, we gauge seasonal liquidity risk in the regional banking system by (1) the variance in and correlation between the seasonal cycles of distinct commercial activities that constitute the regional economy and (2) their relative economic importance. The more extreme seasonal variation in the outlays and receipts of a particular sector would significantly add to the seasonality of banks' liquidity positions, but only when it accounted for a relatively large share of the regional economy and its seasonal peaks and troughs were not offset by the complementary flows of other sectors. What mattered, in other words, was the correlation between, not just the variation in, these flows.

We first dispel the simplistic notion that explains the extreme seasonal liquidity demands in the Cotton South by the natural seasonal cycle of its fleecy staple. To illustrate this point, in Figure 9.3 we plot data on the percentage of the annual crop harvested and then marketed by month for three important staples: cotton, corn, and wheat.[17] The harvest series show the timing of farmers' demands for extra seasonal labor to gather and process their crops for sale, while the marketing stage delineates the timing of crop sales to local buyers and subsequent shipments to major commercial centers. As noted above, the effective liquidity pressures on banks depended on the sequencing of these two stages, which ultimately determined the length, and hence liquidity, of outstanding bank loans tied to current crop production.

For all three crops the harvesting stage was highly seasonal. Farmers reaped the bulk of each crop over a three-month period, September through November for cotton versus June through August for wheat.

FIGURE 9.3   *The Seasonality of Harvesting and Marketing Cotton, Corn, and Wheat Crops*

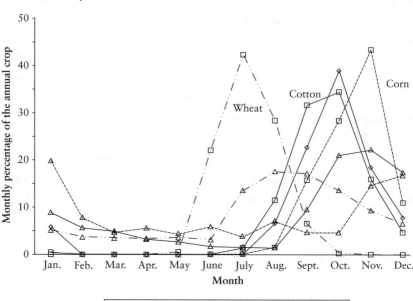

Sources: U.S. Department of Agriculture, Bureau of Crop Estimates (1916), p. 99 for cotton marketing in 1915; U.S. Department of Agriculture, Bureau of Statistics (1920), table 289, pp. 727–728 for the crop harvesting series over the period from 1909 to 1919; U.S. Department of Agriculture, Bureau of Statistics (1920), table 11, p. 516 and table 26, p. 527 for wheat and corn marketing in 1914–1915; U.S. Department of Agriculture, Bureau of Statistics (1922), table 32, p. 529 for wheat marketing over the period from 1916 to 1921; and Macklin (1922), p. 149 for cotton ginning over the period from 1915 to 1918 and shipments in 1919.

The seasonal peaks and overall seasonal variation in the corn and wheat culture were actually greater in magnitude than in the case of cotton. The standard deviation in the monthly shares of crops harvested—a simple measure—was 14.3 percent for the two Midwestern commercial crops but only 12.7 percent (or 11 percent less) for cotton.

In the ensuing marketing stage, however, these rankings are inverted. Even though cotton was not an intrinsically perishable crop especially in comparison to corn and wheat, producers tended to "rush" their harvested crops to local markets for sale. In the peak three-month marketing period just after the harvest, cotton producers sold just over 60 percent of their crops, as opposed to 51.3 percent of the corn and 48.1 of the wheat crops sold in their respective peak quarters. So, despite the greater seasonal variation in harvesting corn and wheat, the standard deviation in the monthly shares of crops marketed was 6.88 percent for cotton but only 5.47 percent (or 20 percent less) for corn and wheat. Viewed another way, the correlation between the monthly shares of crops harvested and marketed was nearly two-thirds in cotton (0.656) but only one-half in wheat and just under one-quarter in corn (see also Kuznets 1933, pp. 372, 386, 388).

In addition to the temporal relationship between the harvesting and marketing of crops, the liquidity demands on banks also depended on farmers' diversification of their commercial, not just total, agricultural production.[18] For this step, our analysis relies on monthly indices of commodity shipments to final markets, compiled by the Federal Reserve for the period 1919 to 1928.[19] The cotton series is composed mainly of cotton fiber shipments. The other series for grains, animal products, and livestock are composites and so may already capture some of the benefits of diversification. Still, these indices reflect a small number of products, which were typically produced in mixed farming regions—for example, wheat (60 percent), corn (24 percent), and oats (6 percent) for the grain index and dairy (55 percent) and poultry (40 percent) products for the animal product index.

We estimate the seasonal index for each product type by the monthly deviations in shipments relative to the evident trend growth over the entire period (see Figure 9.4).[20] All product types followed the same seasonal pattern with a peak in local sales and shipments after the harvest period and a sharp decline in activity afterward. The variation in shipments was most extreme in the case of the cotton culture, and mildest for a more year-round activity like livestock production. The standard deviation in shipments for each product type corroborates this implied ranking from most to least seasonal; it varies from 74.2 for cotton to only 12.3 for livestock.

The graphs in Figure 9.4 also illustrate the potential economic benefits to farmers and their banks from commercial diversification in products with complementary seasonal patterns. As a relevant example,

FIGURE 9.4   *The Seasonality of Agricultural Shipments by Product Type,*
1919–1926

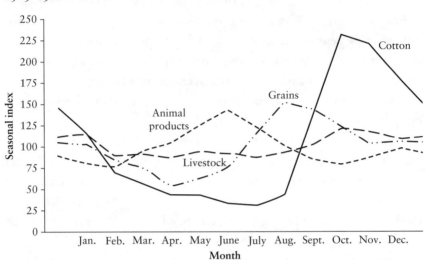

Source: *Federal Reserve Bulletin* (1924–1927).

consider the joint production of grains and animal products. The shipments of each were significantly less seasonal than those for cotton, but
as important they were staggered over the course of the year with the
peak shipments of animal products occurring in the late spring and early
summer and for grains in the late summer and early fall. In other words,
because their seasonal indices were negatively correlated with each other
(equal to −0.366), the joint production of these products in mixed farming regions would generate a smoother distribution of market activity
and so of net demands on banks and other intermediaries over the course
of the year.

To gauge the actual impact of commercial diversification by region,
we estimate the relative importance of the agricultural sector and of each
product in the mix of total farm output in the Cotton South and two
states representing diversified and more specialized agricultural regions in
the Midwest and Plains states, respectively (see Table 9.1). The Cotton
South at the turn of the century, as Wright noted, was not literally a staple
monoculture, but its economy was dominated by the agricultural sector

TABLE 9.1 *State Agricultural Economies, 1899*

State	Agricultural Share of Output[1]	Crops					Animals	
		All Crops	Cotton	All Cereals	Wheat	Corn	Livestock	Animal Products
Cotton South[2]	62.7	75.7	43.7	20.1	1.5	16.4	10.9	11.1
Alabama	57.2	77.4	46.0	20.2	0.6	18.7	7.8	12.1
Arkansas	69.6	71.3	35.2	25.4	1.7	22.1	10.9	14.7
Georgia	54.1	79.7	47.0	19.6	1.5	16.5	7.3	10.0
Louisiana	48.7	84.3	37.2	19.9	0.0	14.2	4.1	9.7
Mississippi	76.5	79.9	52.7	18.9	0.0	18.4	6.9	10.3
South Carolina	56.5	83.5	50.6	18.6	1.4	13.4	5.2	8.5
Texas	71.5	68.2	40.3	19.7	2.9	14.4	18.9	11.5
Mixed Farming								
Iowa	68.6	52.6	0.0	40.5	3.1	26.6	33.3	13.2
Spring Wheat								
North Dakota	88.1	83.9	0.0	62.5	49.4	0.6	8.5	7.4

Notes: 1. Agricultural share of output measures the value added of agricultural products (net of livestock feed) relative to the total value added of agricultural and manufacturing (net of intermediate goods) output.
2. States are included in the Cotton South, if the cotton crop accounted for at least 30 percent of value of agricultural output.

Sources: U.S. Census Office (1902a, 1902b, 1902c).

and in particular the cotton culture. Just over 60 percent of the value of regional output as enumerated in the census was produced on farms, and cotton accounted for 43.7 percent of the total (and so 27.4 percent of total commodity production). This figure probably understates the importance of cotton in the agricultural sector, as other crops and farm products such as corn and hogs were often consumed domestically or locally, not sold in long-distance markets (Ransom and Sutch 1977; Wright 1978, 1986). In turn, they put less pressure on the banking system, because farmers could stagger their production to avoid using seasonal peak labor and did not require credit to finance storage and shipment costs.

Iowa affords a striking contrast of a more diversified agricultural economy. Like the states of the Cotton South, the Iowa economy was relatively dependent on its agricultural sector, which accounted for just over two-thirds of the value of agricultural and manufacturing output. Yet, its farmers produced a greater mix of products, which combined corn and other feed crops (52.6 percent of agricultural output) with commercial livestock (an additional 33.3 percent) and dairy farming (13.2 percent). The Plains States like North Dakota most closely resembled the Cotton South because of their economic dependence on the highly seasonal wheat culture.

The U.S. Department of Agriculture (1915, p. 70) monthly crop report provides related evidence corroborating our results. For each state and region, it contains estimates of the monthly shares of the gross "receipts" from the sale of farm output, total and by type. Focusing on Georgia and Iowa on the eve of World War I, we compare the seasonal variation in gross proceeds from the sale of crops and all farm products. For both series, the standard deviation in monthly shares was much greater in Georgia than in Iowa, 7.15 versus 3.70 percent for crops and 9.00 versus 2.76 for all farm products. More relevant to our argument, monthly crop and total revenues were highly correlated in Georgia (equal to 0.998) but not in Iowa (only 0.395). In Georgia 59.1 percent of crop and 68.1 percent of total revenues were concentrated in the last quarter of the year, the peak cotton marketing season.[21] In Iowa, by contrast, there was no real seasonal peak in revenues. Farmers recorded their highest rate of sales from December through February, but even so their receipts during this period accounted for 30.2 percent of their crop and only 35 percent of their total revenues.

MEDIATING SYSTEMIC SEASONALITY

With data on bank clearings and balance sheets, we analyze the impact of systemic seasonality on country banking in the Cotton South. The clearings data record the monthly value of check and draft payments and receipts settled through a local clearinghouse, in this case in Augusta, Georgia and Des Moines, Iowa. Because both cities were regional commercial centers, their clearings data serve as an accurate barometer of the pace of economic activity in their surrounding agricultural hinterlands (Odell and Weiman 1998).

In Augusta, not surprisingly, the monthly variation in bank clearings directly parallels the seasonality of the cotton harvest and sales-shipments. From the trough (June through August) to the peak (October through December) of cotton's economic cycle, the value of payments and receipts processed by Augusta banks more than doubled. They reached a slightly lower peak at the spring planting-purchasing season, and then diminished steadily until the start of a new cycle. To underscore the point, we find a strong correlation between the seasonal patterns of Augusta bank clearings in the late postbellum period and the Department of Agriculture estimates of crop (equal to 0.867) and farm (equal to 0.852) sales in Georgia in 1914.

Des Moines banks mediated the smoother monthly flows of payments and receipts generated by the mixed cereals-livestock agricultural sector in its hinterland (Garlock 1932). Accordingly, local clearings fluctuated within a much narrower band, only 36.3 percentage points from peak to trough versus 95.6 percentage points for Augusta. Moreover, the two seasonal peaks in clearings, in March and October, were caused by customary arrangements for tax, rent, and mortgage payments and not by the purchases and shipments of farm products per se.[22]

The *Annual Report* of the Comptroller of the Currency furnishes the most direct evidence on the impact of seasonality on banks' operations.

For each state it publishes the aggregate balance sheets of country banks on five call dates spread out evenly over the year. Over the period from 1885 to 1892 we estimated the average deviation from trend in total deposits and loans (relative to average total loans) on each call date for country banks in the Cotton South and Iowa.[23] The results, plotted in Figure 9.5, depict the broad seasonal movements in deposits and loans and so the actual synergies between banks' dual depository and credit functions.

In the case of the Cotton South, the strong negative correlation between the two indices (equal to −0.780) implies that country banks faced recurrent seasonal local funding deficits and surpluses. The deficits mounted

FIGURE 9.5   *Seasonal Variation in Deposits and Loans of Georgia and Iowa Country Banks, 1885–1892*

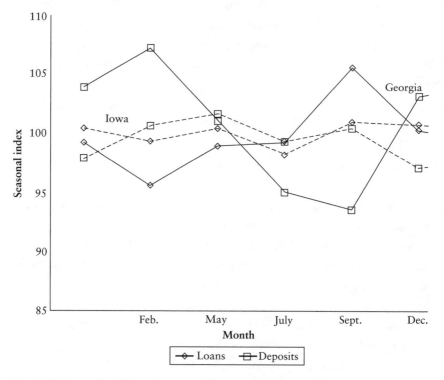

Source: U.S. Comptroller of the Currency (1884–1893).

during the crop growing through the marketing seasons (between the mid-February and late December call dates), when outstanding loans grew by 6.7 percent but deposits fell by 7.5 percent. During the rest of the year, banks faced the opposite condition of current account surpluses. The deposit index jumped by 13.7 percentage points but the loan index fell by an almost equal and opposite amount, 10.0 percentage points.

Our analysis of the balance sheet data also shows how country national banks managed their seasonal funding gaps and surpluses. The relevant items (not shown here) are their excess reserves (including bankers' balances) and interbank borrowing (referred to as "rediscounts" and "bills payable"). Banks met their local funding gap in two steps. They first depleted their excess cash reserves and bankers' balances by around 6.5 percent (mainly from late February to late July) and then increased their short-term borrowing from correspondents by 8.7 percentage points (from late July through September). After the harvest and marketing seasons, they quickly repaid their loans and replenished their correspondent balances (by late December) and then more gradually accumulated cash reserves.

Systemic seasonality more directly affected the operations of smaller, state-chartered banks which diffused further down the urban hierarchy to transport and distribution hubs.[24] When broken down by location, the variation in key balance sheet items of Georgia state banks over three call dates from early winter to early fall clearly evince this city-size effect (Table 9.2). For banks in local market centers with fewer than 1,000 people, the gap between loans and deposits more than doubled over the cotton cycle as compared to a less than 10 percentage point increase for banks in the largest cities.[25] The seasonal indexes for interbank borrowing and deposits also varied more widely for these truly "country" banks. This finding is consistent with later Federal Reserve data, showing a seasonal variation in demand deposits of 26.3 percentage points for member banks in smaller centers as compared to only a 10.1 percentage point range for banks in centers with at least 15,000 people (Wall 1937).

Iowa country banks, by contrast, more closely realized the necessary condition for a truly "revolving fund" of reserves to fund customers'

TABLE 9.2 Selected Balance Sheet Indexes of Georgia State Banks, 1892

Population in 1890	Number of Banks	Loans – Deposits[1]			Interbank Borrowing			Interbank Deposits		
		Jan. 2	June 30	Sept. 30	Jan. 2	June 30	Sept. 30	Jan. 2	June 30	Sept. 30
<1,000[2]	12	59.8	122.2	117.9	84.4	105.4	110.1	110.0	90.9	99.1
1,000–2,499	17	85.8	105.8	108.5	93.4	100.0	106.6	106.5	97.9	98.6
2,500–4,999	7	86.2	104.6	109.2	95.4	100.0	104.6	105.6	98.1	96.4
5,000–9,999	8	85.7	107.8	106.5	94.8	101.8	103.4	103.6	97.8	98.6
10,000+	19	96.8	98.3	104.9	97.9	99.2	102.9	101.9	98.9	99.2
All centers	63	92.7	101.1	106.1	96.5	99.8	103.7	102.8	98.4	98.9

Notes: 1. All of the indexes are computed as a percentage of the balance sheet averages for the three dates. The tabulations include the records of all banks that reported at all three dates and for which there were no significant data problems. The dates of the reports varied somewhat; the most common dates are used for the table headings.
2. Includes places that were not separately returned in the population census.

Sources: Georgia, Treasury Department (1892); U.S. Census Office (1895).

withdrawal and short-term borrowing demands. The loan and deposit indices across the five call dates were weakly correlated (equal to −0.025). For example, the March peak in clearings discussed above hardly appears as a funding problem for Iowa banks (in Figure 9.5), precisely because these payments largely involved transfers between local banks and so tended to offset each other. Moreover, the funding gap between the two varied by only 4.9 percentage points from the trough in late February to the peak in late December and was met mainly by banks' excess reserves especially in the form of surplus bankers' balances (Davis, Hanes, and Rhode 2009).

Unlike in the Cotton South, these seasonal patterns were roughly comparable across all Iowa banks, whether located in small or large population centers. As measured by the standard deviation, the seasonal variation in demand deposits was only marginally greater for FRS member banks in lower-order transport versus higher-order market-money centers. For state banks in Michigan (various years) where we can track seasonal fluctuations in balance sheet items along the same lines as in Table 9.2, lending in small agricultural communities also appeared to be fairly steady over the course of the annual cycle.

SYSTEMIC SEASONALITY, THE NEW YORK MARKET,
AND MONETARY REFORM

New York correspondents constituted a national clearinghouse, mediating payments and financial flows between banks throughout the country, especially in regional centers (James and Weiman 2010a). Consequently the varying demands for their payments and credit services and so the net flow of funds into and out of the New York money market reflected systemic seasonality at the national level, that is, the residual seasonal demands net of offsetting flows within and across regions. These seasonal pressures were clearly evident in the sharp fluctuations in the benchmark call loan interest rate. Varying inversely with the cash reserves of New York banks, loan rates increased from their trough of 2 to 3 percent in late July and August to a peak of 6 to 7 percent in late November and December (Kemmerer 1910, p. 15).

Despite the relatively small size of the banking sector in the Cotton South, its systemic seasonal demands had a disproportionate impact on the New York and hence national money markets. Southern banks accounted for 30 percent of the net cash flow of funds into New York during the late winter and early spring months, and about a quarter of the cash outflows in the fall.[26] And they had a voracious appetite for interbank loans to finance seasonal deficits in the harvest and crop-moving seasons. On the September 1904 call date, for example, over one-half of national banks in the cotton-growing states reported at least some interbank borrowing, and they accounted for just over one-half of the total amount ($37.3 million) borrowed by all national banks.[27] By way of comparison, only 30.1 percent of Iowa national banks reported any interbank borrowing on that date. Moreover, their interbank borrowings—and that of national banks in other mixed-farming states—did not exhibit a strong seasonal pattern and so did not reinforce the liquidity pressures on New York banks from the strong seasonal demands for cash shipments.

Our analysis confirms Laughlin's diagnosis of a "fundamental defect" of the national banking system, especially in peripheral regions like the Cotton South (Laughlin 1912, p. 12). The peak demands of Cotton South banks reinforced the liquidity strains on Wall Street in the late fall and early winter months and as a result magnified the premium on interbank and local lending at this time of the year. Faced with these credit terms, farmers, merchants, and local buyers in the region accelerated the sale and shipment of their crops and so their seasonal credit demands.

Laughlin's solution—greater cooperation among banks through the pooling of their reserves in regional "associations"—could mitigate but not fully resolve this twofold problem (Laughlin 1912, pp. 16–21). A blueprint for the FRS, Laughlin's reserve associations would operate a discount window and more elastically supply reserves to member banks in response to their peak seasonal demands. Just like private correspondents, they would turn banks' loan "assets into cash," but at lower, more uniform discount rates and without the macroeconomic side effects. This reform, he predicted, would reduce the cost of bank credit in peripheral regions and relieve the financial strains on New York and other money center banks. The evidence from the early Federal Reserve years bears out his predictions. Its policies during the 1920s virtually eliminated the seasonality in interest rates in Federal Reserve Bank and branch cities as well as bank panics, and regional differences in national bank loan rates narrowed sharply (see *Federal Reserve Bulletin*, August 1918–January 1934; Miron 1986; Redenius 2007a).

The Cotton South remained a spatial economic outlier, however, with rates stubbornly higher than those in the Northeast and the Midwest. This chronic problem attests to the systemic limits to national banking reform especially in peripheral regions. On the one hand, relatively few southern banks had direct access to the Fed's discount window, because they could not or would not comply with its stricter national standards.[28] As a result, only about a third of all banks in the Richmond, Atlanta, and Dallas Federal Reserve districts had joined the system by 1926. On the other, a purely monetary reform could not lessen cotton's grip on the regional economy, and with it the systemic seasonality that increased banks' liquidity costs and default risks in accommodating their customers' short-term loan demands. Overcoming this structural constraint would call for a more profound economic revolution, whose foundations were laid in the New Deal era (Wright 1986; Olmstead and Rhode 2003; Fleck, this volume).

NOTES

Earlier versions of this chapter were presented at the 2002 Economic History Association meetings, the 2006 Monetary and Financial History Workshop at the Federal Reserve Bank of Atlanta, and a recent conference at Stanford University on "Historical Approaches to Economics." For comments on these earlier drafts, we thank Charles Calomiris, Timothy W. Guinnane, Jon Moen, Harriet B. Newburger, and editors of this volume. We are grateful to Barnard, Bryn Mawr, and Knox Colleges for financial support.

    1. "Currency Reform" (1911), p. 8.

    2. For an alternative view on U.S. banking panics, see Calomiris and Gorton (1991).

    3. On the design of the National Banking Acts and their impact on peripheral regions, see Sylla (1969); Ransom and Sutch (1972), pp. 643–651; Redenius (2007b). Along similar lines, Wright (1986, esp. chap. 7) refers to New Deal labor policies as an "assault on the low wage economy" of the South (see also Fleck, this volume).

    4. Haney (1914), p. 14; Carson (1923), p. 322; Moulton (1931), pp. 98–107; Wickens and Jensen (1931); Garlock (1932); Wall (1932, 1937). Many of these sources also provide evidence on the role of banks and other sources in financing longer-term investments.

    5. Our analysis of the complementarity between banks' dual payments and credit services draws on Kashyap, Rajan, and Stein (2002). For alternative views that emphasize banks' other distinctive role in supplying information-intensive lending, see Calomiris and Kahn (1991) and McAndrews and Roberds (1999).

6. Following the theoretical literature, we couch the argument in terms of an individual bank. More realistically, however, it applies to an integrated regional banking network, a hub-and-spoke system focused on a local market center (Chang et al. 2008). Banks at these sites often formed a clearinghouse and pooled their reserves, which more effectively smoothed out any large transitory or seasonal net withdrawal shocks. Individual banks in turn could benefit from this network externality by forming a local funds market for borrowing and lending excess reserves (Garber and Weisbrod 1990; James and Weiman 2010a).

7. Lockhart (1921, pp. 156–158) specifies the terms of seasonal correspondent lending; see also Watkins (1929), pp. 151–164; James (1976); Gendreau (1983). The interest rate spread roughly corresponds to the seasonal range in the New York call loan rate (Kemmerer 1910, p. 15; Miron 1986). The call loan rate is the relevant benchmark because it represented the opportunity cost of excess reserves for New York banks (Myers 1931, p. 271; Morrison 1966, pp. 83–88; Goodfriend and Whelpley 1998, p. 17; James and Weiman 2010a).

8. See especially Carson (1923) and Moulton (1931), pp. 195–196. Woodman (1968), Ransom and Sutch (1977), and Weiher (1977) analyze the changing channels of cotton distribution after the Civil War.

9. Expressed in terms of Figure 9.1, the marketing stage extended the peak loan period from late August when farmers began to sell their crops and repay their loans to late November and December (Moulton 1931, pp. 105, 190–201). The process in fact required a few more steps, involving the bundling and shipping of crops from local markets to compress centers and then to larger "concentration" markets where they were graded, sorted, and aggregated. Only at this final stage—about three months after the harvest—were the crops issued a certified bill of lading that could back a financial instrument recognized in national and international money centers.

10. Carson (1923), pp. 446–449; U.S. Department of Agriculture (1922), pp. 134, 403–404. The "chaotic" conditions in the cotton distribution system prompted direct federal intervention through the passage of the Cotton Futures Act of 1914 and the Warehouse Act of 1916. The former established a uniform system of standards for grading cotton. The latter created an inducement for states to license and regulate warehouses based on federal standards, as their bonded receipts would constitute eligible paper for discounting at a regional Federal Reserve Bank.

11. Wang (this volume) makes a similar argument about the coevolution of cotton textile production and marketing firms and the local banking sector in Boston and Philadelphia. This institutional perspective on the Cotton South is developed in Wright (1986), Weiman (1990), and Olmstead and Rhode (this volume).

12. Copeland (1912), pp. 182–192. On the connection between technology of textile production and cotton quality, see Copeland (1909); Saxonhouse and Wright (1984).

13. Rothstein (1965, 1966). The development of these standards in the cotton economy ultimately depended on federal policy innovations during the interwar period from the Cotton Futures (1914) and Warehouse (1916) Acts to the Smith-Doxey Act of 1937 to develop uniform marketing standards, as well as the U.S. Department of Agriculture and local extension agents to improve production conditions on the ground (Olmstead and Rhode 2003).

14. Rockoff (2003), Redenius (2007b), and James and Weiman (2010b) analyze the problematic origins of the U.S. common currency union. Wright (1986, p. 7) and Carlton

(1990) explicitly recognize the constraints on the Cotton South because of its location in a political economic union, adjacent to a more developed urban industrial region to its north.

15. Laughlin (1912) as well as Kemmerer (1910), pp. 76–79 and Lockhart (1921), pp. 226–227. In the conclusion we return to this point and present quantitative evidence to support these claims.

16. Historically, these demand deposit accounts routinely included a credit line or over-draft facility and so captured a customers' total demand for and supply of bank liquidity.

17. See Figure 9.3 for the list of sources. We thank Paul Rhode for bringing them to our attention.

18. We emphasize farmers' commercial production, because diverse income sources could increase cash flows over the year, which would enable farmers and their banks to use these internal sources to finance current production at least partially. Self-sufficient production, of course, reduced cash outlays and so farmers' credit-liquidity demands on banks; on the role of self-sufficient production on the farm, see Wright (1986), pp. 107–115.

19. These data were published in the *Federal Reserve Bulletin* over the period (see, for example, pp. 183–188 of the March 1924 issue). Kuznets (1933, appendix I) had access to and analyzed these data disaggregated by crop and stage in the production and distribution cycle.

20. Our indexes were constructed to "wrap around" to form a continuous series over the year. All calculations are based on monthly estimates, not those after December and before January, which are artifacts of the statistical method.

21. The more relevant correlation, perhaps, is between the monthly shares of crop and total revenues and the monthly shares of the cotton crop shipped or marketed. Regardless of the latter series chosen, the correlation was 0.979 for crops and 0.972 for total farm revenues.

22. Garlock (1932), pp. 10–13. To underscore our point, the correlation between Des Moines bank clearings in the late postbellum period and total sale of farm products in Iowa in 1914 was only 0.30.

23. National banks were required to submit balance sheets to the Comptroller of the Currency on five call dates each year. The comptroller published only one individual country bank balance sheet per year, but five aggregate balance sheets per state, one on each call date. The 1885–1892 period was chosen because the call dates most closely tracked the crop cycle. Still, these data will tend to understate the effects of seasonality on bank operations, because there are only 5 observations per year and they do not exactly coincide with the turning points in the seasonal cycle.

24. Odell and Weiman (1998). In late September 1892 none of Georgia's 32 national banks operated in cities with fewer than 1,000 people, and only three were located in cities with 1,000 to 2,499 people. By contrast, 16 state banks (20.0 percent) operated in places with fewer than 1,000 people and 17 (21.3 percent) in those in the next size category.

25. The June 30 figure is actually higher than the one for September. The difference likely reflects the fact that the harvest was well under way by September 30. For state banks as a whole, the range in the loan-deposit index over the year was only 13.4 percent, comparable in magnitude to that for Georgia national banks (13.8 percent).

26. Kemmerer (1910), pp. 76–79. These banks accounted for less than 4 percent of total bank assets in the United States in 1900.

27. This evidence was reproduced in the testimony by Charles N. Fowler to the U.S. Senate, Committee on Banking and Currency (1913, pp. 1888–1890) during its hearings on the proposed Federal Reserve Act. See also various issues of the *Annual Report* of the U.S. Comptroller of the Currency. According to Fowler's evidence, Cotton South banks borrowed $35.1 million from New York correspondents as of June 1913, which was again about one-half of the total amount borrowed by all national banks.

28. If regional banks joined the fledgling system, their access to the discount window was limited, because they often lacked the requisite collateral. For this reason as well as others (such as the Fed's mandate for par clearing), the vast majority saw few benefits and significant costs from membership and so did not join the system (Watkins 1929, p. 122; Jessup 1967; White 1983, esp. chap. 3).

REFERENCES

Baltensperger, Ernst (1974). "The Precautionary Demand for Reserves." *American Economic Review* 64: 205–210.

Baltensperger, Ernst (1980). "Alternative Approaches to the Theory of the Banking Firm." *Journal of Monetary Economics* 6: 1–37.

Bodenhorn, Howard (1995). "A More Perfect Union: Regional Interest Rates in the United States, 1880–1960." In *Anglo-American Financial Systems: Institutions and Markets in the Twentieth Century*, edited by Michael D. Bordo and Richard Sylla. New York: Irwin Professional Publishing, pp. 415–454.

Bradstreet's (1896–1913).

Calomiris, Charles W., and Gary Gorton (1991). "The Origins of Banking Panics: Models, Facts, and Bank Regulation." In *Financial Markets and Financial Crises*, edited by R. Glenn Hubbard. Chicago: University of Chicago Press, pp. 108–173.

Calomiris, Charles W., and Charles M. Kahn (1991). "The Role of Demandable Debt in Structuring Optimal Banking Arrangements." *American Economic Review* 81: 497–513.

Carlton, David L. (1990). "The Revolution from Above: The National Market and the Beginnings of Industrialization in North Carolina." *Journal of American History* 77: 445–475.

Carson, W. J. (1923). "Cotton Financing." *Federal Reserve Bulletin* 9: 162–171, 319–327, 442–454, 566–576, 679–683.

Chang, Howard H., Marina Danilevsky, David S. Evans, and Daniel D. Garcia-Swartz (2008). "The Economics of Market Coordination for the Pre-Fed Check-Clearing System: A Peek into the Bloomington (IL) Node." *Explorations in Economic History* 45: 445–461.

Copeland, Melvin T. (1909). "Technical Development in Cotton Manufacturing since 1860." *Quarterly Journal of Economics* 24: 109–159.

Copeland, Melvin Thomas (1912). *The Cotton Manufacturing Industry of the United States*. Cambridge, MA: Harvard University Press.

Cronon, William (1991). *Nature's Metropolis: Chicago and the Great West*. New York: Norton.

"Currency Reform: Its Popular Side" (1911). *New York Times*, July 26, p. 8.

Davis, Joseph H., Christopher Hanes, and Paul W. Rhode (2009). "Harvests and Business Cycles in Nineteenth-Century America." *Quarterly Journal of Economics* 124: 1675–1727.

Egnal, Marc (2009). *Clash of Extremes: The Economic Origins of the Civil War*. New York: Hill and Wang.

Federal Reserve Bulletin (August 1918–January 1934).

Fox-Genovese, Elizabeth, and Eugene D. Genovese. (1983). *Fruits of Merchant Capital: Slavery and Bourgeois Property in the Rise and Expansion of Capitalism*. New York: Oxford University Press.

Garber, Peter, and Steven Weisbrod (1990). "Banks in the Market for Liquidity." National Bureau of Economic Research Working Paper No. 44. Cambridge, MA: National Bureau of Economic Research.

Garlock, Fred L. (1932). "Effect of Seasonality of Agriculture on Iowa Banking." Washington, DC: United States Department of Agriculture, Bureau of Agricultural Economics.

Gendreau, Brian C. (1983). "The Implicit Return on Bankers' Balances." *Journal of Money, Credit and Banking* 15: 411–424.

Georgia, Treasury Department (1892). *Annual Reports*. Atlanta: State Printer.

Goodfriend, Marvin, and William Whelpley (1998). "The Federal Funds Market." In *Instruments of the Money Market*, edited by Timothy Q. Cook and Robert K. Laroche. Available at www.richmondfed.org/publications/research/special_reports/instruments_of_the_money_market/pdf/chapter_02.pdf.

Haney, Lewis H. (1914). "Farm Credit Conditions in a Cotton State." *American Economic Review* 3: 47–67.

Harris, Siebel (1911). "Methods of Marketing the Grain Crop." *Annals of the American Academy of Political and Social Science* 38: 36–57.

James, John A. (1976). "Banking Market Structure, Risk, and the Pattern of Local Interest Rates in the United States, 1893–1911." *Review of Economics and Statistics* 58: 453–462.

James, John A. (1981). "Financial Underdevelopment in the Postbellum South." *Journal of Interdisciplinary History* 11: 443–454.

James, John A., and David F. Weiman (2010a). "From Drafts to Checks: The Evolution of Correspondent Banking Networks and the Formation of the Modern U.S. Payments System, 1850–1914." *Journal of Money, Credit and Banking* 42: 237–265.

James, John A., and David F. Weiman (2010b). "Towards a More Perfect American Payments Union: The Civil War as a Political Economic Watershed." Unpublished manuscript, Barnard College.

Jessup, Paul F. (1967). *The Theory and Practice of Nonpar Banking*. Evanston, IL: Northwestern University Press.

Kashyap, Anil K., Raghuram Rajan, and Jeremy C. Stein (2002). "Banks as Liquidity Providers: An Explanation for the Coexistence of Lending and Deposit-Taking." *Journal of Finance* 57: 33–73.

Kemmerer, Edwin Walter (1910). *Seasonal Variations in the Relative Demand for Money and Capital in the United States: A Statistical Survey*. Washington, DC: Government Printing Office.

Kuznets, Simon Smith (1933). *Seasonal Variations in Industry and Trade*. New York: National Bureau of Economic Research.

Laughlin, J. Laurence, ed. (1912). *Banking Reform*. Chicago: National Citizens' League for the Promotion of a Sound Banking System.

Lockhart, Oliver C. (1921). "The Development of Interbank Borrowing in the National System, 1869–1914." *Journal of Political Economy* 29: 138–160, 222–240.

Macklin, Theodore (1922). *Efficient Marketing for Agriculture: Its Services, Methods, and Agencies*. New York: Macmillan.

McAndrews, James, and William Roberds (1999). "Payment Intermediation and the Origins of Banking." *Federal Reserve Bank of New York Staff Report*. New York: Federal Reserve Bank of New York.

Michigan (1890–1914). *Annual Report of the Commissioner of the Banking Department*. Lansing, MI: n.p.

Miron, Jeffrey A. (1986). "Financial Panics, the Seasonality of the Nominal Interest Rate, and the Founding of the Fed." *American Economic Review* 76: 125–140.

Morrison, George R. (1966). *Liquidity Preferences of Commercial Banks*. Chicago: University of Chicago Press.

Moulton, Elma S. (1931). *Cotton Production and Distribution in the Gulf Southwest*. Washington, DC: Government Printing Office.

Myers, Margaret G. (1931). *The New York Money Market*, vol. 1: *Origins and Development*. New York: Columbia University Press.

Odell, Kerry A., and David F. Weiman (1998). "Metropolitan Development, Regional Financial Centers, and the Founding of the Fed in the Lower South." *Journal of Economic History* 58: 103–125.

Olmstead, Alan L., and Paul W. Rhode (2003). "Hog-Round Marketing, Seed Quality, and Government Policy: Institutional Change in U.S. Cotton Production, 1920–1960." *Journal of Economic History* 63: 447–488.

Piatt, Andrew A. (1910). *Statistics for the United States, 1867–1909*. Washington, DC: Government Printing Office.

Ransom, Roger L., and Richard Sutch (1972). "Debt Peonage in the Cotton South after the Civil War." *Journal of Economic History* 32: 641–669.

Ransom, Roger L., and Richard Sutch (1977). *One Kind of Freedom: The Economic Consequences of Emancipation*. Cambridge: Cambridge University Press.

Redenius, Scott A. (2007a). "New National Bank Loan Rate Estimates, 1887–1975." *Research in Economic History* 24: 55–104.

Redenius, Scott A. (2007b). "Designing a National Currency: Antebellum Payment Networks and the Structure of the National Banking System." *Financial History Review* 14: 207–227.

Rockoff, Hugh (2003). "How Long Did It Take the United States to Become an Optimal Currency Area?" In *Monetary Unions: Theory, History, Public Choice*, edited by Forrest H. Capie and Geoffrey E. Wood. New York: Routledge, pp. 76–103.

Rothstein, Morton (1965). "International Market for Agricultural Commodities, 1850–1873." In *Economic Change in the Civil War Era*, edited by David T. Gilchrist and W. David Lewis. Greenville, DE: Eleutherian Mills–Hagley Foundation, pp. 62–72.

Rothstein, Morton (1966). "Antebellum Wheat and Cotton Exports: A Contrast in Marketing Organization and Economic Development." *Agricultural History* 40: 91–100.

Saxonhouse, Gary R., and Gavin Wright (1984). "New Evidence on the Stubborn English Mule and the Cotton Industry, 1878–1920." *Economic History Review* 37: 507–519.

Sprague, O. M. W. (1910). *History of Crises under the National Banking System*. Washington, DC: Government Printing Office.

Sylla, Richard (1969). "Federal Policy, Banking Market Structure, and Capital Mobilization in the United States, 1863–1913." *Journal of Economic History* 29: 657–686.

U.S. Census Office (1895). *Eleventh Decennial Census of the United States, 1890: Population*, part 1. Washington, DC: Government Printing Office.

U.S. Census Office (1902a). *Twelfth Decennial Census of the United States, 1900*, vol. 5: *Agriculture*, part 1: *Farms, Livestock, and Animal Products*. Washington, DC: Government Printing Office.

U.S. Census Office (1902b). *Twelfth Decennial Census of the United States, 1900*, vol. 6: *Agriculture*, part 2: *Crops and Irrigation*. Washington, DC: Government Printing Office.

U.S. Census Office (1902c). *Twelfth Decennial Census of the United States, 1900*, vol. 7: *Manufactures*, part 1: *United States by Industries*. Washington, DC: Government Printing Office.

U.S. Comptroller of the Currency (1863–1941). *Annual Report*. Washington, DC: Government Printing Office.

U.S. Department of Agriculture, Bureau of Crop Estimates (1915). "Monthly Rate of Sales from Farms, Averages for Recent Years, Estimates Based upon Reports of Actual Monthly Sales Made by Crop Correspondents of Bureau of Crop Estimates." *Monthly Crop Report* 1: 70.

U.S. Department of Agriculture, Bureau of Crop Estimates (1916). "Monthly Disposition of Cotton Producers." *Monthly Crop Report* 2: 99.

U.S. Department of Agriculture, Bureau of Statistics (1920). *Yearbook of Agriculture, 1919*. Washington, DC: Government Printing Office.

U.S. Department of Agriculture, Bureau of Statistics (1922). *Yearbook of Agriculture, 1921*. Washington, DC: Government Printing Office.

U.S. Senate, Committee on Banking and Currency (1913). *Hearings before the Committee on Banking and Currency on H.R. 7837 (S. 2639)*, vol. 2. Washington, DC: Government Printing Office.

Wall, Norman J. (1932). "Agricultural Credit and the Economic Organization." *Journal of Farm Economics* 14: 138–151.

Wall, Norman J. (1937). "Demand Deposits of Country Banks." Technical Bulletin, No. 575. Washington, DC: U.S. Department of Agriculture.

Watkins, Leonard L. (1929). *Bankers' Balances: A Study of the Effects of the Federal Reserve System on Banking Relationships*. Chicago: A. W. Shaw.

Weiher, Kenneth (1977). "The Cotton Industry and Southern Urbanization, 1880–1930." *Explorations in Economic History* 14: 120–140.

Weiman, David F. (1990). "Staple Crops and Slave Plantations: Alternative Perspectives on Regional Development in the Antebellum Cotton South." In *Agriculture and National Development: Views on the Nineteenth Century*, edited by Lou Ferleger. Ames: Iowa State University Press, pp. 119–161.

White, Eugene N. (1983). *The Regulation and Reform of the American Banking System, 1900–1929*. Princeton, NJ: Princeton University Press.

White, Horace (1911). *Money and Banking, Illustrated by American History*. New York: Ginn and Company.

Wickens, David L., and Ward C. Jensen (1931). *Agricultural Finance in South Carolina*. Clemson College: South Carolina Agricultural Experiment Station.

Wicker, Elmus (2005). *The Great Debate on Banking Reform: Nelson Aldrich and the Origins of the Fed*. Columbus: Ohio State University Press.

Woodman, Harold D. (1968). *King Cotton and His Retainers: Financing and Marketing the Cotton Crop of the South, 1800–1925*. Lexington: University of Kentucky Press.

Wright, Gavin (1978). *The Political Economy of the Cotton South: Households, Markets, and Wealth in the Nineteenth Century*. New York: Norton.

Wright, Gavin (1986). *Old South, New South: Revolutions in the Southern Economy since the Civil War*. New York: Basic Books.

CHAPTER 10

Rural Credit and Mobility in India

SUSAN WOLCOTT

AGRICULTURE CONSTITUTES an unusually large part of the Indian economy even relative to other poor Asian economies. In 2000 agriculture generated 27 percent of Indian gross domestic product (GDP); the regional average was 17 percent. Agriculture's share of employment was 60 percent. Productivity growth in agriculture was flat between 1980 and 2000 (Dasgupta and Singh 2005). This is not a new phenomenon. There is some debate as to whether the overall availability of calories per capita deteriorated or merely stagnated over the British colonial period, but there is certainly no strong case to be made for a substantial improvement (Guha 1992). Given the importance of agriculture in the Indian economy, it is hard to see how India can move away from poverty without significant improvements in its performance.

Kessinger claimed to paraphrase the official critique from the 1890s to the 1970s when he wrote that Indian agriculture suffered from "the density of rural population, the size and fragmentation of holdings, technical backwardness, low levels of capitalization, and dependence on the fickle monsoon" (Kessinger 1975, p. 303). It is no surprise then that there have been government attempts to stimulate agricultural investment for more than a century. With their preferences for limited government, late nineteenth-century British officials pushed for agricultural cooperatives in India modeled on German Raiffeisen's Banks. Postindependence Indian administrators took a more direct approach and mandated that commercial banks expand the number of branches and extent of credit in rural areas. None of these attempts have been fully satisfactory. For whatever reasons, poor Indian cultivators do not seem to fully take advantage of the government programs which are available.[1]

In Bangladesh the Grameen (Village) Bank is seen as a singularly successful attempt to provide rural credit on more reasonable terms. It was founded in 1976 and now has a portfolio of over $3 billion and 2.3

million members. It disperses an average of $170 to each member, which is 60 percent of Bangladesh's per capita GDP. It has spawned imitators in Africa, Asia, Latin America, and even the United States and Europe (Schreiner 2003). The Grameen Bank has an unusual structure. The founder, Muhammad Yunus, writes that he was inspired by meeting a 21-year-old woman who tried to support herself by making bamboo stools. Daily she borrowed 25 cents from a moneylender at rates equivalent to 10 percent per day, and then sold the stools to the moneylender at below market rates. Yunus loaned her the money directly himself, and this was the beginning of his bank. Today, the Grameen Bank still loans to those with no collateral. It has operations throughout Bangladesh. Field representatives go to the village and form lending groups of five members. The groups will continue to receive loans only if all of the members repay previous loans. Thus the incentive to repay is access to future loans and standing within the village. The Grameen Bank has what is perceived to be an astounding 98 percent repayment rate. Yunus received the Nobel Prize in 2006 for his awareness of the needs of the poor.

No one would consider giving such an honor to a moneylender, yet moneylenders have been indispensable in village India at least as long as records have been kept. Malcolm Darling, a British colonial administrator as well as a scholar, wrote:

Financing the village, marketing its produce, and supplying its necessities, the moneylender in India frequently stood between the cultivator and death. . . . Whenever, therefore, we are tempted to revile him, we should remember that by his assistance to agriculture for 2,500 years he has made life possible for millions who must otherwise have perished or never been born. (Darling 1947, p. 168)

Moneylenders in colonial India followed many of the same practices that have been praised in the Grameen Bank. They loaned without collateral based purely on their personal knowledge of the borrower. They lent very small amounts. Colonial moneylender rates were similar to the rates charged by the Grameen Bank today. There was a fully understood, if implicit, system of collective liability.

I will argue this collective liability underpinned colonial rural credit markets. Less heralded, but according to Armendáriz and Morduch

(2007) equally important, features of microfinance such as weekly repayment and "dynamic incentives" created by repeated and increasing loans were also common features of colonial moneylending.[2] While these features were present, it is unlikely that they were as critical for stability in either the colonial or modern period. Very recently, some microfinance institutions have moved away from the group lending model, and even the Grameen Bank now offers some individual liability loans. But collective liability institutions continue to dominate in South Asia, and in other geographic regions when the aim of the institution is to serve the poorest members of the community (Cull, Demirgüç, and Morduch 2007).

I compare the colonial Indian agricultural credit market not only to the Grameen Bank but also to the postbellum U.S. South credit markets. The reason for the comparison to the Grameen Bank is obvious. It is a comparison between what is considered to be a poorly functioning historical system with a well-functioning modern system. The comparison to the credit markets of the U.S. South is perhaps even more important. Both systems have been described as painfully lacking in capital overall (Reserve Bank of India 1956; Woodman 1968). And the problems in both colonial India and the postbellum South were most severe for the large numbers of poor cultivators with limited or no land holding. Both credit markets have been accused of leading to the "debt peonage" of these cultivators. Against these similarities there is one glaring difference. Southern farmers' credit was backed by the cotton growing in the field. When that cotton was harvested, there was no longer any asset to act as a guarantee of repayment. Consequently, landless farmers had access only to seasonal credit. And when the season ended, as they did not have long-term ties to any one area, there were frequent population shifts. Free movement of labor leads to production efficiency in the typical economic model. The lack of stability, however, was a significant reason for the inability to provide long-term credit and kept the farmers from being able to settle profitably in one location (Haney 1914). By contrast, there was almost no population movement in India. The caste system created a tight interconnectedness among the members of Indian villages. This connectedness was a long-lived asset which could be borrowed against to gain access to long-term credit. The Indian system of collective responsibility thus solved at least this one important problem faced by postbellum southern credit markets. Yet the Indian system was associated with even less productivity growth than the postbellum U.S. South, itself hardly a model of agricultural dynamism (Olmstead and Rhode, this volume). The comparison with the postbellum U.S. South illustrates the paradox of the Indian system. A chief use of borrowing in India was to fund the ceremonial expenditures which sustained the social system, which allowed the borrowing. There is one final and potentially interesting similarity between India and the postbellum U.S. South. The U.S. South had a credit and production system which was stable though not dynamic from the 1870s through the 1930s. Thus in both India and the postbellum U.S. South there existed what appeared to be a sustained long-term equilibrium associated with very little growth. In both areas analysts thought solving the credit shortage would invigorate stagnant agricultural productivity, and both regions experimented extensively, especially with cooperative banking and marketing. The U.S. South did not solve the credit problem; it was if anything more acute in the late 1930s than it had been previously (Woodman 1968). What ultimately brought the South out of its stable pattern were large external shocks. The sharp quotas on immigration put into place after World War I combined with high labor demands during World War II pulled the poor out of the South, just as the major policy changes of the New Deal pushed southern tenants off the land (Collins 1997; Whatley 1983). What can bring Indian agriculture out of its low growth pattern? There is a great deal of excitement surrounding the apparent innovations of microfinance. But I will argue that marginal changes to the way credit is provided are unlikely to significantly change centuries-old patterns of investment and expenditure.

In this chapter I first exploit the records of the 1929–1930 Provincial Bank Enquiry Committees (PBECs) and a remarkable data set on Indian rural expenditures and finance from 1951–1952, the All-India Rural Credit Survey (AIRCS), to analyze the nature of agricultural credit in colonial India and make the comparisons to the Grameen Bank and the credit system of the postbellum U.S. South.[3] The second section explores the way in which the caste network supported the credit system, and the third section explores the way in which the credit system supported the caste network. I conclude with a discussion of the potential for credit to change the behavior of Indian cultivators.

CHARACTERISTICS OF COLONIAL INDIA'S RURAL CREDIT MARKETS

We can estimate the structure of credit markets in colonial India from the All-India Rural Credit Survey (Reserve Bank of India 1956). This survey was undertaken to "reveal the broad patterns of the working of agricultural credit in the different regions of the country." As it was undertaken before the massive postindependence attempts to increase rural credit in order to spur agricultural investment, it is indicative of the behaviors of Indian villagers in the absence of significant government intervention; such a regime would describe most of preindependence Indian history.[4] The survey took place between November 1951 and August 1952, and questions were asked relating to the previous 12 months. The unit of observation was the commensal family, that is, the family that shared one kitchen. This is standard in the analysis of Indian cultivators where the farm was owned and operated by an extended family which almost always included multiple generations and frequently included more than one adult sibling. There is no information given about the average size of the family. There were two parts to the survey. Both parts used the same random selection of eight villages in each of 75 randomly chosen Indian districts, or roughly a fourth of India's then 302 districts total. These districts span India geographically as well as culturally. The first part of the survey, the General Survey, obtained information from all residents of each of the villages on levels of expenditure and how they financed those expenditures. For the General Survey, the data are reported for each village and aggregated for each district. The second part, the Intensive Survey, focused on a stratified sample of 15 cultivating families of each village. Detailed data were gathered on family assets, expenditure, and finance.

Data from the AIRCS on extent and sources of cash borrowing of Indian cultivators in 1951–1952 are in Table 10.1. Heston (1982) estimates that in 1947 rupees (Rs.), per capita income in India in 1945 is Rs. 166. Thus per family rural cash borrowing, Rs. 163, is approximately the same as per capita income. Data from the 1961 census indicate the commensal

TABLE 10.1 *Per Family Cash Borrowing in Rural Villages in India*

State	Districts	Total Borrowed (Rs.)	Banks and Cooperative Banks	Money Lenders	Landlords, Informal Money Lenders	Relatives
			Amount Borrowed by Source (Rs.)			
Assam	3	93	0.7	15	21	68
Bhopal	1	148	0.0	41	89	29
Bihar	4	141	0.3	138	21	7
Bombay	7	145	40.1	48	51	53
Himachal Pradesh	1	97	5.0	17	37	44
Hyderabad	4	144	2.0	92	81	22
Madhya Bharat	4	204	7.0	193	6	8
Madhya Pradesh	6	117	6.8	107	28	27
Madras	7	286	18.7	98	268	9
Mysore	2	196	3.0	12	175	9
Orissa	3	72	2.0	66	4	5
PEPSU	2	355	1.5	67	311	42
Punjab	3	192	11.7	60	7	112
Rajasthan	6	193	0.0	183	2	29
Saurashtra	1	185	1.0	173	24	27
Travancore-Cochin	1	197	31.0	94	84	61
Tripura	1	148	0.0	23	20	34
Uttar Pradesh	13	170	4.0	109	48	34
Vindhya Pradesh	2	83	1.0	42	48	1
West Bengal	4	87	1.3	66	14	43
India	75	163	6.9	82	67	33
Shares			3.6%	45.2%	27.3%	17.5%

Note: These figures are per commensal family. The data include all cultivating families in the sampled villages. The "India" row is a simple unweighted average of the state figures. The "Shares" row is the average of the shares of these loan sources in each district. The shares do not sum to 100 because not all sources are listed in this table.

Source: Reserve Bank of India (1956), table 11 (General Schedule District Tables).

family in India is between 5.0 and 5.4 persons, on average (Kolenda 1987, table 7). Thus on average each family is borrowing nearly a fifth of its income every year. Professional moneylenders supplied an average 45.2 percent of all loaned funds in the sample districts, and nonprofessionals supplied a further 27.3 percent. A professional moneylender was defined for the purpose of the survey as "all those who, though primarily cultivators, loaned considerable sums of money to others, and those, whether cultivators or not, who earn a substantial part of their income from moneylending" (Reserve Bank of India 1956, p. 2). I have included in nonprofessional moneylenders landlords, who supplied 2.8 percent of borrowed funds, and traders, "wholesale and commission agents but not retailers and shopkeepers," who supplied 4.5 percent, and agriculturist moneylenders, who supplied 20 percent of the borrowed funds of cultivating families, an impressive level of lending for what must have been a small-scale activity.

These data make it clear that professional and nonprofessional moneylenders supplied large amounts of funds to Indian cultivators throughout India. Just as Malcolm Darling wrote, moneylenders were indispensable. What these raw data cannot indicate, however, is whether this was a productive relationship that should be accepted by the government or an exploitative one that should be strongly discouraged and replaced. The main academic critique of moneylenders is that they abuse their monopoly position either to obtain the cultivator's lands at below-market prices or to simply drain the cultivator of resources (Bhaduri 1973, 1977).

Empirical evidence suggests, however, moneylenders did not enjoy monopoly positions to be exploited. Rural moneylenders were a diverse group. Jain writes, "So far as moneylending is concerned, any one and every one takes to it. A member of any caste who may have a little money in hand can hardly resist the temptation of lending it out to neighbours" (Jain 1929, p. 28). This is a common theme in official documents. An 1860s statement of the deputy commissioner of Rae Bereli in the United Provinces, north India, states: "Almost every man appears to be in debt, and he who saves a rupee puts it out upon interest" (Musgrave 1978, p. 219). A similar comment is in a 1916 settlement report of the Junnar *taluka*, or administrative subdivision, of the Poona District in Western India. "Outside the towns and large villages the professional moneylenders are very few. Agriculturists and the artisan classes borrow and lend amongst themselves" (Charlesworth 1978, p. 102). Evidence given at the Madras PBEC also suggests that moneylenders do not form a special class. "Roughly speaking all those who have spare money—ryots, merchants, retired officials, shopkeepers and vakils—lend it" (Baker 1984, p. 279). William Crooke in his report on the Etah district in the United

Provinces in 1888 listed these income sources for a Muslim Teli [oilmen] family: pressing oilseeds, Rs. 100 per annum; returns from 3 acres, 2 roods of land (an average-size Indian farm), Rs. 50, 6 annas; and from money-lending, Rs. 3,500 per annum. (Rs. 1000 per year was the minimum income required to pay income tax and was considered very wealthy by Indian standards of the time.) A Thakur family—Thakur's are a rich agriculturist caste—held 98 acres. Their income from agriculture was Rs. 1,231 per annum, and that from moneylending was Rs. 750 (Whitcombe 1972, pp. 166–167). Musgrave gives a long list of lenders in the United Provinces:

In the 1920s, telis continued to lend money. . . . Although the 570 cultivators also borrowed from a *zamindar* in a neighboring village, from *banias* [small-scale shopkeepers, moneylenders], Brahmins, Thakurs and Chamars [an "untouchable," leatherworking caste]. Elsewhere . . . much of the money lending was in the hands of the Brahmin family priests, while in Edalpur, the local shrine was, through its *pandit* [priest], the leading source of credit. In Arrana, . . . the school teacher established a very considerable lending business on his government salary, while the subordinate agents of the estate bureaucracies sometimes used their salaries—and sometimes the estates' money—in credit dealings. In Bhensa, . . . the difficulties of the professional *mahajans* and *salukars* [large-scale moneylenders] in the neighbouring village of Mawana led them to abandon the loaning of money to the Jat cultivators, who were constrained to borrow from the *behwaris* (butchers). (Musgrave 1978, p. 219)

It was not just the rich who engaged in rural moneylending. Prominent among India's credit sources for the poor were widows, who apparently operated the equivalent of pawn shops. Jain was particularly impressed with the widows' ability to keep track of their many very small loans despite their almost complete illiteracy (Jain 1929, pp. 66–67). Jain is not the only one to write of women lenders. Ahmed Shah, an inspector for a cooperative in the Punjab, gave evidence before the Punjab PBEC on the loans of women, here not restricted to widows, in amounts from Rs. 25 to 300, usually on the security of jewelry (Bhatacharya 1994, p. 199).

The rural credit market had easy entry, which would suggest that credit provision was competitive. There is still the question of whether individuals had access to more than one moneylender. The historical accounts from the 1930s PBECs suggest that villagers had loans outstanding with more than one private individual, but no systematic data were gathered on this point. Aleem (1993) gathered the most detailed information. He interviewed 14 moneylenders in rural Pakistan as to their business practices during 1980–1981. Of his 14, only 4 were prepared to lend to clients who had other lenders. Binswanger et al. (1985) found that in the villages with traditional large-scale moneylending, the moneylenders would supply all of the significant credit for their client, though clients might have small loans with other lenders. The authors report that though it was infrequently done, one could change moneylenders, but only by paying off past debt. Hardiman (1996) reports the same for the colonial period. Ruthven and Kumar (2002) undertook a detailed study of the credit relations of 68 households in two villages in Koraon Block, Allahabad District (Uttar Pradesh) in 2000 and 2001. They found that households would simultaneously borrow at interest from shopkeepers, wealthy agriculturist lending on a nonprofessional basis, and professional moneylenders, as well as significant borrowing from friends and relatives interest free. In this sample the loans from professional moneylenders were the most high-priced and were to be avoided, and so it seems doubtful that one would have more than one such loan outstanding at a time. The Ruthven and Kumar description of the borrowing patterns of households seemed to greatly resemble the historical discussions, even to the extent that poor cultivators "save" by lending to others. Overall, the impression is that the moneylending business, either in the colonial or the modern period, was not a pure monopoly even if one had major loans outstanding with just one moneylender at a time.

The final piece of evidence against the monopoly position of moneylenders is the relatively low price of credit. Table 10.2, extracted from the report of the PBEC for Bombay, is illustrative. These rates were similar for most provinces, where rural moneylending rates varied from 18 to 36 percent. There were a few cases where the rates were as low as 9 or 12 percent, such as for lending on the collateral of jewelry, and for wealthier borrowers. Grain was typically borrowed at rates of 50 percent. There were also a very few cases where the rates were as high as

TABLE 10.2   *Interest Rates for Rural Moneylending in the Bombay Province, 1931*

Region	Sowcar's Rates (percent)	Co-operative Societies' Rates (percent)
Maharashtra (irrigated)	12 to 24	$10^{15}/_{16}$
Maharashtra (famine)	$18^{3}/_{4}$ to 36	$12^{1}/_{2}$
Karnatak	12 to 24	$9^{3}/_{8}$ to $10^{15}/_{16}$
Gujarat	9 to 18	$9^{3}/_{8}$ to $10^{15}/_{16}$
Khandesh	12 to 18	$9^{3}/_{8}$ to $10^{15}/_{16}$
Sind	12 to 36	$10^{15}/_{16}$

Note: *Sowcar* is another word for professional rural moneylender.
Source: India, Banking Enquiry Committee (1930a), p. 67.

100 or even 300 percent. But these were rare. The various PBECs indicate that such rates were limited to itinerant moneylenders such as Pathans and Kabulis, who were truly hated by the Indian peasant, not like the majority of moneylenders, who were domiciled in the village or a nearby market town and were part of the local community.

The AIRCS gives more comprehensive information. All but 3 percent of loans had a recorded rate of interest, and only 1.6 percent of the loans for which rates had been recorded had rates of 50 percent or greater. The rates, however, vary across districts and within the district across income levels. The authors identified the districts as completely commercialized, monetized but not necessarily commercialized, and subsistence (Reserve Bank of India 1954, pp. 190–191). Wealthier, more commercialized districts had lower rates than monetized or subsistence districts, and within the districts, wealthier cultivators faced lower rates than poorer cultivators. The data are summarized in Table 10.3. The AIRCS does not report the rates charged separately by source of credit. The higher rates in the poorer districts, however, are unlikely to be due to differences in the sources of borrowed funds. The share of formal sector borrowing was never larger than 10 percent and was actually relatively high, 7.5 percent, in the subsistence regions. The share of professional and agriculturalist moneylending was fairly stable across the districts, averaging just under 60 percent. The rates are very similar to those reported in the 1930 PBEC reports.

TABLE 10.3 *Weighted Average Rates Reported in the All-India Rural Credit Survey, 1951*

| District Type | Income Group | Per Commensal Family (Rs.) | | | Average Positive Interest Rate | Modal Interest Rates in Districts and Income Groups |
		Family Assets	Gross Value of Farm Production	Amount Borrowed		
Commercialized	First 5 Deciles	9,576	1,415	433	14.6	10–12.5
	Last 5 Deciles	2,479	366	149	17.0	10–12.5
Monetized	First 5 Deciles	6,293	1,197	282	16.4	10–12.5; 18–25
	Last 5 Deciles	2,102	437	168	18.9	18–25
Subsistence	First 5 Deciles	4,226	881	163	23.3	18–25
	Last 5 Deciles	1,046	254	82	27.0	18–25; 25–35

Source: Reserve Bank of India (1956), tables 12.1.1 and 12.1.2 (for data on average loans and their use) and table 17 (for data on average family assets).

Compare these to the rates of the Grameen Bank. The inflation rate in Bangladesh is about 4 percent. There was no persistent inflation in the interwar period. The standard Grameen loan rate for an income-producing loan is 20 percent, though as the loan must be repaid within the loan period and the interest charge is on a "declining basis," the bank reports that the effective rate is only 10 percent. On the other hand, there are fees and forced saving associated with Grameen Bank loans, and that will bid up the real cost of the loan. Shreiner estimates that 30 percent is a more accurate figure (Schreiner 2003, p. 362). Thus the rates of the Grameen Bank are certainly not significantly below colonial moneylender rates.

One significant difference is that in the colonial period, rates increase with the poverty of the borrower. It is unlikely that this was due to greater risk, as total default to moneylenders was and is infrequent, as I discuss in a later section. It could be evidence of local monopolies in moneylending, but it is more likely that differential prices simply reflected differential costs. The poorer the borrower, typically the lower the loan amount. Though pure default was uncommon, rescheduling payment appears to have been frequent. Transaction costs associated with originally contracting and subsequently rescheduling loans would be a fixed cost and would disproportionately drive up the costs of smaller loans. Armendáriz and Morduch (2007, p. 121) report that across a range of microlenders, transaction costs increase with the percentage of small loans in the portfolio.

The spread between lending and borrowing might also suggest local monopolies. Rural colonial moneylenders could obtain funds at 12 percent, and typically loaned at rates between 18 and 35 percent, with the majority of the loans being at rates between 18 and 25 percent. The spread for the Grameen Bank, however, is very similar. It has deposit rates of 8.5 to 12 percent, and loans at rates equivalent to 30 percent. Armendáriz and Morduch (2007, pp. 240–242) suggest that the Grameen Bank as well as most other microfinance lenders rely on grants and subsidized loans to fund their activities. Thus the reported premium between deposit and loan rates is an underestimate of the true premium. On the other hand, I have less information on fees by moneylenders in the colonial period, though they existed. In Western India, Hardiman (1996) reports there was a "purse opening" charge of a few annas per loan (an anna is 1/16 of a rupee). In the absence of more information, I would suggest that it is not unlikely that the capital subsidies of the Grameen Bank counterbalance the fees of colonial moneylenders. As the Grameen Bank is not at present generating significant profits despite large deposits to lending spreads, it is unlikely that similar spreads for colonial moneylenders indicate monopoly profits.

Ultimately, the test of a credit system is its ability to provide a wide range of users funds for productive activities. The postbellum U.S. South offers a useful point of comparison as it was another agricultural system based on sharecropping and small farms. Identifying the differences in credit provision in the two economies will bring into sharp relief the factors that identify the Indian colonial system as a relatively well-functioning rural credit system.

There is little systematic quantitative information on credit markets in the postbellum South, though there is extensive qualitative discussion. The agents of the newly formed bureaucracies in two southern states, North Carolina and Georgia, contacted farmers and bankers on a regular basis in the late nineteenth century to determine the status of credit for small farms. The main complaint of the bureaucrats was that too much money was borrowed for foodstuffs, fertilizers, and animal feed. Even in a bad year, the authors of the North Carolina report argued returns could be positive if "grasses and stock were reported as a special feature of farming, and also in instances where crops were diversified, and home supplies raised" (p. 383). The authors continue that though this had been the advice given for some time, "it is not generally pursued. The reason assigned in many instances for not doing so is poverty, and no doubt that has a great deal to do with it. Farmers frequently are under obligations which compel them to raise a money crop—that is to satisfy creditors" (p. 384). Thus the discussion of credit in the North Carolina government documents is largely restricted to whether or not farmers grew their own supplies or purchased them on credit. For example, in the 1887 survey of laborers and tenants, there is a table drawn from "reliable parties" in each county that includes answers to the following questions, among others: whether or not "tenants buy supplies on time"; the cost of credit; and the security necessary for the loan. The answers suggest that tenants did typically buy on time, that interest rates varied from 10 to 70 percent, and that some type of collateral was almost always required. There were 96 North Carolina counties. In seven of these no security is listed, though no reason is given. It could be because no security was required, or simply that that question had not been answered. For the remaining 89 counties, the security required was listed as either a "lien" or a crop mortgage. The lien also involved borrowing against a crop in the field. The situation was the same in Georgia, where between 1888 and the early 1890s the Department of Agriculture issued reports of similar surveys of knowledgeable farmers. The discussions in these reports center on credit used for supplies of food or fertilizers. There is no suggestion of credit being used for other ends, such as agricultural implements, livestock, or land. All credit in Georgia as in North Carolina was secured with crop liens. It is seasonal credit, closely tied to the presence of crops in the field, primarily provided by local stores.

There was another, private survey, conducted by Lewis H. Haney in 1912 of conditions in the cotton-growing districts in Texas (Haney 1914). This market was somewhat different in that in about 95 percent of the Texas counties covered in the survey, most credit was supplied by banks rather than stores. Despite that, only 15 percent of the loans were for agricultural investments in such things as land, livestock, buildings, or machinery (p. 48). The modal loan period was only six months; so-called long-term loans were only for nine months (p. 49). A very few of the "more substantial farmers" were able to roll over short-term loans to use the funds for investment purposes. Most of the short-term loans, 75 to 90 percent, were secured; 90 percent of secured loans had "chattel mortgages," chiefly mules but also crops in the field. Haney does not blame banks for their inability to provide funds for investment. He argues that it is an "inherent impediment in the activities of commercial banks as directed to the needs of farm credit" (p. 56). Though he argues "relatively short time loans, largely based on personal security, are the most pressing need in Texas" (p. 63), he does not think this will come about without government assistance. The problem in Texas, in Haney's view, was that, in addition to the futility of such institutions supplying any of the needs of the "negro population due to racism," there was also the problem that "fully 10 per cent of the white tenant farmers of Texas are hopeless." It was not just that land security was not available; another problem was that these farmers were a "shifting and shiftless group" (p. 61). They did not reside long enough in one locality to build up the ties that were required for functioning cooperative credit.

The long-term effect of the credit system in the U.S. South on the lives of those who began their careers as landless cultivators is linked to the typical career path of such men, what historians call the "agricultural ladder." In the U.S. postbellum South, young men who had not inherited land typically began their agricultural careers as wage laborers and worked closely under the supervision of the landlord or his agent. As a young man acquired experience, assets, and a reputation for trustworthiness, he would advance to "cropper," then share tenant, then cash or fixed amount tenant, and finally owner. A cropper meant someone who was given land to farm but was provided by the landlord with a mule to plow it, as well as implements and supplies. Once the farmer saved the money to buy his own mule or horse, he became a "true tenant," and received a higher portion of the crop. Both croppers and share tenants typically were still subject to close supervision. After some years in the same area, a share tenant might be given a contract involving no supervision, and rent paid in cash, or as a fixed amount (not share) of the crop. Each rung up the ladder involved a substantial increase in income. In 1913 a cropper's annual income would be $333, a share tenant's $398, and a cash tenant's $478 (Ferleger 1993). Although cropper contracts were common shortly after the Civil War, it was not until 1920 that the U.S. Census started to collect systematic data distinguishing croppers from share tenants.[5] According to the 1920 Agricultural Census, croppers constituted 17.5 percent of all farmers in the South. Among blacks, 36.2 percent of farmers were croppers. Croppers and share tenants together constituted nearly half of southern farmers. Not all farmers advanced up the agricultural ladder. Survey data from the 1930s suggest that roughly 50 percent of those who had started their careers as laborers or sharecroppers ended their career no higher than share tenants (Alston and Ferrie 2005).

The limitations of the U.S. postbellum credit system delayed cultivators at several rungs of the ladder. As credit was not available to poor farmers to buy plow animals, they had to save enough funds to move from croppers to share tenants. On this point, Gavin Wright asks, rhetorically, "Would you lend $100 to an impoverished but highly mobile wage laborer in a declining county? To buy a horse?" (Wright 1987, p. 111). Then there is the move from share tenant to cash tenant. The accumulating debt of landless southern farmers to landlords and local stores has been described as debt peonage. Farmers were, it has been argued, immobilized by their debts. But Wright argues that view is exactly backward. Farmers could and did walk away from their debt. Those who did remain year after year paying off debt were not in bondage. They were the successes. Only stable farmers could establish reputations for trustworthiness and responsible stewardship of the owner's land and receive the coveted cash contracts. The credit system failed when it was not available in sufficient amounts to allow a landless farmer to continue to accumulate debt, forcing him to move to another location and forfeit his hard-won reputation.

Colonial Indian cultivators faced a similar lack of collateral. But credit was still available, and not just seasonal credit, and not just with good security. Table 10.4, drawn from the AIRCS, indicates that even poor

TABLE 10.4   *Types of Security for Cash Loans Reported in the All-India Rural Credit Survey*

District Type	Income Group	Annual Loans as a % of Family Assets	Share of Loans Reported Used for		Share of Loans Secured by		
			Agricultural Investment	Current Farm Expenditure	Personal Security	Land	Ornaments
Commercialized	First 5 Deciles	5.1	24.7	22.9	81.5	11.7	2.1
	Last 5 Deciles	7.9	28.7	17.5	82.4	9.2	3.3
Monetized	First 5 Deciles	6.7	29.7	6.9	86.3	8.8	1.7
	Last 5 Deciles	12.5	23.9	6.0	91.0	6.1	0.9
Subsistence	First 5 Deciles	4.8	29.1	8.6	83.8	6.8	5.4
	Last 5 Deciles	9.9	25.9	8.6	80.2	7.6	4.1

Sources: Reserve Bank of India (1956), tables 12.2.1 and 12.2.2 (for data on average loans and their use), tables 12.3.1 and 12.3.2 (for data on types of security for loans), and table 17 (for data on average family assets).

farmers in subsistence regions contracted cash loans which were on average as much as a third of the average gross product of their farms, and the majority of those loans were based on personal security. The bottom half of cultivators secured between 80.2 and 91 percent of their loans with no physical collateral. As in the postbellum U.S. South, some of these cash loans were probably for sustenance between harvests. Current farm expenses were a significant cause for cash borrowing in all Indian districts. In addition, there were grain loans; most of those would have fallen into that category, though cultivators also might be borrowing grain for seed. Grain loans were less important in 1951 India than cash loans. In only 23 of the 75 sampled districts were grain loans 10 percent or more of the cash loans. And even in those districts, only an average of 38.8 percent of the families reported grain loans, while 44.2 percent reported cash loans. The average ratio of grain to cash loan was 0.68, but that is mostly due to Mirzapur, Uttar Pradesh, which had a not unusually high average Rs. 43 per cultivator family in grain loans, but an unusually low Rs. 15 per cultivating family in cash loans. The median ratio of grain loans to cash loans for these 23 districts was 0.28 (Reserve Bank of India

1955, pt. 1, table 8.12). In no part of India were loans for current expenditure as important as borrowing to fund agricultural investment. The largest share of loans, between 23 and 30 percent, was used for long-term investments.[6]

Consider one final point on Indian cultivators' borrowing patterns. In the U.S. South it appears that the chief reason poor cultivators borrowed was to see them through the period between the planting and the harvest. They would only accumulate debt if ex post they found it impossible to completely repay their loans. The result of repeated miscalculations coupled with high interest rates would be "debt peonage." Bose makes similar claims for colonial India. He writes that credit and finance were critical "mode of appropriation" (Bose 1994, p. 3). The AIRCS gathered data on the extent of loans that were taken out and repaid within the year, and the expenditure on repaying debt, where this last category was broken down into payments for debt acquired this year but still outstanding, and amounts borrowed a previous year but still outstanding. Monies borrowed and repaid within the year were a relatively small portion of the total amount borrowed; on average these constituted only 18 percent of the total amount borrowed within the year. But this could have been caused by a miscalculation, though a very large one. Perhaps the cultivators intended to repay but were unable. The AIRCS also asked how much the cultivators had spent that year paying off old debt. This constituted a substantial share of expenditures but was not as large as agricultural investment. For cultivators as a whole, average expenditure on the "repayment of old debt" was Rs. 65.47, while average agricultural investment was Rs. 189. For small cultivators in subsistence regions, those one would assume would be most at risk of "debt" peonage, average repayment expenditures were Rs. 31.5 while average agricultural investments were Rs. 64.3.

CASTE AND THE INDIAN CREDIT SYSTEM

I argue that the caste system allowed the provision of long-term debt in rural India. Though caste has many aspects, most economists have focused on just two: the hereditary assignment of some occupations such as priests and manure collectors or sweepers, and the hierarchy that separated, socially and economically, the high castes from the lower castes. However important these may be for both the speed and the morality of Indian economic development, they are not my focus. I want to concentrate on a different aspect of caste. Whatever else it was, caste is an extended, somewhat formalized kinship network. Srinivas argues that despite the scorn heaped upon it, few Indians would want to abandon the caste system as "joint family and caste provide for an individual in our society some of the benefits which a welfare state provides for him in the industrially advanced countries of the West" (Srinivas 1962, p. 70). But continued membership in the network required meeting certain obligations. If a member failed to meet his obligations, he *and his family* would be formally outcasted and lose all benefits of membership. In India there were accepted, formal means of adjudicating cases in which members failed in their obligations to the social network. Each caste had its own *panchayat*, or council, over which the headman of the caste officiated. Cases taken up by the caste-*panchayat* dealt with personal matters that would lower the reputation of the caste, such as irregular unions and family quarrels, with land disputes, and with other disputes between caste members. The *panchayat* had other functions such as planning community festivals or reforming the subcaste, or *jati*, customs (Kolenda 1978, p. 89). The decisions of the *panchayats* were upheld by the group. The punishment meted out for grievous violations of caste rules was to "deprive a casteman of the right to receive water, or the tobacco pipe, from the hands of his fellow castemen and forbids them likewise to receive it from them." This effectively expelled him from the community. He would not receive help in time of difficulty, and there would be no one for his children to marry. Kolenda (1978, p. 11) writes that the resulting "social control of members is unusually strong and effective."

This collective responsibility gave caste a role in maintaining credit and credibility in the rural market. Nehru examined the surveys of 54 rural villages in the Mid-Gangetic Valley which had been conducted for the PBEC. He noted that 50 percent of the debt was not secured. "Patently they are unsecured, as there is no tangible security behind them. But in fact as in a business proposition, they are based on the strongest security, *the borrowers caste and credit*" (Nehru 1932, p. 115; emphasis in original). Nehru asserted that caste supported credit, but he did not describe the mechanism. The AIRCS gave more specific details. "The social compunction [to repay moneylenders] is connected with considerations such as loss of 'face' or local prestige, caste disapproval, possible pressure through the caste *panchayat* and a variety of other social sanctions which, because they happen to be intangible, are not on that account any the less powerful" (Reserve Bank of India 1954, p. 171). Binswanger et al. (1985, p. 35) note this mechanism operating in 1979–1980. "In most villages, village elders will assist recovery [by moneylenders] by mediating between borrowers and lenders in public meetings. The threat to ask for such a meeting is definitely used to speed up recovery." In marked contrast, Binswanger et al. (1985, p. 51) found no stigma associated with failure to repay government loans.

The rigidities of the caste structure would imply that, ceteris paribus, the Indian moneylending market would be less risky. In modern Indian village credit markets, risk does appear to be minimal. Walker and Ryan were involved in creating the ICRISTAT data, an intensive study of three villages in South India by the International Crop Research Institute for the Semi-Arid Tropics in Hyderabad stretching from 1975 to 1985. Walker and Ryan believed that a "crude, upper bound estimate" of the default rate in the informal market was 5 percent in any given year even though the great majority of loans were unsecured (Walker and Ryan 1990, p. 204). Their estimate accords with that of Aleem (1993), for the Chambar area in Sind, Pakistan, who also found a default rate of less than 5 percent. Note that these rates are not very different from the 98 percent repayment of the Grameen Bank.

It was not only caste structure that secured loans in India; it was also the relative immobility of rural Indians. The report for the 1931 census states that 959 out of 1,000 Indians reside in their district of birth, an outmigration rate from the district of less than 5 percent! (There were roughly 300 districts in British India.) Indian migration rates remain quite low. Munshi and Rosenzweig (2009) report that from a representative sample of rural Indian households, which is newly available, they found that in rural areas migration rates for men out of their origin villages were 8.7 percent in 1999. This can be compared to the figures of Graves,

Sexton, and Vedder (1983) of migration in the U.S. South in the mid-nineteenth century. They found outmigration rates *out of the state*, not out of the village, of between 16 and 23 percent for Alabama, Georgia, Mississippi, and North and South Carolina. Only Louisiana, at 6 percent, had rates as low as the Indian rates. Caste may also have a role to play in this relative immobility. Munshi and Rosenzweig (2009) in fact attribute the low levels of migration to the Indian peasant's need to maintain caste connections for credit purposes.

And even if the individual moved, in India his family probably would not. Kessinger (1975) showed for at least one village that the core community of an Indian village changes little over very long periods of time. To my knowledge, he is the only one to prove this point, though it is widely accepted on an anecdotal basis. He made an exhaustive analysis of manuscript censuses, revenue records, and family genealogies, stretching from 1848 to 1968 for Vilyatpur in the Punjab. Though there were a few land sales every year, typically of very small lots, Kessinger found land ownership changed very little over this period (ignoring the fact that fathers were replaced by their sons), or in the family composition of his village. What this means is that even if one member of the family moved away, the rest of the family could provide guarantee for the loan. This was especially true in India because, at least according to Hardiman (1996, pp. 92–117) for western India, family members considered themselves collectively responsible for debt. The lack of mobility and the extremely solid kinship connections in India would have greatly raised the returns to rural lending in India relative to, for example, the postbellum U.S. South.

THE BUDGET CONSTRAINT OF THE
RURAL INDIAN CULTIVATOR

Table 10.5 summarizes the average expenditure of an Indian cultivator in 1951, illustrating the uses of rural India's well-functioning credit system . Even the poorest Indian cultivators spent a remarkable portion of their income on festivals, weddings, and death ceremonies. I have reported all India figures and divided India into the three production categories used earlier. For all of India, ceremonial expenditures for one year on average constituted 18 percent of annual crop values. Expenditures on gross agri-

TABLE 10.5 *Ceremonial Expenditure and Gross Capital Agricultural Investment,*
1951

Area		Districts	Average per Family (Rs.)		Average Ratio of Ceremonial Expenditures to	
			Ceremonial Expenditure	Gross Agricultural Capital Investment	Value of Crops	Gross Agricultural Capital Investment
All India	All Cultivators	75	117	192	18%	76%
	First 5 Deciles	75	162	296	16%	69%
	Last 5 Deciles	75	73	87	24%	120%
Commercial	All	20	99	263	16%	45%
	First	20	148	421	15%	46%
	Last	20	49	106	20%	73%
Monetized	All	28	158	205	22%	84%
	First	28	208	305	19%	74%
	Last	28	108	106	29%	130%
Subsistence	All	27	89	124	16%	89%
	First	27	125	195	15%	80%
	Last	27	52	53	22%	143%

Note: I use information drawn from the Intensive Survey so that these expenditures can be compared to the value of crop production, though the relationship between ceremonial expenditure and gross agricultural capital investment is virtually identical if data from the General Survey are used.

Source: Reserve Bank of India (1956), table 17.

cultural capital investment were larger, but the average district expenditure on ceremonies constituted 76 percent of the expenditure on gross agricultural capital investment. It is also interesting that poorer families, though they spent absolutely less on ceremonial expenditures, have a much higher ratio of ceremonial expenditures to gross agricultural investments, 120 percent. For these families, this type of consumption clearly crowded out investment.

There is no pattern of ceremonial expenditures across the "types" of regions. There is, however, an interesting pattern in the ratio of ceremonial expenditures to gross agricultural capital investments. In commercialized districts there are more investments in agricultural capital. There is no "type" where ceremonial expenditures were not very large, especially relative to expenditures on gross agricultural capital investments. And it is a fairly consistent pattern that poorer cultivators in each "type" spend much more on ceremonies relative to agricultural investments than their richer regional counterparts.

Several modern data sets show a similar ratio of ceremonial expenditure to income among poor Indian cultivators, including Banerji and Duflo (2007), Ruthven and Kumar (2002), and Kochar (2005). Rao (2001b) provides a firsthand description of rural spending patterns. While personally collecting a data set among the potter caste in a village in the southern Indian state of Karnataka in the 1990s, he was struck by the large expenditures he observed on dowries, wedding feasts, and festivals. The members of this caste, who are largely agriculturists, are all quite poor, below India's poverty line. Their day-to-day lives are difficult, even grim. But Rao was struck by the lavishness of their celebrations. Dowries, including the exchange of ornaments and clothes, were up to six times annual income. The costs of the wedding feast were roughly 20 percent of annual income. And expenditures celebrating annual festivals constituted an additional 15 percent of annual income.

One might suspect that these feasts did not represent true excess consumption. As most villagers and kin are invited to the feasts, they could represent a sharing of resources to which all eventually contributed. But Rao's description suggests there was a significant difference between day-to-day consumption and these feasts. Clothing, food, and drink were all above the norm.

One might also suspect that the large colonial wedding expenditures masked dowry expenditures, which might include tangible assets. What appear to be consumption expenditures might simply be a transfer of assets to the new couple. The AIRCS data do not allow me to separate out the cash and gold portions of the dowry from the pure consumption aspects of these expenditures. But I can be certain that the festivities alone constituted a relatively large expenditure for the Indian cultivator. For the General Survey, data were gathered separately on expenditures for "Death Ceremonies" and "Marriage and Other Ceremonies." Death ceremonies would not typically have a monetary transfer component. The ratio of Death Ceremony expenditures relative to Marriage and Other Ceremony expenditures is 19 percent for the "All Cultivators" category. It seems reasonable to assume that the pure festivities associated with a marriage would be at least as great as the festivities associated with a burial. In this case we can double the expenditure on death ceremonies to get an estimate of the pure consumption aspects of ceremonial expenditures. For most parts of India, the pure consumption portion of ceremonial expenditures would be about half as large as was estimated before. Such a figure is still quite large as a share of crop value.

The large sums spent on ceremonies were noted by the AIRCS authors. They wrote that "the occasions [for borrowing] which figure most prominently in all regions are marriages and similar ceremonies on which disproportionate amounts are usually spent almost as a matter of conventional necessity" (Reserve Bank of India 1954, p. 186). They were not surprised by this finding. The perception that the Indian cultivator engaged in excessive spending on ceremonies was commonly held long before this survey. The survey authors themselves cite the observations on this point made in the 1921 Indian census. The authors do not suggest the possibility of eliminating ceremonial expenditures.

If ceremonial expenditures could have been eliminated, the Indian cultivators' problems of fragmented landholdings and insufficient livestock could have been greatly mitigated. Consider just the bottom fifth percentile. Average annual ceremonial expenditure was Rs. 73. That is 5.02 percent of the value of their total land holdings, 69 percent of the value of their plow animals, and 70 percent of the value of their milch animals.[7] Plow animals are the second most important asset of Indian cultivator households, land being the first. And the average farm holding of plow animals for all Indian cultivators was just 2.5. Purchasing just one plow animal would push an Indian cultivator from the lowest fiftieth percentile in terms of this asset category to the top fiftieth percentile. Guha (1985, pp. 62–70), who made a careful survey of the agricultural technology of the Deccan, argued the fall in bullocks per acre in the Deccan was associated with the observed fall in yield over this period (1880–1920).

IMPLICATIONS AND DISCUSSION

Growth requires investment. Credit is supposed to spur growth because of its potential to spur investment. The history presented here suggests widely available credit in colonial India did not spur growth. Colonial cultivators were constrained, either by improvidence or by fear of seemingly inappropriate behavior, to use excess funds for consumption. When they did not have immediate funds for this purpose, they borrowed. What credit spurred in colonial India was ceremonies. I am hardly the first to make this point. My contribution has been the comparative analysis of the credit markets. I have shown that the Indian colonial credit system was superior to that of the postbellum U.S. South at least in the sense that it allowed for long-term borrowing even by landless or nearly landless cultivators. It could have mitigated the capital constraints of colonial Indian farmers with regard to farm fragmentation and the shortage of livestock, but it did not in part because of spending on ceremonies. It is worth pointing out that another part of the Indian cultivator's problem was the absolute severity of the capital shortages he faced. Figure 10.1 depicts the relationship between the average size of cultivated holdings per commensal family and the proportion of families with at least one plow animal in each of the eight villages covered by the 1951 AIRCS survey in 27 "Subsistence" districts. Most commensal family farms were quite small, and many families did not own a plow animal. It should not be thought that the villages with larger farms and a higher proportion of plow animal ownership were financially better off than the others. None of the villages depicted in Figure 10.1 were well off. Data on the value of the gross product of farms are available only from the Intensive Study, and thus only at the district level. The correlation between gross value of farm output and average acres sown for the bottom 50 percent of cultivators across the 76 districts surveyed is only 0.11. It is likely that the larger farms had less fertile land and required more acres just to maintain the family at subsistence levels. Larger farms meant that they needed to own their own plow animal, as it was impossible to share or rent animals for these larger farms. One might argue that what my discussion has really shown is that improving the lives of these cultivators would have required a substantial increase in the resources available. An additional plow animal or a slightly larger farm would have improved the family's welfare, but it would not have eliminated risk. Under these circumstances, it seems reasonable to argue as Charlesworth has that "the certain return in social prestige from a lavish wedding made that, often, a

FIGURE 10.1 *Percent of Cultivating Families with Plow Animals versus Average Acres Cultivated per Commensal Family in the Villages of the 27 "Subsistence" Districts of India*

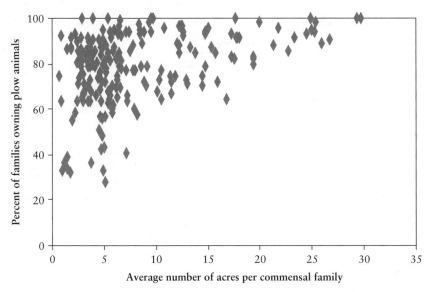

Source: Reserve Bank of India (1956).

more attractive and 'rational' investment than sinking funds in agricultural innovation where output levels and market demand were subject to such vacillation" (Charlesworth 1985, p. 81).

Modern surveys suggest that the spending patterns of Indian cultivators are similar to those of the colonial period. It is not clear if the advent of microfinance can have a substantial impact on these patterns. Microfinance is still of marginal importance, at least in India. In 2001, though there were between 800 and 1,000 nongovernmental organizations assisting the poor with their credit and saving needs, Sinha and Patole (2003) estimate that fewer than 3 million Indian families were reached. Given that widely available credit to poor cultivators in the colonial period was not associated with growth, even supposing that microfinance expanded its outreach, it is questionable if the limited amounts of resources which these institutions provide to individuals would have much of an effect. In their study of modern caste networks, Munshi and Rosenzweig (2009) speculate that only a large change, something that substantially lowered the riskiness of life in India or provided a substantially improved insurance mechanism over caste networks, would lessen the importance of caste in India. The U.S. South today is very different from what it was in the 1930s, but not due to marginal changes in policy or credit availability. India is still waiting for the significant shock that will allow it to break from the past.

NOTES

I thank participants at seminars at the University of Toronto, Queens College, McGill University, and Stanford University as well as the World Cliometrics Conference in Edinburgh and the South Asia Conference in Madison, Wisconsin, for helpful comments.

1. Burgess and Pande (2005) find that the extension of bank branches to the rural sector was associated with a reduction in rural poverty, but they could not identify a specific cause. In particular, they found no associated increase in agricultural productivity. Two important papers that directly address demand for rural credit are Kochar (1997) and Bell, Srinivasan, and Udry (1997). Kochar argues that there is relatively little demand for formal credit, in part because poorer farmers believe correctly that they will not be allowed access, or perhaps they prefer informal credit. Bell, Srinivasan, and Udry, on the other hand, believe that formal credit rationing remains a problem, in part because of the type of loans available in the informal market.

2. Repeated and increasing loans to clients from moneylenders were and are the norm. Weekly repayment with equal installments was not the norm, but such repayment schemes were hardly a major "innovation" of microlenders, as might be suggested by the discussion of Armendáriz and Morduch (2007, pp. 129–134). The 1930 PBEC of the United Provinces of Agra and Oud described the "qist" business, in which loans were repaid in equal installments, either by the month or day. The authors of the report write, "This kind of investment is prevalent almost all over the provinces [of Agra and Oud] in different forms and is showing a great tendency towards increase . . . as it is found attractive in view of the easy installments in which repayments are made" (India, Banking Enquiry Committee 1930d, p. 297). I did not see references to such loans in other parts of India at that time. Microlenders, however, overwhelmingly lend to women. This is a real break from the moneylenders of the colonial period. Lending to women, however, is unlikely to unleash their entrepreneurial talents as what appears to happen most often in India is they pass on their loans to their husbands or brothers (Goetz and Gupta 1996). On the other hand, Ligon (2002) has argued that the fact that the loans are "pipelined" through the women raises the bargaining power of married women in the relationship, and that may have beneficial effects for both the women and their children.

3. See India, Banking Enquiry Committee (1930a, 1930b, 1930c, 1930d) and Reserve Bank of India, Committee of Direction of the All-India Rural Credit Survey (1954–1956), hereafter referred to as Reserve Bank of India.

4. There were government-sponsored agricultural cooperatives. Cooperatives furnished only 2 percent of all rural loans in the AIRCS. This is an upper bound estimate as half the villages chosen in each district were required to have cooperatives, as the Reserve Bank of India was exploring cooperatives' effectiveness.

5. A cropper in the census was defined as anyone who answered yes to the question "Does the person from whom you rent furnish all the work animals?" (U.S. Department of Commerce, Bureau of the Census 1922, p. 121).

6. The Intensive Survey reports data only for the first or last five deciles. The General Survey reports data for smaller groups, including "Small Cultivators," which was the last three deciles. I do not know the value of farm income for this group, but the "Small Cultivators" in subsistence regions borrowed on average Rs. 71.5 per family and reported that 19.4 percent of this was for agricultural investments.

7. The price of milch and plow animals is derived from a regression of the values of a farm's livestock holding on their number. The values are Rs. 149 (35.13) and Rs. 135 (40.88), respectively, with standard errors in the parentheses.

REFERENCES

Aleem, Irfan (1993). "Imperfect Information, Screening, and the Costs of Informal Lending: A Study of a Rural Credit Market in Pakistan." In *The Economics of Rural Organization: Theory, Practice and Policy*, edited by Karla Hoff, Avishay Braverman, and Joseph E. Stiglitz. New York: Oxford University Press, pp. 131–153.

Alston, Lee J., and Joseph P. Ferrie (2005). "Time on the Ladder: Career Mobility in Agriculture, 1890–1938." *Journal of Economic History* 65: 1058–1081.

Armendáriz, Beatriz, and Jonathan Morduch (2007). *The Economics of Microfinance*. Cambridge, MA: MIT Press.

Baker, Christopher John (1984). *An Indian Rural Economy 1880–1955: The Tamilnad Countryside*. New York: Clarendon Press.

Banerji, Abhijit V., and Esther Duflo (2007). "The Economic Lives of the Poor." *Journal of Economic Perspectives* 21: 141–167.

Bell, Clive, T. N. Srinivasan, and Christopher Udry (1997). "Rationing, Spillover, and Interlinking in Credit Markets: The Case of Rural Punjab." *Oxford Economic Papers* 49: 557–585.

Bhaduri, Amit (1973). "A Study in Agricultural Backwardness under Semi-Feudalism." *The Economic Journal* 83: 120–137.

Bhaduri, Amit (1977). "On the Formation of Usurious Interest Rates in Backward Agriculture." *Cambridge Journal of Economics* 1: 341–352.

Bhatacharya, Neeladri (1994). "Lenders and Debtors: Punjab Countryside, 1880–1940." In *Credit, Markets, and the Agrarian Economy of Colonial India*, edited by Sugata Bose. New York: Oxford University Press, pp. 197–247.

Binswanger, Hans, T. Balaramaiah, V. Bashkar Rao, M. J. Bhende, and K.V. Kashirsagar (1985). "Credit Markets in Rural South India: Theoretical Issues and Empirical Analysis." Agriculture and Rural Development Department, World Bank, Report No. ARU45. Washington, DC: World Bank.

Bose, Sugata, ed. (1994). *Credit, Markets, and the Agrarian Economy of Colonial India*. Delhi: Oxford University Press.

Burgess, Robin, and Rohini Pande (2005). "Do Rural Banks Matter? Evidence from the Indian Social Banking Experiment." *American Economic Review* 95: 780–795.

Charlesworth, Neil (1978). "Rich Peasants and Poor Peasants in Late Nineteenth-Century Maharashtra." In *The Imperial Impact: Studies in the Economic History of Africa and*

India, edited by Clive Dewey and A. G. Hopkins. London: University of London, the Athlone Press, pp. 97–113.

Charlesworth, Neil (1985). *Peasants and Imperial Rule: Agriculture and Agrarian Society in the Bombay Presidency, 1850–1935*. New York: Cambridge University Press.

Collins, William J. (1997). "When the Tide Turned: Immigration and the Delay of the Great Black Migration." *Journal of Economic History* 57: 607–632.

Cull, Robert, Asli Demirgüç, and Jonathan Morduch (2007). "Financial Performance and Outreach: A Global Analysis of Leading Microbanks." *Economic Journal* 117: F107–F133.

Darling, Malcolm (1947). *The Punjab Peasant in Prosperity and Debt*, 4th ed. Columbia, MO: South Asia Books.

Dasgupta, Sukti, and Ajit Singh (2005). "Will Services Be the New Engine of Indian Economic Growth?" *Development and Change* 36: 1035–1057.

Ferleger, Louis (1993). "Sharecropping Contracts in the Late-Nineteenth-Century South." *Agricultural History* 67: 31–46.

Georgia, Department of Agriculture (various years). *Publications of the Georgia State Department of Agriculture*. Atlanta, GA: State Printer.

Goetz, A. M., and R. Sen Gupta (1996). "Who Takes the Credit? Gender, Power and Control over Land Use in Rural Credit Programs in Bangladesh." *World Development* 24: 45–63.

Graves, Philip E., Robert L. Sexton, and Richard K. Vedder (1983). "Slavery, Amenities, and Factor Price Equalization: A Note on Migration and Freedom." *Explorations in Economic History* 20: 156–162.

Guha, Sumit (1985). *The Agrarian Economy of the Bombay Deccan, 1818–1941*. New York: Oxford University Press.

Guha, Sumit (1987a). "The Land Market in Upland Maharashtra c. 1820–1960—I." *Indian Economic and Social History Review* 24: 117–144.

Guha, Sumit (1987b). "The Land Market in Upland Maharashtra c. 1820–1960—II." *Indian Economic and Social History Review* 24: 291–322.

Guha, Sumit (1992). *Growth, Stagnation or Decline? Agricultural Productivity in British India*. New York: Oxford University Press.

Guinnane, Timothy W. (1994). "A Failed Institutional Transplant: Raiffeisen's Credit Cooperatives in Ireland, 1895–1914." *Explorations in Economic History* 31: 38–61.

Haney, Lewis H. (1914). "Farm Credit Conditions in a Cotton State." *American Economic Review* 4: 47–67.

Hardiman, David (1996). *Feeding the Baniya: Peasants and Usurers in Western India*. New York: Oxford University Press.

Heston, Alan (1982). "National Income." In *The Cambridge Economic History of India*, vol. 2: *c. 1757–c. 1970*, edited by Dharma Kumar with the editorial assistance of Meghnad Desai. New Delhi: Orient Longman, pp. 376–462.

India, Banking Enquiry Committee (1930a). *Report*. Bombay: Government Central Press.

India, Banking Enquiry Committee (1930b). *Report of the Madras Provincial Banking Enquiry Committee, 1929–1930*. Madras: Madras Government Press.

India, Banking Enquiry Committee (1930c). *Report of the Punjab Provincial Banking Enquiry Committee, 1929–30*, vol. 1. Lahore: Superintendent of Government Printing.

India, Banking Enquiry Committee (1930d). *Report of the United Provinces Provincial Banking Enquiry Committee, 1929–30*, vol. 3. Allahabad: Superintendent of the Government Press.

India, Census Commissioner (1933). *Census of India, 1931*. Delhi: Manager of Publications.

Jain, Lakshmi C. (1929). *Indigenous Banking in India*. London: Macmillan.

Kessinger, Tom G. (1975). "The Peasant Farm in North India, 1848–1968." *Explorations in Economic History* 12: 303–323.

Kochar, Anjini (1997). "An Empirical Investigation of Rationing Constraints in Rural Credit Markets in India." *Journal of Development Economics* 53: 339–371.

Kochar, Anjini (2005). "Parental Benefits from Intergenerational Coresidence: Empirical Evidence from Rural Pakistan." *Journal of Political Economy* 108: 1184–1209.

Kolenda, Pauline (1978). *Caste in Contemporary India: Beyond Organic Solidarity*. Menlo Park, CA: The Benjamin/Cumming Publishing Co.

Kolenda, Pauline (1987). *Regional Differences in Family Structure in India*. Jaipur: Rawat Publications.

Ligon, Ethan (2002). "Dynamic Bargaining in Households (with Application to Bangladesh)." Working Paper, Department of Agricultural and Resource Economics, University of California, Berkeley.

Munshi, Kaivan, and Mark Rosenzweig (2009). "Why Is Mobility in India So Low? Social Insurance, Inequality, and Growth." National Bureau of Economic Research Working Paper No. 14850. Cambridge, MA: National Bureau of Economic Research.

Musgrave, Peter J. (1978). "Rural Credit and Rural Society in the United Provinces, 1860–1920." In *The Imperial Impact: Studies in the Economic History of Africa and India*, edited by Clive Dewey and A. G. Hopkins. London: University of London, The Athlone Press, pp. 216–232.

Nehru, S. S. (1932). *Caste and Credit in the Rural Area: A Survey*. Bombay: Longmans, Green.

North Carolina, Bureau of Labor Statistics (1887). *First Annual Report*. Raleigh, NC: Josephus Daniels.

North Carolina, Bureau of Labor Statistics (1888). *Second Annual Report*. Raleigh, NC: Josephus Daniels.

Rao, Vijayendra (2001a). "Celebrations as Social Investments: Festival Expenditure, Unit Price Variation and Social Status in Rural India." *Journal of Development Studies* 38: 71–97.

Rao, Vijayendra (2001b). "Poverty and Public Celebrations in Rural India." *Annals of the American Academy of Political and Social Science* 573: 85–104.

Reserve Bank of India. Committee of Direction of the All-India Rural Credit Survey (1954). *All-India Rural Credit Survey: Report of the Committee of Direction*, vol. 2: *General Report*. Bombay: Reserve Bank of India.

Reserve Bank of India. Committee of Direction of the All-India Rural Credit Survey (1955). *All-India Rural Credit Survey: Report of the Committee of Direction*, vol. 1: *Survey Report*. Bombay: Reserve Bank of India.

Reserve Bank of India. Committee of Direction of the All-India Rural Credit Survey (1956). *All-India Rural Credit Survey: Report of the Committee of Direction*, vol. 3: *Technical Report*. Bombay: Reserve Bank of India.

Ruthven, Orlanda, and Sushil Kumar (2002). "Fine Grain Finance: Financial Choice and Strategy among the Poor in Rural North India." Finance and Development Research Programme Working Paper Series, University of Manchester.

Schreiner, Mark (2003). "A Cost-Effectiveness Analysis of the Grameen Bank of Bangladesh." *Development Policy Review* 21: 357–382.

Sinha, Sanjay, and Meenal Patole (2003). "Microfinance and the Poverty of Financial Services: A Perspective from Indian Experience." *South Asian Economic Journal* 4: 301–318.

Srinivas, M. N. (1962). *Caste in Modern India and Other Essays*. New York: Asian Publishing House.

U.S. Department of Commerce, Bureau of the Census (1922). *Fourteenth Census of the United States of America taken in 1920*, vol. 5: *Agriculture*. Washington, DC: Government Printing Office.

Walker, Thomas S., and James G. Ryan (1990). *Village and Household Economies in India's Semiarid Tropics*. Baltimore: Johns Hopkins University Press.

Whatley, Warren C. (1983). "Labor for the Picking: The New Deal in the South." *Journal of Economic History* 43: 905–929.

Whitcombe, Elizabeth (1972). *Agrarian Conditions in Northern India*, vol. 1: *The United Provinces under British Rule, 1860–1900*. Berkeley: University of California Press.

Woodman, Harold D. (1968). *King Cotton and His Retainers: Financing and Marketing the Cotton Crop of the South, 1800–1925*. Lexington: University of Kentucky Press.

Wright, Gavin (1987). "Postbellum Southern Labor Markets." In *Quantity and Quiddity: Essays in U.S. Economic History*, edited by Peter Kilby. Middletown, CT: Wesleyan University Press, pp. 98–134.

PART THREE

Revolution in Labor Markets

VIEWED OVER long time spans, the course of economic development appears to be characterized by episodes of relative institutional stability punctuated by periods of dramatic, even revolutionary, change. An important characteristic of these episodes of revolutionary change is that while their occurrence can be rationalized ex post, they are rarely predictable ex ante. In Chapter 11, Joshua L. Rosenbloom and William A. Sundstrom argue that this dynamic of institutional stability punctuated by revolutionary change in what they call "labor-market regimes" is an inherent characteristic of labor markets created by the role that market institutions play in facilitating coordination among economic agents. As their narrative history of labor market regimes in U.S. history documents, institutional complementarities mean that once a coherent set of formal and informal institutional arrangements is arrived at, it becomes difficult to change them. As a result, changes tend to occur episodically and in response to more or less exogenous shocks.

Robert K. Fleck (Chapter 12) extends the argument advanced by Rosenbloom and Sundstrom by elaborating on the mutual interaction between labor markets and the broader economy. Writing about the causes and consequences of the New Deal, Fleck shows how the truly revolutionary consequences of this political event were transmitted through their effect on labor markets. By severing the ties that had kept blacks in the South and initiating their large-scale migration to the North, the New Deal initiated a political realignment that in turn had profound consequences for the entire country.

The remaining chapters in Part Three broaden and deepen these observations in a number of important ways. Stacey M. Jones (Chapter 13) offers an interpretation of the discontinuous shift in female labor force participation that took place during the late 1960s and early 1970s. Specifically, she argues that the dramatic shift in women's career choices from homemaker to professional should be viewed as a transition from one labor market regime to another and that this transition was precipitated by a transitory event: the decline in employment opportunities in teaching.

Frank Levy and Peter Temin's analysis (Chapter 14) of the reasons why inequality has increased in the United States since 1980 further illustrates both the discontinuous nature of labor market regime changes and the self-reinforcing mechanisms that help support regimes once they are established. As Levy and Temin describe, the labor market institutions that they term the "Treaty of Detroit" were forged in the Great Depression and World War II but prevailed into the late 1970s, giving way only under the pressure of stagflation and growing international economic competition. The emergence of a new regime, the "Washington Consensus," was in their view instrumental in undermining forces promoting wage equality and initiating the era of rising inequality.

Richard Sutch (Chapter 15) examines more closely one element of the postwar labor market regimes considered by Levy and Temin, minimum wage legislation. While most of the conventional economic analysis of the minimum wage has focused on measuring the disemployment effects of imposing a wage "floor," Sutch argues that the most important effect of this intervention was in altering school attendance behavior. By making low-skilled workers more expensive and limiting employment, increases in the minimum wage encouraged greater investment in education. These investments, in turn, helped support the tendency of the Treaty of Detroit regime to encourage greater wage equality. With the breakdown of this regime and the emergence of the Washington Consensus, real minimum wages began to decline, discouraging school attendance.

Because labor markets are the mechanisms that coordinate the allocation of human effort, the ways in which they operate and the outcomes they produce have broad consequences for choices about investments in education, decisions about migration, family formation, fertility, and retirement. And once a particular labor market regime becomes established, it may well be the case that it is easier to adjust along these other margins than to alter the labor-market regime. Susan B. Carter (Chapter 16) illustrates how these characteristics of the labor market influenced the employment opportunities of Chinese Americans through a history of the spread of Chinese restaurants in America. As she argues, this remarkably culinary revolution can be traced back to the effects of the Chinese Exclusion Act of 1882 on the location decisions of Chinese immigrants and their offspring.

P. W. R., J. L. R., and D. F. W.

CHAPTER 11

Labor-Market Regimes in
U.S. Economic History

JOSHUA L. ROSENBLOOM
AND WILLIAM A. SUNDSTROM

THE 30-YEAR TREND of rising income inequality in the United States has led to heightened interest among labor economists in assessing the role of labor-market institutions in the determination of wages and other market outcomes. The central role of institutions governing work and compensation is a venerable theme in economics. Adam Smith famously held that the incentives associated with labor systems could explain the relative success of countries like England and the backwardness of economies based on slavery or sharecropping. Karl Marx based his stages theory of economic development on the nature of the relationship between workers and property holders under different economic regimes. Recently, economists and economic historians have revisited the long-run impact of institutions on economic growth and performance in an effort to understand the divergent fortunes of different countries and regions.[1]

The economic history of the United States presents a kind of laboratory for research on labor-market institutions and their impact. The contrast between the labor systems of chattel slavery in the Cotton South and free wage labor in the industrializing North plays a leading role in our understanding of patterns of regional development in the antebellum period. After the Civil War, regional differences persisted, but much of the action shifted to the evolution of industrial and postindustrial labor markets, from the relatively unfettered competitive environment of the late nineteenth century to the emergence of a federally regulated and more centralized bargaining system by the 1950s. The partial unraveling of that system in recent decades is one of the prime suspects in the trend toward greater inequality.

No economist has spent more time in this laboratory, or produced more significant results, than Gavin Wright. In this chapter our goal is to sketch a broad interpretation of the evolution of American labor markets, building on a key concept that informs Wright's work on both southern economic history and the growth of the U.S. industrial economy since the late nineteenth century—namely, what we will refer to as labor-market *institutional regimes*. We begin by providing a conceptual framework, defining what we mean by institutions and making a case for why labor-market institutions may be expected to exhibit both coherence and persistence—the defining traits of an institutional regime. We then begin our historical narrative with the familiar contrast between the labor systems of the antebellum northern and southern economies, and proceed through the dramatic changes in labor-market regimes wrought by the Civil War and later by the world wars and the Great Depression. These regime shifts shaped not only important labor-market outcomes, such as wages, working conditions, and employment, but also the dynamics of technology and human capital accumulation. An important conclusion, which we draw from Wright's work and from the events recounted in our narrative, is that trends in the underlying economic "fundamentals" that are often given causal primacy are themselves partly the endogenous product of institutional regimes.

LABOR-MARKET REGIMES

The institutions of the labor market can be defined as the principal rules and organizations governing the transactions between the buyers and sellers of labor. In this context rules should be conceived broadly to include both formal laws and property rights—enforceable in the courts— and implicit or informal behavioral norms. Familiar examples of formal legal rules affecting the U.S. labor market would be the Thirteenth Amendment to the Constitution, which by abolishing involuntary servitude established free labor as the standard form of property rights in labor nationwide, and the Fair Labor Standards Act of 1938, which set broad, legally enforceable minimum wages and maximum hours for most workers. An example of an informal rule, widely observed in labor markets of the pre–civil rights South, was the requirement that in mixed-race workplaces a black worker may never supervise a white worker (Dewey 1952).

In the sizable literature that has emerged in recent years attempting to classify and describe the variation of labor-market institutions across countries and assess their impact on economic performance, as measured by growth, unemployment, and inequality, the term "institutions" is often used as shorthand for the extent of governmental regulation of labor markets and the relative influence of unions or collective bargaining. We should be clear that while these factors are an important dimension of labor-market institutions, we intend a broader definition here.

The distinction between institutions on the one hand and what are merely widespread contractual arrangements or patterns of behavior on the other is a fuzzy one. If almost all workers receive paid vacation time as part of their employment contract, are paid vacations "institutionalized," or merely an equilibrium form of nonwage compensation? We take the view here that institutions are something more than common patterns of behavior; they must constrain individual choices and contracts beyond the constraints determined by prices and endowments. In the case of legal regulations such as the minimum wage, the constraint is a rule that can be enforced by the state. Informal norms are not legally enforceable but may be enforced through extralegal social sanctions, such as ostracism or reciprocity. Finally, we include standardization of contractual terms as additional institutional constraints. Given transaction costs and bounded rationality, participants in the market may adhere to a coordinating equilibrium in which the range of contractual options is narrowed by convention—a familiar example from economic history is the conventional 50–50 split of the harvest between worker and landlord under sharecropping, with adjustment to changing market conditions being made along other margins, such as plot size.

The institutional features of labor markets differ considerably across political settings as well as industries and even individual firms. There is widespread acknowledgment that in the universe of developed economies, labor markets in the United States tend to lie at the laissez-faire end of the spectrum, but the implications for economic outcomes remain in dispute. In a useful survey, Freeman (2007) suggests that the one robust finding from studies of comparative labor-market performance is that institutions have significant effects on income distribution, with the more regulated and centralized wage-setting regimes of continental Europe exhibiting less inequality than the less-regulated Anglo-American regimes. The wage regulation and employment rigidities associated with European labor institutions have also often been blamed for higher rates of unemployment and sluggish employment growth, although the evidence is more mixed for these effects.

As we document in this chapter, it is also clear that within a given national setting labor-market institutions are subject to considerable temporal change. U.S. labor markets may now be thought of as a relatively unregulated "wild west" by developed capitalist standards, but even in America centralized federal regulation increased substantially over the course of the past century. These changes did not occur along a steady, continuous path; rather, periods of relative stasis in the basic rules of the game were punctuated by episodes of rapid change. Emancipation and the New Deal are perhaps the most obvious instances of such "revolutionary" episodes in U.S. labor-market history. Furthermore, the direction of change is not necessarily monotonic. While U.S. labor markets are subject to more government regulation today than they were a century ago, it is certainly arguable that the same period witnessed the rise and then fall of centralized wage bargaining institutions, and therefore that U.S. labor markets more closely resembled those of contemporary continental Europe in the 1950s than they do today.

Although labor-market institutions vary across countries, regions, and periods of time, the question arises whether it makes sense to think of the configuration of institutional elements in a particular time and place as constituting a coherent institutional regime or system rather than a mere collection of rules and laws. The idea of such an institutional regime should be familiar to readers of Gavin Wright's seminal work on slavery and the postbellum American South. In contrasting the developmental paths of the slave South and the free-labor North, Wright stresses ways in which each region's system of property rights over labor shaped private incentives as well as political interests and behavior, with profound implications for the path of economic development (Wright 1978,

2006a). With the Civil War and emancipation, the labor-market institutions of South and North necessarily converged in terms of basic property rights, but Wright (1986) argues that the South retained a distinctive regional labor-market regime for decades, one that rested on geographical isolation, political domination by the planter class, disfranchisement of African Americans, inferior education, and low wages.

We argue here that an institutional regime must exhibit two characteristics: coherence and persistence (or path dependence). By coherence we mean that important institutional elements are complementary and mutually reinforcing and therefore tend to occur together as a set. For example, the mid-twentieth-century high-wage regime depicted by Wright (2006b) emerged behind the protective barrier of restrictive immigration policy, which not only contributed to the high-wage equilibrium itself by reducing labor supply and making it less elastic but also helped protect organized labor from immigrant strikebreaking and thus complemented the legal protection and sometimes active governmental promotion of collective bargaining. It is at least arguable that a regime with widespread collective bargaining is incompatible in the long run with free immigration. By contrast, in the labor regime of the early twentieth-century South, lower state spending on education was consistent with the regional political-economic strategy of maintaining a comparative advantage in low-wage industries and an isolated low-wage labor market by limiting information and opportunities for mobility of the workforce.

Once established, institutional regimes are sticky, with periods of relative institutional stability punctuated by crisis periods of relatively rapid change. David (1994) notes three important factors that make institutions path dependent, or as he puts it the "carriers of history." First, institutions facilitate coordination among agents by creating mutually consistent expectations; in other words, institutional rules and norms are standards. Common language, social conventions, and the delineation of social roles all permit agents to economize on information gathering and learning in social transactions. In the context of labor markets, exchange is facilitated if workers can expect that the basic contractual rules of the game are common across employers. These rules could include legal rights, such as common-law rules governing workplace liability, or terms and conditions of the employment relationship, such as standard hours of labor and pay periods or labor's share of the harvest. Standards serve to reduce the dimensionality of the labor contract (which could otherwise be extraordinarily complex), thereby reducing the costs of evaluating and negotiating terms. Because the gains from adopting a behavioral standard or convention are a function of how many others have adopted the same standard, such conventions are subject to increasing returns and potential lock-in effects (David 1985).

A second, related source of historical persistence in an institutional regime is learning. The information channels, codes, and conventions that facilitate labor transactions must, like a language, be learned by individuals and organizations. These investments in human and organizational capital are largely irreversible, in the sense that the stock of knowledge is not readily transferable to new institutional settings.[2] Third, institutional complementarities themselves can increase rigidity by increasing the costs of adjusting any single institutional element. During the 1960s and 1970s, for example, racial integration of job ladders in some southern industries was hampered not only by lingering racial hostilities on the part of white workers but also by vested interests created under the seniority system (Minchin 2007).

The path dependence of institutional regimes obviously does not imply that institutions are completely exogenous to broader historical and economic forces, but it does give them an important codetermining role in shaping economic outcomes over fairly long periods of time. Institutional regimes affect not only the static equilibrium of the labor market—the level and distribution of wages, employment, and unemployment—but the dynamics of the market as well. In particular, institutions shape the evolution of the technologies and endowments often considered to be market fundamentals.

In this chapter we discuss several important illustrative cases from U.S. labor-market history, including the impact of slavery on southern economic development and the contrasting role of free labor in the industrializing North, and the implications of the "high-wage" institutional regime of the mid-twentieth century for productivity growth and human capital accumulation. With regard to the latter case, Wright (2006b, p. 158) argues that "the primary causal influence ran from the labor market to productivity rather than the other way round," with labor-market outcomes affecting not only the choice of technique along a static isoquant but also the very pace of technological progress. At the risk of oversimplifying some complex arguments, we suggest that this neo-institutionalist view may be contrasted with the important work of Goldin and Katz, summarized in their recent book (2008), which emphasizes a more conventionally neoclassical causal story: technological change is the fundamental driver of labor demand, the existing stock of skills determines labor supply, and investment in education responds endogenously in the long run to the relative price of skills. But even in the Goldin and Katz narrative, political institutions play a central role in the accumulation of human capital, and labor-market institutions such as unions and regulation play at least a supporting part in determining the wage structure in the medium run. As in many cases where there are competing institutional and neoclassical narratives, historical studies can help sort out the relative importance of these causal influences.

LEGAL FOUNDATIONS OF AMERICAN LABOR MARKETS

The legal foundations of employment law in the United States and Britain developed from common precedents in the seventeenth century, but different circumstances led to divergent practices. This divergence was sharpened in the wake of the American Revolution, when the abolition of slavery across the northern states led Americans toward a distinctive conception of the meaning of "free labor." In many respects these legal foundations have exerted a persistent effect on American labor markets even into the present day, contributing to the relatively high levels of mobility and competition that characterize American labor markets.

In colonial British North America a variety of different and overlapping arrangements concerning property rights in labor coexisted with one another. At one extreme, the legal system accepted the right of European Americans to own African Americans. Slave owners enjoyed a largely unrestricted authority over the allocation of time and effort of their slaves and their offspring, and this property was freely transferable, just as other property. At the other extreme, free colonists were able to sell their labor effort for a limited period of time in ways that resembled modern labor-market transactions. In between these extremes, however, were a number of intermediate relationships, the numerically most important of which was indentured servitude. Like free laborers, indentured servants were seen as having entered "voluntarily" into their employment relationship, but once they had indentured themselves to a master they became for the period specified in their contract the property of that master. Law and custom provided servants some protection, but ownership of their labor could be freely transferred, the master could enforce obedience to his wishes, and servants were not free to leave their owner before the conclusion of their term of service.[3]

Before American independence these varying systems of property rights coexisted throughout all of the colonies that would become the United States. Slavery was most prevalent in the southern colonies, but there were slaves and slave owners in every colony prior to the Revolution. In the wake of the American Revolution, however, all of the northern states adopted some form of abolition. Writing about changing attitudes toward slavery, Kolchin (1993, pp. 63–70) argued that the rhetoric of the American Revolution appears to have contributed to changing views of the legitimacy of slavery and thus to northern abolition. Although many southern states did ease restrictions on voluntary manumission following the Revolution, southerners also developed increasingly elaborate intellectual defenses of slavery in response to the emerging northern critique of the institution.

The North-South divide over slavery that emerged after the Revolution was formalized in the Northwest Ordinance. Passed in 1787 to govern the settlement of western territories, the ordinance prohibited the introduction of slavery into areas north of the Ohio River. On the frontier, slavery offered the possibility of more rapid settlement, a faster transition to commercial agriculture, and a quicker rise in property values, all of which appealed strongly to early settlers. The restraints of the Northwest Ordinance, however, prevented them from legalizing slavery, and as the number of free settlers in the territories increased, political opposition to slavery grew in the region (Wright 1978, pp. 12–13).[4] As a result, by the beginning of the nineteenth century, the United States was characterized by two distinct labor-market regimes: one in the South that allowed slavery and one in the North that prohibited it.

The geographic division between the slave South and the free North contributed to the emergence in the early nineteenth century of an increasingly sharply drawn and uniquely American conception of "free" labor. In the late eighteenth and early nineteenth centuries this emerging sense of what it meant to be a free worker was manifested in growing tensions between masters and journeymen in a variety of skilled crafts. As one visitor to the country observed at the time: "There is no such relation as *master* and *servant* in the United States: indeed the name is not permitted;—'help' is the designation of one who condescends to receive wages for service" (quoted in Steinfeld 1991, p. 127; emphasis in original). At the same time, court decisions were gradually exposing the logical contradictions between the abolition of slavery and the persistence of voluntary servitude. The culmination of this trend came in 1821, when the Indiana Supreme Court concluded in the case of *Mary Clark, a Woman of Color* that employers could not impose specific enforcement of a labor contract.

Other court decisions in the early nineteenth century reflect the formation of a uniquely American regime of high labor turnover and worker mobility. For example, while English courts continued to hold that an indefinite labor contract was an annual one and that the worker was entitled to compensation only at the completion of the entire year's work, northern courts increasingly ruled that workers who left prior to the termination of their contract were nonetheless entitled to compensation for the time that they had served. They also increasingly ruled in ways that set strict limits on an employer's ability to physically discipline employees. The confluence of these trends helped to establish in the antebellum North the notion of "employment at will," in which the employment relationship was viewed as a kind of lease but one that could be maintained only so long as both parties assented to its perpetuation (Steinfeld 1991, 147–172; Steinfeld 2001). Even when a legal contract might in principle have bound a worker to an employer for a limited duration, the geographic mobility of American workers and availability of the frontier "escape valve" often rendered such contracts unenforceable from the employer's perspective. This problem is a recurring theme in explanations of the weakness of apprenticeship in North American labor markets, although its significance has been questioned (Elbaum 1989; Hamilton 1995). The norms of low attachment and high mobility established the context in which the initial stages of American industrialization took place.

NORTHERN LABOR MARKETS IN THE
NINETEENTH CENTURY

At the beginning of the nineteenth century, the United States remained a predominantly agricultural economy, and industrial employment competed directly with agricultural opportunities. Native-born white males concentrated in farming, shopkeeping, the professions, and independent craft work (Gordon, Edwards, and Reich 1982, p. 48). When textile manufacturing began to expand in New England after the Embargo Act of 1807, the proprietors of these businesses were obliged to turn to other sources of labor. The early Rhode Island manufacturers relied primarily on children drawn from nearby farms to run the small spinning mills they established. This source of labor proved inadequate, however, for the larger, integrated spinning and weaving mills built on the model introduced by the Boston Manufacturing Company in 1814. Faced with the challenge of securing several hundred workers to staff a large-scale production process, Frances Lowell and his partners chose to recruit young women from the surrounding region, dispatching labor recruiters to rural areas and building dormitories to house the women who came to work in the mills (Rosenbloom 2004). Industrialization thus depended from the outset on expanding the scope of labor markets, both geographically and in the definition of the labor force, rather than accepting the prevailing labor supply conditions at a particular location.

The growth of the American textile industry depended not only on expanding the geographic scope of labor markets but also on technological innovations that were conditioned by the nature of the available labor. The mutual interaction between labor supply and innovation jointly shaped the emerging northern labor-market regime. Rothbarth (1946) and Habakkuk (1962) were among the first to seek to link the direction of American technological innovation in the nineteenth century to American labor supply conditions, arguing that relative labor scarcity led to capital-intensive (labor-saving) technological innovations. This conjecture has prompted both theoretical arguments seeking to rationalize this conjecture (e.g., David 1975) and a large empirical literature.

Although the burden of the empirical evidence suggests that Habakkuk was mistaken in his argument that the United States adopted more capital-intensive methods of production than Britain (Field 1983; James and Skinner 1985), careful examination of a number of industries does support the causal connection between labor supply and the direction of technological innovation. Rather than substituting capital for labor, it appears that American innovators sought to develop ways of conserving on traditional craft skills, which were in short supply in the United States. They did this by substituting raw materials and special-purpose machinery, which could be used by the less skilled workers who were available in greater abundance (Ames and Rosenberg 1968; Rosenberg 1976). One of the chief examples of this substitution is provided by the production of firearms. By the 1850s American innovations in this industry had attracted significant attention from the British, who sent engineers to inspect American factories with the goal of transferring American advances back to Britain. As Rosenbloom (1993) notes, the central feature of American innovations in the manufacture of firearms was the use of specialized machine tools and systems of measurement in lieu of the all-around craft skills of British gunsmiths.

Another, and quantitatively more significant, illustration of this pattern of technological response comes from the development of the American textile industry. Initially borrowing British spinning technologies, this industry grew to prominence through the development of a distinct technological paradigm uniquely adapted to American conditions. Following the British model, the earliest textile ventures spun yarn in small factories and then shipped this yarn to hand-loom weavers in the surrounding countryside to be made into cloth. But the shortage of skilled weavers (compared to Britain) imposed significant limits on the possible scale of production. To overcome the shortage of skilled weavers that constrained earlier ventures, Francis Lowell developed a mechanical loom and de-signed an integrated factory method of production to supply yarn that could be woven by this loom. The Boston Manufacturing Company, which Lowell and his associates established in 1814, proved enormously success-ful, and the production technology they introduced became the model for the industry's rapid expansion in the following decades.

The success of the New England textile manufacturers depended on securing an adequate supply of labor to operate the new factories, and it was the genius of Lowell's approach that his technological innovations were adapted to take advantage of the labor that was available at that time. As Field (1978) has pointed out, in the early decades of the nine-teenth century, westward migration and the growth of midwestern ag-riculture created a labor surplus on New England farms. Competition from midwestern agricultural products was undermining markets for the less efficient farms of New England, and the selective migration of young men in response to the opportunities created on the frontier was produc-ing a surplus of young women on these declining eastern farms. To take advantage of this *potential* source of labor, however, Lowell had to build dormitories to house them and develop a network of recruiters through-out the region to encourage them to take factory jobs. That the majority of the young women attracted in this way viewed industrial work as a temporary episode had two important effects. First, factory labor systems were shaped by the need to continually attract and train new workers, thus reinforcing the tendency of American employment relationships to-ward low attachment and high mobility. Second, technological innovation was directed in ways that sought to minimize reliance on employer- and job-specific skills.

By the 1840s demographic shifts in New England combined with the continued expansion of textile production produced a new episode of labor shortage. But the organization of the factories made it relatively easy to introduce new sources of labor as they became available. Respond-ing to the rising tide of Irish immigration at this time, mill owners adapted by hiring the newly arrived immigrants. As Wright (1979, pp. 676–679) has observed, the causes of rising immigration in the 1840s—the Irish potato famine, European political unrest, and falling transatlantic passage rates—were largely exogenous to the American textile industry. But the fact that many immigrants were drawn to New England reflects the fact that the region's textile mills created an attractive destination for migrants lacking resources to go into farming and thus seeking industrial employment.

By the middle of the nineteenth century a distinctive northern labor-market regime had emerged from the interaction of the legal framework of free labor, technological innovations that reduced the need for craft skill and facilitated the integration of new factory workers through on-the-job training, and the purposeful expansion of the sources of labor supply. This regime facilitated the rising volume of European migration that continued until World War I and provided the foundation for American industrialization in the second half of the century. It also resulted in a high degree of geographic integration across the northeastern and midwestern regions of the country, and linked labor markets in the United States increasingly closely with European ones (Rosenbloom 2002; Hatton and Williamson 2005). Meanwhile, an entirely distinct and largely isolated labor-market regime took shape in the American South.

ANTEBELLUM SOUTHERN LABOR MARKETS

Coincident with developments in the North, a very different labor-market regime was developing in the southern United States under the influence of slavery. The divergent course of economic development in the two regions comes as close to providing a "natural experiment" in institutional development as economic history is likely to offer. "In 1790, the two economies were nearly equal in population, area, and levels of wealth," notes Wright (2006a, p. 49). "Broadly speaking they shared a similar culture and legal heritage. So the economic competition boiled down to the institutional differences between them." Having started with relatively similar economies and populations, the two regions had diverged markedly on the eve of the American Civil War. In comparison to the North, the southern states in 1860 had a smaller, more rural, and less dense population, as well as substantially lower levels of manufacturing employment, immigration, and railroad miles per capita (Bateman and Weiss 1981; Wright 1986). The point is not that one path of development was superior to the other, but rather that the differences in regional development can be traced to the different labor-market regimes that emerged as a result of the differences in property rights in the two regions.

In comparison to the northern states, slavery facilitated westward migration and settlement, and by doing so deprived southern industry of the labor supply necessary for expansion. Individual preferences, attachments to family, aversion to risk, and the challenges of obtaining capital and information, all of which slowed migration in the North, created no obstacle to the movement of slaves to western lands where they were more productive.[5] Moreover, because male and female slaves were both used for fieldwork, there was no difference in migration response by gender. The circumstances of individual slave owners posed no barrier to mobility either, as owners who could not finance a move to the West or preferred to remain in the East could easily sell their slaves to planters in the West. In effect, while northern manufacturers were able to recruit within a fairly localized labor market, southern manufacturers found themselves competing on a region-wide level for slave labor. Given the extremely high value of labor on western cotton plantations, the price of labor that potential southern industrialists faced was much higher than in the North. If employers chose instead to rely on free labor, the lower density of population in the South Atlantic region meant that recruitment costs were higher. Additionally, because free southern farmers were less involved in production for the market than their northern counterparts, they were less subject to the dislocations created by competition from western producers that Field identifies as a key factor in releasing labor to industry in the Northeast (Field 1978; Wright 1979).

Beyond its direct labor-market effects, slavery altered the incentives of property owners in the South. In the North, property owners had a broadly unified interest in promoting immigration, because immigrants raised real property values, expanded markets for domestic manufactures, and drove down unit labor costs. In the South, by contrast, slaves dominated the portfolios of wealthy property owners, and immigration threatened to reduce the value of these assets. Rather than promoting immigration, they opposed any action that would increase the labor supply. As an 1859 editorial in the *Southern Banner* of Athens, Georgia, opposing the reopening of the slave trade observed: "We want to see labor high. . . . No country can be really prosperous and happy where it is otherwise. . . . Cheap labor is a curse to any country. We wish it was twice as high in the country as it is" (quoted in Wright 1979, p. 678). The regional difference in the economic interests of the propertied elite could be summarized, in Wright's (2006a) terminology, as a contrast between southern "labor-lords" and northern "landlords." These differences resulted in vastly different conditions of labor supply and ultimately economic development.

Perhaps the clearest indication of the role that slavery played in affecting the course of southern development is the marked shift in the nature of southern development after abolition. With this dramatic shift in property rights, wealthy southerners displayed a much greater interest in investment in railroads, town promotion, and industry. Urban growth and industrialization, which had lagged behind the North before 1860, grew faster than in the North after 1880 (Wright 1986, pp. 17–26).

EMANCIPATION AND POSTBELLUM SOUTHERN LABOR MARKETS

The Civil War and emancipation imposed an abrupt and sudden shift in labor-market regimes in the South. The end of slavery transferred property rights in labor from planters to their former slaves. To produce a crop it was necessary to develop new ways of combining labor with land and capital. Southerners' efforts to forge a solution provide a graphic illustration of how many characteristics of the employment relationship we ordinarily take for granted. A list compiled by an official of the Freedmen's Bureau in 1866 and reproduced by Harold Woodman notes these issues: whether the freedpeople would work on Saturdays, whether the contract would end on a set date, or when the crops were gathered, whether those working for a portion of the crop would be required to do other work and whether they would receive any payment in advance of the harvest, who was responsible for maintaining fences, whether a physician is to be employed, whether an overseer is to be employed, if the land owner furnishes tools or stock animals, who will be responsible if the tools are broken or the animals die, the kind and quantity of rations, quarters, and clothing to be provided, the number of hours to be worked, whether women and children will work, if wages are paid when they will be paid and what portion will be retained until the crop is harvested (Woodman 1984, p. 535; cited in Wright 1987, p. 320).

The dominant labor-market regime of the postbellum South, sharecropping, emerged from a process of competition between a number of alternative labor arrangements, including wage labor and cash tenancy, and it continued to coexist with these alternatives throughout the late nineteenth and early twentieth centuries. Once established, however, sharecropping exerted an important influence on the technological evolution of southern agriculture.

Sharecropping has often been portrayed as effectively reinstating slavery through the debt obligations that the croppers undertook. Yet sharecropping coexisted with a highly competitive wage labor market in the South, and croppers displayed a considerable degree of geographic mobility, suggesting that the situation was more fluid and less constraining than this traditional view implies (Jaynes 1986; Wright 1986, pp. 84–107; Ransom 1989, pp. 216–253). Settling in one place and becoming a sharecropper was a conscious choice that southerners, both black and white, made as the first step up an agricultural ladder that led to cash tenancy and ultimately independent farming. Climbing this ladder required that they obtain access to capital to finance seed, equipment, and other short-term borrowing, and access to capital required that they establish their creditworthiness by committing themselves to a particular locale.

For both landowners and laborers, wage labor was an alternative to sharecropping. But for landowners the seasonal nature of labor inputs required in cotton cultivation made wage labor impractical except near urban areas where the supply of labor was sufficiently elastic that they could meet their need for temporary workers. For laborers, wage work offered higher pay but greater uncertainty, and it did not provide a means to put other family members to work. Thus the wage labor force was composed primarily of young, single men.

Sharecropping emerged out of an initial period of flexibility, but once established, this labor-market regime imposed significant constraints on subsequent technological developments. In wheat farming, mechanical harvesters had from the 1840s begun to reduce labor requirements in agriculture. In contrast, however, cotton picking was not mechanized until nearly a century later, in the 1940s. An important reason for this delay was that while the peak labor demand in wheat production occurred at harvest time, cotton growing had two peak periods of labor demand—the first occurring in June when the crops were cultivated, and the second at harvest time. Sharecropping effectively ensured that labor effort would be available to meet both of these peaks, and efforts to mechanize cotton foundered on the fact that unless they reduced labor demand throughout the growing cycle they would not be of much value. As Whatley (1987) documents, International Harvester did not begin to seriously explore development of a mechanical cotton picker until the diffusion of tractors in the 1920s had made it feasible to mechanize cultivation, and the first successful mechanical cotton pickers were introduced during World War II.[6]

By this time, however, the stability of sharecropping had been significantly undermined by the severe economic contraction of the 1930s. As alternative employment opportunities dried up, landowners were able to shift a greater proportion of their land to wage labor, reducing the number of sharecropping contracts. But the major factor in displacing croppers came from New Deal agricultural policies that encouraged landowners to displace croppers to collect agricultural subsidy payments for idling the land (Whatley 1983). Not only did this shift create further incentives for efforts to mechanize cotton picking, but it also severed the ties holding many poor blacks to southern agriculture. There were scant opportunities to induce them to move in the 1930s, but once labor demand began to expand during World War II, and given the context of restrictive immigration policies that choked off old sources of supply (Collins 1997), the Great Migration of African Americans to northern cities in search of industrial employment commenced, as did the integration of southern labor markets more fully into the national economy.

THE EVOLUTION OF INDUSTRIAL LABOR MARKETS TO WORLD WAR I

By the turn of the twentieth century the United States (more specifically the northeastern and midwestern regions of the country) was emerging as the world's preeminent industrial economy, although still an economy with sizable agricultural and mineral extraction sectors. The period between the Civil War and World War I is often seen as an era of unfettered, competitive labor markets, characterized by a legal regime of employment at will, loose attachments between workers and employers, mass immigration of low-skilled workers, weak unions, flexible wages, and minimal government regulation—in other words, the kind of market well-suited to the standard theory of supply and demand (Fishback 1998).

The general validity of this view as a snapshot of the institutions at a point in time is hard to deny. But it also obscures some important dynamics that became forces for institutional change. Production technologies and ultimately labor-market institutions evolved during these decades under the pressure of four interrelated influences: relatively inelastic and scarce supply of skilled labor; conflict between employers and skilled workers over control of the production process; the growing scale of firms as organizations, with attendant problems of monitoring and incentives; and emerging forms of government regulation of labor markets, particularly at the state level.

Labor historians and radical economists have often interpreted the technological and institutional trajectory of late nineteenth-century America as the result of a purposeful effort by employers to forestall or weaken organized labor and wrest control of the production process from skilled artisans (Edwards 1979; Gordon, Edwards, and Reich 1982; Montgomery 1987). While the evidence of such class struggle in the workplace is plentiful, the same developments also reflect the fact that the labor-market regime was more effective in mobilizing unskilled labor than in providing workers with traditional craft skills. During the second half of the nineteenth century, large-scale factory production was associated with more intensive use of low-skilled labor, as Atack, Bateman, and Margo (2004) have documented. Technological innovation and capital investment thus appear to have had an overall skill-saving bias. Nonetheless, over the same period wage premiums for skilled craft workers were actually rising, suggesting that however much employers had "deskilling" in mind, overall growth in the demand for skills continued to outpace supply (Dawson 1979; Rosenbloom 2002). Experimentation with

various methods of attaching workers to the firm and training them internally, such as rudimentary promotion ladders and welfare capitalism,
can also be seen as responses to perceived skill shortages, attacking the
problem from the supply side. These developments were reflected in the
job-tenure data: despite overall high rates of labor turnover, sizable mi-
norities of workers in industrial establishments could expect to have a
job with the same employer for many years (Carter and Savoca 1990).

Indeed, by the turn of the century the advanced industrial sectors of
the U.S. economy were increasingly characterized by technology-skill
complementarity (Goldin and Katz 1998). New technologies were more
"skilling" than deskilling. Goldin and Katz (2008) argue that this complementarity, initially associated with the rise of large-scale batch and
continuous process production technologies, would impart a skill bias to
technological change that persisted across the twentieth century and beyond. That the relative wages of skilled workers failed to rise steadily
during the twentieth century is evidence of the extraordinary increase in
the supply of skills, largely driven by rising educational attainment.

In the advanced sectors of the industrial economy, growing organizational scale created other challenges—most notably, management of the
employment relationship had to be delegated to a growing cadre of sub-
ordinates. In many industries this was accomplished by leaving labor
management in the hands of first-line supervisors, a system that Nelson
(1975) referred to as the "foreman's empire." Delegation created growing
principal-agent problems, and firms began to experiment with reforms
that removed some of the foreman's discretion over hiring and firing, pay,
training, and task assignments. Still, the bureaucratic managerial revolution would not have a widespread impact on the employment relationship until well after World War I (Jacoby 1985).

As for the role of government, late nineteenth-century U.S. labor markets undoubtedly came closer to the laissez-faire ideal than they would
50 years later, but as in other areas of economic life, the decades leading
up to World War I witnessed a flurry of regulatory activity. Under the
federalist system, government regulation of labor-market institutions
was largely left to the states. States passed laws limiting the work hours
of children and women and established bureaus of labor statistics, factory

inspection systems, and arbitration boards. By 1915 all of the major industrial states had established workers' compensation programs (Fishback and Kantor 1996). These regulations set the stage for broader interventions to come but on the whole were fairly weak. Comparing the United States with advanced European countries during the same period, Robertson (2000) contends that the purported exceptionalism of American labor laws and institutions did not emerge until after World War I. While state policies and programs were piecemeal and often ineffectual, labor regulation was similarly weak elsewhere in the western world as well.

To summarize, the period between the Civil War and World War I was one during which the elements of the institutional regime were becoming increasingly discordant. While mass immigration, high mobility, and employment at will fostered a labor market of readily available unskilled labor and posed challenges for training skilled workers, new technological opportunities militated toward increased organizational scale and greater importance of skills that were learned on the job or in school. Much of the labor conflict of this era can thus be seen as symptomatic of the search for a solution to these challenges within the constraints of the existing labor-market institutions. The eventual institutional regime shift would come in response to the series of severe shocks to the system generated by two world wars, the Great Depression, and a dramatic realignment of the government's role in the economy.

THE COMMAND ECONOMY AND THE GREAT DEPRESSION: THE EMERGENCE OF A HIGH-WAGE REGIME

World War I is often seen as a watershed in the evolution of labor-market institutions in the United States. With the onset of the war, mass immigration from Europe was curtailed. This reduction in supply, coupled with the wartime stimulus to industry, caused the scissors of demand and supply to close, driving unemployment down and wages dramatically up. Tight market conditions increased the bargaining power of labor, and strikes and unionization rates spiked. In an effort to minimize the disruption to critical war production, the federal government implemented a short-lived but historically influential experiment in regulating industrial labor markets and arbitrating disputes, in the form of the National War Labor Board. The corporatist character of the board, which sought to bring captains of industry together with labor leaders under the guiding umbrella of the federal government, would be echoed in the implementation of the National Industrial Recovery Act (NIRA) of 1933 as well as similar efforts during World War II.

At the end of the war the influence of organized labor in most industries fell apart rapidly with some disastrous strikes—such as the steel strike in 1919—and the short but deep postwar recession of 1921. Still, some of the war's effects on labor markets were lasting. Most importantly, perhaps, restrictive immigration quotas passed in 1921 and 1924—spurred in part by xenophobia and concerns about European radicalism—made permanent the wartime cutoff of mass immigration of low-skilled labor. Given this restriction of labor supply growth and ongoing productivity advances, labor earnings rose quite dramatically. Indeed, Gavin Wright has argued that the 1920s witnessed the emergence of a "high-wage national regime" that would last half a century and coincide with the "one big wave" of twentieth-century productivity growth (Gordon 1999; Wright 2006b). Wright argues that high wages induced a set of institutional and technological responses that drove further productivity changes; hence the correlation between the great wave of productivity growth and high wages is not mere coincidence.

The evidence on real wages is striking. Standard manufacturing wage series show that real hourly wages of production workers were nearly stagnant between 1890 and the Great War, but by the early 1920s they had risen by more than 50 percent and then continued to grow modestly until further increases occurred during the 1930s (Wright 2006b; see also Goldin and Katz 2008). Figure 11.1 traces the history of average earnings of production workers in manufacturing (including nonwage benefits) relative to average output per worker hour in the private economy from 1889 to 2006. This ratio is comparable to the ratio that Levy and Temin (this volume) label the Bargaining Power Index (BPI). It can also be interpreted as a reflection of the purchasing power of an hour of manufacturing labor relative to the rising productivity of the overall

FIGURE 11.1 *Ratio of Average Hourly Compensation of Production Workers in Manufacturing to GDP per Labor Hour in the Private Economy, 1889–2006*

Sources: Average hourly compensation of production workers in manufacturing: Officer (2009). The data are also available at Lawrence H. Officer and Samuel H. Williamson, "Annual Wages in the United States, 1774–2008," MeasuringWorth, 2009, http://www.measuringworth.org/uswage/. GDP per labor hour in the private economy: We first created a linked series of real GDP per labor hour. For 1950–2006 this series was obtained by dividing GDP in constant dollars by total hours worked, using series reported in the Conference Board's Total Economy Database, http://www.conference-board.org/economics/database.cfm. This series was then extrapolated backward to 1889 using year-to-year changes in the index of real gross domestic product per labor hour reported in Carter et al. (2006, series Cg265). Finally, the resulting linked real productivity series for 1889–2006 was converted to current prices using the GDP deflator reported by Louis D. Johnston and Samuel H. Williamson, "What Was the U.S. GDP Then?" MeasuringWorth, 2008, http://www.measuringworth.org/usgdp/.

economy.[7] From 1889 to 1907 this ratio fell by nearly a third, reaching its nadir during the decade before World War I, ratcheted up significantly in the aftermath of the war, and then stabilized during the 1920s. Relative to the economy's mean capacity to pay (productivity), production workers' wages were indeed "high" in the 1920s compared with earlier in the century, although they would rise higher still during the 1930s.

The implications of the high-wage regime for labor relations during the 1920s, even before the dramatic labor-law reforms of the New Deal, were nicely summarized by Slichter (1929). Employers faced with high wages sought to "upgrade" their employees to match productivity to pay; fear of the return of labor unrest and high turnover spurred not only efficiency wages but experimentation with more systematic personnel management, internal labor markets, and various incentives designed to attach workers to firms. These schemes elaborated on and bureaucratized some of the practices developed by the welfare capitalism and scientific management movements of the late nineteenth century. The extent to which these reforms were widely adopted by U.S. firms before World War II remains subject to some debate (see Jacoby 1985; Moriguchi 2003, 2005). Large corporate employers were generally the leaders in adopting more formal, systematic methods, but there was considerable heterogeneity across firms of all sizes, and informal modes of personnel management were remarkably persistent (see esp. Licht 1991).

There seems little doubt, however, that the advent of the high-wage regime coincided with changes in other broad measures of labor-market structure and performance. After peaking in 1919 or 1920, both union density and strike activity fell throughout the 1920s. Data on labor turnover rates are spotty before 1920, but the available evidence suggests that turnover fell dramatically between the teens and 1920s, led by falling rates of voluntary quits. Because the quit rate tended to be dominated by a fairly small, unstable segment of the workforce (Woytinsky 1942) and was sensitive to short-run fluctuations in business-cycle conditions, its movements are not necessarily indicative of changes in the prevalence of long-term labor attachments. Still, Owen (1995) builds a case for the view that changes in employment management practices were a significant contributing factor. Programs that increased incentives for worker attachment to firms necessarily reduced the attractiveness of the exit option, spurring workers to demand greater voice in the employment relationship. Fairris (1995) argues that the formation of so-called company unions in many firms during this period was a response to these demands, and an unintended consequence of the success of turnover reduction efforts.

The broader institutional manifestation of labor upgrading was the continuing rapid development of the American system of mass public education—in this period, largely the high-school movement. Goldin and Katz (2008) attribute the United States' global leadership in secondary education to a set of long-standing social and political "virtues"—including social and political egalitarianism and local political control—that facilitated publicly funded schooling for the masses, as well as the strong price incentive provided by a substantial educational wage premium. The extent to which mass schooling in America was shaped predominantly by economic forces and interests (cf. Bowles and Gintis 1976) may be debated, but the apparent complementarity between educational and labor-market institutions is nicely illustrated by the regional contrast between the American South and the rest of the country. Public support of schooling in the South lagged substantially, a phenomenon attributable in considerable measure to the disfranchisement of African Americans but also to the commitment of political and economic elites in the region to maintaining an isolated, low-wage labor-market regime (Wright 1986; Margo 1990).

By the late 1920s it seemed that U.S. industrial labor-market institutions were settling into a stable regime of relatively high wages, managerial paternalism, minimal government intervention, and low rates of unionization and labor unrest—what might be referred to as corporate welfarism. The economic crisis of the 1930s, however, brought an early demise to this episode. Two well-known and interrelated developments characterize labor-market institutions in the 1930s: the resurgence of mass unionism and the advent of significant federal regulation. As Wright (2006b) notes, these developments helped to ratchet up real wages again during the early 1930s—a truly remarkable phenomenon within the context of massive excess supply of labor. Although productivity gains were also remarkable during the 1930s (Field 2003), wages actually surged ahead of the increase in labor productivity, as is indicated in Figure 11.1. By 1940 average manufacturing wages relative to labor productivity had recovered all of the ground lost between 1889 and 1907. Whether or not blame for the depth and duration of the Depression can convincingly be placed on the high-wage regime, as some have argued (Vedder and Gallaway 1993; Cole and Ohanian 2004; Ohanian 2009), there can be little doubt that the 1930s saw a strengthening of the high-wage regime rather than its demise, as might have been expected under the circumstances.

The surges in labor unrest and union membership during the 1930s are often attributed to changes in the legal environment, especially protective labor legislation, such as Section 7(a) of the 1933 National Industrial Recovery Act (NIRA) and its successor, the 1935 Wagner Act. It is also true that some cracks in the generally anti-union, open-shop orientation of American labor law had begun to appear by the late 1920s (see Ebell and Ritschl 2008). But, as Brody (1980) has argued, labor organizing in the 1930s was initially spurred as much by economic conditions and changes in employer behavior as it was by a more favorable political climate. In particular, the abandonment of welfare capitalist benefits by financially strapped corporations was viewed by many workers as reneging on an implicit contract that had maintained the peace, and it led to the collapse of the prior institutional equilibrium (Moriguchi 2005).

The expanded role of federal regulation also included a national minimum wage and the set of social insurance measures associated with the Social Security Act of 1935: unemployment insurance, retirement insurance, and welfare support for single mothers. The social safety net was undoubtedly emblematic of labor's increased political power but may in turn have served to strengthen labor's bargaining power by improving workers' threat points.

The key role of the federal government in shaping labor-market institutions continued during World War II. As Jacoby (1985, p. 261) puts it, "During the war the nation came close to having a command labor market." Building on the precedent of World War I, a National War Labor Board (NWLB) was reestablished with the primary goal of avoiding strikes that could undermine the war effort; the NWLB compelled bargaining between firms and unions, the latter's right to bargain collectively now legally protected by the National Labor Relations Act. Government reporting requirements and the dissemination of best-practice personnel management practices served to standardize and bureaucratize labor relations in large firms (Jacoby 1985; Baron, Dobbin, and Devereaux 1986). In the aftermath of the war the power and influence of American industrial unions were at their zenith. Levy and Temin (this volume) argue that the postwar agreements between the United Auto Workers and the Big

Three auto firms, the so-called Treaty of Detroit, were particularly important in establishing the practice of pattern bargaining, whereby key contracts had wide spillover effects on wages and working conditions across industries. In this interpretation, during the 1950s U.S. labor markets had in important respects come to resemble the collective, centralized wage-setting institutions often associated with labor markets in continental Western Europe.

Coinciding with these institutional changes was a dramatic reduction in the dispersion of wages between 1940 and 1950, a phenomenon dubbed the "Great Compression" by Goldin and Margo (1992). Wage differentials declined rapidly both between and within observable skill groups, as classified by education and experience. The new wage structure persisted well beyond the wartime period of tight labor markets. The fact that wage inequality ratcheted downward, rather than exhibiting a temporary wartime compression followed by a postwar decompression, suggests that neither tight wartime markets nor wartime wage controls offer a complete explanation. Rather, the evidence is consistent with a significant role of more long-lived institutional change, including the power of organized labor and advances in the legal minimum wage, which relative to labor productivity reached an all-time high during the 1950s (Levy and Temin, this volume; Sutch, this volume). Trends in labor-market fundamentals, especially the relative supply of human capital, may have been at least as important in the long run: Goldin and Katz (2008) emphasize changes in educational attainment that served to compress the skill premium during the immediate postwar decades. It would be a mistake, however, to assume that investment in human capital was exogenous to labor-market institutions; as Sutch (this volume) argues, increases in the legal minimum wage may have reduced job opportunities for youths at the margin, thereby lowering the opportunity cost of staying in school longer.

THE DEMISE OF THE HIGH-WAGE REGIME?

Developments in U.S. labor markets since 1970 have suggested to many observers an unraveling of the postwar institutional regime. Much of the work by labor economists has stressed the dramatic increase in wage and income inequality, both within and across skill groups, but the paradox of slow median wage growth, even as productivity growth accelerated during the 1990s, is another piece of the puzzle. Figure 11.1 and the analogous Bargaining Power Index constructed by Levy and Temin (this volume) document the slowdown in wage growth. This ratio deteriorated fairly steadily beginning in the late 1960s, with the decline especially pronounced for low-skilled men. By 2006 the ratio of production workers' wages to productivity was as low as it had been since 1919.[8]

The widening of the gap between median worker pay and productivity is not, as one might surmise, the result of a change in the distribution between labor and capital; labor's share of national income has in fact been remarkably stable over time. Rather, pay at the top of the wage distribution has steadily pulled away from the middle for some 30 years (Piketty and Saez 2003; Autor, Katz, and Kearney 2006). At the same time, especially during the 1980s, the pay of workers in the lower deciles of the wage distribution stagnated, further contributing to the "polarization" of the labor market.

Explaining the trends in wages and inequality since the late 1970s remains an active and contentious area of research. Wright (2006b) and others have pointed to an institutional regime change in response to the economic crisis of the 1970s, characterized by deregulation, the erosion of the real minimum wage, weakened private-sector unionism, increased low-skilled immigration, increased international trade, and, more vaguely, the weakening of distributional norms that placed constraints on the acceptable degree of wage inequality.[9] A competing, neoclassical account stresses the changing structure of labor demand due largely to skill bias in the impact of computerization, coupled with a significant slowdown in the rate of growth of human capital, as the educational attainment of recent cohorts has stagnated (Autor, Katz, and Kearney 2006, 2008; Goldin and Katz 2008).

These debates relate to two fundamental and unresolved issues regarding the role of institutions in capitalist labor markets. The first is the extent to which specific institutional arrangements can have a significant and long-term impact on market outcomes, such as wages, working conditions, and employment, beyond what is determined by the underlying fundamentals of technology and human capital. Although Goldin and

Katz (2008) acknowledge a significant supporting role for such labor-market institutions as labor unions and regulations during certain histori-cal episodes, in the longer run these institutions are merely waves riding the larger tidal force of the race between education and technology—that is, between supply and demand. Still, we know from international com-parisons that wage distributions, hours, and employment can vary dra-matically (and persistently) across economies with apparently similar technologies and levels of educational attainment, for what seem to be institutionally driven reasons. Regulatory regimes clearly matter across countries, but their significance in explaining temporal change within the U.S. setting is debatable.

A dimension of the impact of institutions on labor-market outcomes deserving greater attention is their potential role in determining the size and distribution of economic rents. An important body of work in the 1980s and 1990s suggested that rent sharing has been a significant factor in wage determination in the United States, at least for interindustry wage patterns (Krueger and Summers 1988; Blanchflower, Oswald, and Sanfrey 1996). The importance of rent sharing implies a role for noncompetitive—and thus perhaps "institutional"—forces in labor markets, whether unions, personnel management practices, or social norms. How institutional change may have affected economic rents and their distribution is poorly understood, in part because of the difficulty of identifying and measuring the rents themselves.

The second issue in assessing the role of institutions is the extent to which the underlying economic fundamentals of technologies and en-dowments (such as human capital) are endogenously determined by in-stitutions. If, for example, as Acemoglu (2002) and Wright (2006b) con-tend, the skill bias of technological change is endogenous to the pattern of relative prices, and institutional regimes help determine relative prices, the identification strategy of treating technological change as an exoge-nous residual is problematic.

CONCLUSION

In much economic analysis it is a convenient fiction to suppose that wages and employment are determined by shifts in supply or demand within a more or less competitive market framework. And indeed this framework can be conveniently deployed to understand many episodes in American economic history. Thus, for example, within the northern United States the influx of relatively unskilled European immigrants between the end of the Civil War and the beginning of World War I raised skill premia while promoting spatial wage equalization. Similarly, within the postbellum South, adjustments in acreage farmed by sharecroppers can be understood as a response to variations in relative supply and demand.

As the foregoing account demonstrates, however, the interaction of supply and demand takes place within an institutional context that is, itself, endogenously determined. And the prevailing institutional context can profoundly alter the wage and employment outcomes produced by markets, a point that is starkly illustrated by the divergent development of northern and southern labor markets in the antebellum period. Although labor-market institutional regimes are determined endogenously, they tend to be persistent, reflecting the interdependent nature of the institutions that support market exchange.

As a result, the history of American labor markets can best be characterized as a sequence of relatively stable arrangements punctuated by abrupt changes in institutional regimes. Such a narrative suggests that policy advice that focuses solely on efforts to influence supply and demand conditions and ignores the role of institutional regimes in conditioning the operation of supply and demand ignores one of the central features of the labor market.

NOTES

1. On the role of institutional heritage on long-run economic development see Engerman and Sokoloff (1997); Acemoglu, Johnson, and Robinson (2001).

2. The role of irreversible investments in generating path dependence is stressed by Arrow (2004).

3. See Steinfeld (1991, chaps. 1–2) on the status of servants. Indentures were entered into in Europe prior to passage, and the merchants carrying the servants recouped their investment by selling the contracts once they had reached the colonies. In another, closely related contractual form, immigrants would borrow money from merchants to finance their passage and repay this on arrival by selling themselves into long-term labor contracts in the colonies. These so-called redemptioners retained greater freedom to select between potential employers, but they also bore additional risks as they did not know when they embarked what labor market conditions would be like once they arrived.

4. The self-reinforcing impact of the institutional environment on the composition of state population offers an interesting contrast to the mechanisms described by Fleck (this volume) through which New Deal policies initiated patterns of migration that tended to upset the institutional equilibrium that had prevailed in the South since emancipation.

5. On the interaction between westward migration and productivity growth within the South, see the chapter by Olmstead and Rhode in this volume.

6. Because tractors were of general utility throughout northern and southern agriculture, the limitations of cotton cultivation did not significantly impede development of this technology.

7. To the extent that the pay of production workers is representative of pay near the median of the wage distribution, trends in the wage-productivity ratio should also track broad trends in the income share of the middle deciles of the income distribution, a prediction largely confirmed by a comparison of our index with trends in the share of the bottom 90 percent of income earners (see Piketty and Saez 2003). The wage-productivity ratio is also known as the "adjusted real wage" in the neo-Austrian literature on unemployment (Vedder and Gallaway 1993).

8. Because the wage-productivity ratio used in Figure 11.1 is generated from wages in manufacturing only, it might be surmised that postwar trends in the ratio are not representative of the economy as a whole, as the employment share of manufacturing has steadily declined. However, the trend in the ratio is actually very similar if one uses instead the average hourly wages of all production and nonsupervisory workers in the private economy as a whole.

9. On institutional explanations, see also Levy and Temin (this volume), Piketty and Saez (2003), and the recent survey by Lemieux (2008).

REFERENCES

Acemoglu, Daron (2002). "Directed Technical Change." *Review of Economic Studies* 69: 781–809.

Acemoglu, Daron, Simon Johnson, and James A. Robinson (2001). "The Colonial Origins of Comparative Development: An Empirical Investigation." *American Economic Review* 91: 1369–1401.

Ames, Edward, and Nathan Rosenberg (1968). "The Enfield Arsenal in Theory and History." *Economic Journal* 78: 827–842.

Arrow, Kenneth J. (2004). "Path Dependence and Competitive Equilibrium." In *History Matters*, edited by Timothy W. Guinnane, William A. Sundstrom, and Warren C. Whatley. Stanford, CA: Stanford University Press, pp. 23–35.

Atack, Jeremy, Fred Bateman, and Robert A. Margo (2004). "Skill Intensity and Rising Wage Dispersion in Nineteenth-Century American Manufacturing." *Journal of Economic History* 64: 172–192.

Autor, David H., Lawrence F. Katz, and Melissa S. Kearney (2006). "The Polarization of the U.S. Labor Market." *American Economic Review* 96: 189–194.

Autor, David H., Lawrence F. Katz, and Melissa S. Kearney (2008). "Trends in U.S. Wage Inequality: Revising the Revisionists." *Review of Economics and Statistics* 90: 300–323.

Baron, James N., Frank R. Dobbin, and P. Devereaux Jennings (1986). "War and Peace: The Evolution of Modern Personnel Administration in U.S. Industry." *American Journal of Sociology* 92: 350–383.

Bateman, Fred, and Thomas Weiss (1981). *A Deplorable Scarcity: The Failure of Industrialization in the Slave Economy.* Chapel Hill: University of North Carolina Press.

Blanchflower, David G., Andrew J. Oswald, and Peter Sanfey (1996). "Wages, Profits and Rent-Sharing." *Quarterly Journal of Economics* 111: 227–251.

Bowles, Samuel, and Herbert Gintis (1976). *Schooling in Capitalist America: Educational Reform and the Contradictions of Economic Life.* New York: Basic Books.

Brody, David (1980). *Workers in Industrial America: Essays on the 20th Century Struggle.* New York: Oxford University Press.

Carter, Susan B., Scott Sigmund Gartner, Michael R. Haines, Alan L. Olmstead, Richard Sutch, and Gavin Wright, eds. (2006). *Historical Statistics of the United States: Earliest Times to the Present, Millennial Edition.* New York: Cambridge University Press.

Carter, Susan B., and Elizabeth Savoca (1990). "Labor Mobility and Lengthy Jobs in Nineteenth-Century America." *Journal of Economic History* 50: 1–16.

Cole, Harold L., and Lee E. Ohanian (2004). "New Deal Policies and the Persistence of the Great Depression: A General Equilibrium Analysis." *Journal of Political Economy* 112: 779–816.

Collins, William J. (1997). "When the Tide Turned: Immigration and the Delay of the Great Black Migration." *Journal of Economic History* 57: 607–632.

David, Paul A. (1975). *Technical Choice Innovation and Economic Growth: Essays on American and British Experience in the Nineteenth Century.* London: Cambridge University Press.

David, Paul A. (1985). "Clio and the Economics of QWERTY." *American Economic Review, Papers and Proceedings* 75: 332–337.

David, Paul A. (1994). "Why Are Institutions the 'Carriers of History'? Path Dependence and the Evolution of Conventions, Organizations and Institutions." *Structural Change and Economic Dynamics* 5: 205–220.

Dawson, Andrew (1979). "The Paradox of Dynamic Technological Change and the Labor Aristocracy in the United States, 1880–1914." *Labor History* 20: 325–351.

Dewey, Donald (1952). "Negro Employment in Southern Industry." *Journal of Political Economy* 60: 279–293.

Ebell, Monique, and Albrecht Ritschl (2008). "Real Origins of the Great Depression: Monopoly Power, Unions and the American Business Cycle in the 1920s." Centre for Economic Performance Discussion Paper No 876. London: London School of Economics and Political Science.

Edwards, Richard (1979). *Contested Terrain: The Transformation of the Workplace in the Twentieth Century.* New York: Basic Books.

Elbaum, Bernard (1989). "Why Apprenticeship Persisted in Britain but Not in the United States." *Journal of Economic History* 49: 337–349.

Engerman, Stanley L., and Kenneth L. Sokoloff (1997). "Factor Endowments, Institutions, and Differential Paths of Growth among New World Economies: A View from Economic Historians of the United States." In *How Latin America Fell Behind*, edited by Stephen Haber. Stanford, CA: Stanford University Press, pp. 260–304.

Fairris, David (1995). "From Exit to Voice in Shopfloor Governance: The Case of Company Unions." *Business History Review* 69: 494–529.

Field, Alexander J. (1978). "Sectoral Shifts in Antebellum Massachusetts: A Reconsideration." *Explorations in Economic History* 15: 146–171.

Field, Alexander J. (1983). "Land Abundance, Interest/Profit Rates, and Nineteenth-Century American and British Technology." *Journal of Economic History* 43: 405–431.

Field, Alexander J. (2003). "The Most Technologically Progressive Decade of the Century." *American Economic Review* 93: 1399–1413.

Fishback, Price V. (1998). "Operations of 'Unfettered' Labor Markets: Exit and Voice in American Labor Markets at the Turn of the Century." *Journal of Economic Literature* 36: 722–765.

Fishback, Price V., and Shawn Everett Kantor (1996). "The Durable Experiment: State Insurance of Workers' Compensation Risk in the Early Twentieth Century." *Journal of Economic History* 56: 809–836.

Freeman, Richard B. (2007). "Labor Market Institutions around the World." National Bureau of Economic Research Working Paper No. 13242. Cambridge, MA: National Bureau of Economic Research.

Goldin, Claudia, and Lawrence F. Katz (1998). "The Origins of Technology-Skill Complementarity." *Quarterly Journal of Economics* 113: 693–732.

Goldin, Claudia, and Lawrence F. Katz (2008). *The Race between Education and Technology*. Cambridge, MA: Harvard University Press.

Goldin, Claudia, and Robert A. Margo (1992). "The Great Compression: The Wage Structure in the United States at Mid-Century." *The Quarterly Journal of Economics* 107: 1–34.

Gordon, David M., Richard Edwards, and Michael Reich (1982). *Segmented Work, Divided Workers: The Historical Transformation of Labor in the United States*. Cambridge: Cambridge University Press.

Gordon, Robert J. (1999). "U.S. Economic Growth since 1870: One Big Wave?" *American Economic Review* 89: 123–128.

Habakkuk, H. J. (1962). *American and British Technology in the Nineteenth Century: The Search for Labour-Saving Inventions*. London: Cambridge University Press.

Hamilton, Gillian (1995). "Enforcement in Apprenticeship Contracts: Were Runaways a Serious Problem? Evidence from Montreal." *Journal of Economic History* 55: 551–574.

Hatton, Timothy J., and Jeffrey G. Williamson (2005). *Global Migration and the World Economy: Two Centuries of Policy and Performance*. Cambridge, MA: MIT Press.

Jacoby, Sanford M. (1985). *Employing Bureaucracy: Managers, Unions, and the Transformation of Work in American Industry, 1900–1945*. New York: Columbia University Press.

James, John A., and Jonathan S. Skinner (1985). "The Resolution of the Labor-Scarcity Paradox." *Journal of Economic History* 45: 513–540.

Jaynes, Gerald David (1986). *Branches without Root: The Genesis of the Black Working Class in the American South, 1862–1882*. New York: Oxford University Press.

Kolchin, Peter (1993). *American Slavery, 1619–1877*. New York: Hill and Wang.

Krueger, Alan B., and Lawrence H. Summers (1998). "Efficiency Wages and the Inter-industry Wage Structure." *Econometrica* 56: 259–293.

Lemieux, Thomas (2008). "The Changing Nature of Wage Inequality." *Journal of Population Economics* 21: 1432–1475.

Licht, Walter (1991). "Studying Work: Personnel Policies in Philadelphia Firms, 1850–1950." In *Masters to Managers: Historical and Comparative Perspectives on American Employers*, edited by Sanford Jacoby. New York: Columbia University Press, pp. 43–73.

Margo, Robert (1990). *Race and Schooling in the South, 1880–1950.* Chicago: University of Chicago Press.

Minchin, Timothy J. (2007). *From Rights to Economics: The Ongoing Struggle for Black Equality in the U.S. South.* Gainesville: University Press of Florida.

Montgomery, David (1987). *The Fall of the House of Labor: The Workplace, the State, and American Labor Activism, 1865–1925.* Cambridge: Cambridge University Press.

Moriguchi, Chiaki (2003). "Implicit Contracts, the Great Depression, and Institutional Change: A Comparative Analysis of U.S. and Japanese Employment Relations, 1920–1940." *Journal of Economic History* 63: 625–665.

Moriguchi, Chiaki (2005). "Did American Welfare Capitalists Breach Their Implicit Contracts during the Great Depression? Preliminary Findings from Company-Level Data." *Industrial and Labor Relations Review* 59: 51–81.

Nelson, Daniel (1975). *Managers and Workers: Origins of the New Factory System in the United States, 1880–1915.* Madison: University of Wisconsin Press.

Ohanian, Lee E. (2009). "What—or Who—Started the Great Depression?" National Bureau of Economic Research Working Paper No. 15258. Cambridge, MA: National Bureau of Economic Research.

Officer, Lawrence H. (2009). *Two Centuries of Compensation for U.S. Production Workers in Manufacturing.* New York: Macmillan.

Owen, Laura (1995). "Worker Turnover in the 1920s: What Labor Supply Arguments Don't Tell Us." *Journal of Economic History* 55: 822–841.

Piketty, Thomas, and Emmanuel Saez (2003). "Income Inequality in the United States, 1913–1998." *Quarterly Journal of Economics* 118: 1–39.

Ransom, Roger L. (1989). *Conflict and Compromise: The Political Economy of Slavery, Emancipation, and the American Civil War.* Cambridge: Cambridge University Press.

Robertson, David Brian (2000). *Capital, Labor, and State: The Battle for American Labor Markets from the Civil War to the New Deal.* Lanham, MD: Rowman and Littlefield.

Rosenberg, Nathan (1976). "Technological Change in the Machine Tool Industry, 1840–1910." In Nathan Rosenberg, *Perspectives on Technology.* New York: Cambridge University Press, pp. 9–31.

Rosenbloom, Joshua L. (1993). "Anglo-American Technological Differences in Small Arms Manufacturing." *Journal of Interdisciplinary History* 23: 683–698.

Rosenbloom, Joshua L. (2002). *Looking for Work, Searching for Workers: American Labor Markets during Industrialization.* Cambridge: Cambridge University Press.

Rosenbloom, Joshua L. (2004). "Path Dependence and the Origins of Cotton Textile Manufacturing in New England." In *The Fibre That Changed the World: The Cotton Industry in International Perspective, 1600–1990s*, edited by Douglas A. Farnie and David J. Jeremy. Oxford: Oxford University Press, pp. 365–391.

Rothbarth, Erwin (1946). "Causes of the Superior Efficiency of U.S.A. Industry as Compared with British Industry." *Economic Journal* 56: 383–390.

Slichter, Sumner H. (1929). "The Current Labor Policies of American Industries." *Quarterly Journal of Economics* 43: 393–435.

Steinfeld, Robert J. (1991). *The Invention of Free Labor: The Employment Relation in English and American Law and Culture, 1350–1870.* Chapel Hill: University of North Carolina Press.

Vedder, Richard, and Lowell E. Gallaway (1993). *Out of Work: Unemployment and Government in Twentieth-Century America.* New York: Holmes & Meier.

Whatley, Warren C. (1983). "Labor for the Picking: The New Deal in the South." *Journal of Economic History* 43: 905–929.

Whatley, Warren C. (1987). "Southern Agrarian Labor Contracts as Impediments to Cotton Mechanization." *Journal of Economic History* 47: 45–70.

Woytinsky W. S. (1942). *Three Aspects of Labor Dynamics*. Washington, DC: Committee on Social Security, Social Science Research Council.

Wright, Gavin (1978). *The Political Economy of the Cotton South: Households, Markets, and Wealth in the Nineteenth Century*. New York: Norton.

Wright, Gavin (1979). "Cheap Labor and Southern Textiles before 1880." *Journal of Economic History* 39: 655–680.

Wright, Gavin (1986). *Old South, New South: Revolutions in the Southern Economy since the Civil War*. New York: Basic Books.

Wright, Gavin (1987). "Labor History and Labor Economics." In *The Future of Economic History*, edited by Alexander J. Field. Boston: Kluwer-Nijhoff, 1987, pp. 313–348.

Wright, Gavin (2006a). *Slavery and American Economic Development*. Baton Rouge: Louisiana State University Press.

Wright, Gavin (2006b). "Productivity Growth and the American Labor Market: The 1990s in Historical Perspective." In *The Global Economy in the 1990s: A Long-Run Perspective*, edited by Paul W. Rhode and Gianni Toniolo. Cambridge: Cambridge University Press, pp. 139–160.

CHAPTER 12

The Political Economy of Progress: Lessons from the Causes and Consequences of the New Deal

ROBERT K. FLECK

THIS CHAPTER sets out to explain the New Deal's place in the transformation of the Old South into the New South. My scholarly contribution here is neither new theory nor new empirical evidence. Rather, it is to propose a way to interpret the previous literature—including theoretical, empirical, and historical analysis of New Deal policy and the vast literature of southern politics—in a manner that demonstrates the breadth of its implications. More specifically, the literature on the political economy of the New Deal and the South informs our general understanding of democratic processes and complements the currently booming literature on the political economy of franchise expansion and economic development.

For scholars seeking to understand institutional change and economic performance, the evolution of the South has long been an obvious candidate for study. And for an economist today, it would be difficult to read American history without noticing that the South successfully escaped from both widespread poverty and what the modern economic development literature considers "bad" institutions, including the unequal treatment of citizens under the law, poor educational opportunities for many children, and, most infamously, the disenfranchisement of so many citizens in a country famous for its democratic institutions (e.g., Key 1949).[1] Moreover, it is clear that national-level policy—notably the New Deal and, in later years, efforts to improve the treatment of African Americans— played a key role in changing the South. This makes the South especially appealing for studying the ways in which policy reforms can help bring about a transition from an outcome with poor institutions and low income to an outcome with better institutions and higher income.

That said, it is easy to identify major challenges for those who study the South in an effort to draw general lessons for political and economic transitions. Looking around the world today, the typical scenario for seriously derailed economic development is not that of a region with poor institutions and low income in an otherwise wealthy democracy; rather, it is that of an entire country in which poor institutions (and the consequent poor policy) hinder overall economic progress. As Wright (1986, p. 16) stated:

The southern case is often seen as an economic success story to be held out as an example to the poor countries of the world, a region that managed to "break the vicious circles that thwart development." Perhaps it is more accurate to say that a new economy has moved into the geographic space formerly occupied by the old one.

In this light, if an explanation of the South's successful changes is to have broad relevance, it must be balanced in the following way. The argument cannot rest excessively on political or economic circumstances unique to the South, or even circumstances specific to a less developed region of a wealthy country. Nor can the explanation be wedded too closely to particular politicians or events specific to the United States. Yet the explanation must keep the nature of the South at the forefront, because the South truly was unique. As I argue in this chapter, economic historians have, through a large literature that includes theoretically grounded empirical work and careful analysis of institutional change, provided this kind of balanced explanation.

More specifically, this chapter draws on the economic history literature to develop a three-part explanation of the New Deal's role in the political economy of southern progress. The first section reviews the economic explanation of New Deal policy decisions. On this point, the most relevant literature includes Wright (1974) and related work by other scholars, and it takes a standard applied microeconomics approach: exogenous institutions, optimizing agents, and testable predictions derived from the constraints faced by those agents. The second section reviews how and why southern institutions, specifically those related to the political system and labor markets, evolved. The most important research on this topic has, by necessity, focused far less on generating comparative statics from theoretical models and far more on the subtleties of southern institutions. The third section builds on the first two in a manner that relies on core economic principles yet can account for institutional change: persistent attributes of institutions influenced the outcomes generated by individuals' (i.e., politicians' and voters') optimizing behavior, and this behavior in turn brought long-run institutional change. When viewed in this light and related to the broader topic of economic development, the economic history of the New Deal and the South provides insight into what one could easily describe, and Mukand and Rodrik (2005) do describe, as the Holy Grail in economics: why some countries (or regions of countries) succeed, while others fail, to establish good institutions and policies.

INSTITUTIONS AS EXOGENOUS DETERMINANTS OF NEW DEAL POLICIES

The design of New Deal policies can be modeled usefully with standard microeconomic tools. The seminal work on the topic, and an excellent example of a broadly informative analysis of the New Deal, is Wright (1974). Wright models a president who allocates federal funds among states in the manner that maximizes his or her expected electoral vote total. The model is a straightforward application of constrained optimization and generates two key predictions about spending patterns. First, swing states (relative to loyally partisan states) will receive more money, ceteris paribus, because competition between political parties gives those states more electoral weight. Second, states with more electoral votes per capita (i.e., states with few people) will obtain more federal spending per capita, ceteris paribus, because the apportionment of electoral college votes and congressional seats gives those states more weight per capita.

Wright tests his model using a cross-section of state-level data on per capita New Deal spending over the years 1933–1940.[2] To measure a state's weight in the electoral college, he uses electoral votes per capita (denoted V/POP). To test his model's predictions with respect to swing states, he develops the variable SD: the standard deviation around the trend in the Democratic vote share in presidential elections, 1896–1932. Because this variable measures the propensity of a state's electorate to switch with respect to the party it supported in presidential elections, it proxies for the extent to which additional spending would change election margins. Wright also develops a proxy for the political productivity of spending in a state (denoted VL32); this variable summarizes the way in which Wright's theoretical model predicts that V/POP and SD, along with a forecast of the Democratic vote share, would influence spending (Wright 1974, pp. 31–33). To control for other factors, Wright employs a variety of economic variables, including measures of income decline, unemployment, the size of the farm population, and the amount of federal land in the state (as a percentage of total land in the state).

The empirical support for Wright's model is striking. For a variety of specifications, Wright found substantial estimated effects of his political variables on spending: higher spending per capita in swing states and in states with more electoral votes per capita; or, in alternative specifications, higher spending in politically productive states (as indicated by VL32). Moreover, Wright's political variables can account for much of the variation in per capita spending, and this holds across the alternative specifications.[3] In short, Wright showed that the New Deal distributed funds in line with what his model predicts.

More recent research on the New Deal has built on Wright's work in several ways. Many papers have reexamined the state-level data in an effort to identify the extent to which Wright's political variables and/or other variables can explain New Deal spending patterns.[4] Several other papers develop formal theoretical models related to Wright's and use state-level or county-level New Deal data to test those models.[5] Another set of papers estimates the effects of New Deal policy, using the logic of Wright's theoretical model to identify potential instrumental variables and, hence, sort out the directions of causality between policy and economic conditions.[6]

Given the long-running ideological debates over the New Deal, it is unsurprising that Wright's findings caught the attention of scholars who sought to understand what motivated Roosevelt and other New Dealers.[7] For example, Anderson and Tollison (1991, p. 175) interpret Wright's findings (and their own extensions of his empirical analysis) as evidence that "the New Deal was not big government's Garden of Eden, but rather the more familiar stomping ground of *Homo economicus*." Even within the less pro/anti New Dealer literature, there has been a prominent effort to infer New Dealers' objectives from spending patterns. As Wallis (1998) puts it, "The fundamental question in the New Deal spending literature has been: Did Roosevelt and the New Dealers allocate money between states to achieve their stated goals of relief and reform by giving more money to states with lower employment and lower incomes, or did they promote their own interests and allocate more money to states that were politically sensitive?" More recently, Fishback, Kantor, and Wallis's (2003) econometric analysis of county-level data asks (in the paper's title): "Can the New Deal's Three Rs Be Rehabilitated?"—where the three "Rs" are the New Deal's famously stated objectives of relief, recovery, and reform.

Although Wright's findings have generated great interest among scholars who seek to identify what New Dealers were trying to do, for scholars who seek broadly useful implications, Wright's major contribution is about the way institutions shape policy. To make my point, I will discuss three reasons to view politicians' motives as tangential to what Wright's paper actually shows. Each of these reasons is straightforward if one considers Wright's and similarly styled papers on the New Deal (e.g., Fleck 1999a, 1999c, 2001a, 2008; Strömberg 2004) to be standard microeconomics applied to a *positive* political economy topic.

The first reason is the logic of the theoretical models (Wright's, Fleck's, and Strömberg's). The models do not identify the marginal effect on spending that occurs in response to, say, a change in some parameter characterizing a politician's utility function. Wright's model, for example, makes predictions about the effects of the apportionment of electoral votes (equivalently, congressional seats) and the electorate's responsiveness to policy. This is analogous to predicting the effects of *prices* (as they reflect opportunity costs), not preferences, on a consumer's decision. Note that an alternative, preference-uncovering theoretical foundation for Wright's empirical findings is far from obvious. Even if politicians acted purely on the basis of their own personal ideology, we would expect policy to be set in a manner similar to the way reelection-seeking politicians would set policy. Why? Because ideologically driven politicians whose ideologies matched the induced policy preferences of reelection-seeking politicians would be the ones selected into office and reelected.

The second reason is the nature of the empirical relationships between New Deal spending, proxies for "need" (e.g., unemployment, the depth of the Depression), and proxies for political productivity. One could read several analyses of New Deal spending and come away thinking that the received wisdom has long been (or for a long time was) that New Dealers bought votes and all but ignored their stated objectives. But what the data actually show is that New Deal spending allocations are positively and substantially correlated with plausible proxies for need and, especially at the state level, with land area (which was an explicit criterion in formulas for land-related projects).[8] Thus, even if one is willing to operate on the assumption that weak correlations between spending and proxies for relief, recovery, and reform would provide strong evidence that New Dealers were unconcerned with those stated objectives, that evidence would be missing.

The third reason pertains to what types of findings have the most relevance to economic research. Someone interested in history for history's sake (a reasonable interest) might want to know what New Dealers sought to do. But even if the New Deal spending literature did actually reveal New Dealers' preferences, it is not obvious how that would inform our understanding of policy issues today. By contrast, understanding the way that incentives, especially as they are shaped by institutions, affect policy remains highly relevant.[9] This point has not been lost in the broader political economy literature: Wright's paper has been cited in work on post–New Deal federal spending in the United States, USAID contracting, and distributive policy in Australia, Israel, Japan, Mexico, Peru, Spain, Sweden, and the United Kingdom.[10]

Interpreting New Deal econometric findings in this general context is an essential prerequisite for understanding how those findings illuminate the major changes brought by the 1930s. To see the relevance of New Deal spending patterns to those major changes, the key point is this: The New Deal sent relatively large allocations of funds to swing states and small-population states, and that (combined with other policies) changed the Democratic Party's base of electoral support.[11] This is different from saying that New Dealers did much in the way of tweaking allocations in a state-by-state manner to target funds to electorally important states. In fact, such state-by-state tweaking did not drive the politically productive spending patterns; it was spending in line with plausible proxies for need that drove the politically productive spending patterns (Fleck 2008). Put simply, for New Dealers to allocate funds to the states Wright's model identifies as politically productive, there was no need to rely on state-by-state adjustments when distributing funds. Given the severity of the Depression and concurrent droughts, the electorate supported programs that spent money on relief, roads, conservation, and reclamation. Spending on such programs could easily be directed toward states that suffered more severe economic downturns and had more land. And these states happened to have been the most politically productive according to Wright's measures—so much so that even a basic formula (which allocated more per capita to states in which the Depression was very severe and more to states with vast amounts of land) could have generated high spending levels in states that Wright's model predicts would have had a high expected electoral value of spending.[12]

In sum, when the New Dealers came to power in 1932, they set policy that won votes in the politically productive states. The extent to which New Dealers did so in an effort to win votes, rather than to alleviate the effects of the Depression or improve the nation's infrastructure, is not a central issue for understanding how the Depression gave rise to the New Deal. Nor does it matter much for understanding how the New Deal, by delivering policy favored by swing states' electorates, changed the nature of partisan alignments and political competition. This latter insight is especially informative when combined with what the economic history literature can tell us about institutional changes in the South—the topic for the third section of this chapter.

INSTITUTIONAL CHANGE IN THE SOUTH:
LABOR MARKETS, POLITICS, AND THE NEW DEAL

This section explains a few highlights from the enormous literature on the South's transition from its low-wage, poor-institutions era. Of course, there has long been an extensive historical literature on the topic, but the economic literature differs in its focus and methodological approach.[13] When economic historians set out to explain the demise of the old southern institutions, a key starting point was to identify what caused the pre–New Deal stability.[14] This is not to say that the Old South was completely unchanging prior to the New Deal; rather, it is to say that despite political and economic links to the rest of the country, the South maintained political institutions and economic conditions that made it distinct. Described in the terms used to frame the theme of this book, an observer in the pre-Depression years might have seen some evolution (not revolution) in progress with respect to race, class, and political relationships. Moreover, an economic explanation of the stability of southern institutions requires an understanding of southern history, not just the concept of equilibrium.

To expand on this point, note that on the surface the stability of the southern system may, in one sense at least, seem obvious: a subset of the population, once in power and obtaining rents from being in power, has an incentive to choose economic policies that avoid upsetting the status quo. That simple observation has some legitimacy in explaining the South. Notably, employers of low-wage labor had disproportionate influence in the southern political system and had an incentive to avoid actions that would raise wages and/or enfranchise the masses. Yet that really only touches on the core issue. Put loosely, even if we accept that the South was at an "equilibrium" state with low wages and disenfranchisement, why was it at *that* equilibrium?

The answer is not obvious in the absence of the historical context. Note, for example, that if the entire U.S. economy had been highly integrated at the national level (essentially, if one supply-and-demand diagram per good or service could explain market behavior throughout the entire country), then it would be difficult to explain why one region could lag so far behind in terms of wages. Also note that if Tiebout (1956) competition had operated effectively and on a national scale, it would have generated an exodus of African Americans from locales with policies flagrantly unfavorable to African Americans. To understand why neither the interregional integration of markets nor Tiebout competition was sufficient to undo the southern system, history is essential.[15]

Turning to the historical facts, one fundamental characteristic of the South was the relative isolation of its labor market. The issue here is not merely that Depression-era southerners earned wages below those of their counterparts elsewhere in the country (a fact that even a quick glance at labor market data makes clear). The aspect of isolation that really matters is the lack of convergence.[16] Between the South and the rest of the country, decades went by without convergence. Examining northern-southern differences, Wright (1987, p. 163) concludes that the farm wage "shows no tendency toward convergence before World War II. Both the absolute and relative differentials were higher in the 1920s than at any time since the Civil War." This persistent regional gap does not merely reflect wage differentials related to race: The gap is apparent when examining wage differences between northern and southern whites. Furthermore, the gap held for industrial as well as agricultural wages.[17]

Another fundamental characteristic of the South was the nature of the relevant output markets for southern producers (e.g., Wright 1987, pp. 164–165). The importance of considering output markets follows from basic economic theory: even in the absence of labor mobility, if firms throughout the United States had mobile capital and sold their output in the same markets, that would tend to equalize the returns to inputs. In fact, however, much of the South's output (e.g., cotton) was sold in international markets where the competing producers were foreign, not from elsewhere in the United States. Given the South's regionally isolated labor market *and* sufficiently different output market, the mechanisms that would otherwise have caused North-South factor price convergence were absent.

To put the persistence of the regional wage gap in perspective, examining what happened with respect to convergence *within* regions is particularly informative. Markets did tend to be integrated within regions. Essentially, convergence occurred when gaps existed in the east-west direction (both within the South and within the North), but not when gaps existed in the north-south direction (Wright 1987, pp. 162–164). This point is critical for understanding the South because it shows that the nature of the regional isolation was very different from southern markets just "not working" in some sense. Thus it is reasonable to view the long-run regional wage gap as a comparison between *different* markets.

Naturally, this points to the question of why there would be a persistent North-South gap despite convergence in the case of east-west gaps. This makes sense in terms of basic economic theory if and only if one considers the role of history. The legacy of slavery and southern industry made the South unique in terms of what can be viewed usefully as the initial conditions that led to a stable equilibrium that lasted until the New Deal (e.g., Wright 1986). For example, from the perspective of a slaveholder, a slave was a highly mobile asset (especially in contrast to the major agricultural asset elsewhere—land); this reduced incentives to engage in technological development and location-specific investment (e.g., Wright 1978, 1986). Thus the South started the post–Civil War era as the relatively less educated region of the country, with plentiful labor and natural resources, but not much physical or human capital. Very importantly, the South *remained* relatively less educated, lacking engineers and centers for technological innovation—things it would have needed in order to develop rapidly by utilizing its local resources. In addition, the flow of migrants into the South was small, and providing a southerner with a better education generally led to a greater likelihood of that southerner emigrating. Both of these factors put downward pressure on the South's stock of human capital, and the second factor reduced the incentives for southern leaders to fund education.[18]

Moreover, to understand the South it is important to consider which factors underpinning its isolated labor market were endogenous and why, a point emphasized by Wright (1986). Notably, migration out of the South depended largely on information and personal connections. Consequently, where emigrants would go depended largely on where previous emigrants had gone. Thus a historically low rate of emigration would lead to continued low rates of emigration, and east-west migration in the past would help maintain east-west integration of labor markets within regions, while also helping to maintain the North-South isolation of labor markets. Similarly, the lack of technological advance was endogenous; low education levels were a function of the southern political economy as well as a contributing factor to sustaining the southern political economy.

What this all meant for the South's unique institutions was a long period with little pressure to change—hence, the exceptional stability. The southern system perpetuated low wages, factor prices that were little affected by competition elsewhere in the country, political decisions that gave small weight to the desires of the poor, and few technological advances. When viewed by today's generally accepted standards, this was not a good system. Yet because those who dominated the southern political system obtained substantial rents from investments complementary to low-wage labor, they had little reason to pursue change.

Eventually the system did change, in part because of the New Deal.[19] The Agricultural Adjustment Act (passed in 1933) created incentives to reduce agricultural output and, hence, agricultural employment. The way government payments were disbursed under the act also created incentives for landlords to change the way they contracted for labor, thus driving sharecroppers and tenant farmers off the land (e.g., Whatley 1983; Wright 1986, pp. 226–238). In addition, the minimum wage provisions included first in the National Industrial Recovery Act (passed in 1933) and later in the Fair Labor Standards Act (passed in 1938) were binding for many southern workers. Thus, when southern workers left farms, many could not find new employment in the South. The combined effect of these policies was to spur migration out of the South, largely undo the low-wage labor market in key industries (such as timber and textiles), and speed the mechanization process in agriculture, most importantly cotton.[20]

Of course, the changes did not stop when the New Deal ended. This is partly because of new shocks, most notably World War II. But it is also because the processes (emigration and mechanization) accelerated by the New Deal kept going through the postwar years. Indeed, the extent to which New Deal policies would change the South was not apparent during the New Deal years. Wright (1986, p. 236) offers a compelling account:

At the end of the decade [the 1930s], many observers thought that little had changed. An authoritative 1940 survey on *The Plantation South Today* stated:

"Cotton is still king in the South, and the plantation remains an important form of organization in the Cotton Belt. . . . It is chiefly the outward aspects that have changed"; a 1942 prize-winning essay held that "the plantation is as deeply rooted today as at any time in the history of the South." These views were reasonable at the time. Yet with the aid of hindsight, we can see that they were wrong. The "outward aspects" of southern economic life had changed much less than the "inward aspects." The economic underpinnings and social glue that had kept the regional economy isolated were no longer present in 1940.[21]

In short, the full effects of the shocks that brought major changes to the South were not obvious until long after those shocks occurred, demonstrating the importance of taking a longer, historical view when seeking to identify such shocks.

The end result was a change in the southern economy. With employers no longer operating in a low-wage labor market isolated from the rest of the nation, the incentives for those who dominated the southern political system had changed. After decades of resisting economic integration, southern leaders actively sought industrialization and inflows of northern capital (e.g., Wright 1986, pp. 257–264).

THE POSITIVE POLITICAL ECONOMY
OF SOUTHERN PROGRESS

The end of the southern labor market's isolation is a key factor in the account of how the South eventually got on a path to higher wage rates and expanded civil rights, but to explain the political economy of southern progress, two additional questions require consideration. First, why did New Dealers enact the wage regulations that they did? Second, why did ending the isolation of the southern labor market lead, in the long run, to such sweeping changes? Answering these questions brings us back to theoretical models.

Although federal spending data have been featured prominently in papers that apply political economy models to the New Deal (e.g., Wright 1974; Fleck 1999a, 1999c, 2001a; Strömberg 2004), the theoretical predictions can be interpreted more generally to explain why the New Deal, to be effective for keeping the Democratic Party in power at the national level, had to deliver policies that won votes in electorally important states. In other words, the same logic that underlies Wright's (and related) predictions with respect to spending patterns can be generalized to other types of policy.[22] And this includes labor-market regulations. Most importantly, there is good reason to believe that establishing a nationwide minimum wage, a prominent part of the New Deal, was an effective policy for winning swing-state support. First, the policy was widely popular with the general public (e.g., Schulman 1991, p. 60). Second, although electoral data do not provide an opportunity for scholars to observe directly the way the electorate of that era responded to minimum wages, it is clear that minimum wage laws won legislative support in swing states. Most notably, when Congress passed the Fair Labor Standards Act (FLSA), southern Democrats were divided, but swing-state Democrats overwhelmingly favored the act, and some northern proponents of the act specifically sought to impose a wage floor in the South.[23] In sum, the basic mechanism first formalized in Wright's model of distributive politics also helps explain why New Dealers set the regulatory policies that helped undo the southern labor market's isolation.

With the end of the isolated low-wage southern labor market, the South had to change, but why did it change the way it did? The integration of the labor market did not by itself create incentives sufficient to induce southern politicians (or employers) to push for enfranchising the poor and ending racial segregation. Indeed, the medium-run effects (i.e., 1930–1960) of the Depression and New Deal labor regulations strengthened the incentives for southern whites to support continued segregation (e.g., Wright 1986, p. 265). For example, a binding price floor will generally reduce the cost that buyers incur for engaging in an arbitrary form of discrimination between types of sellers. Thus, in the presence of a minimum wage, such as those imposed by the National Recovery Administration (NRA) and the Fair Labor Standards Act (FLSA), one would expect the unemployment burden to fall disproportionately on discriminated-against groups, including African Americans.[24] So the key question is how the New Deal and the end of the old southern economic conditions led *indirectly* (and in the long run) to the demise of the old southern politics. The basic logic of political economy models (e.g., Wright 1974;

Fleck 1999a, 2008) points to a key mechanism: when disenfranchised African Americans left the South in large numbers, many moved to swing states where they could vote.[25] This increased the weight of African Americans' preferences in federal policy decisions, and federal policy was critical to the demise of disenfranchisement and segregation (Wright 1986, p. 265).[26]

BROADER IMPLICATIONS

This section illustrates how understanding the causes and consequences of the New Deal can inform the broader literature on political economy, institutional change, and economic development. Perhaps the most obvious question is whether the models applied to the New Deal have relevance to modern politics and to political systems outside the United States. As discussed earlier in this chapter, the scholarly literature on distributive politics continues to build on the logic of Wright's model, and similar empirical tests have been conducted using modern data from around the world (Australia, Israel, Japan, Mexico, Peru, Spain, and Sweden).[27]

Turning to the big question of what circumstances lead to a previously disenfranchised group's acquiring voting rights, the recent political economy literature suggests several potential mechanisms. For example, Acemoglu and Robinson (2000, 2001) explain why elites, when facing a potential threat of revolt, may expand the franchise as a way to commit credibly to future wealth redistribution. Lizzeri and Persico (2004) consider how a future expansion of the franchise can benefit groups within the currently enfranchised, even when the established political order faces no threat of revolt. Llavador and Oxoby (2005) also model an elite that is divided by economic interests (more specifically, a society composed of stylized landlords, capitalists, and workers). They examine incentives for the elite to expand the franchise, and consider how an expanded franchise will affect the character of industrialization and, hence, economic growth. Fleck and Hanssen (2006) consider the role of expanded democracy as a commitment device, analyzing the conditions when the ruling group can gain by committing to refrain from confiscating wealth, because such a commitment will, along the lines of North and Weingast's (1989) argument, promote investment.

Each of these mechanisms has some relevance to the South. For example, the nature of the southern landscape made it possible for southern "laborlords" (under slavery) and landlords to obtain substantial rents from plantation-style agriculture. Under such circumstances, Fleck and Hanssen's (2006) model predicts narrow democracy (e.g., the landlords vote) rather than universal voting rights. And the civil rights movement may have had an effect similar to signaling an increasing threat of revolt in Acemoglu and Robinson (2000, 2001). But especially for explaining the *expansion* of the franchise in the South, the most relevant theoretical approach is the combination of a divided-elite model (either Lizzeri and Persico's or Llavador and Oxoby's) with the key insights from Wright's (1974) model.

To see why, recall that electoral pressure to end southern disenfranchisement came largely from a group of northern voters who (by adding African Americans to the southern electorate) stood to get policy changes they desired, including expanded civil rights. This is in line with a key component of the divided-elite model: among those already enfranchised (whom one can consider part of the stylized "elite" here), some, including African American voters in the North, had substantial interests in line with the disenfranchised citizens of the South. But another critical factor is that those voters had gained influence because, in line with models such as Wright's (1974) and Fleck's (1999a, 1999c, 2001a, 2008), they had become recognized as a large group of swing voters in swing states (e.g., Freidel 1965, p. 90; Sundquist 1973, p. 248; Miller and Schofield 2003).

This points to an interesting variation on the previous divided-elite models. Note, for example, that in the Lizzeri and Persico model, franchise expansion is favored not by swing voters, but by non-swing voters (because non-swing voters receive relatively few benefits from the incumbent politicians, who court swing voters). Here, the key feature to take from Wright's model (and related ones) is the effect of having winner-take-all elections at the state level; when applied to the post–World War II United States, this explains the incentives for the federal government (more accurately, politicians seeking support for their party in national elections) to act on the preferences of the swing-state voters who sought expanded civil rights in the South. Also note that the Llavador and Oxoby model implies expansion of the franchise when the stylized landlords are not politically strong. This can explain the expansion of voting rights in the South if (and only if) one also has an explanation for why landlords lost their political strength. Once again, the key insight is from the implications of general models applied in a historically informed manner: the incentives faced by New Dealers led to policies that, in the long run, eroded the political power of southern landowners.

Finally, consider some additional lessons that the political economy of the New Deal teaches us about mechanisms for overcoming obstacles to economic development. Wright (1986, 1987) pointed out, for good reason, that the South was not a case study in economic development. But in the years since he made that point, there have been changes in what economists look for as a case study in development. The emphasis is no longer focused on what policies are good or bad, or on which institutions are good or bad, but on what leads to good institutions, and what conditions (e.g., institutional environment, presence or absence of commitment problems) will enable a given set of policies to work well. In this context the South provides a fascinating case study—even more so because the South and North took different economic paths while operating under many of the same formal institutions.

For example, what does the eventual end of the southern labor market's isolation tell us about the effects of freer trade on economic growth and convergence? Even though the Constitution has provisions that guarantee relatively free flows of goods (and labor) between states, for decades the South did not show convergence in terms of either income levels or institutional quality. (This is not to suggest that mutual gains from trade were absent; they could have been large without causing convergence.) As Wright explains, however, the cause of the eventual convergence was closely linked to the free flow of goods and labor between states. This matters for two reasons. First, it illustrates why the effects of freer trade will depend critically on the institutional environment, which of course depends on history. Second, it underscores the importance of considering that phenomena appearing at first glance to be basic supply-and-demand issues (e.g., generic gains from free trade) may have much larger long-run effects if they promote (or hinder) institutional change.

This parallels the thinking among development economists who see improved institutions as the most important potential benefit of free-trade agreements. For example, Rodrik (2002, p. 10) advises that "the first question that policymakers contemplating trade reform should ask is not whether the reform will result in higher volumes of trade, render their trade regime more liberal, or increase market access abroad but whether it will improve the quality of institutions at home." The way the South progressed provides evidence consistent with that advice. It also highlights the importance of looking within countries (and regions) to see how history and current institutions shape the potential routes for improving institutions in the future.

CONCLUSION

By employing a set of general models *and* paying careful attention to institutions, the economic history literature has provided a broadly useful explanation of the political economy of the New Deal and its long-run influence on the progress of the South. This fills in a critical chapter in the story of how the United States—the *whole* United States—eventually evolved into the wealthy democracy it is. And that, in turn, contributes to our understanding of the possible paths for moving from an outcome with poor institutions and low income to an outcome with better institutions and higher income.

NOTES

1. For recent work on franchise expansion and its relationship to economic performance, see Acemoglu and Robinson (2000, 2001); Lizzeri and Persico (2004); Engerman and Sokoloff (2005); Llavador and Oxoby (2005); Mukand and Rodrik (2005); Fleck and Hanssen (2006). To illustrate how the modern literature's view of institutions relates to southern history, it is useful to consider the South from the perspective of modern development aid policy. For example, the U.S. Millennium Challenge Corporation (MCC) explicitly links aid eligibility to criteria based on the quality of policy and institutions. As the MCC (2009) explains: "MCC is based on the principle that aid is most effective when it reinforces good governance, economic freedom and investments in people. MCC's mission is to reduce global poverty through the promotion of sustainable economic growth. Before a country can become eligible to receive assistance, MCC looks at their performance on independent and transparent policy indicators." The Old South's political and educational institutions, along with its record on civil rights, would score poorly (compared to the rest of the country or compared to the New South) on MCC criteria. Of course, many of the Old South's institutions were related to the legacy of slavery. For new work (and an overview

of previous arguments) on the relationship between slavery, technological advances, and southern economic development, see Olmstead and Rhode (this volume).

2. Arrington (1969) found that per capita spending varied greatly between regions and appeared to favor states with higher incomes. He suggested a variety of explanations, including the possibility that electoral concerns produced low per capita spending in the South because "the South was safe in the Democratic fold and did not need as much economic bribing" (Arrington 1969, p. 312). As a potential explanation for low spending in the low-income South, Reading (1973) argued that spending appeared to be designed to restore incomes to pre-Depression levels rather than to equalize incomes between regions.

3. Indeed, using just two of Wright's variables (V/POP and SD) accounts for 78 percent of the variance in per capita New Deal spending (Fleck 2008). Furthermore, Wright's findings are not just an artifact of regional differences (e.g., Wright 1974, p. 34; Fleck 2008).

4. Wallis (1998) reviews the literature and criticizes Wright's conclusions. Arguing that small state populations may lead to high per capita spending, Wallis introduces a new explanatory variable, 1/population (denoted 1/POP). According to Wallis, adding 1/POP to the analysis provides an apolitical explanation of spending patterns and overturns many previous findings, including Wright's (1974) large estimated effects of political variables. Fleck (2001b) demonstrates that the vast majority of the cross-sectional variation in per capita spending can be accounted for econometrically with a few land and income variables, most importantly land area. Controlling for land area greatly reduces the ceteris paribus explanatory power of Wright's political variables and 1/POP. In addition, Fleck (2001b) explains that Wallis's "apolitical" 1/POP is the econometric equivalent of senators per capita (which equals 2/POP), a "political" variable in the distributive politics literature. Fleck (2008) explains why the logic of Wright's model is still central to the political economy of the New Deal, even though land and income variables explain so much of the variation in spending. Among the many other papers building on Wright are Wallis (1987, 2001); Anderson and Tollison (1991); Fishback, Kantor, and Wallis (2003); Wallis, Fishback, and Kantor (2005).

5. See, e.g., Fleck (1999a, 1999c, 2001a, 2008); Strömberg (2004).

6. See, e.g., Fleck (1999b); Fishback, Haines, and Kantor (2001); Fishback, Horrace, and Kantor (2005).

7. Since the 1930s, critics have accused the Roosevelt Administration of using distributive policy for the purpose of winning votes. For example, Roosevelt's adversaries argued that New Deal programs manipulated spending and relief employment to win votes in politically sensitive regions, and that the Works Progress Administration (WPA) temporarily provided relief jobs in order to influence close elections (e.g., see Howard 1943).

8. In the literature based on county-level data, there has never been much (if any) question that allocations of relief funds and relief jobs tended to be greater, ceteris paribus, where the Depression was more severe. In a study of county-level Federal Emergency Relief Administration (FERA) allocations in the South, Fleck (1999c, p. 619) reports: "The regressions suggest that need had a strong influence on FERA spending. Most important, the coefficient on UNEMPL37 [unemployment in 1937, measured by the number of totally unemployed plus partially unemployed workers per capita] indicates that, all else equal between two counties, the county with an additional individual unemployed could expect its FERA allocation to be about \$70 [t = 8.59] greater." Note that an additional \$70 (this is measured in 1930s dollars) flowing to a county is a substantial estimated effect, especially

given that the mean of per capita FERA spending in the sample is $13. Employing a country-wide, county-level data set, Fleck (1999b) reports substantial estimated effects of male unemployment (from 1930, which is reasonably exogenous with respect to the New Deal) on relief employment reported in the 1940 census and on relief employment reported in the 1937 special census. In another study with a country-wide, county-level data set, Fleck (2001a) again reports substantial estimated effects of unemployment (using several measures) on FERA spending and on relief employment from 1937 and from 1940: "As expected, the unemployment-related variables, which should indicate the need for relief, have a substantial effect: more funds and jobs went to counties with higher unemployment rates, higher layoff rates, and fewer people in the workforce, ceteris paribus" (p. 92). Fishback, Kantor, and Wallis (2003) present a program-by-program analysis of county-level data. The comprehensive nature of their study makes it difficult to summarize, but in general they conclude that the major relief-oriented programs appear to have been responsive to "relief, recovery, and reform" objectives (though other programs appear less responsive). In contrast to the literature using county-level data, the literature that focuses on state-level data has been far more contentious (see, e.g., Wright 1974; Anderson and Tollison 1991; Wallis 1998, 2001; Fleck 2001b, 2008). Although a detailed summary of the arguments and evidence must (for space reasons) remain beyond the scope of this chapter, the essential points are covered in notes 2, 3, 4, 11, and 12, along with the main text of the second section.

9. For a more general exposition of this point, see Stigler and Becker's (1977) famous critique.

10. Studies using post-1930s U.S. spending data include Levitt and Snyder (1995); Levitt and Poterba (1999); Fleck and Kilby (2001); Bateman and Taylor (2003a, 2003b); Lowry and Potoski (2004); Hoover and Pecorino (2005); and Ansolabehere and Snyder (2006), among others. Studies examining the allocation of funds in other countries include Rozevitch and Weiss's (1993) analysis of Israeli data, Worthington and Dollery's (1998) analysis of Australian data, Ward and John's (1999) and John, Ward, and Dowding's (2004) analyses of English data, Schady's (2000) analysis of Peruvian data, Johansson's (2003) analysis of Swedish data, and Castells and Solé-Ollé's (2005) analysis of Spanish data. Kawaura (2003) examines spending data from Japan and the United States. Diaz-Cayeros (2008) examines spending data from Mexico and the New Deal.

11. Wright (1974) demonstrates that the high-spending states—and perhaps more importantly, high relief-employment states—showed intertemporal increases in the Democratic vote share.

12. Fleck (2008) uses hypothetical spending formulas to show that allocating dollars in proportion to income and land variables could have generated state-level spending with a close correlation to Wright's political variables. Indeed, a simple formula can generate hypothetical spending data that are correlated with Wright's political variables to a degree even higher than Wright found using real spending data.

13. Key (1949) is the classic text on southern politics. More recent work provides very careful analyses of the way individual southern politicians (see, e.g., Patterson 1967) and Congress as a whole (see, e.g., Brady 1988) reacted to the Depression and New Deal policies.

14. My discussion here draws on Wright (1978, 1986, 1987, 1999); Whatley (1983, 1985, 1987); Rosenbloom (1990, 1996); Alston and Ferrie (1999). Also see Rosenbloom and Sundstrom (this volume) on the way labor markets have evolved over the long run.

15. The research on Tiebout sorting most relevant to this chapter is Rhode and Strumpf (2003); they employ an exceptionally rich panel data set (all counties from 1850 to 1990).

16. In his highly influential work on the topic, Wright (1987, p. 162) explains that his "analysis of Southern economic history is built around the proposition that the region's distinctive culture and economic life were rooted in the regionalization of the labor market." One essential factor here is that the nature of southern output (including the seasonality of cotton production) shaped the formation and evolution of southern institutions, including financial institutions (e.g., Redenius and Weiman, this volume).

17. For more discussion of the wage gaps, see Wright (1986, 1987); Rosenbloom (1990, 1996); Sundstrom (2007). Also see Foote, Whatley, and Wright (2003) on the existence of, and nature of, discrimination along nonwage margins.

18. In particular, see Wright (1986, pp. 78–80). For complementary perspectives related to this issue, see Key (1949); Alston and Ferrie (1999).

19. As Wright (1987, p. 162) explains, "The modern period of equilibration only began in earnest when the institutional foundations of that regional labor market were undermined, largely by federal farm and labor legislation dating from the 1930s." Also see Rosenbloom and Sundstrom (this volume).

20. On factors delaying mechanization in cotton production, see Wright (1986); Whatley (1985, 1987). Also see Alston and Ferrie (1999) on southern agricultural labor relations, and Grove and Heinicke (2005) on why cotton workers left the fields in the years after World War II.

21. Wright is quoting from the following: T. J. Woofter and A. E. Fisher, The Plantation South Today (WPA Social Problems Series no. 5) (Washington, DC: Government Printing Office, 1940), p. 3; Donald Chrichton Alexander, The Arkansas Plantation 1920–1942 (New Haven, CT: Yale University Press, 1943).

22. Fleck (1999a, 2008) makes this point more formally.

23. On the political divisions over the FLSA, see Patterson (1967); Wright (1986), pp. 219–225; Poole and Rosenthal (1991); Seltzer (1995); Fleck (2002). As mentioned earlier, the vast majority of the public favored a national minimum wage; Schulman (1991, p. 60) notes that "public opinion polls indicated as much as 70 percent of the electorate in favor of the legislation." To understand why such strong public support led to particularly strong legislative support among swing states (and less strong legislative support among loyally Democratic states), one should consider why popularity among the public need not generate popularity among legislators. Quite simply, elected officials may represent opponents of the minimum wage, even if those opponents compose a minority of the public. One reason for this is that partisan positions reflect logrolled policy interests, and this is consistent with the long-standing partisan division over minimum wages (e.g., Poole and Rosenthal 1991). Another reason is that policy decisions made by representative governments place more weight on the policy preferences of voters than on those of nonvoters. This matters for my discussion here because the popularity of the FLSA among the public generated strong congressional support among non-southern Democrats, while congressional support among Democrats within the loyally Democratic South (where many citizens who supported a minimum wage law could not vote) was divided. For evidence on this point, see Fleck's (2002) analysis of congressional voting; most importantly, among members of the House from southern districts, those representing the higher-turnout districts had, ceteris paribus, a higher probability of voting in favor of passing the FLSA.

24. Indeed, the NRA was referred to as the "Negro Removal Act" in African American newspapers and elsewhere (e.g., Wright 1986, p. 224).

25. From 1920 to 1940, the share of the African American population who lived outside the South increased from 15 percent to 23 percent (Fleck 2008, p. 25). Given the political configuration of the country, the movement of African Americans out of the South would generally increase the number of African Americans in states that were more electorally competitive. Fleck (2008, p. 26) provides an empirical measure of this, reporting a .33 correlation between Wright's electoral variability measure (SD) and growth (from 1930 to 1940) in the share of a state's population that was African American. Of course, the presence of African Americans in the North became a critical component of the coalition that later formed the basis of the Democratic Party—and it seems safe to presume that the migration-caused increase in the number of African Americans in the North increased the weight of African Americans in that coalition. See Miller and Schofield (2003) on the long-run transformation of the Democratic Party's base of support, including "The Decline of Class and the Rise of Race" from 1960 to 2000.

26. Estimating the influence of African Americans (or, more generally, any group of voters) is by nature difficult, but the increased influence of African Americans in the post-Depression Democratic Party is quite clear from historical accounts. Note, for example, that the potentially swing role of African American voters was explicitly considered by African American leaders and by politicians, even while Roosevelt was still in power. For example, Walter White, secretary of the NAACP, made the following argument to Roosevelt: "The Secretary [Walter White] then called the President's attention to the tables . . . in which 17 states, with a total electoral vote of 281, have a Negro voting population, 21 years of age and over, sufficient to determine the outcome in a close election." My source here is Freidel (1965, p. 90), quoting White's memoirs. Truman, of course, faced similar circumstances, and his civil rights policy positions weakened his electoral support in the South (e.g., Sundquist 1973). Also see Sitkoff (1978); Miller and Schofield (2003).

27. The second section cites the studies using data from these countries. Other work on the effects that the apportionment of legislative seats has on spending includes Bennett and Mayberry (1979); Atlas et al. (1995); and Lee and Oppenheimer (1999).

REFERENCES

Acemoglu, Daron, and James A. Robinson (2000). "Why Did the West Extend the Franchise? Democracy, Inequality and Growth in Historical Perspective." *Quarterly Journal of Economics* 115: 1167–1199.

Acemoglu, Daron, and James A. Robinson (2001). "A Theory of Political Transitions." *American Economic Review* 91: 938–963.

Alston, Lee J., and Joseph P. Ferrie (1999). *Southern Paternalism and the American Welfare State: Economics, Politics, and Institutions in the South, 1865–1965.* New York: Cambridge University Press.

Anderson, Gary M., and Robert D. Tollison (1991). "Congressional Influence and Patterns of New Deal Spending." *Journal of Law and Economics* 34: 161–175.

Ansolabehere, Stephen, and James M. Snyder Jr. (2006). "Party Control of State Government and the Distribution of Public Expenditures." *Scandinavian Journal of Economics* 108: 547–569.

Arrington, Leonard J. (1969). "The New Deal in the West: A Preliminary Statistical Inquiry." *Pacific Historical Review* 38: 311–316.

Atlas, Cary M., Thomas W. Gilligan, Robert J. Hendershott, and Mark A. Zupan (1995). "Slicing the Federal Government Net Spending Pie: Who Wins, Who Loses, and Why." *American Economic Review* 85: 624–629.

Bateman, Fred, and Jason E. Taylor (2003a). "The New Deal at War: Alphabet Agencies' Expenditure Patterns, 1940–1945." *Explorations in Economic History* 40: 251–277.

Bateman, Fred, and Jason E. Taylor (2003b). "Was 'V' for Victory or Votes? A Public Choice Analysis of World War II Federal Spending." *Public Choice* 114: 161–174.

Bennett, James T., and Eddie R. Mayberry (1979). "Federal Tax Burdens and Grant Benefits to States: The Impact of Imperfect Representation." *Public Choice* 34: 255–269.

Brady, David W. (1988). *Critical Elections and Congressional Policy Making.* Stanford, CA: Stanford University Press.

Castells, Antoni, and Albert Solé-Ollé (2005). "The Regional Allocation of Infrastructure Investment: The Role of Equity, Efficiency, and Political Factors." *European Economic Review* 49: 1165–1205.

Diaz-Cayeros, Alberto. (2008). "Electoral Risk and Redistributive Politics in Mexico and the United States." *Studies in Comparative International Development* 43: 129–150.

Engerman, Stanley L., and Kenneth L. Sokoloff (2005). "The Evolution of Suffrage Institutions in the New World." *Journal of Economic History* 65: 891–921.

Fishback, Price V., Michael R. Haines, and Shawn Kantor (2001). "The Impact of the New Deal on Black and White Infant Mortality in the South." *Explorations in Economic History* 38: 93–122.

Fishback, Price V., William C. Horrace, and Shawn Kantor (2005). "Did New Deal Grant Programs Stimulate Local Economies? A Study of Federal Grants and Retail Sales during the Great Depression." *Journal of Economic History* 65: 36–71.

Fishback, Price V., Shawn Kantor, and John Joseph Wallis (2003). "Can the New Deal's Three Rs Be Rehabilitated? A Program-by-Program, County-by-County Analysis." *Explorations in Economic History* 40: 278–307.

Fleck, Robert K. (1999a). "Electoral Incentives, Public Policy, and the New Deal Realignment." *Southern Economic Journal* 65: 377–404.

Fleck, Robert K. (1999b). "The Marginal Effect of New Deal Relief Work on County-Level Unemployment Statistics." *Journal of Economic History* 59: 659–687.

Fleck, Robert K. (1999c). "The Value of the Vote: A Model and Test of the Effects of Turnout on Distributive Policy." *Economic Inquiry* 37: 609–623.

Fleck, Robert K. (2001a). "Inter-Party Competition, Intra-Party Competition, and Distributive Policy: A Model and Test Using New Deal Data." *Public Choice* 108: 77–100.

Fleck, Robert K. (2001b). "Population, Land, Economic Conditions, and the Allocation of New Deal Spending." *Explorations in Economic History* 38: 296–304.

Fleck, Robert K. (2002). "Democratic Opposition to the Fair Labor Standards Act of 1938." *Journal of Economic History* 62: 25–54.

Fleck, Robert K. (2008). "Voter Influence and Big Policy Change: The Positive Political Economy of the New Deal." *Journal of Political Economy* 116: 1–37.

Fleck, Robert K., and F. Andrew Hanssen (2006). "The Origins of Democracy: A Model with Application to Ancient Greece." *Journal of Law and Economics* 49: 115–146.

Fleck, Robert K., and Christopher Kilby (2001). "Foreign Aid and Domestic Politics: Voting in Congress and the Allocation of USAID Contracts across Congressional Districts." *Southern Economic Journal* 67: 598–617.

Foote, Christopher L., Warren C. Whatley, and Gavin Wright (2003). "Arbitraging a Discriminatory Labor Market: Black Workers at the Ford Motor Company, 1918–1947." *Journal of Labor Economics* 21: 493–532.

Freidel, Frank (1965). *F.D.R. and the South.* Baton Rouge: Louisiana State University Press.

Grove, Wayne A., and Craig Heinicke (2005). "Better Opportunities or Worse? The Demise of Cotton Harvest Labor 1949–1964." *Journal of Economic History* 63: 736–767.

Hoover, Gary A., and Paul Pecorino (2005). "The Political Determinants of Federal Expenditure at the State Level." *Public Choice* 123: 95–113.

Howard, Donald S. (1943). *The WPA and Federal Relief Policy.* New York: Russell Sage Foundation.

Johansson, Eva (2003). "Intergovernmental Grants as a Tactical Instrument: Empirical Evidence from Swedish Municipalities." *Journal of Public Economics* 87: 883–915.

John, Peter, Hugh Ward, and Keith Dowding (2004). "The Bidding Game: Competitive Funding Regimes and the Political Targeting of Urban Programme Schemes." *British Journal of Political Science* 34: 405–428.

Kawaura, Akihiko (2003). "Public Resource Allocation and Electoral Systems in the U.S. and Japan." *Public Choice* 115: 63–81.

Key, V. O., Jr. (1949). *Southern Politics.* New York: Alfred A. Knopf.

Lee, Frances E., and Bruce I. Oppenheimer (1999). *Sizing Up the Senate: The Unequal Consequences of Equal Representation.* Chicago: University of Chicago Press.

Levitt, Steven D., and James M. Poterba (1999). "Congressional Distributive Politics and State Economic Performance." *Public Choice* 99: 185–216.

Levitt, Steven D., and James M. Snyder Jr. (1995). "Political Parties and the Distribution of Federal Outlays." *American Journal of Political Science* 39: 958–980.

Lizzeri, Alessandro, and Nicola Persico (2004). "Why Did the Elites Extend the Suffrage? Democracy and the Scope of Government, with an Application to Britain's 'Age of Reform.'" *Quarterly Journal of Economics* 119: 707–765.

Llavador, Humberto, and Robert J. Oxoby (2005). "Partisan Competition, Growth, and the Franchise." *Quarterly Journal of Economics* 120: 1155–1192.

Lowry, Robert C., and Matthew Potoski (2004). "Organized Interests and the Politics of Federal Discretionary Grants." *Journal of Politics* 66: 513–533.

Millennium Challenge Corporation (2009). "About MCC." Available at http://www.mcc .gov/about/index.php.

Miller, Gary, and Norman Schofield (2003). "Activists and Partisan Realignment in the United States." *American Political Science Review* 97: 245–260.

Mukand, Sharun, and Dani Rodrik (2005). "In Search of the Holy Grail: Policy Convergence, Experimentation, and Economic Performance." *American Economic Review* 95: 374–383.

North, Douglass C., and Barry R. Weingast (1989). "Constitutions and Commitment: The Evolution of Institutions Governing Public Choice in Seventeenth Century England." *Journal of Economic History* 49: 803–832.

Patterson, James T. (1967). *Congressional Conservatism and the New Deal.* Lexington: University of Kentucky Press.

Poole, Keith T., and Howard Rosenthal (1991). "The Spatial Mapping of Minimum Wage Legislation." In *Politics and Economics in the 1980s*, edited by Alberto Alesina and Geoffrey Carliner Chicago: University of Chicago Press, pp. 215–246.

Reading, Don C. (1973). "New Deal Activity and the States, 1933 to 1939." *Journal of Economic History* 36: 792–810.

Rhode, Paul W., and Koleman S. Strumpf (2003). "Assessing the Importance of Tiebout Sorting: Local Heterogeneity from 1850 to 1990." *American Economic Review* 93: 1648–1677.

Rodrik, Dani (2002). "Trade Policy Reform as Institutional Reform." In *Development, Trade, and the WTO: A Handbook*, edited by Bernard M. Hoekman, Aaditya Mattoo, and Philip English. Washington, DC: World Bank, pp. 3–10.

Rosenbloom, Joshua L. (1990). "One Market or Many? Labor Market Integration in the Late Nineteenth-Century United States." *Journal of Economic History* 50: 85–107.

Rosenbloom, Joshua L. (1996). "Was There a National Labor Market at the End of the Nineteenth Century? New Evidence on Earnings in Manufacturing." *Journal of Economic History* 56: 626–656.

Rozevitch, Shimon, and Avi Weiss (1993). "Beneficiaries from Federal Transfers to Municipalities: The Case of Israel." *Public Choice* 76: 335–346.

Schady, Norbert R. (2000). "The Political Economy of Expenditures by the Peruvian Social Fund (FONCODES), 1991–95." *American Political Science Review* 94: 289–304.

Schulman, Bruce J. (1991). *From Cotton Belt to Sunbelt: Federal Policy, Economic Development, and the Transformation of the South, 1938–1980*. New York: Oxford University Press.

Seltzer, Andrew J. (1995). "The Political Economy of the Fair Labor Standards Act of 1938." *Journal of Political Economy* 103: 1302–1342.

Sitkoff, Harvard. (1978). *A New Deal for Blacks*. New York: Oxford University Press.

Smith, Adam (1976 [1776]). *The Wealth of Nations*. Edited by Edwin Cannan. Chicago: University of Chicago Press.

Stigler, George J., and Gary S. Becker (1977). "De Gustibus Non Est Disputandum." *American Economic Review* 67: 76–90.

Strömberg, David (2004). "Radio's Impact on Public Spending." *Quarterly Journal of Economics* 119: 189–221.

Sundquist, James L. (1973). *Dynamics of the Party System*. Washington, DC: The Brookings Institution.

Sundstrom, William A. (2007). "The Geography of Wage Discrimination in the Pre–Civil Rights South." *Journal of Economic History* 67: 410–444.

Tiebout, Charles (1956). "A Pure Theory of Local Expenditures." *Journal of Political Economy* 64: 416–424.

Wallis, John J. (1987). "Employment, Politics, and Economic Recovery in the Great Depression." *Review of Economics and Statistics* 69: 516–520.

Wallis, John J. (1998). "The Political Economy of New Deal Spending Revisited, Again: With and without Nevada." *Explorations in Economic History* 35: 140–170.

Wallis, John (2001). "The Political Economy of New Deal Spending, Yet Again: A Reply to Fleck." *Explorations in Economic History* 38: 305–314.

Wallis, John Joseph, Price Fishback, and Shawn Kantor (2005). "Politics, Relief, and Reform: The Transformation of America's Social Welfare System during the New Deal."

National Bureau of Economic Research Working Paper No. 11080. Cambridge, MA: National Bureau of Economic Research.

Ward, Hugh, and Peter John (1999). "Targeting Benefits for Electoral Gain: Constituency Marginality and the Distribution of Grants to English Local Authorities." *Political Studies* 47: 32–52.

Whatley, Warren C. (1983). "Labor for the Picking: The New Deal in the South." *Journal of Economic History* 43: 905–929.

Whatley, Warren C. (1985). "A History of Mechanization in the Cotton South: The Institutional Hypothesis." *Quarterly Journal of Economics* 100: 1191–1215.

Whatley, Warren C. (1987). "Agrarian Labor Contracts as Impediments to Cotton Mechanization." *Journal of Economic History* 47: 45–70.

Worthington, Andrew C., and Brian E. Dollery (1998). "The Political Determination of Intergovernmental Grants in Australia." *Public Choice* 94: 299–315.

Wright, Gavin (1974). "The Political Economy of New Deal Spending: An Econometric Analysis." *Review of Economics and Statistics* 56: 30–38.

Wright, Gavin (1978). *The Political Economy of the Cotton South: Households, Markets, and Wealth in the Nineteenth Century*. New York: Norton.

Wright, Gavin (1986). *Old South, New South: Revolutions in the Southern Economy since the Civil War*. New York: Basic Books.

Wright, Gavin (1987). "The Economic Revolution in the American South." *Journal of Economic Perspectives* 1: 161–178.

Wright, Gavin (1999). "The Civil Rights Revolution as Economic History." *Journal of Economic History* 59: 267–289.

CHAPTER 13

Teachers and Tipping Points: Historical Origins of the Teacher Quality Crisis

STACEY M. JONES

A MARCH 2008 front-page article in the *New York Times* opened with the question, "Would six-figure salaries attract better teachers?"[1] A new charter school in New York City aimed to attract a high-quality teaching force by offering annual salaries of $125,000. The school's founder contended that schools must compete for talented workers with other high-paying professions and that the key to attracting high-quality teachers is offering competitive salaries.

A current line of the economic literature contrasts present-day concerns over teacher quality with a past in which high-ability women entered teaching careers despite relatively low pay because gender discrimination barred them from more lucrative professions. Temin (2002) suggests that the opening of broader job opportunities to women may have resulted in an exodus of the most talented women from teaching to the greener pastures of business, law, and medicine. Following up on this line of argument, empirical examinations of teacher quality, as measured by standardized test scores, provide some evidence of a decline in teacher quality over recent decades (Corcoran, Evans, and Schwab 2004; Bacolod 2007). A variant on the argument makes the claim that union-driven wage compression within teaching is to blame for the unwillingness of high-ability college graduates to enter teaching (Hoxby and Leigh 2004). Throughout this discussion of teacher quality, the opening of broader and better nonteaching opportunities to college women is taken to be exogenous.

The aim of this chapter is to argue that changing labor market conditions in the teaching profession played an integral role in the opening of broader professional opportunities to college women. From the beginning of women's higher education in the United States in 1837, teaching was both the central rationale for women's higher education and the overwhelmingly likely occupational destination for women college graduates. For most of the history of women's participation in higher education, a relative balance existed between the supply of women college graduates and the demand for teachers. In the first half of the twentieth century this balance was preserved by the growth of the public school system as well as population growth. In the 1950s and 1960s the arrival of the baby-boom generation in the public school system kept demand for teachers high even as the number of college-educated women was growing rapidly. Along the lines of Rosenbloom and Sundstrom (this volume), one might characterize the first century of higher education for women as one element of a coherent labor force regime, in which the complementary forces of growing demand for teachers, rising levels of education for women, and restricted opportunities for educated women outside of teaching were mutually reinforcing.

However, in the late 1960s the balance between the demand and supply of teachers ceased to hold. The number of women graduating from college soared past the demand for teachers. Faced with a growing oversupply of teachers, college women shifted their occupational choices to other professional occupations such as business, law, and medicine. As the number of women desiring to enter predominantly male professions grew, women were able to leverage civil rights legislation as well as the contemporary political climate to challenge discriminatory practices in both higher education and the labor market. The gender composition of many traditionally male professional occupations tipped such that women were no longer isolated pioneers in these occupations. By the mid-1970s college women had broken down many of the barriers, both explicit and implicit, to their participation in well-paying professions such as business, law, and medicine. From that point forward, teaching was on an equal footing with other occupations in competing for high-ability educated women.

Economic historians have emphasized the role of changes in contraceptive technology in initiating a shift in the labor force behavior of more educated women (Goldin and Katz 2002; Bailey 2006). The "pill hypothesis" contends that the increased certainty and convenience of oral contraceptives ("the pill") relative to previously available forms of contraception tipped the balance for some young women from early marriage and limited investment in careers to delayed marriage and greater investment in careers. Empirical studies have found small but statistically significant links between legal access to the pill at ages 18 to 21 and the delay of first marriage (Goldin and Katz 2002) and increases in women's labor supply (Bailey 2006). Neither study, however, finds effects of legal access to oral contraception of sufficient magnitude to explain more than a small fraction of the large changes in women's educational choices and labor market behavior observed in the late 1960s and early 1970s.

This chapter counters, or potentially complements, this supply-side explanation for women's push into the professions with an explanation based on change in labor demand. The chapter brings together national educational statistics on teaching and the historical literature on women's push into the professions in the early 1970s to argue that women were not pulled out of teaching by the exogenous opening of lucrative nonteaching opportunities. Instead, demographic and economic trends came together in the late 1960s in such a way as to end a long-standing balance between the supply of college women and the nation's growing demand for teachers. In the late 1960s, as the numbers of college-educated women soared far beyond the number of job opportunities in teaching, women gained the critical mass to push their way into high-paying traditionally male professions. Once this generation of college women had lowered barriers for women in traditionally male professions, the teaching profession could no longer attract high-ability new entrants by relying on its status as the default occupational choice for college women.

TIPPING POINTS AND WOMEN'S RAPID MOVEMENT INTO CAREERS

The first piece of the argument is a multiple-equilibrium model of social change. The model is based on a theory of social change articulated by Timur Kuran that predicts long periods of stability in societal expectations, punctuated by occasional episodes of unexpected, rapid change (see Kuran 1995). An illustrative example of this sort of societal shift is the transformation of societal attitudes regarding racial discrimination that took place in the United States in the 1960s (Wright 1999). Here, the model is used to explain a rapid, unexpected shift of societal expectations regarding women's career choices (Jones 2009). Suppose that two social equilibria are possible among college women, the *homemaking equilibrium* and the *career equilibrium*. The term "homemaking" is used to summarize a set of complementary behaviors: low earnings expectations, educational investments in low-paying, predominantly female fields, limited labor force attachment, and relatively early marriage and childbearing. These choices on the part of college women are mutually reinforcing. A woman whose training is in a low-paying field, for example, has less incentive to enter or remain in the labor force. When the homemaking equilibrium holds, women might train for jobs but do not pursue careers.[2]

The *career equilibrium* describes a state of affairs where the pursuit of a career is widely held to be appropriate and desirable for college women. When "career" prevails, college women make educational investments in high-skill, high-pay fields and exhibit tenacious labor force attachment. As in the homemaking equilibrium, these choices are mutually reinforcing. Women whose educations provide them high earnings potential are more likely to remain in the labor force, for example. With the career equilibrium in place, social pressures and externalities work in favor of, rather than against, women's pursuit of careers.

Suppose also that for all but the most determined homemakers or career women, the choice between homemaking and career depends not only on their private preferences but also on the choices made by other women. Social pressure may not sway those with the strongest commitments to homemaking or career, but it influences the choices of the ambivalent majority. The likelihood that a woman chooses "career" over "homemaking" increases as the expected share of women choosing career increases. Several justifications can be provided for this claim, among them: (1) a woman's information about potential choices regarding family and career is a function of the prevailing social climate, (2) social pressures surrounding career and family decisions may tend to favor currently prevalent choices, and (3) the smaller the share of women seriously pursuing careers, the greater the likelihood of discrimination against those women who did intend to seriously pursue careers.

In the presence of these externalities, the model predicts two equilibriums: one with a large majority of women pursuing homemaking, and another with a large majority of women pursuing careers. When the homemaking equilibrium prevails, externalities deter most women from pursuing careers. The low numbers of women in nontraditional careers are self-perpetuating. For all but the most determined careerists, it is optimal to choose homemaking *given that they expect everyone else to*. Externalities and social pressures hold the equilibrium in place in the face of rising incentives to enter careers. Externalities help explain why in the 1950s and 1960s we do not see women pushing to enter more lucrative careers in business, law, and medicine. Societal expectations and women's own expectations reinforce women's remaining in traditionally female jobs and placing their primary emphasis on homemaking.

However, when the incentives to pursue a career are strong enough, the system can tip from the homemaking to the career equilibrium. A gradual shift of economic incentives may not increase the share of women in careers, but it can lower the threshold at which individuals would be willing to dissent from the prevailing equilibrium of public opinion. In the case of college women, a small increase in the economic incentives to pursue nontraditional careers could result in an unexpected surge in the share of women choosing "career" over "homemaking," as the share pursuing careers achieves critical mass. The revolution moves the system from one equilibrium of public preferences to another. In the new equilibrium expectations and externalities reinforce women's choice of career over homemaking. Law school professor Thelma Lavine described the shift in the social climate as follows: "College women of the late 1960s and early 1970s may feel they *should* want a professional career, just as . . . in the 1940s and 1950s, whether women wanted babies or not, they felt they *should* want them."[3]

WOMEN'S HIGHER EDUCATION AND TEACHING

The second piece of the argument is that the viability of the teaching career was essential to holding the "homemaking equilibrium" in place throughout most of the history of women's participation in higher education. From the time women first entered American colleges in 1837 until the late 1960s, to quote one college counselor, "teaching was ubiquitous."[4] The need for teachers served as the key justification for the initial provision of higher education to women in the mid-nineteenth century. Because the expansion of women's higher education roughly coincided with the expansion of the nation's public school system, a sizable share of college women were able to find positions as teachers through much of the history of women's higher education.[5] Figure 13.1 compares the number of women college graduates to the change in the size of the nation's public school teaching force. Through the early decades of the twentieth century, growth in the number of teachers was positive and outpaced growth in the number of women college graduates. In the 1930s and early 1940s, growth in the teaching force was slow, and at times even negative. Not surprisingly, a majority of school districts imposed bars on hiring and retaining married teachers during the 1930s and 1940s.[6] However, growth in the teaching force picked up again after World War II. Although women's college participation shot upward at this time, teaching demand did so as well, as grade schools stretched to accommodate the postwar baby boom.

With booming demand for new teachers, the 1950s and 1960s gave women little reason to broaden their range of educational choices. Figure 13.2 shows the percentage of college graduates majoring in education from 1950 to 1990. Teaching was an exceptionally popular occupational choice for women attending college in the postwar decades. A third of college women in 1950–1951 and almost half by 1960–1961 graduated with a major in education. These figures do not include the significant number of women majoring in the humanities, sciences, and social sciences that also planned to pursue careers in teaching. A brief wartime movement of women into science, engineering, and medicine ended in the post–World War II decades. According to David Riesman, in 1964 college women felt "diffident about identifying themselves with a specialized occupational achievement that would stamp them as perhaps not 'feminine': thus the helping professions are open to them (teaching, social work, in rare cases psychiatry or pediatrics) but the old feminist drive to enter engineering and architecture, law and business, economics and archeology is much attenuated."[7] The strong emphasis on women's

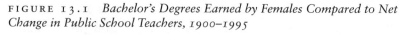

FIGURE 13.1 *Bachelor's Degrees Earned by Females Compared to Net Change in Public School Teachers, 1900–1995*

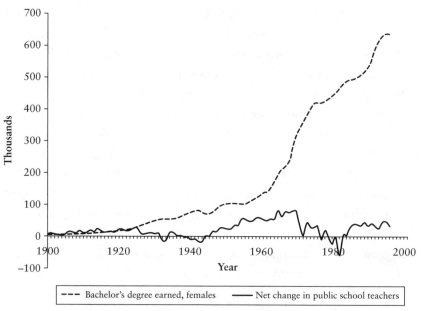

Sources: Bachelor's degrees earned by females: From table Bc565-587, "Degrees Conferred by Institutions of Higher Education, by Degree and Sex: 1869–1994," In Carter et al. (2006). Through 1959, first professional degrees are included with bachelor's degrees. The reported figures represent the number of bachelor's degrees earned by women in the academic year ending in a given year. For example, bachelor's degrees earned in the academic year 1949–1950 are plotted at 1950. Table Bc565-587 does not report the degrees earned in 1916–1917 and other academic years ending in odd years through 1946–1947; the figures reported for those years were constructed by averaging the number of bachelor's degrees awarded in the previous and subsequent academic years. For all other years, annual figures are reported. Net change in public school teachers: From table Bc97-106, "Public Elementary and Secondary Day School Teachers and Instructional Staff—Average Salary and Number," In Carter et al. (2006). The series represents the annual increase or decrease in the total number of elementary and secondary classroom teachers. The figures represent the change over the previous year for the academic year beginning in the reported year. For example, the number reported for 1950 represents the increase in the total number of classroom teachers from the 1949–1950 academic year to the 1950–1951 academic year. Table Bc97-106 does not report the number of classroom teachers in 1916–1917 and other academic years ending in odd years through 1958–1959, nor does it report figures for 1962–1963. For those years, figures were constructed by averaging the number of classroom teachers reported in the previous and subsequent academic years.

role in the family reduced, or at least postponed, many women's investment in careers.

The long-standing balance between the demand for teachers and the supply of college-educated women was essential to keeping the home-making equilibrium in place in the face of rising levels of women's educa-

FIGURE 13.2   *Percent of College Graduates Majoring in Education, 1950–1990*

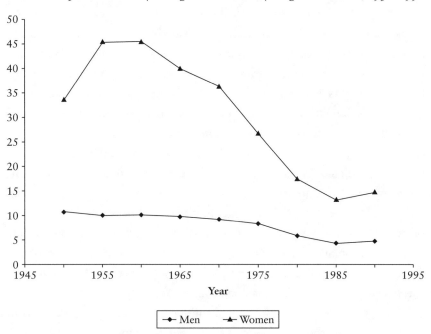

Sources: College major percentages calculated from data on college majors published in U.S. Department of Education (1948–1962), U.S. Department of Education (1963–2001), and from unpublished data on college majors provided by W. Vance Grant of the National Center for Education Statistics.

tion and labor force participation. Women's participation in college and the labor force rose sharply in the 1950s and 1960s. However, expanding demand for teachers allowed the labor force to absorb a growing number of educated women without challenging prevailing norms regarding women. Teaching was viewed as a vocation compatible with women's primary homemaking role.[8] As late as 1974 a college counselor listed the following advantages of teaching as an occupation for women: (1) it was a respected white-collar occupation, (2) it was in line with parents' expectations of their daughters, (3) "no matter where a husband might move, a school system of some kind was nearby," (4) teaching allowed time for family vacations, and (5) "a woman could teach a few years, transfer her experience into raising her own children, then return to teaching other people's children later."[9]

THE END OF TEACHING

By 1970, however, it was becoming increasingly clear that teaching could no longer be the predominant occupational choice of college women. This was for two reasons: grade schools were shrinking and the number of college women was expanding. Grade schools were shrinking because the bulge of enrollment caused by the baby boom had passed. Elementary and secondary school enrollment peaked in 1971, after which enrollment declined 15 percent between 1971 and 1984.[10] In 1970 the Bureau of Labor Statistics predicted only a 2 percent increase in the number of school teachers between 1970 and 1980, leading economist Margaret Gordon to describe it as "imperative" that colleges advise would-be teachers to train for other fields.[11] Despite some decrease in student-teacher ratios, the decline in school populations not surprisingly brought about a softening of demand for teachers. Beginning in the fall of 1969 several states observed a surplus of persons seeking teaching jobs.[12] According to a congressional report, only 52 percent of the record number of 338,000 graduates from teacher training programs found teaching positions in 1972.[13]

A straightforward regression analysis of the size of the teaching force relative to the number of children in school reveals the importance of enrollment changes in driving the demand for teachers. Table 13.1 shows the results of a regression of the number of public school teachers on the average number of students in attendance daily in the nation's public schools from the academic year beginning in the fall of 1900 to that beginning in the fall of 1975: while retirement and other sources of turnover certainly would have resulted in some new teaching positions, enrollment declines were strongly associated with a shrinking of the overall size of the teaching force. The correlation between the size of the teaching force and the number of students in school over this period is positive and nearly perfect: 0.97. Separate regressions for teachers of each gender show a decline in enrollment of 1,000 students to be associated with a predicted decline of 19 male teachers and 32 female teachers. The correlation of daily enrollment to the size of the male teaching force is 0.91 as compared to 0.98 for the female teaching force, suggesting that the employment level of female teachers was slightly more sensitive to changes in enrollment

TABLE 13.1   *Regressions of Size of the Teaching Force on Daily Attendance,*
1900–1975

	Dependent Variable		
	All Classroom Teachers (1,000s)	Male Teachers (1,000s)	Female Teachers (1,000s)
Independent Variable	Parameter Estimates (standard errors in parentheses)		
Intercept	−173.25* (29.04)	−175.22* (21.60)	0.657 (15.22)
Average daily attendance (1,000s)	0.051* (0.001163)	0.019* (0.000865)	0.032* (0.000609)
R^2	0.976	0.912	0.984
Sample size	48	48	48

Note: *P < 0.01.

Source: U.S. Department of Education, National Center for Education Statistics (1993), table 14. Data are sometimes biennial, sometimes annual, with values recorded for 48 years over the 75-year period.

than that of male teachers. Nonetheless, both male and female college students rapidly moved out of the field of education in the 1970s in response to signs of declining demand. The popularity of the education major among both men and women fell by half between 1970 and 1980.[14]

The expansion of the number of women attending college was also a factor in reducing the ubiquity of teaching as a career destination for college women. Figure 13.1 shows the sharp increase in the number of women enrolled in college in the 1960s and 1970s. Growth in the number of women college graduates far outpaced growth in the teaching force. The public school teaching force grew only 8 percent between 1970 and 1980; women's higher education enrollment grew 81 percent over the same period. By 1970 the Bureau of Labor Statistics was recommending that career counselors encourage college women to enlarge their range of occupations, because the traditional "women's" fields, especially teaching, would not be able to absorb the increase in the number of women college graduates.[15] In the words of career counselor John Parrish, "the traditional steps of 'from high school to college to teaching,' which served both talented women and counselors so well for so long, could no longer be taken for granted."[16] Throughout the 1970s continued poor labor markets in teaching reinforced women's movement into a broader range of occupations.

By the late 1960s college women correctly perceived that opportunities in teaching were shrinking. Surveys of incoming college women reveal this shift in women's occupational aspirations away from teaching. Figure 13.3 shows the occupational intentions of incoming freshmen from 1966 to 1985, surveyed annually by the Comparative Institutional Research Program (CIRP). The share of women planning to enter elementary or secondary teaching plummeted beginning in 1968, from a peak of 38 percent, bottoming out at about 10 percent by 1975, and remaining roughly at this level through 1985. Over the same period there was more gradual growth in the share of women aspiring to careers in business, engineering, law, and medicine. Combined interest in those fields rose from a low of 5 percent in 1968 to 29 percent by 1985. The broadening of women's vocational aspirations continued through the 1970s and into the 1980s. The continued poor market for teachers in the 1970s helped sustain women's movement into nontraditional fields.

FIGURE 13.3 *Intended Careers of Freshman Women Entering College, 1966–1985 (percent)*

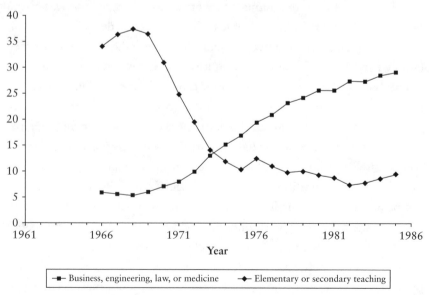

Source: Calculated from data reported in Astin (1987), p. 106.

WHERE DID ALL THE TEACHERS GO? THE PUSH
INTO PROFESSIONAL SCHOOLS

With growing numbers of college women seeking occupations other than teaching, the movement of college women into traditionally male professions gained momentum. Women reached the critical mass to challenge discriminatory policies and practices that had kept them out of more lucrative professions, smoothing the way for new entrants. Women's representation in business, dental, law, and medical schools took off around 1970 and grew rapidly through the 1970s and 1980s. By 1974 observers of academe were commenting on the "astonishing and unexplained" increase in women's professional school participation.[17] The nation's schools of dentistry, for example, graduated a total of only 34 women in 1970; this total grew to 700 by 1980. The share of professional degrees earned

FIGURE 13.4 *Percent of Degrees Awarded to Women in Dentistry, Medicine, Law, and Business, 1950–1995*

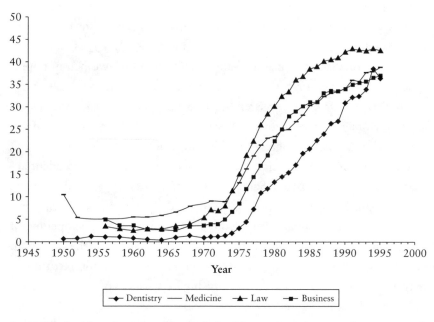

Source: Calculated from the number of first professional degrees awarded to men and women reported in *Digest of Educational Statistics* (1997), p. 290, table 260. The year in the figure refers to the school year ending in that year.

by women from 1950 to 1995 is plotted in Figure 13.4. The number of female graduates from business, dental, law, and medical schools increased twelve-fold between 1970 and 1980, while the total number of graduates from these schools only doubled.[18]

The record shows that the increase in women's participation in professional schools came from an increase in the number of applications rather than an increase in acceptance rates. Part of the explanation for the sudden upswing in women's applications to professional schools around 1970 was a general surge of interest in professional occupations. Women shifting their aspirations from "homemaking" to "careers" joined a stampede into professional schools. Enlarging the picture to include men shows a jump in the number of applications of both men and women to law and medical schools in the late 1960s and early 1970s. Contemporary commentators cite a decline in federal support for graduate students and a shift of funding from other areas of science to medicine as factors that shifted enrollments away from graduate school toward the professions.[19] They also speculate that the idealism and social movements of the 1960s drew young people to public service careers in medicine and law.[20]

Growing interest in professional occupations meant steep competition for admission to professional schools in the early 1970s. Why then did professional schools begin in about 1970 to admit women in unprecedented numbers, at a time when admissions conditions were extremely competitive? Part of the answer lies in a voluntary shift in policies regarding women in professional schools. There existed what one historian described as a "new progressivism in education in the late 1960s that emerged in response to racial unrest, antiwar sentiment, and student activism."[21] Darmouth's Tuck School of Business, for example, admitted its first woman, Martha Fransson, in 1968, and the law school of the University of Notre Dame admitted its first women in 1969. The opening of Princeton and Yale to women in 1969 may have signaled the end of an era of gender division in higher education. Higher education institutions may also have seen women as a promising new source of tuition revenue as budgets became tighter in the late 1960s.

Having gained a foothold in professional schools by 1970, women increased their representation to unprecedented levels during the rest of the decade. The increase in women's representation in professional schools continued through the 1970s and into the 1980s, as shown in Figure 13.4. The importance of group pressures and externalities in driving social change can explain why women's applications to professional schools kept growing when men's applications leveled off. Women in professional schools gained the critical mass to overcome barriers to their participation. One effect of critical mass was in removing informal barriers to women's participation such as isolation and harassment. At Harvard law school, for example, there had been a tradition of "ladies day," when professors called on women students "for the sole purpose of embarrassing them." Women students of the early 1970s mounted a joint protest to end this practice. Growing numbers of women in professional school facilitated the organization of concerted action to protest discriminatory practices.[22] The sheer presence of greater numbers of women could also signal a more welcoming atmosphere. One Stanford Business School professor recalls, "As soon as women found they were welcome here, they began to apply in large numbers."[23]

As their numbers increased, women in the professional schools were able to organize more formal attacks on discriminatory practices. The inclusion of sex in the 1964 Civil Rights Act provided women a means of challenging discrimination in professional employment. In 1968 the first woman law students group was formed, the Women's Rights Committee at New York University. In the years that followed the group organized women law students in the New York City area to gather information about the hiring practices of local law firms. This information allowed them later to file complaints alleging sex discrimination with the New York State Commission on Human Rights. Women at the University of Chicago adopted similar tactics. The Women's Law Caucus at the University of Chicago sued the law school under Title VII of the Civil Rights Act, charging that the school in its function as an employment agency allowed firms that have explicitly refused to hire women to use the law school premises for recruitment purposes.

To fight discriminatory admissions policies and practices, women in the professions put new federal policy measures to use in unanticipated ways. As women's rights activist Bernice Sandler described it, women enlisted "a little help from our government" in gaining admission to professional education.[24] Executive Order 11375, effective October 13, 1968, was used as a lever to open the doors of professional school more widely to women. Although Executive Order 11375 did not explicitly address discriminatory admissions practices, it prohibited sex discrimination in employment, including training, on the part of any institutions with federal contracts of over $10,000 and required affirmative action plans of all contractors with contracts of $50,000 or more and 50 or more employees.

On January 31, 1970, the Women's Equity Action League (WEAL) filed a class action complaint with the Department of Labor under Executive Order 11375 against all universities and colleges in the country. WEAL asked the Department of Labor to investigate admissions quotas and discrimination in financial assistance, hiring practices, promotions, and salary differentials. The attack on the admissions policies of professional schools continued in 1970 and 1971. WEAL successfully campaigned Congress to pressure the Department of Labor to take action regarding its complaint regarding higher education; the first investigation concerning sex discrimination began at Harvard in the spring of 1970. In October 1970 WEAL filed a class action suit against all the medical schools in the country. Other women's organizations joined the effort; in 1970 Ann Scott, head of the Campus Coordinating Committee of the National Organization for Women (NOW), issued 2,500 "Academic Discrimination Kits" with instructions on how to file a complaint of discrimination against one's own university and how to formulate an affirmative action plan. In April 1971 the Professional Women's Caucus filed a suit charging all of the nation's law schools with sex discrimination. NOW also filed charges against Harvard University and against the state university system of New York in 1971. By 1973, 360 charges had been filed against universities and colleges, 260 initiated by WEAL and the rest by other national women's organizations, campus associations, and individuals.

In 1970 Congress responded to the charge of sex discrimination in higher education. Congresswoman Edith Green, a member of WEAL's advisory board, held the first congressional hearings on sex discrimination. In 1971 and 1972 Congress passed measures explicitly prohibiting sex discrimination in professional school admission. The Comprehensive Health Manpower Act and the Nurse Training Amendments Act of 1971 banned discrimination in admission of students on the basis of sex on the part of "all institutions receiving or benefiting from a grant, loan guarantee, or interest subsidy to health personnel training programs or receiving a contract under Title VII or VIII of the Public Health Services Act."[25] The act prohibited sex discrimination in medical school admission, with the threat of the withdrawal of federal funds from institutions in violation of the prohibition. Title IX of the Education Amendments of 1972 included a more global, although not universal, ban on sex discrimination in admissions. Title IX prohibited admissions discrimination on the part of graduate and professional institutions, vocational institutions, and public undergraduate coeducational institutions. It exempted public single-sex institutions, private undergraduate institutions, religious institutions, and military schools from its coverage.

By 1972, at least in the letter of the law, the path was cleared for women to expand their participation in professional schools. The share of women in the professions continued to grow through the 1970s and 1980s. In this way the slight widening of women's opportunity to enter professional schools that grew out of the egalitarian movements of the 1960s resulted in a very large and unanticipated increase in the share of women in the professions. The inflow of women fed on itself, reducing the isolation of women and stimulating further efforts to reduce discrimination. Women were able to put federal policy to use in unanticipated ways to further open doors to women in professional occupations. Because of the rapid increase on the supply side, women's presence in the professions continued its rapid increase without a heavy thumb on the scale in favor of women or intensive recruitment efforts. Rather, their presence increased quickly and dramatically because the tentative movement toward "diversity" in the professions found a latent bandwagon of women awaiting their opportunity to move into careers.

CONCLUSION

This chapter has argued that a system of supply and demand in teaching that remained in approximate balance for more than a century of women's higher education moved dramatically toward oversupply in the late 1960s, resulting in women's rapid push into professional occupations and in the near-elimination of gender distinctions within higher education. Whereas a current strain in the literature on teacher quality contends that the exogenous opening of opportunities in high-paying professions pulled women out of teaching, this chapter counters that women (and men) were pushed out of teaching by a dearth of job openings. This emphasis on labor-market conditions in teaching as the source of change in women's employment and education is supported by the timing of change at a national level as well as by the fact that the decline in interest in teaching in the late 1960s occurred among both college men and women.

From the late nineteenth century through the late 1960s, steady growth in the demand for teachers allowed for a large increase in women's educational attainment and employment levels without a rethinking of women's role. This coherent and persistent labor-market regime supplied the growing U.S. public school system with a steady stream of highly qualified female teachers. However, the labor market for teachers moved dramatically toward oversupply in the late 1960s. This crisis in women's employment led to a dramatic tipping of societal norms regarding women's role. Women's own expectations regarding career and family, as well as society's expectations of women, shifted to place a much greater emphasis on career. The generation of women graduating from college in the late 1960s and early 1970s drew on civil rights legislation and a social climate favorable to change to push their way into traditionally male occupations. This produced rapid growth in the share of women in the professional schools and the near-elimination of gender divisions within U.S. higher education.

The essence of the argument is that while discrimination against women may have played a role in maintaining the quality of the teaching force prior to the 1960s, it was not the exogenous elimination of discrimination that resulted in the flight of highly qualified women from teaching. Rather, highly qualified women accurately perceived an extremely weak labor market for teachers and placed their efforts into preparing for and gaining access to occupations where job opportunities were stronger. With a broader set of occupational doors open to women, the teaching profession since about 1970 has had to compete for new entrants with a more lucrative and diverse set of occupations.

The argument has implications for the discussion of teacher quality. It was not the case, as some have argued, that women deserted teaching for the greener pastures of more lucrative occupations. Rather, teaching might be said to have deserted women: teaching jobs became extremely scarce relative to the supply of female college graduates. In periods of low teacher demand it may be more important to emphasize the professional development and retention of existing well-qualified teachers than to lament the very rational decision on the part of young people not to enter an occupation where jobs are scarce. Any rethinking of the tenure and pay system in teaching might also take into consideration the need to ensure adequate pay to compete with alternative occupations and adequate turnover in the stock of teachers so that there is in fact demand for new entrants at higher pay levels.

Finally, the argument has implications for the debate as to the causes of rapid change in women's education and employment in the 1970s and 1980s. Existing arguments emphasize supply-side factors, in particular, the increased availability of oral contraception, as the source of shifts in women's choices regarding career and family. This argument takes a more historical approach, citing the central role of teaching in the historical development and growth of women's higher education as a crucial piece of the explanation for the rapid changes of the 1970s and as an important part of the answer to the question, "Why did change take so long?"

NOTES

1. Gootman (2008).

2. Historian William Chafe makes the distinction between a "job" and a "career" as follows: "A job has limits. The time it consumes, the energy it requires, and the rewards it brings can all be fairly well defined in advance, and in most cases the bargain is based on the assumption that the woman is an incidental wage-earner, that her *primary* role is still in the home. A career, in contrast, requires a commitment of energy and spirit that is inconsistent with such an arrangement" (Chafe 1972, p. 251).

3. Lavine (1974), p. 190.

4. Parrish (1974), p. 12.

5. The theory that the expansion of women's higher education drove the expansion of public education in a virtuous circle, holding teaching wages down, is explored in detail in Carter (1986).

6. Goldin (1990), pp. 160–178.

7. Riesman (1964), p. 91.

8. See Perlman and Margo (2001) on the feminization of teaching. They describe significant regional variation in the timing of the feminization of teaching, with the South lagging the rest of the country in the proportion of women teachers.

9. Parrish (1974), pp. 12–13.

10. U.S. Department of Education, National Center for Education Statistics (1993), p. 26.

11. Gordon (1974), p. 64.

12. Ibid.

13. Parrish (1974), p. 12.

14. Jones (2009), table 1.

15. U.S. Bureau of Labor Statistics (1970).

16. Parrish (1974), p. 11.

17. Lavine (1974), pp. 187–188.

18. In 1970 the U.S. Department of Education's National Center for Education Statistics (NCES) reported a total of 47,969 graduates of business, dental, law, and medical schools, of whom 2,303 were women. In 1980 the total was 110,291, which included 27,136 women (NCES 1997).

19. Goldhaber (1972), p. 332; Pye and Cramer (1984), p. 463.

20. Lavine (1974, p. 189) writes, "The current competition to gain admission to law school applies, of course, to men as well as to women and is partially triggered by the utility of legal knowledge and skills in the liberal-activist spectrum of reform-revolution within the student culture, as well as by the decline in academic job opportunities."

21. Wandersee (1988), p. 103.

22. O'Connor (1980), p. 4.

23. Zich (1992), p. 23.

24. See Sandler (1973), pp. 439–462.

25. Ibid., p. 457.

REFERENCES

Astin, Alexander (1987). *The American Freshman: Twenty Year Trends, 1966–1985.* Los Angeles: Higher Education Research Institute, UCLA.

Bacolod, Marigee (2007). "Do Alternative Opportunities Matter? The Role of Female Labor Markets in the Decline of Teacher Quality." *Review of Economics and Statistics* 89: 737–751.

Bailey, Martha (2006). "More Power to the Pill: The Impact of Contraceptive Freedom on Women's Life-Cycle Labor Supply." *Quarterly Journal of Economics* 121: 289–320.

Carter, Susan (1986). "Occupational Segregation, Teachers' Wages, and American Economic Growth." *Journal of Economic History* 46: 373–383.

Carter, Susan B., Scott Sigmund Gartner, Michael R. Haines, Alan L. Olmstead, Richard Sutch, and Gavin Wright, eds. (2006). *Historical Statistics of the United States: Earliest Times to the Present, Millennial Edition.* New York: Cambridge University Press.

Chafe, William (1972). *The American Woman: Her Changing Social, Economic, and Political Role, 1920–1970.* Oxford: Oxford University Press.

Corcoran, Sean, William Evans, and Robert Schwab (2004). "Changing Labor-Market Opportunities for Women and the Quality of Teachers, 1957–2000." *American Economic Association Papers and Proceedings* 94: 230–235.

Goldhaber, Samuel (1972). "Medical School Admissions: A Raw Deal for Applicants." *Science* 177: 332–334.

Goldin, Claudia (1990). *Understanding the Gender Gap*. New York: Oxford University Press.

Goldin, Claudia, and Lawrence Katz (2002). "The Power of the Pill." *Journal of Political Economy* 110: 730–770.

Gootman, Elissa. (2008). "At Charter School, High Hopes and Even Higher Teacher Pay." *New York Times*, March 17, p. 1.

Gordon, Margaret S. (1974). "The Changing Labor Market for College Graduates." In *Higher Education and the Labor Market*, edited by Margaret S. Gordon. San Francisco, CA: McGraw-Hill, pp. 62–77.

Hoxby, Caroline, and Andrew Leigh (2004). "Pulled Away or Pushed Out? Explaining the Decline of Teacher Aptitude in the United States." *American Economic Association Papers and Proceedings* 94: 236–240.

Jones, Stacey M. (2009). "Dynamic Social Norms and the Transformation of Women's Higher Education, 1965–1975." *Social Science History* 33: 247–291.

Kuran, Timur (1995). *Private Truths, Public Lies: The Social Consequences of Preference Falsification*. Cambridge, MA: Harvard University Press.

Lavine, Thelma (1974). "The Motive to Achieve Limited Success: The New Women Law School Applicant." In *Women in Higher Education*, edited by W. Furniss and P. Graham. Washington, DC: American Council of Education, pp. 187–191.

O'Connor, Karen (1980). *Women's Organizations' Use of the Courts*. Lexington, MA: Lexington Books.

Parrish, John (1974). "Women, Careers and Counseling: The New Era." *Journal of the National Association for Women Deans, Administrators and Counselors* 38: 11–19.

Perlman, Joel, and Robert Margo (2001). *Women's Work? American School Teachers 1650–1920*. Chicago: University of Chicago Press.

Pye, A. Kenneth, and John Kramer (1984). "Solvency and Survival after the Boom: A Different Perspective." *Journal of Legal Education* 34: 462–478.

Riesman, David (1964). "Two Generations." In *The Woman in America*, edited by R. J. Lifton. Boston: Beacon Press, pp. 72–97.

Sandler, Bernice (1973). "With a Little Help from Our Government." In *Academic Women on the Move*, edited by A. Rossi and A. Calderwood. New York: Russell Sage Foundation, pp. 439–462.

Temin, Peter (2002). "Teacher Quality and the Future of America." *Eastern Economic Journal* 28: 285–400.

U.S. Bureau of Labor Statistics (1970). *College Educated Workers: 1968–80: A Study of Supply and Demand*. Bulletin 1676. Washington, DC: Government Printing Office.

U.S. Department of Education (1948–1962, biennial). *Earned Degrees Conferred*. Washington, DC: Government Printing Office.

U.S. Department of Education, National Center for Education Statistics (1963–2001, annual). *Digest of Education Statistics*. Washington, DC: Government Printing Office.

U.S. Department of Education, National Center for Education Statistics (1993). *120 Years of American Education: A Statistical Portrait.* Edited by T. Snyder. Washington, DC: Government Printing Office.

Wandersee, Winifred (1988). *On the Move: American Women in the 1970s.* Boston: Hall and Co.

Wright, Gavin (1999). "The Civil Rights Revolution as Economic History." *Journal of Economic History* 59: 267–289.

Zich, Janet (1992). "A Woman's Place." *Stanford Business Magazine* (June): 22–24.

CHAPTER 14

Inequality and Institutions in Twentieth-Century America

FRANK LEVY AND PETER TEMIN

A CENTRAL FEATURE of post–World War II America was mass upward mobility: individuals seeing sharply rising incomes through much of their careers and each generation living better than the last. The engine of that mobility was increased labor productivity.

It therefore is problematic that recent productivity gains have not significantly raised incomes for most American workers.[1] In the quarter century between 1980 and 2005 business sector productivity increased by 71 percent. Over the same quarter century median weekly earnings of full-time workers rose from $613 to $705, a gain of only 14 percent (figures in 2000 dollars).[2] Median weekly compensation—earnings plus estimated fringe benefits—rose from $736 to $876, a gain of 19 percent.[3]

Because productivity growth expands total income, slow income growth for the average worker implies faster income growth elsewhere in the distribution. In the U.S. case, growth occurred at the very top.[4] Piketty and Saez estimate that the share of gross personal income claimed by the top 1 percent of tax filing units—about 1.4 million returns—rose from 8.2 percent in 1980 to 17.4 percent in 2005. Among tax returns that report positive wage and salary income, the share of wages and salaries claimed by the top 1 percent rose from 6.4 percent in 1980 to 11.6 percent in 2005. These data imply that fully half of the gain in pretax, pretransfer income from 1980 to 2005 went to the top 1 percent of taxpayers.[5]

Many economists attribute the average worker's declining bargaining power to skill-biased technical change: technology augmented by globalization heavily favors better-educated workers. In this explanation the broad distribution of productivity gains during the Golden Age of 1947–1973 is often assumed to be a free-market outcome that can be restored by creating a more educated workforce. We argue instead that the Golden Age relied on market outcomes strongly moderated by institutional factors. Following the literature on economic growth that emphasizes the role of institutions in economic outcomes, we argue that institutions and norms affect the distribution of economic rewards as well as their aggregate size.

Our argument leads to an explanation of earnings levels and inequality in which skill-biased technical change, globalization, and related factors function within an institutional framework. In our interpretation the recent impacts of technology and trade have been amplified by the collapse of the institutions of the postwar years, a collapse that arose because economic forces led to a shift in the political environment over the 1970s and 1980s. If our interpretation is correct, no rebalancing of the labor force can restore a more equal distribution of productivity gains without government intervention and changes in private-sector behavior.

We combine data and history in a way that permits telling a more complete story including the likely origins of institutional shifts. By emphasizing the interplay among productivity, inequality, and the earnings growth of average workers we are also better able to describe the impact of current trends on economic life. We call the post–World War II institutional arrangements the Treaty of Detroit, after the most famous labor-management agreement of that period. This agreement was replaced in the 1980s and surrounding years by another set of institutional arrangements we call the Washington Consensus.[6] Wright (2006) described this policy shift as a "regime change," and it is discussed in Rosenbloom and Sundstrom (this volume). As we describe, the decisions to strengthen or to abandon these institutions were made by many people in complex economic and political settings.

We develop this argument in the sections that follow. The second section presents the underlying data that show stagnating real wages even for well-educated men. The third section describes the institutional arrangements that originated in the Great Depression and helped to distribute productivity gains broadly from 1947 to 1973. The fourth section describes the way in which the post-1973 productivity slowdown and associated stagflation ultimately led to the arrangements' collapse, to be replaced by institutions that made the labor market particularly vulnerable to extreme effects of technical change and trade—a vulnerability that is not as evident in most other industrialized countries. The fifth section provides evidence that connects our story and the wage data. The sixth section concludes by considering the implications of our story for policy.

EVIDENCE OF STAGNATING WAGES

To focus our historical discussion, we construct the following ratio:

$$\frac{\text{Median Annual Compensation for Full-Time Workers}}{\text{Annualized Value of Output per Hour in the Business Sector}}$$

The numerator is the sum of median annual earnings of full-time workers and the value of fringe benefits estimated from the National Income and Product Accounts. [7] The denominator is Business Sector Productivity expressed as an annual dollar amount. In each year both figures are in nominal dollars. We can think of the ratio as a bargaining power index (BPI), the share of total output per worker that the median full-time worker captures in compensation.[8]

Figure 14.1 displays this Bargaining Power Index for 1950–2005.[9] For purposes of comparison, the figure also displays the Piketty-Saez estimate of the 99.5th income percentile on federal tax returns—the median income of the top 1 percent of reported incomes normalized by Business Sector Productivity.[10] This graph summarizes 55 years of economic history. In the "Golden Age" labor productivity and median family income each roughly doubled. The Golden Age is illustrated in Figure 14.1 by the relatively steady BPI. The median compensation of full-time workers (the numerator) and labor productivity (the denominator) grew at the same rate from 1950 to the late 1970s. Simultaneously, income equality increased as very high incomes (illustrated by the 99.5th percentile) grew more slowly than labor productivity. The BPI series is too short and noisy to give more than 10 percent probability to a change in slope around 1980; it is more illuminating to note that the BPI was as high around 1980 as in 1950, after which time it steadily lost ground.

In the 1970s stagflation, median compensation of full-time workers began to lag behind productivity growth, a trend that accelerated after 1980. In Figure 14.1 the lag is illustrated by the BPI declining from 0.6 in

FIGURE 14.1 *Bargaining Power Indexes for the Median Full-Time Worker and for the Piketty-Saez 99.5th Percentile of Income*

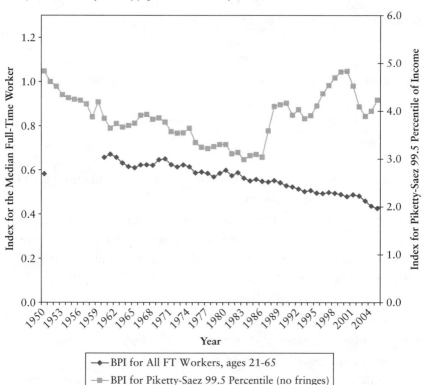

Source: Levy and Temin (2007).

1980 to 0.53 in 1990 and to 0.43 in 2005. This declining bargaining power of the typical full-time worker is a useful way to describe why significant productivity growth since 1980 has translated into weak growth in earnings and compensation. Very high incomes also lagged productivity growth through the 1970s and early 1980s. They began to increase rapidly in 1986 and have outstripped productivity growth up to the present.

For over a decade the economist's primary explanation for income inequality has been skill-biased technical change.[11] While the explanation has been refined over time, its core is unchanged.[12] Technology, perhaps augmented by international trade, is shifting demand toward more skilled workers faster than the supply of skilled workers is increasing.

This explanation of earnings inequality has resonated strongly with the public as well as public policy. Educational improvement has been a central policy focus at all levels of government. Equally important, many government officials describe educational differences as the central driver of inequality, as in the August 1, 2006 remarks of Treasury Secretary Henry Paulson:

We must also recognize that, as our economy grows, market forces work to provide the greatest rewards to those with the needed skills in the growth areas. This means that those workers with less education and fewer skills will realize fewer rewards and have fewer opportunities to advance. In 2004, workers with a bachelor's degree earned almost $23,000 more per year, on average, than workers with a high school degree only. This gap has grown more than 60 percent since 1975.[13]

This view is echoed in the recent book by Goldin and Katz (2008). They argue that inequality is a race between education and technology, citing evidence from Lemieux (2006a) that the returns to education have increased in recent years, particularly for college education. They define inequality more narrowly than we do, however. Goldin and Katz focus on the divergence of earnings between the tenth and ninetieth percentiles of wages and salaries as reported in the census. We are concerned also about the rising incomes of people at the top of the income distribution, whose incomes are not captured in census data on wages and salaries. This is why we relate median wages not to other wage income, but to the growth of per capita income.

Our broader measure calls for a more compressive view than previous literature. We do not challenge the existence of technology's and trade's effects on labor demand (Card and DiNardo 2002), or the papers finding relationships between inequality and measurable institutional variables including the rate of unionization, the minimum wage, and tax policy (e.g., Bound and Johnson 1992; Feenberg and Poterba 1993; DiNardo, Fortin, and Lemieux 1996; Lee 1999; Gordon and Slemrod 2000; Saez 2004; Reynolds 2006; Autor, Katz, and Kearny 2008).[14] Instead, we argue that all of these specific factors are embedded in a larger institutional story.

We argue that important aspects of inequality—such as the rapid increase in salaries associated with the financial sector—are not revealed in a comparison of census data on wages and salaries. A case in point is, for example, a starting associate lawyer at Cravath, Swain and Moore in 1967 earned about $49,500 in 2005 dollars. This salary, which excludes bonuses, was 24 percent lower than median earnings reported in the Current Population Survey (CPS) for all U.S. male lawyers and judges, ages 25 to 64, a result one would expect given that associates were beginning their careers. In 2005 a starting associate at Cravath earned about $135,000, excluding bonuses, a salary 35 percent *more* than U.S. median earnings for all male lawyers and judges (Galanter and Palay 1991, p. 24; Marin Levy, personal communication; CPS).

The salaries of Wall Street lawyers, from associate to partner, often are described as winner-take-all salaries: an extreme form of skill-based demand. In fact, Alfred Marshall used lawyers as an example when he first described winner-take-all markets in 1890s England.[15] The question is why such winner-take-all salaries were far less common in 1950s and 1960s America than they are today. This comparison also raises the possibility that as more people attend college (and more college graduates go to graduate school), today's median BA is "less skilled" than the BA of 10 or 20 years ago. We show in the longer version of this essay that the change in the BPI that we describe in Figure 14.1 is evident for men when correcting for the increase of income. It does not hold for women, whose educational and occupational opportunities changed dramatically (Levy and Temin 2007).

Who received the rest of the gain? The data are not good at the top of the income distribution, but data on Saez's Web site enable a rough calculation to be made. We compare the gain since 1980 in the average income per tax unit and the average income of the top 1 percent of tax filing units. In a random sample of 100 tax filing units, the gain in average income of the top tax filer equals fully half of the total gains of the group. This is in agreement with Saez's table 1, which reports that the fraction of total growth captured by the top 1 percent from 1993 to 2006 was almost exactly 50 percent.[16]

We argue that while the relatively weak demand for BA's is fairly recent, it represents an old phenomenon: the periodic inability of the free market to broadly distribute the gains from productivity. In particular, the potential for this problem existed in the Golden Age but was largely overcome by economic institutions and norms. The composition of the labor force was, of course, much different then. In 1940 only 5 percent of the labor force had a bachelor's degree. Unemployment in the Depression had been concentrated among the less educated and less skilled members of the labor force, and it was largely for these workers that the New Deal erected a new structure of institutions and norms (U.S. Bureau of the Census 1975, 380; Margo 1991).

The result was a decline in income inequality that was reinforced by the controls of World War II and produced a broad distribution of productivity gains for at least another quarter century. Piketty and Saez (2003, pp. 33–34) write that the stability of income distribution followed by the growth of inequality is "indirect evidence that nonmarket mechanisms such as labor market institutions and social norms regarding inequality may play a role in setting compensation at the top." We agree and in the sections that follow, we show how these nonmarket mechanisms distributed productivity gains broadly while limiting the extent of very high incomes—at least until the mechanisms broke down.

NORMS, INSTITUTIONS, AND THE GOLDEN AGE

The nonmarket mechanisms that shaped the postwar Golden Age had roots in the Great Depression and the New Deal. At first glance, it is surprising that norms and institutions—microeconomic policies—grew out of a macroeconomic crisis. But macroeconomic policy as we now understand it did not exist in the Great Depression; Keynes's General Theory was not published until 1936. The New Deal initiated a series of federal government actions that altered the relative bargaining power of labor and management.

In 1933, Franklin Delano Roosevelt's first year in office, unemployment stood at nearly 25 percent and microeconomic policies were apparently the only tools at hand. Lacking a theory of aggregate demand,

Roosevelt's New Deal policies focused on other goals—in particular trying to stop what the administration saw as ruinous price deflation (Eggertsson 2006). This effort was implicit in the first major piece of New Deal legislation, the 1933 National Industrial Recovery Act (NIRA) that gave the government control over employer contracts, and encouraged labor and industry to negotiate industry codes that shortened work hours, increased wages significantly, and raised prices. The NIRA also gave workers the right to organize and bargain collectively with their employers, and this was a bone of contention. Roosevelt supported union organizing, but Johnson, charged with administering the NIRA, was eager to get industry codes with or without collective bargaining. Roosevelt formed the National Labor Board led by Senator Wagner that mediated the resulting conflicts. The confusing implementation of the NIRA made both sides tense and combative (Gross 1974).

The Supreme Court outlawed the NIRA in 1935, citing it as an overreach of federal power into state interests and probably easing passage of the National Labor Relations Act (NLRA)—the "Wagner Act." Congress passed the Wagner Act in 1935, endorsing the rights of labor, limiting the means employers could use to combat unions, and transforming the informal National Labor Board into the legislatively directed National Labor Relations Board (NLRB). Unions grew dramatically under the NLRA, but the postwar system of collective bargaining had its origins as much in workers' reactions to the unemployment of the Depression as in congressional actions (Freeman 1998).

The minimum wage was introduced in 1938, and was set to raise wages significantly in concert with other supports of unions and collective bargaining. We compared the minimum wage to average output per worker in the economy (as we did with the median wage earlier). In 1938 annual earnings at the first minimum wage represented 27 percent of the economy's average output per worker. Between 1947 and 2005 the value of the minimum wage exceeded that percentage in only four other years, as shown in Figure 14.2, and stands at something less than half that percentage today.[17]

New Deal policy also raised taxes on very high incomes. On the eve of Roosevelt's election, Hoover raised the top bracket rate sharply from

FIGURE 14.2   *Ratio of Annual Earnings at the Minimum Wage to Economy-Wide Labor Productivity*

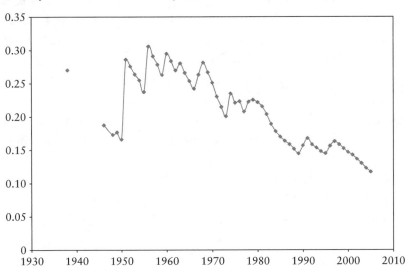

Source: U.S. Department of Labor, http://www.dol.gov/esa/minwage/chart.htm.

25 percent to 63 percent in an effort to reduce the federal deficit under the impression that the Depression was over. In 1936, after the economy began to recover more robustly, Roosevelt raised the top bracket rate further to 79 percent. This additional increment was part of a general tax rise that included a tax on undistributed profits, based on the presumption that the economy had progressed into a normal recovery—a presumption speedily abandoned in the recession that followed hard on the heels of the higher taxes (E. Rosen 2005). Nonetheless, Roosevelt compressed the income distribution using unions and the minimum wage to raise low incomes and tax rates and moral suasion to hold down incomes at the top (Goldin and Margo 1992). While it is dangerous to impute too much intellectual coherence to the New Deal, the increasing regulation of industry and utilities in the 1930s can be seen as creating oligopoly rents that would provide a basis for union bargaining. Among many other innovative programs, the Federal Housing Authority helped workers buy houses, Social Security added to workers' retirement income, and enhanced antitrust enforcement sought to protect workers from monopoly pricing.

When the United States entered World War II, mobilization and production became the focus of the economy. The military saw unions as detrimental to the war effort, and they took several initiatives to undercut union power (Koistinen 2004). The government created the National Defense Mediation Board in 1941 to settle labor disputes and replaced it a year later with the National War Labor Board (NWLB). NWLB initiatives achieved no-strike and no-lockout pledges from unions and companies and effectively froze wages for the duration of the war. The agreement created an uneasy peace, with continuing tension between unions, the government, and industry, throughout the war.

As the war drew to a close, many feared that the end of wartime strike controls would bring labor market disruption and the potential for a second Great Depression. Truman retained a high top-bracket income tax rate on labor income in an extension of Depression-era policy. Econometric results in a historical study of executive compensation suggest that if tax rates been at their year 2000 level for the entire sample period, the level of executive compensation would have been 35 percent higher in the 1950s and 1960s (Frydman and Saks 2010). Despite Truman's best efforts, however, the postwar transition was difficult. At the war's end, organized labor erupted with work stoppages involving over 3 percent of the workforce each year between 1947 and 1949.[18] Business supported the Taft-Hartley Act of 1947, which established restrictive administrative policies to constrain unions. Although the Taft-Hartley Act clearly rolled back some union gains from the Depression and war, it fell far short of dismantling the Wagner Act and the NLRB.

It was in this context, in late 1948, that Walter Reuther and his advocates assumed control over the United Auto Workers (UAW). The relationship between the UAW and the "Big Three" automakers (Ford, GM, and Chrysler), previously plagued by turmoil, entered a new phase of negotiation. Reuther, an experienced labor leader, hoped to overhaul industrial relations in favor of labor interests, but the postwar setting created significant obstacles for his social vision. Workers faced price inflation while wages remained inert, and the government's division between Truman and Congress indicated the situation would not improve. Reuther also had recently survived several assassination attempts, which indicated dramatically labor's internal fissures.

Charles Wilson, the CEO of GM, was aware that inflationary pressures generated by cold war military spending promised to be a permanent feature of the economic scene. GM had recently begun a $3.5 billion expansion program that depended on production stability. Stress created by inflation could instigate the unions to interrupt production with devastating strikes, and Wilson thought a long-term wage concession would be a profitable exchange for guaranteed production stability (Lichtenstein 1995).

GM's two-year proposal to the UAW included an increase in wages and two concepts intended to keep wages up over time. The first, a cost-of-living adjustment (COLA), would allow wages to be influenced by changes in the Consumer Price Index, adjusting for rising inflation. Second, a 2 percent annual improvement factor (AIF) was introduced, which would increase wages every year in an attempt to allow workers to benefit from productivity gains. The UAW, in exchange, would allow management control over production and investment decisions, surrendering job assignment seniority and the right to protest reassignments. Reuther and his advisors initially opposed the plan, believing the AIF formula to be too low and the deal to be a profiteer's bribe signaling the end of overall reform. Workers needed assistance, however, and Reuther agreed to the plan and wage formulas, but "only because most of those in control of government and industry show no signs of acting in the public interest. They are enforcing a system of private planning for private profit at public expense" (UAW press release, quoted in Lichtenstein 1995, p. 279). The contract was signed in May 1948.

Labor saw wage increases and gains from productivity for the next two years. GM enjoyed smooth, increasing production, and it established a net income record for a U.S. corporation in 1949 (Amberg 1994). When the time period for the contract ended, the UAW and GM readily agreed to a similar plan that included several changes. A pension plan was added, initially through Ford in 1949, which had an older workforce and progressive managers (Lichtenstein 1987). The resulting plan was presented to GM as a precedent to create industrial conformity in a process known as pattern bargaining. GM agreed quickly, and the last of the "Big Three," Chrysler, agreed after an expensive strike. Agreements to the pension plan ultimately spread to other industries like rubber and steel (Amberg 1994). In addition to the pension plan, GM increased the COLA/AIF formulas and paid for half of a new health insurance program. The final, five-year UAW-GM agreement was named the "Treaty of Detroit" by *Fortune* magazine: "GM may have paid a billion for peace but it got a bargain. General Motors has regained control over one of the crucial management functions . . . long range scheduling of production, model changes, and tool and plant investment." Wage adjustments and productivity gains became recognized as necessary and just, union membership increased, and industry reaped the profits from the Treaty of Detroit's stability (Lichtenstein 1995).

The Korean War's outbreak in 1950 immediately threatened the agreement as the UAW and GM had to intervene to prevent the government from freezing wages. Inflationary adjustments during Korea were not fully reflected by the COLA formula, causing disappointment in the UAW. Other issues created by the Treaty of Detroit also caused friction, specifically the emphasis on debating national policy over local factory floor issues. The UAW shifted its focus, fighting for standardized monetary and fringe benefits while workers became frustrated over shop terms and job assignments. The problem was exacerbated by the bureaucratization of grievance disputes, which created a backlog of complaints about daily working conditions.

Despite these problems, the Treaty of Detroit initiated a stable period of industrial relations. The use of collective bargaining spread throughout industry, and even nonunion firms approximated the conditions achieved by unions in an extension of pattern bargaining. Although the strict application of this term refers to the dynamics of union negotiations in large firms, a looser version was pervasive (Chamberlain and Kuhn 1986). The NLRA provided a regulatory framework for labor to organize a significant part of the industrial labor force.

This framework was administered by the National Labor Relations Board (NLRB). Congress explicitly rejected a partisan board composed of labor and management representatives in the NLRA and opted instead for "impartial government members." This concept lasted only two decades, however, and President Eisenhower, the first Republican president after Roosevelt, appointed management people to the NLRB. This violation of the original intent of the board was controversial, and the seeds of future controversy were planted, although the neutrality of the board was more or less preserved (Flynn 2000).

Unions acknowledged the exclusive right of management to determine the direction of production in return for the right to negotiate the impact of managerial decisions. Unions crafted an elaborate set of local rules that constrained management in its allocation of jobs and bolstered the power of unions over jobs (Kochan 1980; Weinstein and Kochan 1995). Managers used the framework of the Treaty of Detroit to tighten their grasp on production decisions. The inclusion of supplementary unemployment benefits in production decisions in 1955 gave managers even more control over job descriptions and workplace decisions, as unions conceded these rights in exchange for direct welfare. Labor complaints had to go through paperwork, and the burden to oppose or modify change was placed on the workers (Brody 1980).

The impact of this framework is clear in the pattern of relative wages. Eckstein and Wilson found in a study of nominal wages in the 1950s that

wages in a group of heavy industries, which we call the key group, move virtually identically because of the economic, political and institutional interdependence among the companies and the unions in these industries. . . . Wages in some other industries outside this group are largely determined by spillover effects of the key group wages and economic variables applicable to the industry. (Eckstein and Wilson 1962)

Changes in these pattern wages were determined by economic variables, according to Eckstein and Wilson, but the same forces that kept industrial wages in a stable pattern likely affected the extent of overall wage changes as well. Erickson (1996) extended the concept of pattern bargaining to include other contract provisions. He found that they also were remarkably similar at both inter- and intraindustry levels in the 1970s, although not in the 1980s, as we will see. Katznelson (2005), however, reminds us that this pattern of stable conditions and wages did not extend to all corners of the economy. Black workers and other minority groups were largely ignored in these negotiations.

This pattern came under strain in the 1960s. While initially successful, the Kennedy tax cut was soon overwhelmed as the government began deficit-financing the Vietnam War in an economy already near full employment. By 1969 unemployment had fallen to 3.5 percent and inflation had risen to a high of 5.4 percent. In a tight labor market, debates over automation became increasingly common as new technology fueled the power struggle between unions and management for control of decision making and the right to adapt to change (Lichtenstein 2002).

1970–2005: INSTITUTIONAL CHANGE AT THE END OF THE GOLDEN AGE

As with the Great Depression, policy makers faced stagflation in the 1970s with little relevant history to serve as a guide. Economic theory had followed Keynes in focusing on demand shifts, and there was no theory of the supply side that related to economic policy. Only in the mid-1970s was the concept of aggregate supply integrated with the standard IS-LM model. And as with the Great Depression, the resulting policy agenda was heavily microeconomic. To combat slow productivity growth, some economists began to argue for economic restructuring including removing what they saw as the rigidities of New Deal institutions: unions imposing work rules; a regulatory regime covering most of the nation's utilities, telecommunications, and interstate transportation; and high marginal tax rates that they assumed reduced work effort.

Jimmy Carter argued in 1978, "The two most important measures the Congress can pass to prevent inflation . . . [are] the airline deregulation bill . . . [and] hospital cost containment legislation." He appointed Alfred E. Kahn, chairman of the Civil Aeronautics Board, to head the administration's anti-inflation program. Kahn's field was government regulation, and his plans were to reduce regulations that supported monopoly pricing (Carter 1978; Cowan 1978). We do not want to equate Carter and Roosevelt or economic theory in the 1970s and 1930s. Instead, we note that unusual macroeconomic events sometimes transcend existing macroeconomic theory. Before macroeconomics could be expanded to include the aggregate supply curve in the 1970s, public policy appears to have focused on perceived microeconomic problems.

In what is now known as the Washington Consensus on economic policy, deregulation plays a prominent role. The impact of deregulation on wages was not much discussed in the 1970s because blue-collar wages, in particular, continued to do fairly well. On the labor market's supply side, male high school graduates remained heavily unionized (42 percent, authors' tabulations) with unionization among female high school graduates at 17 percent. On the labor market's demand side, food and oil supply shocks stimulated the energy and agricultural industries while a declining international value of the dollar expanded global demand for U.S. manufacturing goods.[19] Strong manufacturing, energy, and agricultural sectors created what economic geographers called a "Rural Renaissance" (Long and DeAre 1988) in which the nation's heartland was doing well, with resulting demand for blue-collar workers, while the east and west coasts were stagnant.[20]

In reality the Rural Renaissance was a blue-collar bubble. High demands for agriculture and domestic energy were temporary while the falling dollar was masking manufacturing's competitive weakness. Unions, perhaps lulled by this temporary prosperity, largely ignored the need to organize a changing labor market. As labor force composition shifted toward women and college graduates, many in the service sector, union membership fell to about 27 percent of all wage and salary workers (private and public), down from 35 percent at the peak of their postwar strength (Osterman 1999; Hirsch and Macpherson 2004).

While the bubble existed, however, wage-setting norms interacted with inflation to markedly increase labor's share of national income. The ideas embodied in the Treaty of Detroit were developed in the time of low inflation and high productivity that followed World War II. From the end of the war through the mid-1960s, real wages rose dramatically and labor's share of national income cycled narrowly around 67 percent (Dew-Becker and Gordon 2005). In subsequent years inflation accelerated, productivity growth declined, and wage-setting norms—for example, money wages rising roughly in line with the Consumer Price

Index—helped labor's share to rise to 0.74 in 1973 and 0.76 in 1980. Capital's weak prospects were summarized in the performance of the Dow Jones Industrial Average: 903 in January 1965 falling to 876 in January 1980 while the general price level had more than doubled. The effectiveness of COLA contracts in this inflationary environment put pressure on the Treaty of Detroit system.

While Carter advanced deregulation and increased competition as solutions to the stagnant economy, others attacked unions directly. An example was the 1978 failure of a bill reforming labor law. The bill proposed a set of small, technical changes in labor law that would have preserved the legal framework in which the Treaty of Detroit labor system had operated. Despite the small scale of the bill, business mounted a large, inflammatory public campaign against it. The bill passed the House by a vote of 257 to 163, and it would have passed the Senate as well, but employers took a hard line against the bill and arranged to have it stopped by a filibuster. After a 19-day filibuster, the bill's supporters failed in their sixth try to muster 60 votes to stop it and sent the bill back to committee to die (Mills 1979).

The economy continued to limp along for the remainder of the 1970s. Unemployment fell slowly, and weak productivity growth translated economic expansion into additional inflation. By 1979, consumer prices were increasing at 12 percent annually. Shaken financial markets forced Carter to appoint Paul Volcker, an inflation hawk, as chairman of the Federal Reserve. Volcker quickly instituted a strong, tight money policy to break inflation quickly. When, in 1980, Carter was defeated by Ronald Reagan, Volcker's and Reagan's policies combined to help dismantle much of what remained of New Deal institutions and norms.

Reagan made three decisions in his first year in office that proved central to the wage-setting process. He gave Volcker's tight-money anti-inflation policy his full backing. He introduced a set of supply-side tax cuts including lowering the top income tax on nonlabor income from 70 to 50 percent to align it with the top rate on labor income. And when the air traffic controllers union, one of the few unions to support Reagan, went out on strike, he gave them 48 hours to return to work or be fired. His stance ultimately led to the union's decertification.

The 1978 defeat of labor law reform, the lowering of tax rates, and the firing of the air traffic controllers were signals that the third man—government—was leaving the ring.[21] From that point on, business and labor would fight over rewards in less regulated markets with many workers in an increasingly weak position. Then, in an unanticipated development, Volcker's tight money policy further weakened the position of blue-collar workers.

Volcker's policy reduced inflation far more rapidly than most economists had predicted—from 12.5 percent in 1980 to 3.8 percent in 1982. Reagan's tax cuts led to projections of large future deficits, and the fear that deficits would be monetized kept interest rates high even as inflation fell.[22] High real interest rates increased global demand for U.S. securities and the dollars required to buy them. Between 1979 and 1984, the trade-weighted value of the dollar rose by 55 percent. The result was perhaps fifteen years of normal change compressed into five years. U.S. durable goods manufacturing firms were hit first by the deep recession and then by the high dollar that crippled export sales. The loss of old-line manufacturing jobs together with new employer boldness put unions under siege. The fraction of all private-sector wage and salary workers in unions fell from 23 percent in 1979 to 16 percent in 1985 (Hirsch and Macpherson 2004). The Rural Renaissance of the 1970s became the Rust Belt of the 1980s.

The rise of the financial sector and accompanying high salaries represented a mirror image of these events. Financial innovations had emerged in the 1970s, but the financial sector first attained its current prominence in the macroeconomic events of the 1980s.[23] Blair (1989) argued that the high real interest of the early 1980s restricted profitable investment opportunities for mature firms in many industries, resulting in free cash flows that made these firms takeover targets (Blair and Shary 1993; Jensen 1997). More generally, the period represented a reallocation of capital across firms and industries (Holmstrom and Kaplan 2001; Philippon 2008). In earlier postwar years investment came from mature corporations utilizing their own cash flows. Now, new corporations were financing investment through financial intermediaries. The result was increased demand for financial professionals—the financial sector—to create and sell the new debt involved in the capital reallocation. The financial sector's importance was further increased by the rapidly growing U.S. Treasuries market, a result of the Reagan budget deficits. Between 1975 and 1984 total credit market debt grew from $2.5 trillion to $7.2 trillion (nominal).[24]

Mortgage-backed bonds are a microcosm of these developments. As interest rates rose during the 1970s and early 1980s, savings and loan institutions were under pressure to sell low-interest mortgages in the hope of reinvesting the proceeds at higher returns. There was little investor interest in buying individual mortgages, but mortgage-backed bonds created a market in which these mortgages could be sold. By the early 1980s the mortgage-backed bond market had taken off and, as a by-product, helped to redefine income norms. Lewis (1989, p. 126) tells the story of Howie Rubin, a late 1920s graduate of Salomon Brothers' training program who was assigned to trade mortgage-backed bonds. In 1983, Rubin's first year, he generated $25 million of revenue and was paid $90,000; he moved in his third year to Merrill Lynch for a three-year guarantee of over $1 million a year. Many of Salomon's other successful mortgage bond traders soon left the firm for similar offers.

Similarly, junk bonds had been developed in the late 1970s to finance corporate takeovers, attempts to wrest control of the corporation's assets away from its current managers (Jensen 1997). Here, too, a by-product was very high salaries for both the junk bond salesmen and the investment bankers and lawyers who advised in the transactions. This history is summarized in Figure 14.3, which shows for selected industries the sum of compensation and corporate profits—a surrogate for economic rents—per full-time equivalent employee (FTE). From 1950 through the end of the 1970s, economic rent per FTE in the Finance, Insurance, and Real Estate Industry (FIRE) grew at a rate similar to rates in other industries. Beginning in the mid-1980s, economic rent per FTE in FIRE grew at an accelerating pace in line with the expanding bond market and a revived stock market.[25]

Kaplan and Rauh (2010) estimate that in the period from 1994 to 2005, financial professionals and partners at national law firms are more numerous than CEOs in the top income ranges reported by Piketty and

FIGURE 14.3   *Compensation and Corporate Profits per FTE in Selected Private Industries*

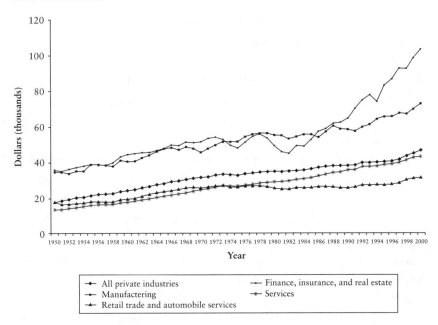

Source: U.S. Department of Commerce, National Income and Product Accounts, http://www.bea.gov/national/nipaweb/SelectTable.asp, tables 6.2, 6.8, and 6.16.

Saez. As financial salaries changed income norms, superstar markets were often invoked to justify large compensation in occupations where high pay arose from nonmarket sources of power, such as CEOs who benefited from compliant compensation committees. In 1984 median CEO compensation in the sample analyzed by Hall and Liebman (1998) was $568,000 (in 1984 dollars). Over the next decade, real median compensation in the Hall and Liebman sample increased by 87 percent. Much of this increase came from the rapidly expanding inclusion of stock options in compensation, a practice relatively unknown before the mid-1980s. While the options' stated purpose was to align managerial and shareholder interests, accounting regulations did not require the value of options to be treated as an expense and boards were reluctant to grant bonuses of comparable value (Hall and Liebman 1998).

Many of Reagan's supporters acknowledged his policies would lead to inequality, but they argued that inequality was the price of revived productivity growth. Most people would see rising incomes while the incomes of the rich would rise faster. The result of the booming financial sector, rapidly rising CEO compensation, and tax reforms in 1986 was that the 99.5th percentile of reported taxpayer income increased from $175,000 (2005 dollars) in 1980 to $220,000 in 1988. At the same time, labor productivity continued its weak growth while the compensation of male high school graduates, in particular, declined sharply.

Because a rising tide was supposed to lift all boats, there was no thought given to ex-post redistribution. To the contrary, Reagan's administration allowed the minimum wage to reach a historical low relative to output per worker, as seen in Figure 14.2. In a similar way the NLRB became more polarized, moving away from the impartial model that characterized the board's early years. The seeds planted under Eisenhower flowered under Reagan when he broke with tradition and appointed a management consultant who specialized in defeating unions to be the chairman of the NLRB. The result is that the NLRB increasingly reflected current political trends (Flynn 2000).

The sharp decline in male high school graduate earnings caused economists to focus their attention on the declining demand for less educated workers and the relationship between growing inequality and educational differences (Levy 1988, 1989; Katz and Murphy 1992; Juhn, Murphy, and Pierce 1993; Goldin and Katz 2008). These analyses ignored the point that began this chapter. Since the mid-1970s a growing fraction of male BA's also now faced demand that was too weak to keep compensation growing in line with productivity.

The outlines of this story have persisted through the present. Clinton, the only Democratic president between 1980 and 2008, encouraged the Washington Consensus in his centrist positions extending deregulation in the United States and—to the extent possible—in the world as a whole. He took important measures of ex-post redistribution by expanding the Earned Income Tax Credit, increasing the minimum wage, and increasing the top income-tax rate, but George W. Bush reversed the trend of these last two elements.

CONNECTING THE DOTS: EVIDENCE OF THE
EFFECTS OF INSTITUTIONAL CHANGE

Two kinds of evidence connect our story and our evidence. The first type concerns the nature of the labor market in the United States, showing that aspects have changed that are unconnected with skill-biased technical change. The second type of evidence is international, demonstrating that the choice of institutional change was in fact a choice; it was not dictated by changes in technology, globalization, and the reduction in the rate of productivity growth.

Our labor market test involves the nature of the wage bargaining process. While skill-biased technical change affects the outcome of this process, it says little about the nature of the process itself.[26] The hypothesis that skill-biased technical change has affected the path of wages is confined to the outcome of the wage bargaining process; it does not have any implications for the bargaining itself. Our story by contrast argues that the nature of wage bargaining has been altered drastically by changing institutions.

Lee (1999) among others argued that the falling value of minimum wage was a significant determinant of inequality during this period. We take the broader position advanced by Autor, Katz, and Kearny (2008) that increased inequality reflected a change in regime of which the falling minimum wage was part. An indicator of this changed regime was the dramatic fall-off in strike activity.[27] In the 1970s an average 1.7 percent of the labor force was involved annually in work stoppages (http://stats .bls.gov/news.release/wkstp.to1.htm); in the 1980s this rate fell to one-half percent. Even as the number of union complaints of unfair labor practices was rising, the politicization of the NLRB sharply reduced the economic return to work stoppages and discouraged workers from attempting them (Roomkin 1981; Flynn 2000). The rapid fall in work stoppages underestimates the decline in expressions of union power as strikes increasingly became expressions of union despair—for example, the strike against the Greyhound Corporation—rather than efforts to improve working conditions (Kochan, Katz, and McKersie 1994).

Another result driven in part by this changed process appears in international comparisons of wage flexibility. A large project has compared the year-to-year flexibility in both nominal and real wages. The United States now is near the bottom of the list in real wage stability. In other words, American workers have lost the ability to preserve their real wages in response to economic shocks. They have ample stability of nominal wages, but at the cost of losing the ability to preserve the purchasing power of their labor (Dickens et al. 2007). Further evidence in process indicates that the stability of American real wages has been falling over time to reach this position. The loss of COLA contracts has eroded the ability of workers to preserve real wages. Fewer workers are in unions, have a realistic opportunity to strike, and have the power to engage in meaningful collective bargaining. The process of wage determination began to change in the 1980s, as we have described, and it has changed the outcome of wage determination.

These changes in the way wages are determined were not inevitable. Labor-market institutions appear to have many national idiosyncrasies. Lindert (2004) showed that different labor-market institutions in Western Europe and America are compatible with similar rates of economic growth. Nickell (1997) demonstrated that different labor-market institutions within Western Europe are compatible with similar rates of unemployment. Saez (2004) showed that rapidly rising incomes among the very rich appear in the United States, England, and Canada (largely in response to U.S. competition) but do not appear in most continental European countries or Japan. Globalization has affected all countries, yet the variety of institutions surveyed by Lindert and Nickell shows no sign of disappearing. Their work suggests that it may not even be costly to preserve a preferred set of labor-market institutions, in contrast to the assertions of globalization enthusiasts.

Economic shocks do not determine institutions. The Vietnam War and the oil shocks disrupted the international economy. Yet countries responded to these shocks in idiosyncratic ways. The contrast between the economic performance of the United States and Japan in the 1970s is only one example of the great diversity. Economic shocks can affect policy, and the shocks of the 1970s may have accelerated institutional change, but there is no indication that it forced countries to adopt homogenous labor-market institutions. It did, however, create opportunities for political choices to change institutions, and we analyze the results in the United States.

Other countries made other choices. Atkinson and Piketty (2007) chronicle the history of top incomes in a variety of countries, finding a peculiar pattern. Of the countries for which they could amass data, the English-speaking countries had U-shaped behavior of the share of income going to the top earners. That is, they look like the United States in recent years as shown in Figure 14.1. Other countries—Germany, France, the Netherlands, Switzerland—did not have this U-shaped behavior of the top income share. There was no trend toward income inequality in these countries in the past few decades. Japan, not covered in their book, also exhibits this European pattern and does not show the rising inequality so apparent in the United States (Moriguchi and Saez 2008).

There could not be a clearer demonstration that external and exogenous events like globalization and technological change do not fully determine the path of income inequality. Instead, people make different choices through their choices of governments and institutions. As we have described here, the government of the United States played an important role in the determination of income inequality over the last half century.

CONCLUSION

We have argued in this chapter that the current trend toward greater inequality in America is primarily the result of a change in economic policy that took place in the late 1970s and early 1980s. The stability in income equality where wages rose with national productivity for a generation after World War II was the result of policies that began in the Great Depression with the New Deal and were amplified by both public and private actions after the war. This stability was not the result of a natural economy alone: it was also the result of policies designed to promote it. We have termed this set of policies the Treaty of Detroit.

The new policies, which we have grouped under the title of the Washington Consensus, also originated in a time of economic distress, albeit

nowhere near the distress of the 1930s. In a process similar to the experience of the Great Depression, policy makers—unable to comprehend the
macroeconomic causes of distress—instituted microeconomic changes in
an attempt to ameliorate the macroeconomic problems. In both cases the
measures taken were only partially successful, and recovery came from
diverse influences. The microeconomic changes, however, had durable
impacts on the distribution of economic production.

The elements of the Washington Consensus—deregulation, floating
exchange rates, international capital mobility, low minimum wages
and taxes, and the destruction of labor unions—were adopted in the
name of improving economic efficiency. But there is growing recognition that the current free-market income distribution—the combination
of large inequalities and stagnant wages for many workers—creates its
own "soft" inefficiencies as people become disenchanted with existing
economic arrangements. The Washington Consensus has come under
fire recently as people suffering from stagnant incomes have begun to
protest.

Our analysis suggests that the trends in the distribution derive in part
from the shift from one complex of policies to another—from the Treaty of
Detroit to the Washington Consensus. There is no single determinant,
whether education, minimum wage, capital, or labor mobility, that determines the path of income distribution. Any specific measure therefore can
alleviate the distress of some people, but it cannot change the overall distributional trends described in this chapter. Only a reorientation of government policy can restore the general prosperity of the postwar boom and
re-create a more equitable distribution of productivity gains where a rising
tide lifts all boats.

NOTES

This chapter is a revision of Levy and Temin (2007, 2009). We thank Nirupama Rao and
Julia Dennett for excellent research assistance and the Russell Sage and Alfred P. Sloan
foundations for financial support. We have benefited from helpful comments from Elizabeth Ananat, David Autor, Jared Bernstein, Margaret Blair, Barry Bosworth, Peter Dia-
mond, Bill Dickens, John Paul Ferguson, Carola Frydman, Robert Gordon, Harry Katz,
Larry Katz, Tom Kochan, David Levy, Richard Murnane, Paul Osterman, Steven Pearlstein, Michael Piore, Peter Rappoport, Dani Rodrik, Emmanuel Saez, Dan Sichel, Jon

Skinner, Robert Solow, Katherine Swartz, Ted Truman, Eric Wanner, and David Wessel and from seminar participants at the University of California at Berkeley, the National Bureau of Economic Research, the Sloan School Institute for Work and Employment Research, and the New America Foundation.

1. See, for example, Dew-Becker and Gordon (2005); Krugman (2006); Pearlstein (2006a, 2006b); and Tritch (2006).

2. To compare earnings and productivity on a consistent basis, earnings and compensation are adjusted using the GDP deflator.

3. Detailed analysis of this period shows that college-educated women are the only large labor force group for whom median compensation grew in line with labor productivity (see Figure 14.3).

4. Slow income growth for the average worker can also mean faster growth of capital income. Labor's share of income was unusually high in 1980, and the share of capital income has grown. The rise in the share of top incomes nevertheless is largely the result of rising wage and entrepreneurial income.

5. See Piketty and Saez (2003) and the updating of their figures to 2005 on Emmanuel Saez's Web site, http://elsa.berkeley.edu/~saez/, particularly tables A0 and A1.

6. This term normally is used for least developed countries (LDCs), but the spirit of this concept applies well to the changing institutions within the United States. We use the term here to refer to the microeconomic policies of deregulation and privatization of the consensus, not the macroeconomic policies of fiscal discipline and stable exchange rates. See Williamson (1990), pp. 7–24.

7. More precisely, we inflate the median weekly earnings of all full-time workers (35 or more hours per week) by the ratio of Supplements to Wages and Salaries to Wages and Salaries taken from the U.S. Bureau of Economic Analysis National Income and Product Accounts (http://www.bea.gov/national/nipaweb/index.asp).

8. The description is not quite accurate, because focusing on output per worker in the Business Sector excludes the value of government output due to difficulties in measuring output.

9. Data come from authors' tabulations of the 1950 and 1960 Decennial Census and Current Population Survey micro data sets for 1961 and 1963 onward. Data are missing for 1951–1959 because Current Population Survey data do not exist in machine-readable form for these years and published summaries of the data do not report full-time workers separately.

10. This income measure excludes capital gains.

11. See Levy and Murnane (1992) for a history of how earnings inequality became a prominent issue in labor economics.

12. In one refinement technology is now assumed to substitute for midskilled workers rather than the lowest-skilled workers (Autor, Levy, and Murnane 2003; Autor, Katz, and Kearny 2006). In a second refinement the steady growth of earnings inequality among observationally similar workers in the Current Population Survey was first described as measuring returns to unobserved dimensions of skill (Juhn, Murphy, and Pierce 1993). It is now identified with increasing year-to-year earnings volatility (Gottschalk and Moffitt 1994) or as an artifact of particular data sets (Lemieux 2006b).

13. Paulson's remarks, delivered at Columbia University, are available at http://www.treasury.gov/press/releases/hp41.htm.

14. Other authors have focused on historical narrative (e.g., Katz and Lipsky 1998; Osterman 1999).

15. Marshall (1947, book VI, chap. VII, para. 43) wrote: "It is the [general growth of wealth], almost alone, that enables some barristers to command very high fees; for a rich client whose reputation, or fortune, or both, are at stake will scarcely count any price too high to secure the services of the best man he can get." Such markets often arise in the provision of a complex high-stakes service that must be done right the first time—a legal defense, a delicate surgery, a financial merger, the performance of a professional athlete—where small differences in skills that cannot be taught can have big consequences. The pay of virtually all partners in Wall Street law firms falls into the top 1 percent of reported incomes on tax returns which began in 2005 at $310,000 (the figure excludes capital gains).

16. "Real Annual Income Growth by Groups, 1993–2006," available at http://elsa .berkeley.edu/~saez/TabFig2006prel.xls.

17. See Wright (2006), p. 152 for a similar graph and Sutch (this volume) for more analysis.

18. See U.S. Bureau of Labor Statistics, "Work Stoppages Involving 1,000 or More Workers, 1947–2009," available at http://stats.bls.gov/news.release/wkstp.t01.htm.

19. In 1971 Richard Nixon had abandoned fixed exchange rates as part of his program to deal with inflation, a recognition of the fact that continuing trade deficits were diminishing the country's exchange reserves.

20. Even at the time it was clear that some of this success was unsustainable. In the early 1970s both the auto workers' and steelworkers' unions had signed new contracts in which full cost-of-living adjustments were exchanged for promises of labor peace. At that time no one anticipated consumer prices doubling over the next 10 years. As a result, auto makers and big steel firms became an island in the economy with real wages far higher than even most other unionized occupations. Had exchange rates fallen far enough to bring overall trade flows into balance, auto and big steel would still have been overpriced on world markets.

21. This refers to the referee in a boxing ring (Goldstein and Graham 1972).

22. By 1982 the *real* interest on three-year government securities exceeded 6 percent—three times its normal postwar value.

23. For example, Michael Milken issued his first junk bonds in the late 1970s. The development of the first mortgage-backed bonds occurred at the same time (Lewis 1989).

24. Board of Governors of the Federal Reserve System, *Flow of Funds Accounts of the United States*, various issues.

25. Between 1980 and 1990 the Dow Jones Industrial Average rose from 875 to 2,785.

26. But see Acemoglu, Aghion, and Violante (2001).

27. Osterman (1999), chapter 2 makes a similar point.

REFERENCES

Acemoglu, Daron, Philippe Aghion, and Gianluca Violante (2001). "Deunionization, Technical Change and Inequality." *Carnegie-Rochester Conference Series on Public Policy* 55: 229–264.

Amberg, Stephen (1994). *The Union Inspiration in American Politics*. Philadelphia: Temple University Press.

Atkinson, Anthony B., and Thomas Piketty (2007). *Top Incomes over the Twentieth Century: A Contrast between Continental European and English-Speaking Countries*. Oxford: Oxford University Press.

Autor, David H., Lawrence F. Katz, and Melissa S. Kearny (2006). "The Polarization of the U.S. Labor Market." *American Economic Review* 96: 189–194.

Autor, David H., Lawrence F. Katz, and Melissa S. Kearny (2008). "Trends in U.S. Wage Inequality: Re-Assessing the Revisionists." *Review of Economics and Statistics* 90: 300–323.

Autor, David H., Frank Levy, and Richard J. Murnane (2003). "The Skill Content of Recent Technical Change: An Empirical Investigation." *Quarterly Journal of Economics* 118: 1279–1334.

Blair, Margaret (1989). "Theory and Evidence on the Causes of Merger Waves." Unpublished PhD diss., Yale University.

Blair, Margaret M., and Martha A. Shary (1993). "Industry-Level Pressures to Restructure." In *The Deal Decade*, edited by Margaret M. Blair. Washington, DC: The Brookings Institution, pp. 149–203.

Bound, John, and George Johnson (1992). "Changes in the Structure of Wages in the 1980s: An Evaluation of Alternative Explanations." *American Economic Review* 92: 371–392.

Brody, David (1980). *Workers in Industrial America*. Oxford: Oxford University Press.

Card, David, and John E. DiNardo (2002). "Skill-Biased Technical Change and Rising Wage Inequality: Some Problems and Puzzles." *Journal of Labor Economics* 20: 733–783.

Carter, Jimmy (1978). "Transcript of the President's Address on Inflation." *New York Times*, April 12. p. A16.

Chamberlain, Neil W., and James W. Kuhn (1986). *Collective Bargaining*, 3rd ed. New York: McGraw-Hill.

Cowan, Edward (1978). "Can Kahn Contain Wage-Price Spiral?" *New York Times*, November 12, p. F1.

Dew-Becker, Ian, and Robert J. Gordon (2005). "Where Did the Productivity Growth Go? Inflation Dynamics and the Distribution of Income." *Brookings Papers on Economic Activity*, no. 2: 67–150.

Dickens, William T., et al. (2007). "How Wages Change: Micro Evidence from the International Wage Flexibility Project." *Journal of Economic Perspectives* 21: 195–214.

DiNardo, John, Nicole Fortin, and Thomas Lemieux (1996). "Labor Market Institutions and the Distribution of Wages, 1973–1992: A Semiparametric Approach." *Econometrica* 64: 1001–1044.

Eckstein, Otto, and Thomas A. Wilson (1962). "The Determination of Money Wages in American History." *Quarterly Journal of Economics* 76: 379–414.

Eggertsson, Gauti B. (2006). "Was the New Deal Contractionary?" Federal Reserve Bank of New York Staff Report No. 264, October.

Erickson, Christopher L. (1996). "A Re-Interpretation of Pattern Bargaining." *Industrial and Labor Relations Review* 49: 615–634.

Feenberg, Daniel, and James Poterba (1993). "Income Inequality and the Incomes of High-Income Taxpayers: Evidence from Tax Returns." *Tax Policy and the Economy* 7: 145–173.

Flynn, Joan (2000). "A Quiet Revolution at the Labor Board: The Transformation of the NLRB, 1935–2000." *Ohio State Law Journal* 61: 1–53.

Freeman, Richard B. (1998). "Spurts in Union Growth: Defining Moments and Social Processes." In *The Defining Moment: The Great Depression and the American Economy in the Twentieth Century*, edited by Michael D. Bordo, Claudia Goldin, and Eugene N. White. Chicago: University of Chicago Press, pp. 265–295.

Frydman, Carola, and Raven E. Saks (2010). "Executive Compensation: A New View from a Long-Term Perspective, 1936–2005." *Review of Financial Studies* 23: 2099–2138.

Galanter, Marc, and Thomas Palay (1991). *Tournament of Lawyers: The Transformation of the Big Law Firm*. Chicago: University of Chicago Press.

Goldin, Claudia, and Lawrence F. Katz (2008). *The Race between Education and Technology*. Cambridge, MA: Harvard University Press.

Goldin, Claudia, and Robert A. Margo (1992). "The Great Compression: The Wage Structure in the United States at Mid-Century." *Quarterly Journal of Economics* 107: 1–34.

Goldstein, Ruby, and Frank Graham (1972). *Third Man in the Ring: Ruby Goldstein*. New York: Funk and Wagnalls.

Gordon, Roger H., and Joel Slemrod (2000). "Are 'Real' Responses to Taxes Simply Income Shifting between Corporate and Personal Tax Bases?" In *Does Atlas Shrug? The Economic Consequences of Taxing the Rich*, edited by Joel Slemrod. Cambridge, MA: Harvard University Press, pp. 240–280.

Gottschalk, Peter, and Robert Mofffit (1994). "The Growth of Earnings Instability in the U.S. Labor Market." *Brookings Papers on Economic Activity*, no. 2: 217–272.

Gross, James A. (1974). *The Making of the National Labor Relations Board*. Albany: State University of New York Press.

Hall, Brian J., and Jeffrey B. Liebman (1998). "Are CEO's Really Paid like Bureaucrats?" *Quarterly Journal of Economics* 113: 653–691.

Hirsch, Barry T., and David. A. Macpherson (2004). *Union Membership and Earnings Data Book: Compilations from the Current Population Survey, 2004 Edition*. Washington, DC: Bureau of National Affairs.

Holmstrom, Bengt, and Steven N. Kaplan (2001). "Corporate Governance and Merger Activity in the United States: Making Sense of the 1980s and 1990s." *Journal of Economic Perspectives* 15: 121–144.

Jensen, Michael C. (1997). "Eclipse of the Public Corporation" (revised version). Available at http://papers.ssrn.com/abstract=146149 (paper originally published in the *Harvard Business Review*, September–October 1989).

Juhn, Chinhui, Kevin M. Murphy, and Brooks Pierce (1993). "Wage Inequality and the Rise in Returns to Skill." *Journal of Political Economy* 101: 410–442.

Kaplan, Stephen N., and Joshua Rauh (2010). "Wall Street and Main Street: What Contributes to the Rise in Highest Incomes?" *Review of Financial Studies* 23, no. 3: 1004–1050.

Katz, Harry C., and David B. Lipsky (1998). "The Collective Bargaining System in the United States: The Legacy and the Lessons." In *Industrial Relations at the Dawn of a New Millennium*, edited by M. Neufeld and J. McKelvey. Ithaca: New York State School of Industrial and Labor Relations. pp. 145–162.

Katz, Lawrence F., and Kevin M. Murphy (1992). "Changes in Relative Wages, 1963–1987: Supply and Demand Factors." *Quarterly Journal of Economics* 107: 35–78.

Katznelson, Ira (2005). *When Affirmative Action Was White: An Untold Story of Racial Inequality in Twentieth-Century America*. New York: Norton.

Kochan, Thomas A. (1980). *Collective Bargaining and Industrial Relations: From Theory to Policy and Practice.* Homewood, IL: Irwin.

Kochan, Thomas A., Harry C. Katz, and Robert B. McKersie (1994). *The Transformation of American Industrial Relations.* Ithaca, NY: ILR Press.

Koistinen, Paul A. C. (2004). *Arsenal of World War II: The Political Economy of American Warfare, 1940–1945.* Lawrence: University Press of Kansas.

Krugman, Paul (2006). "Whining over Discontent." *New York Times,* September 8. p. A29.

Lee, David S. (1999). "Wage Inequality in the United States during the 1980s: Rising Dispersion or Falling Minimum Wage?" *Quarterly Journal of Economics* 114: 977–1023.

Lemieux, Thomas (2006a). "Postsecondary Education and Increasing Wage Inequality." *American Economic Review, Papers and Proceedings* 96: 195–199.

Lemieux, Thomas (2006b). "Increasing Residual Wage Inequality: Composition Effects, Noisy Data, or Rising Demand for Skill?" *American Economic Review* 96: 461–498.

Levy, Frank (1988). "Incomes, Families and Living Standards." In *American Living Standards: Challenges and Threats,* edited by Robert E. Litan, Robert Z. Lawrence, and Charles Schultze. Washington, DC: The Brookings Institution, chapter 4.

Levy, Frank (1989). "Recent Trends in U.S. Earnings and Family Incomes." In *National Bureau of Economic Research Macroeconomics Annual, 1989.* Cambridge, MA: MIT Press.

Levy, Frank, and Richard J. Murnane (1992). "U.S. Earnings Levels and Earnings Inequality: A Review of Recent Trends and Proposed Explanations." *Journal of Economic Literature* 30: 1333–1381.

Levy, Frank, and Peter Temin (2007). "Inequality and Institutions in 20th Century America." National Bureau of Economic Research Working Paper No. 13106. Cambridge, MA: National Bureau of Economic Research.

Levy, Frank, and Peter Temin (2009). "Institutions and Wages in Post–World War II America." In *Labor in the Era of Globalization,* edited by Clair Brown, Barry Eichengreen, and Michael Reich. Cambridge: Cambridge University Press, chapter 1.

Lewis, Michael (1989). *Liar's Poker.* New York: Norton.

Lichtenstein, Nelson (1987). "Reutherism on the Shop Floor: Union Strategy and Shop-Floor Conflict in the USA 1946–1970." In *The Automobile Industry and Its Workers: Between Fordism and Flexibility,* edited by Steven Tolliday and Jonathan Zeitlin. New York: St. Martin's Press, pp. 121–143.

Lichtenstein, Nelson (1995). *Walter Reuther: The Most Dangerous Man in Detroit.* Urbana: University of Illinois Press.

Lichtenstein, Nelson (2002). *State of the Union.* Princeton, NJ: Princeton University Press.

Lindert, Peter H. (2004). *Growing Public: Social Spending and Economic Growth since the Eighteenth Century.* New York: Cambridge University Press.

Long, Larry, and Diana DeAre (1998). "U.S. Population Redistribution: A Perspective on the Nonmetropolitan Turnaround." *Population and Development Review* 14: 433–450.

Margo, Robert A. (1991). "The Microeconomics of Depression Unemployment." *Journal of Economic History* 51: 333–341.

Marshall, Alfred (1947). *Principles of Economics,* 8th ed. New York: Macmillan.

Mills, D. Quinn (1979). "Flawed Victory in Labor Law Reform." *Harvard Business Review* 57: 92–102.

Moriguchi, Chiaki, and Emmanuel Saez (2008). "The Evolution of Income Concentration in Japan." *Review of Economics and Statistics* 90: 713–734.

Nickell, Stephen (1997). "Unemployment and Labor Market Rigidities: Europe versus North America." *Journal of Economic Perspectives* 11: 55–74.

Osterman, Paul (1999). *Securing Prosperity: The American Labor Market: How It Has Changed and What to Do about It*. Princeton, NJ: Princeton University Press.

Pearlstein, Steven (2006a). "New Economy Hurting People in the Middle Most." *Washington Post*, March 8, p. D01.

Pearlstein, Steven (2006b). "Solving Inequality Problem Won't Take Class Warfare." *Washington Post*, March 15, p. D01.

Philippon, Thomas (2008). "Why Has the Financial Sector Grown So Much? The Role of Corporate Finance." Working Paper, New York University, Stern School of Business, January.

Piketty, Thomas, and Emmanuel Saez (2003). "Income Inequality in the United States." *Quarterly Journal of Economics* 118: 1–39.

Reynolds, Alan (2006). "The Top 1% . . . of What?" *Wall Street Journal*, December 14, p. A20.

Roomkin, Myron (1981). "A Quantitative Study of Unfair Labor Practice Cases." *Industrial and Labor Relations Review* 34: 245–256.

Rosen, Elliot A. (2005). *Roosevelt, the Great Depression and the Economics of Recovery*. Charlottésville: University of Virginia Press.

Rosen, Sherwin (1981). "The Economics of Superstars." *American Economic Review* 71: 845–858.

Saez, Emmanuel (2004). "Reported Incomes and Marginal Tax Rates, 1960–2000: Evidence and Policy Implications." *Tax Policy and the Economy* 18: 117–173.

Tritch, Teresa (2006). "Editorial Observer: A Letter to Treasury Secretary Henry M. Paulson Jr." *New York Times*, August 5, p. A12.

U.S. Bureau of the Census (1975). *Historical Statistics of the United States, Colonial Times to 1970*. Washington, DC: Government Printing Office.

Weinstein, Marc, and Thomas Kochan (1995). "The Limits of Diffusion: Recent Developments in Industrial Relations and Human Resource Practices in the United States." In *Employment Relations in a Changing World Economy*, edited by Richard Locke, Thomas Kochan, and Michael Piore. Cambridge, MA: MIT Press, pp. 1–31.

Williamson, John (1990). "What Washington Means by Policy Reform." In *Latin American Adjustment: How Much Has Happened?* edited by John Williamson. Washington, DC: Institute for International Economics. pp. 5–37.

Wright, Gavin (2006). "Productivity Growth and the American Labor Market: The 1990s in Historical Perspective." In *The Global Economy in the 1990s: A Long-Run Perspective*, edited by Paul W. Rhode and Gianni Toniolo. Cambridge: Cambridge University Press, pp. 139–160.

CHAPTER 15

The Unexpected Long-Run Impact of the Minimum Wage: An Educational Cascade

RICHARD SUTCH

> Except perhaps for the Social Security Act, [the Fair Labor Standards
> Act] is the most far-reaching, the most far-sighted program for the
> benefit of workers ever adopted here or in any other country.
>
> FRANKLIN D. ROOSEVELT, "Fireside Chat," June 24, 1938[1]

THE MINIMUM WAGE is a contentious and emotional issue in the United States, and it has been for almost a century.[2] A shorthand version of the issue at stake was famously stated by Milton Friedman in *Playboy* magazine: "A minimum-wage law is, in reality, a law that makes it illegal for an employer to hire a person with limited skills" (Norman 1973, reprinted in Friedman 1983, p. 16).[3] Proponents, of course, argue that the purpose of a minimum wage is to ensure that every (covered) worker earns an income that can purchase at least the bare necessities of good health and a "living decent according to the standard of the time," a living, in the words of Franklin Roosevelt, "which gives man not only enough to live by, but something to live for."[4] Framed in this way, the minimum wage has been a cause for political battle between Democrats (pro) and Republicans (con) whenever it has been raised at the federal, state, or local level.[5] That means it has been almost continuously the object of heated debate. This political passion is a bit curious because most experts for many years have regarded the minimum wage as a largely irrelevant institutional hangover from the New Deal.[6]

The legislated minimum has frequently been so low relative to prevailing wages that few workers or occupations are affected. The U.S. Bureau of Labor Statistics (BLS) estimated the fraction of employed wage and salary workers with earnings at or below the federal minimum wage in 2005 at only 2.5 percent (U.S. BLS 2006, table 1; also see Haugen and Mellor 1990).[7] In 1938 the national minimum wage was set at 25 cents

Year	Month	Day	1938 Fair Labor Standards Act Dollars per Hour	1961 Amendments Dollars per Hour	1966 and Subsequent Amendments		1989 and 1996 Amendments 90-Day Youth Subminimum Dollars per Hour
					Nonfarm Workers Dollars per Hour	Farm Workers Dollars per Hour	
1938	Oct.	24	0.25	—	—	—	—
1939	Oct.	24	0.30	—	—	—	—
1945	Oct.	24	0.40	—	—	—	—
1950	Jan.	25	0.75	—	—	—	—
1956	Mar.	1	1.00	—	—	—	—
1961	Sept.	3	1.15	1.00	—	—	—
1963	Sept.	3	1.25	1.00	—	—	—
1964	Sept.	3	1.25	1.15	—	—	—
1965	Sept.	3	1.25	1.25	—	—	—
1967	Feb.	1	1.40	1.40	1.00	1.00	—
1968	Feb.	1	1.60	1.60	1.15	1.15	—
1969	Feb.	1	1.60	1.60	1.30	1.30	—
1970	Feb.	1	1.60	1.60	1.45	1.30	—
1971	Feb.	1	1.60	1.60	1.60	1.30	—
1974	May.	1	2.00	2.00	1.90	1.60	—
1975	Jan.	1	2.10	2.10	2.00	1.80	—
1976	Jan.	1	2.30	2.30	2.20	2.00	—
1977	Jan.	1	2.30	2.30	2.30	2.20	—
1978	Jan.	1	2.65	2.65	2.65	2.65	—
1979	Jan.	1	2.90	2.90	2.90	2.90	—
1980	Jan.	1	3.10	3.10	3.10	3.10	—
1981	Jan.	1	3.35	3.35	3.35	3.35	—
1990	Apr.	1	3.80	3.80	3.80	3.80	3.35
1991	Apr.	1	4.25	4.25	4.25	4.25	3.61
1993	Apr.	1	4.25	4.25	4.25	4.25	—
1996	Oct.	1	4.75	4.75	4.75	4.75	4.25
1997	Sept.	1	5.15	5.15	5.15	5.15	4.25
2007	July	24	5.85	5.85	5.85	5.85	4.25
2008	July	24	6.55	6.55	6.55	6.55	4.25
2009	July	24	7.25	7.25	7.25	7.25	4.25

Notes: This table revises and updates the table presented in *Historical Statistics of the United States* (Carter et al. 2006, table Ba4422-4425). The original table was contributed by Susan B. Carter.

TABLE 15.1 *(continued)*

Documentation: The federal minimum wage was established with the passage of the Fair Labor Standards Act (FLSA) of 1938. The FLSA was the capstone of the New Deal legislation designed to end the Great Depression of the 1930s. The 1938 act applied to workers engaged in interstate commerce or in the production of goods for interstate commerce.

Series 1.1. Indicates the new minimum level at each successive change. All increases in the minimum wage rate beginning in 1978 covered all nonexempt workers.

Series 1.2. The 1961 amendments to the FLSA extended coverage to employees in large retail and service enterprises as well as to local transit, construction, and gasoline service station employees. The level of the minimum for these workers is shown in this series. After January 30, 1968, the rate for these employees matched that for all covered, nonexempt workers under the 1938 act. In 1990, the new law raised the annual dollar volume test for enterprise coverage. A grandfather clause was established to protect employees who no longer met the tests for individual coverage, whose employers were covered as of March 31, 1990, but who would have become exempt from coverage with the new volume test.

Series 1.3–1.4. The 1966 amendments to the FLSA extended coverage to state and local government employees of hospitals, nursing homes, and schools, and to laundries, dry cleaners, and large hotels, motels, restaurants, and farms. Subsequent amendments extended coverage to the remaining federal, state, and local government employees who were not protected in 1966, to certain workers in retail and service trades previously exempted, and to certain domestic workers in private household employment. After December 31, 1976, the minimum for nonfarm workers covered by the 1966 amendments matched that for all covered, nonexempt workers under the 1938 act. The minimum for farm workers matched that for all covered, nonexempt workers after December 31, 1977.

Series 1.5. Beginning April 1, 1990, a youth subminimum wage ("training wage") was established by the 1989 amendments at 85 percent of the statutory minimum wage (but not less than $3.35 per hour) that applied to employees under 20 years of age during their first 90 continuous days of employment. This provision expired after March 31, 1993. Under the 1996 amendments a youth subminimum wage of $4.25 per hour was established beginning October 1996 that applied to employees under 20 years of age during their first 90 consecutive calendar days of employment. The terms of the two youth subminimum wage plans were confirmed by newspaper accounts at the time. See David E. Rosenbaum, "Bush and Congress Reach Accord Raising Minimum Wage to $4.25," *New York Times*, November 1, 1989, and Eric Schmitt, "Bill to Increase Minimum Pay Clears Hurdle in a New Deal," *New York Times*, August 1, 1996.

Sources: U.S. Department of Labor, Wages and Hours Division (n.d.), "History of Federal Minimum Wage Rates Under the Fair Labor Standards Act, 1938–2009," http://www.dol.gov/whd/minwage/chart.htm (accessed June 8, 2010); U.S. Department of Labor, Wages and Hours Division (n.d.), "History of Changes to the Minimum Wage Law,". http://www.dol.gov/whd/minwage/coverage.htm (accessed June 8, 2010).

per hour, which was raised to 30 cents the following year and, according to Gavin Wright, had a major impact in the South particularly for blacks working in tobacco (1986, pp. 219–220), but soon thereafter the minimum wage was "repealed by inflation," as George Stigler remarked in 1946 (p. 358). From time to time, Congress has increased the nominal minimum wage and expanded the coverage of the law. In 1950 it was increased from 40 to 75 cents per hour. In July 2008 it became $6.55 with a further increase in July 2009 to $7.25 (see Table 15.1 for a tabulation of all of the changes). These periodic decisions by Congress succeeded in increasing the real value of the wage floor until 1968, but thereafter the legislated increases have failed to catch up or keep up with inflation (see Figure 15.1, which plots the federal minimum wage measured in terms of the prices of 2007).

FIGURE 15.1   *Federal Minimum Wage in Real Dollars per Hour*

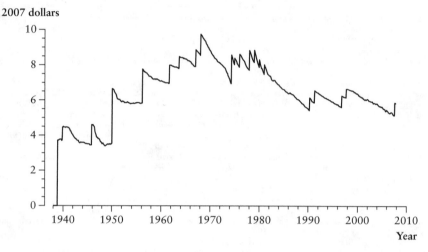

Sources: Table 15.1 and U.S. Bureau of Labor Statistics, Consumer Price Index (online database), http://www.bls.gov/cpi/ (accessed November 15, 2007).

In early studies, econometricians who attempted to measure the impact of the minimum wage on employment generally reported only a small effect, and that only for teenagers. A careful review by Charles Brown, Curtis Gilroy, and Andrew Kohen considered 18 pre-1982 studies, each of which employed a time-series analysis of published data derived from the Current Population Surveys (CPS). All 18 reported a negative impact on teenage employment. The point estimates suggested that a 10 percent minimum wage increase would reduce teenage employment by between 0.5 and 3.0 percent (Brown, Gilroy, and Kohen 1982, p. 505; also see the update in Brown 1999). However, Brown and his coauthors regard the lower part of the range as most plausible because they regard the tests that produced the lower numbers to be the better specified. Studies conducted in the 1980s and early 1990s reduced the estimate of the negative impact on teenage employment induced by a 10 percent increase in the minimum wage to less than 1 percent (Solon 1985; Adams 1989; Wellington 1991; Card and Krueger 1995, pp. 180–182, 194–204). Because the teenage employment rate averages about 45 percent, a reduction of 1 percent corresponds to a reduction of 0.45 percentage points in the employment rate, a small effect. Taken together these studies do not allow us to reject the proposition that the true effect is zero. There seems to be no discernible evidence of an impact on employment overall.[8]

Quite apart from the issue of whether the minimum wage leads to job loss, I suggest that a neglected, but significant, consequence of the minimum wage requirement is its stimulation of capital deepening. This took two forms. First, the engineered shortage of low-skill, low-paying jobs induced teenagers to invest in additional human capital—primarily by extending their schooling—in an attempt to raise their productivity to the level required for employment. Second, employers faced with an inability to legally hire low-wage workers rearranged their production processes to innovate new technology and substitute capital for low-skilled labor. This essay will focus on the first phenomenon, the impact on educational attainment.

I begin from the premise that the debate over the employment effects of the minimum wage has been misfocused. A labor market with a binding minimum wage is out of equilibrium. In that situation the alternative to employment for many teenagers is to stay in school. Thus the long-run impact of the minimum wage might well be to increase the stock of human capital: a clearly beneficial, if unexpected, consequence of the minimum wage policy. Yet the impact of the minimum wage on employment is in any case agreed to be rather slight, so one might suggest that any supposed impact on increasing the level of educational attainment is likely to be slight as well. I suggest, however, that there are two reasons to believe that the effect might be strong. First, the minimum wage does have a significant bite for teenagers. I also propose an additional point. There is a ratchet mechanism through which the initial response to a change in the minimum wage can trigger an "educational cascade," producing a sustained increase in educational attainment.

To visualize how a cascade might operate, consider a cohort of 15-year-old high school students, most of whom would be enrolled in the tenth grade. Each must make a decision about whether to continue to the eleventh grade. The alternative to school is to join the labor force or to voluntarily join the nonemployed.[9] One economic factor that would influence this decision would be the local unemployment rate of teenagers. Because 15-year-olds are not likely to look these statistics up at the library or even read about them in the newspaper, we suppose they form an impression of employment possibilities by observation of the experiences of those like themselves in the local job market. Thus the relevant unemployed rates would be those for individuals of the same race, gender, and locality—those of the individual's likely "role-model" group. Thus a black 15-year-old male would be likely to consider the job-market experiences of the 16- to 19-year-old black men who were not in school in his locality.

There would be another peer effect on the school-versus-labor-force decision coming directly from the student's classmates. Dropping out would be a significant and probably difficult decision. For most it will be irreversible (Card and Lemieux 2000, pp. 8–9 and table 1). In such a situation it is natural that the student would consult and often mimic his peers. If more of the high school students our 15-year-old knows stay in school and go on to the next grade, he will be encouraged to continue as well.

Role-model and peer effects are not the only influences on the school attendance decision. I presume that the opportunity cost of going to school will influence the decision. The opportunity cost will be largely driven by the wage the student can expect if he takes a job. What a binding minimum wage will do is to dramatically lower the opportunity cost of schooling for those whose skills do not yet warrant receiving the minimum wage. In a job market with a high minimum wage, the earning prospects of a student with subminimum skills are nil.[10] Thus an increase in the minimum wage should reduce the dropout rate for this cohort by lowering the opportunity cost of staying in school.

As I envision this mechanism moving forward in time, a feedback would then produce a ratchet effect operating on the next cohort. If the minimum wage increase causes a greater fraction of the tenth-grade class to stay in school, then the next year's tenth graders will see a greater number of their peers staying in school than would have been the case without the minimum wage increase. Thus even without further minimum wage increases the dropout rate will remain lower than it would have been otherwise. In principle this ratchet effect can influence educational trends for several, perhaps many, years. However, if inflation and productivity increases begin to erode the bite the minimum wage takes out of the lower tail of the wage distribution, the forces supporting the reduction in dropout rates would become attenuated. Another increase in the minimum wage would be necessary to revive the effect.

As educational attainment rises over time, it will generate a scarcity of low-skilled laborers whose employment would be warranted at the minimum wage relative to the skill distributions that characterized the past. One consequence is that this relative shortage would induce employers to substitute capital for low-skilled workers. Think about the computer-assisted order kiosk in a fast-food restaurant. The take-out clerk can punch in the customer's order, which immediately flashes on a computer screen in the kitchen and automatically computes the bill and the amount of change to return and even prompts the clerk to ask if the customer would like the order "super-sized" or to suggest a side of fries. A consequence of the capital-labor substitution is to raise the productivity of workers with limited skills. Thus increasing the minimum wage should work to increase the productivity of those at the bottom of the skill distribution.[11]

If not counteracted, a shortage of low-skilled workers combined with a rising productivity of low-skilled workers operating with more sophisticated capital might drive up the market-clearing wage for low-skilled workers and thus erode the bite of the minimum wage and slow down or even halt the educational cascade. However, in a global economy with open borders the shortage of low-skilled domestically educated workers would stimulate the immigration of such workers from abroad, thus widening the wage distribution and increasing the returns to additional education of the native born. Immigration (documented or not) then will serve to prevent a stifling of the long-run educational impact of a minimum wage increase. Another possibility is that the shortage of low-skilled workers will induce producers to import goods and services with low skill content from suppliers abroad, thus producing much the same beneficial impact on school attendance as immigration.

Too much of the theoretical literature on the minimum wage has assumed that low-skilled workers are homogeneous. In the scenario I have just sketched, I assume, as seems realistic, that high school students are heterogeneous in the distribution of their job-relevant skills (I illustrate the point in Figure 15.2). The bell curve represents the hypothesized distribution of skills (in real terms) of students still enrolled in high school in period t facing an increase in the minimum wage from MW_t to MW_{t+1}. For ease of reference, I will place high school students into three groups. Some, whom I will call "the relative skillful," have skills that—in a suitable job—would contribute sufficient product at the margin to warrant more than the proposed minimum wage. At the other extreme are the "subminimal" students who have skills (or a maturity) so low that they could not be productively employed at any job paying the current minimum wage. At an intermediate position, the "marginal group" would be able to secure productive employment at the current minimum but unable to do so at the higher minimum.

The enrollment decision of the skillful and subminimal students would be unaffected by the proposed change in the minimum wage. It would be marginal students who would be shut out of the labor market by an increase in the minimum wage and thus see the opportunity cost of

FIGURE 15.2 *Hypothetical Skill Distribution of High School Students*

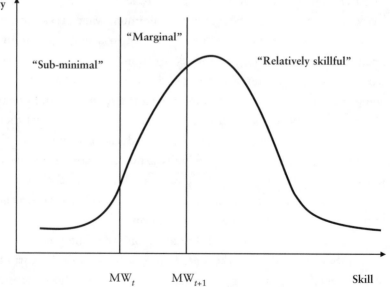

their schooling fall. Note that in periods where the nominal minimum wage is constant, the marginal group collapses to a razor-thin slice.

This distribution of job-relevant skills is not the same as the distribution of academically relevant abilities. An individual student's position in the distribution depicted in Figure 15.2 would not be static. It will shift rightward as time goes on. Additional schooling will enhance job-related skills and move the individual to the right. How effective additional schooling will be in moving the student to higher skill levels will depend, presumably, upon the student's academic abilities. The higher those attributes, the higher the perceived return to continued enrollment. That is why not every relatively skillful student will take a job. Some will, of course, but their lower academic promise may be the cause.[12]

I can also illustrate the influence of the introduction of new technologies and higher capital-labor ratios on the three groups. Labor productivity would be raised by those phenomena, shifting the entire distribution to the right (relative to the MWt and $MWt+1$ lines) and carrying every student with it. That would sweep some marginal students into the relatively skillful group where those with low academic potential will be tempted to drop out. To prevent the consequent decline in enrollments, the minimum wage would have to be adjusted upward to at least keep up with productivity advances.

The educational cascade I am describing is not incompatible with the proposition that a minimum wage increase would have no negative employment consequences. If everyone employed before the increase retained his or her job and if every vacancy created by voluntary attrition were filled, it would still remain the case that a law that makes it illegal for an employer to hire a person with subminimal skills would shut the student in the marginal group just described out of the market and thus lower the opportunity cost of remaining in school.

This chapter will explore the connections linking the minimum wage and educational attainment using a variety of data sources. It will set aside for another project the impact of the minimum wage on inducing investments in physical capital, spurring technological innovation, or stimulating an increase in low-skilled immigration. Compared to the quite extensive literature on the employment effects of the minimum wage, there has been very little empirical work on the impact of the minimum wage on schooling.[13]

To explore the enrollment consequences of an increase in the minimum wage I turn to two different sources of data. For the period from 1968 to the present I use the micro-level data drawn from the public-use files of the October Survey of Current Population (Unicon Research 2007). Although the school enrollment questions associated with the October surveys date back to 1947, only the published summaries are available for the years before 1968. For the period before 1972 I use the micro-level data in the Integrated Public Use Microdata Series (IPUMS) drawn from the enumerators' manuscripts of 1980, 1970, and 1960 censuses of the U.S. population (Ruggles et al. 2008). The two data sources are quite different. They pose unique complications and offer unique opportunities. I will treat them separately, beginning with the more recent. This partition by data source is unfortunate because coincidentally the general trend of the national real minimum wage has been downward since 1968, while it was generally rising between 1950 and 1968 (see Figure 15.1). In what follows I make my best effort to adjust for the changes in my evidentiary bases.

FIGURE 15.3   *Number of States with a Minimum Wage Law*

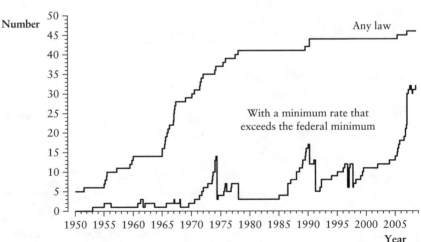

Source: Data appendix available at http://economics.ucr.edu/repec/ucr/wpaper/Appendix%20A%20State%20Laws.pdf.

It should also be noted that throughout the entire period some states enacted minimum wage laws that exceeded the federal minimum established by the Fair Labor Standards Act and its amendments (see Figure 15.3). When the state law established a minimum wage that exceeded the federal minimum, the state law takes precedence. We will exploit the information inherent in the interstate variance in the legal minimum in what follows.

POST-1971 TESTS FOR IMPACT OF CHANGES IN THE FEDERAL AND STATE MINIMUM WAGE LAWS

For parsimony's sake, I begin with a look at changes in the federal minimum wage rate before turning to the variation in state laws. Before the latest (2007–2009) round of minimum wage increases, there are four episodes that we can examine with the October CPS data. For ease of identification, I label the rounds of increases with the name of the president who signed the corresponding minimum wage bill:[14]

Nixon Round—1974–1976 (Enacted: April 1974)

May 1, 1974	from $1.60	to $2.00
January 1, 1975		to $2.10
January 1, 1976		to $2.30

Carter Four Step—1978–1981 (Enacted: November 1977)

January 1, 1978	from $2.30	to $2.65
January 1, 1979		to $2.90
January 1, 1980		to $3.10
January 1, 1981		to $3.35

Bush I Round—1990–1991 (Enacted: November 1989)

April 1, 1990	from $3.35	to $3.80
October 1, 1991		to $4.25

Clinton Round—1996–1997 (Enacted: August 1996)

October 1, 1996	from $4.25	to $4.75
September 1, 1997		to $5.15

Bush II Round—2007–2009 (Enacted: May 2007)

July 24, 2007	from $5.15	to $5.85
July 24, 2008		to $6.55
July 24, 2009		to $7.25

It is important to examine these federal changes by rounds because the second, third, and fourth steps can be anticipated as of the date the first step is enacted. Thus forewarned, the impact of the subsequent steps may influence student decisions before they actually take effect.

I use the October surveys from the CPS because they contain detailed questions about education; in particular there is the response recorded to a question about the school grade currently attended.[15] This information was recorded for everyone age 3 and older. The CPS surveys recognized four grades of "high school" defined as ninth through twelfth grade. By merging the October results for all the available years (1968–2006) I can follow a birth cohort from year to year. A student who was 15 years old in October 1968 would be 16 in 1969, 17 in 1970, and so on. A birth cohort series assembled in this manner describes a "statistical" rather than a true cohort because we have a sample of 15-year-olds in 1968 and a separate sample of 16-year-olds in 1969 that would include many individuals not surveyed in the previous year.[16] But if the samples are representative, then the time series identified as the birth cohort of 1953 can be said to represent the experience of those who were born between October 15, 1952 and October 14, 1953 (1953 + 15 = 1968) and who survived into the following year.

For each cohort I cumulate the average number of years of high school enrollment experienced between ages 13 and 20. A time series of this statistic for men is displayed as the top line in the top panel of Figure 15.4. The shaded bars indicate the cohorts that experienced a change in the minimum wage while of high school age. In an appendix I give an example based on the Nixon round of minimum wage increases to illustrate how the affected cohorts were determined. In that episode the cohort born in 1959 experienced all three minimum wage increases of the Nixon round before they reached 17. That cohort was 17 years old in 1976 and is indicated that way in the figure. That cohort also reported

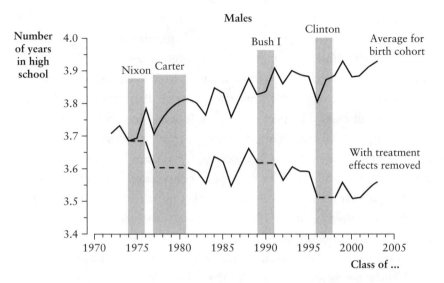

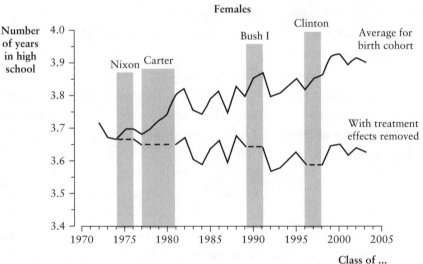

Source: Author's calculations based on the October Current Population Surveys (Unicon Research 2007). Each birth cohort is identified with the nominal year of graduation from high school.

more years of high school enrollment (3.78 years) than the 1957 and 1958 birth cohorts (3.68 and 3.69 years, respectively).

The three other rounds of minimum wage increases appear to have produced a similar ratcheting up in school attendance. All four episodes coincide with a noticeable increase in the average amount of high school experienced.[17] Moreover, much of the gain from each episode persisted. According to my argument, this effect can be attributed to the educational cascade caused by peer emulation. Indeed, the entire upward trend in male high school attainment during the period since 1972 can plausibly be attributed to minimum wage increases.[18] We can illustrate this by removing the gains observed for the treated cohorts and then splice together the changes that remain. This is illustrated diagrammatically by constructing the lower time trend in the upper panel of the figure. Remarkably, that line shows a downward trend.

As the lower panel of Figure 15.4 illustrates, the pattern for women is much the same as that for men. Women also reported increases in attendance at all four rounds. The magnitude of the increase for the Nixon round is less dramatic compared with that for men, but the magnitudes are roughly the same for the following three rounds.[19] An exercise that deletes the periods of minimum wage exposure and splices the remaining years together for women is also presented in the figure. This demonstrates that the upward drift in high school exposure for women since the mid-1970s can be eliminated by removing the ratcheting influence of the cohorts treated by the minimum wage.

TESTING FOR THE IMPACT OF STATE MINIMUM WAGE INCREASES, 1968–2003

One objection to the foregoing analysis is that a number of the states had set minimum wages higher than the federal rate during this period. In those states the relevant rate is the state minimum, not the federal. Moreover, the changes in these state minimums often took place at different dates than the federal changes. I will deal with this concern in two ways. First, I compute the time series on the number of years of high school experienced by each cohort including only states in which the federal law dominated. I compare that series with that for all states which I displayed in Figure 15.4. This exercise is performed separately for each of the four post-1969 rounds because the states included in the first series change as both federal and state laws are revised. The second test examines the schooling enrollments for a selection of states that set minimums at a higher level than the federal government and which changed their minimums on dates that differed from the federal changes. Among this set of state demonstrations it is possible to compare the state change(s) under examination with the experience of states that had no changes in either federal or state law.

The first approach calculates the number of years of high school enrollment experienced by each cohort only for states that *did not* exceed the federal standard. An unpublished data appendix available from the author and online indicates the states that were included in each of the four tests.[20] Figure 15.5 presents the results for men. In two of the cases examined, the Nixon round and the Bush I round, the results are clearly stronger than in the original. In the Carter round the result is somewhat weaker than measured without excluding any states but is still quite substantial. During the Clinton round the expansion of high school experience is measured at approximately the same magnitude.

As illustrated in Figure 15.3, there have been five episodes since 1950 when a significant number of states raised the minimum wage above the federal level. These five episodes preceded five rounds of increases legislated by Congress beginning with the Nixon round of 1974–1976. It would seem at first that this implies that there should be many cases that could be examined individually. However, due to limitations of the CPS data a number of the potential cases cannot be examined. The last cohort we can observe fully at the time of writing was born in 1986 and was 20 in 2006, the last year for which the CPS data are presently available. That cutoff date, a year before the Bush II round, makes the examination of that episode premature. We are constrained when considering the first episode of state increases as well. For the years 1968–1973 the variable indicating the state of residence is aggregated in the public-use data source into regional groupings for most states. Of the 12 states that raised their minimum above the federal level prior to the Nixon round, only four (Connecticut, New York, New Jersey, and Illinois) can be individually

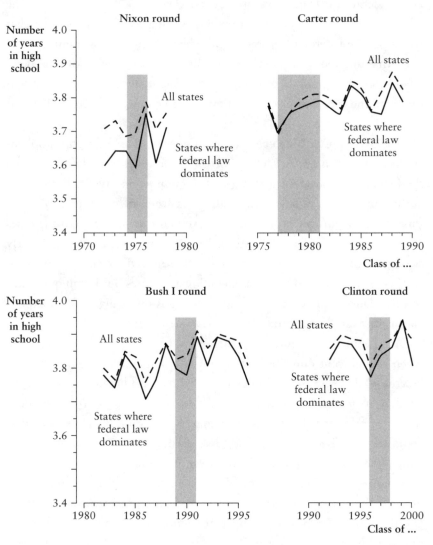

FIGURE 15.5 *Average Number of Years of High School Enrollment, Men: Results Excluding States with Minimum Standards Exceeding the Federal Minimum Wage*

Source: Author's calculations based on the October Current Population Surveys (Unicon Research 2007). Each birth cohort is identified with the nominal year of graduation from high school.

examined. Only one additional state, California, is individually identified during the years prior to the Carter Four Step round of increases.

An additional limitation is produced by the annual nature of the CPS surveys, conducted in October of each year. Some states raised their rates less than a year before the subsequent change in the federal minimum. Illinois, for example, raised its rate in January 1974 only a few months before the federal increase in May of that year. Thus in our annual data source, Illinois's change would appear coincident with the federal change. That leaves only three states for our pre-Nixon test: New York, which changed its law in July 1970; Connecticut, October 1971;[21] and New Jersey, October 1972.

The left-hand panel of Figure 15.6 graphically displays the minimum wage history of these three states for the 1970s. The lower line in each case is the federal minimum; the upper line displays the state's minimum wage when it exceeds the federal rate. The shading indicates the periods when the state minimum exceeded the federal. Note that the vertical scale is logarithmic and measures the wage rates in nominal dollars. The right-hand panel of Figure 15.6 presents the results for these three states taken together and compares them with the results for a selection of states where federal law dominates.[22] As anticipated, the three-state aggregate displays a prominent spike in high school attendance before the Nixon round. And that spike was larger than the reaction to the Nixon round in those states. This makes sense, of course, because the impact of the May 1974 federal increase was muted in those states.[23]

Four states (New York, New Jersey, California, and Hawai'i) raised their rates above the federal level prior to the Carter round initiated in 1978. None of the four can be analyzed separately.[24] The best episode of the four for testing the impact of state increases is the period of the late 1980s. Eleven states raised their rates above the federal level. However, the last of the 11, Iowa, timed the effective date of its increase only four months before the federal change. Three others (Wisconsin, North Dakota, and Oregon) raised rates less than a year before the first increase of the Bush I round. The remaining seven can be divided into three distinct groups. Maine, Vermont, and Rhode Island increased their standards between October 1984 and October 1986; Hawai'i and California

FIGURE 15.6 *Average Number of Years of High School Enrollment for Three States that Exceeded the Federal Minimum in the 1970s, Men*

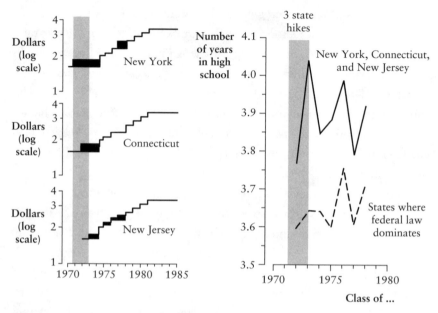

Source: Author's calculations based on the October Current Population Surveys (Unicon Research 2007). The shaded areas in the left-hand panel indicate when the state minimum wage exceeded the federal minimum wage, which is indicated by the lower line.

moved between October 1987 and October 1988; and Washington and Pennsylvania increased their minimum rates in January 1989. In each case an upward shift in enrollment is recorded by the CPS and in each case it was substantially larger than the movement shown for the states that did not raise their minimums above the federal level.

PRE-1972 TESTS FOR IMPACT OF CHANGES IN THE FEDERAL MINIMUM WAGE LAW

The micro-level CPS data used for the post-1971 tests are unavailable before 1968. Thus I need to switch data sets and adopt a different approach to study the impacts of changes in the federal minimum wage during this earlier period.[25] Rather than surveying each cohort annually as they progress through the U.S. school system, I turn to retrospective

reports of educational attainment. For this information I use the 1 percent samples drawn from the 1980, 1970, and 1960 decennial censuses
available from the University of Minnesota's IPUMS project (Ruggles
et al. 2008).[26] Each individual was asked to report to the Census Bureau
the highest grade of school ever attended. The micro-level data files report the highest grade of school completed and identify respondents who
began but did not finish the grade. From these reports I can calculate the
number of years of high school attended by each respondent. Constraining attention to native-born individuals greater than 20 years old and less
than 66 at each census, I was able to produce the cohort data displayed in
Figure 15.7.[27] The line at the right reproduces the CPS data for men
shown earlier in Figure 15.4. Another line covering 1935 to 1975 presents
the data for men constructed from the responses to the 1980 census for
the high school cohorts of 1938 to 1976. A third line is constructed from

FIGURE 15.7 *Average Number of Years of High School Enrollment for
Men: Census Retrospective Cohort Values versus Cohorts Tracted in the
Current Population Survey*

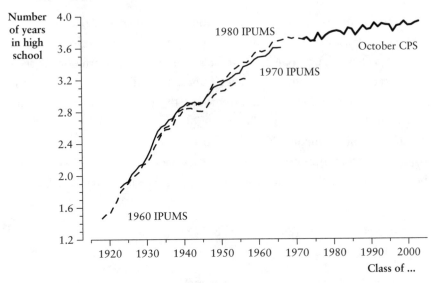

Sources: Author's calculations based on the IPUMS (Ruggles et al. 2008) and the October Current
Population Surveys.

the 1970 census, and the fourth line, pushing the series back to the high school class of 1918, is based on responses to the 1960 census.

Two things are obvious from this graph. First, there was a very rapid rise in high school attendance between 1918 and 1968 (from 1.47 years at the earlier date to 3.73 years at the later date), which was followed by the relatively slower growth evident after 1968. The dramatic educational advance associated with the spread of the high school after World War I is well known, and it suggests that a long-run secular process was at work (Goldin and Katz 2008, chap. 1). The other point that the plot illustrates is that as each cohort aged from one census to the next its members seem to have reported more high school experience than they did at the previous census. Some of this upward drift of the trend line measured at different census dates might be due to selective mortality. At least, we might suppose that the better educated are healthier and live longer than less-educated members of their cohort. But surely most of this educational attainment inflation is caused by selective memory (not to say prevarication) as one is further removed from one's high school days. For this reason we tend to favor the census reports from the respondents when they were younger.

In this analysis I focus on the minimum wage increases between 1950 and 1968. Because of the sharp upward gradient of the lines in Figure 15.7, it is clear that there is more influencing high school attendance than the increases in the minimum wage. To better highlight the impact of the minimum wage changes, I have removed the trend from the data and analyzed the residuals from the trend.[28] I focused on the data from the census sample immediately following each increase. I examined four rounds of federal minimum wage increases between 1947 and 1974.[29] As before, I labeled them with the name of the president who signed the bill.

Truman Increase—1950 (Enacted: October 1949)

    January 25, 1950   from $0.40   to $0.75

Eisenhower Increase—1956 (Enacted: August 1955)

    March 1, 1956   from $0.75   to $1.00

Kennedy Round—1961–1963 (Enacted: May 1961)

September 3, 1961	from $1.00	to $1.15
September 3, 1963		to $1.25

Johnson Round—1967–1968 (Enacted: September 1966)

February 1, 1967	from $1.25	to $1.40
February 1, 1968		to $1.60

For the Truman, Eisenhower, and Kennedy treatments, the residuals from the trend show a marked increase above the trend, supporting the hypothesis of a positive impact of these changes on school attendance. The Johnson round is less clear. If the treated cohorts were thought to be 1967–1970 rather than 1968–1971, then the fit would be better. I could rationalize that by noting that the Johnson bill was signed in September 1966, so it might be that the cohort that was 17 (largely seniors) in 1967 knew that the increase was coming. However, I also should note that there was a significant break in the trend rates displayed in Figure 15.7 sometime in the mid-1960s, and the results are sensitive to the way in which I have modeled the trend.

I can approximate the magnitude of the educational cascade induced by changes in the minimum wage between 1950 and 1972 by sequentially subtracting the estimated residuals from the IPUMS series on the number of years of high school attended. This is done at the left side of Figure 15.8. The line at the top is the original data based on the 1980 IPUMS and the lower line indicates what the trend might have been had there been no minimum wage changes. At the right-hand side of the figure the actual and the counterfactual series are extended to 2003 using the CPS data illustrated in Figure 15.4. If our approximations to the magnitude of the minimum-wage ratchet is accepted, then the average number of years of high school enrollment would have risen to only 3.52 years, rather than 3.73 years, for men born in 1951 (17 in 1968). Thereafter enrollment rates would have trended down to about 3.2 years for the cohort born in 1986 (17 in 2003), rather than slowly rising to around 3.9 years. This is an astonishing result. The cumulative effect of the minimum wage

FIGURE 15.8   *Average Number of Years of High School Enrollment for Males*

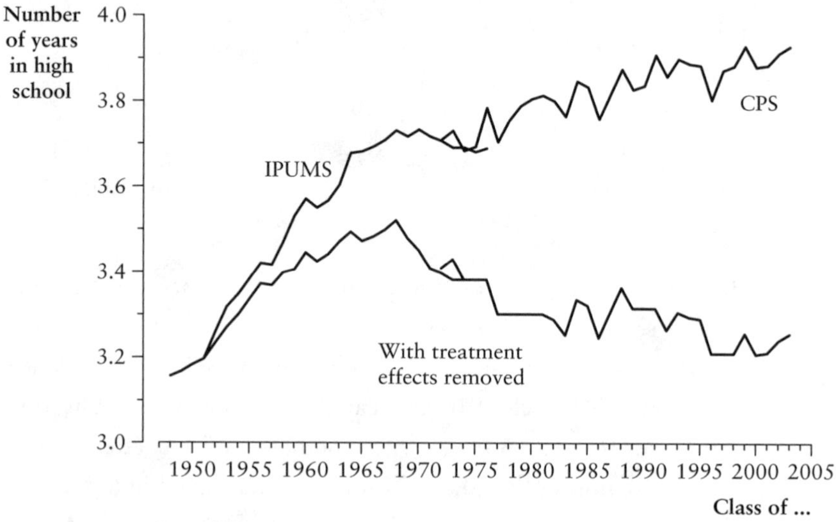

Sources: Author's calculations based on the IPUMS (Ruggles et al. 2008) and the October Current Population Surveys.

increases beginning in 1950 was to add 0.7 years to the average high school experience of men born in 1986.

CONCLUSION

Gavin Wright has suggested that the productivity slowdown that began after 1968 was associated with the rise of "flexible labor markets" and the dismantling of high-wage labor-market institutions that prevailed in the preceding half century (Wright 2006, pp. 152–153). The erosion of the real minimum wage after 1968 (displayed in Figure 15.1) was, according to Wright, a consequence of this labor-market "regime change" from one complex of policies to another. Frank Levy and Peter Temin (this volume) characterize the labor-market policies associated with the high-wage regime "the Treaty of Detroit" and the flexible labor-market policies that followed "the Washington Consensus." One element of the Washington Consensus was the desirability (or acceptability) of low minimum wages. The downward trend of the counterfactual enrollment I have illustrated in Figure 15.8 is consistent with the view that a regime change took place and that labor-market policy is relevant for long-run economic performance, just as Rosenbloom and Sundstrom (in this volume) argue.

Why the regime change? Levy and Temin argue that policy makers, "unable to comprehend the macroeconomic causes of distress" (high unemployment, inflation, economic inefficiency), turned to microeconomic tinkering, dissolving the long-standing understandings embodied in the Treaty of Detroit. The policy makers might have been influenced by that old argument of George Stigler (1946) and the campaign led by Milton Friedman that the minimum wage made the unemployment problem (particularly the teenage unemployment problem) intractable. If so, I might add that the policy makers responsible were also lacking in microeconomic understanding. As Card and Krueger make clear, Stigler and Friedman were wrong. Their microeconomic theory was too simplified and was inconsistent with the macroeconomics of causes of unemployment (Card and Krueger 1995, chap. 11).

The main contribution of this essay, as I see it, is to demonstrate the plausibility of the argument that increases in the minimum wage would increase the amount of schooling attained by a cohort that experiences the increases while in high school. If my empirical estimates are nearly correct,[30] the impact is numerically significant and likely to be economically important. This is not to say that the manipulation of the minimum wage is the most effective, efficient, or fair policy to achieve an increase in high school attendance. But further increases in the minimum wage large enough to counteract the decline in the real value of the minimum wage are likely to be beneficial and (Republicans willing) likely to be politically achievable.

High school dropout rates remain unacceptably high, particularly for minority teenagers. A reconsideration of the impact of the minimum wage would be a welcome component of any reorientation of government policy that attempts to deal with our current economic distress (high unemployment, deteriorating educational attainment).

APPENDIX: SPECIFYING THE AFFECTED COHORTS: THE NIXON ROUND

The Nixon round consisted of three increases in the minimum wage: the first on May 1, 1974, the second on January 1, 1975, and the third on

TABLE 15.A *Example: The Nixon Round of Minimum Wage Increases, May 1974–January 1976*

Percent of Age Class Attending High School—Average for Birth Cohorts of 1957–1959			13 Years	14 Years	15 Years	16 Years	17 Years	18 Years	19 Years	20 Years
			8.0	73.0	91.5	92.6	79.9	21.3	4.4	1.3

Month	Year	Federal Minimum Wage	Year of Birth of Individual in October of Indicated Year							
October	1973	$1.60	1960	1959	1958	1957	1956	1955	1954	1953
May	1974	$2.00								
October	1974	$2.00	1961	1960	1959	1958	1957	1956	1955	1954
January	1975	$2.10								
October	1975	$2.10	1962	1961	1960	1959	1958	1957	1956	1955
January	1976	$2.30								
October	1976	$2.30	1963	1962	1961	1960	1959	1958	1957	1956

January 1, 1976. Note first that the typical ages of high school attendees in October was 14 to 17, though a significant fraction of 18-year-olds (21.3 percent) were also still in high school. Table 15.A gives the birth cohort for each age class, 13 through 20, beginning with the October survey taken before the first rate change (and before President Nixon signed the wage bill[31]) continuing through the October that followed the third increase. I consider the cohorts of 1958 and 1959 to be the most directly affected by the Nixon round. The cohort born in 1957 aged from 16 to 17 years over the year that the first minimum wage change took place. But most 17-year-olds would be seniors (twelfth graders) in 1974, so this cohort had only a brush with the Nixon round. The 1958 cohort, on the other hand, experienced both the first and second increases before they reached 17. The 1959 cohort experienced all three boosts in the minimum during their high school years.[32]

I would expect the 1959 cohort to experience more years of high school education than either the 1957 or 1958 cohorts. This is, indeed, what we find. The 1959 cohort (they were 17 in 1976) reported 3.78 years. The 1958 cohort logged on average 3.69 years of high school enrollment by the time they were 20. The 1957 cohort reported 3.68 years.

NOTES

I have benefited from the suggestions offered by participants at the Washington Area Economic History Seminar (March 2008), the National Bureau of Economic Research's "Development of the American Economy" Summer Institute (July 2008), the Conference on Historical Approaches to Economics at Stanford University (September 2008), and the Bay Area Colloquium on Population (March 2009). Todd Sorensen made helpful suggestions after a close reading of an early draft. Susan B. Carter has followed this project from its inception. Her advice and encouragement are especially appreciated.

1. Moses (2002).

2. Massachusetts was the first state to adopt a minimum wage law in 1912. It was a "recommendatory" law that applied only to women and minors (Kelley 1912). In 1935 this was replaced with a mandatory law, and in 1946 the law was amended to apply to men (U.S. Department of Labor, Bureau of Labor Standards 1967, pp. 93–95). The minimum wage became federal law with the passage of the Fair Labor Standards Act of 1938. The federal minimum wage applied uniformly to all covered employees (male and female) in all regions of the country.

3. The Friedman quote is famous enough to be an entry in the *Yale Book of Quotations* (Shapiro 2006, p. 292).

4. Franklin D. Roosevelt, "Speech before the 1936 Democratic National Convention," Philadelphia, Pennsylvania, June 27, 1936. The speech is more famously titled "A Rendezvous with Destiny."

5. For the political and legal history of the minimum wage through 1996 see Waltman (2000), chaps. 2 and 5. See also U.S. Department of Labor, Bureau of Labor Standards (1967), pp. 69–100, and Nordlund (1997). Wright (2006, pp. 143–147) and Rosenbloom and Sundstrom (this volume) place the origin of the minimum wage in the context of the "high-wage national regime" that lasted for 50 years following World War I and that induced the coinciding period of rapid productivity growth and rising educational attainment (see also Levy and Temin, this volume, and Goldin and Katz 2008).

6. Charles Brown, a University of Michigan labor economist and a veteran of the minimum wage debates in the academy, stated the case for relative unimportance 20 years ago in his paper "Minimum Wage Laws: Are They Overrated?" (1988). Card and Krueger forcefully and persuasively argued that increases in the minimum wage did not lead to a corresponding loss of jobs or an increase in unemployment (1995). Neumark and Wascher are associated with the argument that minimum wages reduce job opportunities for teenagers, yet they report that their 1992 article did "not reveal disemployment effects of minimum wages for teenagers" (1995a, p. 199). For a sampling of journalistic reports see the following, all from the *New York Times* and all suggesting that the minimum wage has or would have minimal economic consequences: Passell (1989, p. D2); Rasky (1989, p. E4); Uchitelle (1990, p. 1; 1995, p. D1); Meredith (1996, p. D1); and Kilborn (1997, p. E5). All page references to the *New York Times* are from ProQuest Historical Newspapers online database. Passell, an economic historian before he became a journalist, cites the research of Alison Wellington, who found little or no impact of the minimum wage on employment (Wellington 1991). Rasky attributed to Isabel Sawhill, a labor economist at the Urban Institute, the opinion that the minimum wage "isn't going to make a big difference one way or the other." Uchitelle (1995) quotes Nobel laureate Robert Solow: "The main thing about this research is that the evidence of job loss is

weak, and the fact that the evidence is weak suggests that the impact on jobs is small." Meredith quotes Barry Bosworth, an economist at the Brookings Institution: " 'The whole issue is overblown."

7. The incidence is much higher for teenagers, the focus of this report. The 2005 estimate for teenagers is 8.8 percent.

8. Card and Krueger launched a devastating critique of the empirical literature I have just summarized (1995, chaps. 6 and 7). They conclude that the previous estimates are not robust and that "the conventional view that increases in the minimum wage necessarily have an adverse effect on employment has very weak empirical foundations" (pp. 236–237).

9. For the student who decides to stay enrolled, part-time (after-school) employment is also a possibility. As a possible motive to drop out, an alternative to a legitimate job is to join the underground economy and to engage in criminal activities with a pecuniary reward (drug dealing, prostitution, theft) (Freeman 1996). My focus is on the enrollment decision, not the labor-force status or occupation of the teenager.

10. I am skirting the issue that not all jobs are covered by the federal minimum wage law. The original law covered workers in private industries engaged in interstate commerce or the production of goods for commerce. It excluded such major sectors as agriculture, retail trade, and service (Douglas and Hackman 1939, pp. 29–33). Effective in 1950 coverage was reduced by narrowing the meaning of production for interstate commerce. In 1961 employees of retail establishments with sales over $1 million were added. In 1967 employees of schools, colleges, hospitals, hotels, restaurants, and laundries and employees of large farms were added. In addition, the retail sales volume test was reduced to $250,000 (Frankel 1966; Waltman 2000, p. 46). By 1968 coverage of wage workers by the federal law was reasonably complete and many states had their own minimum wage laws that extended protection to those not covered by the federal law. Moreover, there is some evidence that many (most?) employers who are not required to pay the minimum wage do so nonetheless (Fritsch 1981; Uchitelle 1990; Katz and Krueger 1991, 1992; Card and Krueger 1995, p. 158).

11. The argument that a minimum wage would stimulate technological innovation was made by Webb (1912, pp. 981–983). The mechanism might also work in reverse. Wright has suggested that the decline in the real minimum wage evident in Figure 15.1 after the 1960s was one element contributing to the productivity slowdown in the 1970s (Wright 2006, pp. 152–153).

12. Poverty or a temporary setback might force some academically promising students in the skillful group to drop out. If so, the fault would be imperfect capital markets that make it impossible or prohibitively expensive to borrow with only academic promise as collateral.

13. I know of only a few prior studies. Ragan in a passing footnote reported a time-series regression in which the unemployment rate and the minimum wage rate had no impact on school enrollment to justify an assumption to that end (1977, p. 131 n. 17). Mattila has made an argument that is in part similar to mine (1981). "There is good reason to believe that school enrollment may be affected. If minimum wages create barriers to employment, then additional schooling may be one strategy for over-coming that barrier" (1981, p. 61). Neumark and Wascher (1995a, 1995b, 2003) reach an opposite conclusion. They report that "the minimum wage reduces the proportion of teenagers in school." However,

they emphasize the preliminary nature of their results and suggest that the topic "merits further scrutiny" (Neumark and Wascher 2003, p. 9).

14. This nomenclature is a bit misleading because each of the five minimum wage bills emerged as a compromise between the supporters of a raise (most Democratic Congress members and presidents Clinton and Carter) and opponents (Republican legislators). The dates of enactment are reported in the *New York Times* (Apple 1974, p. 1; "Carter Signs" 1977; Rosenbaum 1989, p. A1; Stevenson 1996, p. B6; Labaton 2007).

15. This is reported in two variables. One is named *grdatt* and labeled "Grade attending" in the Unicon version of the October data files. The other is named *chgrd* and labeled "Grade or year child is attending." For ages 15 and up the information is recorded in *grdatt*. For ages 13 and 14 the information is recorded in *grdatt* for 1968–1983 and in *chgrd* for 1989–2006. For the period 1984–1988 the information for 13-year-olds is recorded in *chgrd*, while that for 14-year-olds is in *grdatt*. Producing a consistent time series is complicated for 1968–1983 because children (ages 3–13) recorded in *grdatt* are coded with a different set of codes than used for adults (14 and up). The incarcerated population is excluded and beginning in 1994 the universe excludes members of the military. No distinction is made in the CPS between enrollment and attendance.

16. A statistical cohort is not quite the same as a "synthetic" cohort because the latter is derived from a cross-section. The statistical cohort follows an actual birth cohort but draws a different (random) sample from that cohort each year.

17. For the Carter Four Step round the four cohorts born in the years 1961–1964 were the most affected. The cohort of 1961 experienced two Carter steps between ages 16 and 18. Those in the cohort of 1962 experienced three steps between ages 15 and 18. The cohort of 1963 experienced all four steps during their high school years. Those from the cohort of 1964 experienced the last three Carter steps between ages 14 and 17. The Bush I round had two steps. The cohorts of 1973 and 1974 experienced both of those changes between ages 15 and 18. The Clinton round also had two steps, but the first step took place on October 1, 1996, only a few days before the October CPS survey of that year. I take the cohorts of 1980 and 1981 as those that were most affected. Considering the simultaneity of the first step and the October survey, the cohort of 1979 experienced only one upward tick, and that was between ages 17 and 18. The cohort of 1982 witnessed the first step between ages 13 and 14 and the second between ages 14 and 15.

18. Of course, there were several profound shifts in the labor market for those with less educational attainment beginning in the mid-1970s. Of particular importance was the increasing wage gap between those with a high school diploma and those without. It has been suggested that this would explain the upward drift in the average number of years of schooling in the period under study. What I am suggesting is that whatever impact the changing returns to schooling had, they were primarily manifested during the rounds of minimum wage increases.

19. Interestingly, during the Nixon era the graduation rates for women and men measured at age 20 were roughly equal, but following 1975 female graduation rates were consistently higher than that for men.

20. The appendix mentioned can be found at this URL: http://economics.ucr.edu/repec/ucr/wpaper/App%20B%20STATE%20CODES.pdf. For the Nixon round test some states were excluded because of the aggregated geocoding in the CPS files for 1968–1976.

21. Connecticut officially raised its minimum allowable rate above the federal level in May 1971, but it was only by a symbolic one cent. In October the state raised its minimum to 25 cents above the federal level of $1.60.

22. I have aggregated the three states because of the low number of observations in Connecticut and New Jersey.

23. We might also note that these three states were all states that experienced high enrollment rates compared with the rest of the country, making proportional increases in the enrollment rate less likely.

24. Unfortunately, Hawai'i's data cannot be separated from the data for Washington and Alaska. New Jersey's pre-Carter increase was in January 1975 during the middle of the Nixon round. New York and California's increases in October and November 1976 came directly between the Nixon round (May 1974–January 1976) and the Carter Four Step (January 1978–January 1981). Thus California and New York experienced an increase every single year from 1974 to 1981. For New Jersey and the states that did not exceed the federal standard there were also changes every year with the exception of 1977. Thus it would be difficult to discern a distinctly different pattern for these three states.

25. There were few states with minimum wage increases that exceeded the federal minimum before 1970. See Figure 15.3.

26. I cannot use the 1990 or subsequent census samples because they define educational attainment differently than the earlier censuses. In particular they consider the Generalized Educational Development (GED) degree (or high-school equivalency diploma) to be equivalent to graduating from twelfth grade and earning a high school diploma. For a discussion of the problems this change created see Heckman, LaFontaine, and Rodriguez (2008).

27. The foreign born are excluded because I cannot know whether they attended high school in the United States or a foreign country. When examining the CPS data this was not a concern because we were examining residents of the United States attending school (or not) in October of each year.

28. The trends were estimated separately for each IPUMS sample. They are piecewise linear and pass through the observations for 1951, 1957, 1962, and 1974. These dates were chosen to coincide with the first cohort to experience one of the minimum wage increases while 14 to 16 years old. However, 1968 was skipped because the profile from the 1980 IPUMS indicated there was no upward trend between 1963 and 1974.

29. See Table 15.1. For a discussion of the political and legislative history of these episodes see Waltman (2000), pp. 34–41. For the dates of enactment and other details see Stark (1949); "Eisenhower Signs $1 Minimum Pay" (1955); "Kennedy Signs Wage Floor Bill" (1961); Frankel (1966).

30. Of course, my measure of the impact of the educational cascade induced by increases in the minimum wage is only approximate because it is based on several strong assumptions. My procedures for controlling for the underlying trend in the pre-1972 data and the assumption that there are no omitted variables that would influence the results are the most obvious issues. On the other hand, my own hunch is that my preliminary results are likely to underestimate the full effect. High on any list of omitted variables to add are controls for state differences in compulsory education laws and a variable to measure the impact of unemployment rates on the decision to remain in school. Omission of these variables is likely to attenuate the effect I am trying to assess.

31. President Nixon had vetoed the bill the previous September and his change of heart was somewhat of a surprise. "But politicians in both parties suggested that, with possible impeachment hanging over his head, Mr. Nixon could not afford to risk a second veto" (Apple 1974).

32. Recall that the 1958 birth cohort is calculated by subtracting the age of the respondent in October from the year that the survey was conducted. Thus the two cohorts of 1958–1959 consist of those born between October 15, 1957 and October 14, 1959.

REFERENCES

Adams, F. Gerard (1989). "The Macroeconomic Impacts of Increasing the Minimum Wage." *Journal of Policy Modeling* 11: 179–189.

Apple, R. W., Jr. (1974). "President Signs Rise in Pay Base to $2.30 an Hour; He Cites 'Reservations' But Says Higher Minimum Can 'No Longer Be Delayed.'" *New York Times*, April 9, p. 1.

Brown, Charles (1988). "Minimum Wage Laws: Are They Overrated?" *Journal of Economic Perspectives* 2: 133–145.

Brown, Charles (1999). "Minimum Wages, Employment, and the Distribution of Income." In *Handbook of Labor Economics*, vol. 3B, edited by Orley Ashenfelter and David Card. Amsterdam: North-Holland, pp. 2101–2163.

Brown, Charles, Curtis Gilroy, and Andrew Kohen (1982). "The Effect of the Minimum Wage on Employment and Unemployment." *Journal of Economic Literature* 20: 487–528.

Card, David, and Alan B. Krueger (1995). *Myth and Measurement: The New Economics of the Minimum Wage*. Princeton, NJ: Princeton University Press.

Card, David, and Thomas Lemieux (2000). "Dropout and Enrollment Trends in the Post-War Period: What Went Wrong in the 1970s?" National Bureau of Economic Research Working Paper No. 7658. Cambridge, MA: National Bureau of Economic Research.

Carter, Susan B., Scott Sigmund Gartner, Michael R. Haines, Alan L. Olmstead, Richard Sutch, and Gavin Wright, eds. (2006). *Historical Statistics of the United States: Earliest Times to the Present, Millennial Edition*. New York: Cambridge University Press.

"Carter Signs Minimum Wage Bill, Giving Raises of 45 Percent by '81" (1977). *New York Times*, November 2, p. 1.

Douglas, Paul H., and Joseph Hackman (1939). "The Fair Labor Standards Act of 1938: II." *Political Science Quarterly* 54: 29–55.

"Eisenhower Signs $1 Minimum Pay; Rise From 75 Cents an Hour Effective Next March 1 Will Affect 2,000,000" (1955). *New York Times*, August 13, p. 1.

Frankel, Max. (1966). "President Signs Minimum Pay Bill; Hails Rise to $1.60 in '68—Recalls 25-Cent Wage Gained by New Deal." *New York Times*, September 24, p. 1.

Freeman, Richard B. (1996). "Why Do So Many Young American Men Commit Crimes and What Might We Do About It?" *Journal of Economic Perspectives* 10: 25–42.

Friedman, Milton (1983). *Bright Promises, Dismal Performance: An Economist's Protest*. San Diego: Harcourt Brace Jovanovich.

Fritsch, Conrad (1981). "Exemptions from the Fair Labor Standards Act, Retail Trade and Services." In *Report of the Minimum Wage Study Commission*, vol. 5. Washington, DC: Minimum Wage Study Commission.

Goldin, Claudia, and Lawrence F. Katz (2008). *The Race between Education and Technology*. Cambridge, MA: Harvard University Press.

Haugen, Steven E., and Earl F. Mellor (1990). "Estimating the Number of Minimum Wage Workers." *Monthly Labor Review* 113: 70–74.

Heckman, James J., Paul A. LaFontaine, and Pedro L. Rodriguez (2008). "Taking the Easy Way Out: How the GED Testing Program Induces Students to Drop Out." National Bureau of Economic Research Working Paper No. 14044. Cambridge, MA: National Bureau of Economic Research.

Katz, Lawrence F., and Alan B. Krueger (1991). "The Effects of the New Minimum Wage Law in a Low-Wage Labor Market." National Bureau of Economic Research Working Paper No. 3655. Cambridge, MA: National Bureau of Economic Research.

Katz, Lawrence F., and Alan B. Krueger (1992). "The Effect of the Minimum Wage on the Fast-Food Industry." *Industrial and Labor Relations Review* 46: 6–21.

Kelley, Florence (1912). "Minimum-Wage Laws." *Journal of Political Economy* 20: 999–1010.

"Kennedy Signs Wage-Floor Bill; 3.6 Million More Get Coverage" (1961). *New York Times*, May 6, p. 14.

Kilborn, Peter T. (1997). "A Minimal-Impact Minimum Wage." *New York Times*, April 6, p. E5.

Labaton, Stephen (2007). "Congress Passes Increase in the Minimum Wage." *New York Times*, May 25.

Mattila, J. Peter (1981). "The Impact of Minimum Wages on Teenage Schooling and on Part-Time/Full-Time Employment of Youths." In *The Economics of Legal Minimum Wages*, edited by Simon Rottenberg. Washington, DC: American Enterprise Institute, pp. 61–87.

Meredith, Robyn (1996). "Politics Aside, Economy Is Shrugging Off Rise to $4.75." *New York Times*, October 1, p. D1.

Moses, Montrose J., ed. (2002). *The Fireside Chats of Franklin Delano Roosevelt*. Project Gutenberg. Available at www.gutenberg.org/.

Neumark, David, and William Wascher (1995a). "Minimum Wage Effects on Employment and School Enrollment." *Journal of Business and Economic Statistics* 13: 199–206.

Neumark, David, and William Wascher (1995b). "Minimum-Wage Effects on School and Work Transitions of Teenagers." *American Economic Review* 85: 244–249.

Neumark, David, and William Wascher (2003). "Minimum Wages and Skill Acquisition: Another Look at Schooling Effects." *Economics of Education Review* 22: 1–10.

Nordlund, Willis J. (1997). *The Quest for a Living Wage: The History of the Federal Minimum Wage Program*. Westport, CT: Greenwood Press.

Norman, Geoffrey (1973). "*Playboy* Interview: Milton Friedman." *Playboy* 28: 51–68, 74. Reprinted in Friedman (1983), pp. 9–59.

Passell, Peter. (1989). "Minimum Wage: A Reality Test." *New York Times*, March 15, p. D2.

Ragan, James F., Jr. (1977). "Minimum Wages and the Youth Labor Market." *Review of Economics and Statistics* 59: 129–136.

Rasky, Susan F. (1989). "The Minimum-Wage Fight Isn't Really about Pay." *New York Times*, May 7, p. E4.

Roosevelt, Franklin D. (1936). "Speech before the 1936 Democratic National Convention," Philadelphia, Pennsylvania, June 27, 1936. In *The American Presidency Project*, edited by John T. Woolley and Gerhard Peters. Available at www.presidency.ucsb.edu/.

Rosenbaum, David E. (1989). "Bush and Congress Reach Accord Raising Minimum Wage to $4.25." *New York Times*, November 1, p. A1.

Rottenberg, Simon, ed. (1981). *The Economics of Legal Minimum Wages*. Washington, DC: American Enterprise Institute.

Ruggles, Steven, Matthew Sobek, Trent Alexander, Catherine A. Fitch, Ronald Goeken, Patricia Kelly Hall, Miriam King, and Chad Ronnander (2008). *Integrated Public Use Microdata Series*: Version 4.0 (online database). Minneapolis: Minnesota Population Center. Available at http://usa.ipums.org/usa/.

Schmitt, Eric (1996). "Bill to Increase Minimum Pay Clears Hurdle in a New Deal." *New York Times*, August 1, p. D22.

Shapiro, Fred R. (2006). *The Yale Book of Quotations*. New Haven, CT: Yale University Press.

Solon, Gary (1985). "The Minimum Wage and Teenage Employment: The Role of Serial Correlation and Seasonality." *Journal of Human Resources* 20: 292–297.

Stark, Louis (1949). "Minimum Pay Bill Is Sent to Truman; Wage Floor Is Set at 75 Cents But Coverage Is Reduced by Final Compromise." *New York Times*, October 19.

Stevenson, Richard W. (1996). "Clinton Signs a Bill Raising Minimum Wage by 90 Cents." *New York Times*, August 21, p. B6.

Stigler, George J. (1946). "The Economics of Minimum Wage Legislation." *American Economic Review* 36: 358–365.

Uchitelle, Louis. (1990). "Employers Shun Sub-Minimum Wage." *New York Times*, December 31, p. 1.

Uchitelle, Louis. (1995). "A Pay Raise's Impact." *New York Times*, January 12, p. D1.

Unicon Research (2007). *CPS Utilities: Education and School Enrollment, October 1968–2005*, DVD version 5.5, December 6.

U.S. Bureau of Labor Statistics (2006). "Characteristics of Minimum Wage Workers: 2005." May. Available at http://www.bls.gov/cps/minwage2005.htm.

U.S. Bureau of Labor Statistics, Consumer Price Index (online database). Available at http://www.bls.gov/cpi/ (accessed November 15, 2007).

U.S. Department of Labor, Bureau of Labor Standards (1967). *Growth of Labor Law in the United States*, 2nd ed. Washington, DC: U.S. Superintendent of Documents.

U.S. Department of Labor, Wages and Hours Division (n.d.). "History of Changes to the Minimum Wage Law." Available at http://www.dol.gov/whd/minwage/coverage.htm (accessed June 8, 2010).

U.S. Department of Labor, Wages and Hours Division (n.d.). "History of Federal Minimum Wage Rates under the Fair Labor Standards Act, 1938–2009." Available at http://www.dol.gov/whd/minwage/chart.htm (accessed June 8, 2010).

U.S. Department of Labor, Wages and Hours Division (n.d.). *Minimum Wage Laws in the States: January 1, 2010*. Available at http://www.dol.gov/whd/minwage/america.htm (accessed June 8, 2010).

Waltman, Jerold (2000). *The Politics of the Minimum Wage*. Urbana: University of Illinois Press.

Webb, Sidney (1912). "The Economic Theory of a Legal Minimum Wage." *Journal of Political Economy* 20: 973–998.

Wellington, Alison (1991). "Effects of the Minimum Wage on the Employment Status of Youths: An Update." *Journal of Human Resources* 26: 27–46.

Wright, Gavin (1986). *Old South, New South: Revolutions in the Southern Economy since the Civil War*. New York: Basic Books.

Wright, Gavin (1987). "Labor History and Labor Economics." In *The Future of Economic History*, edited by Alexander J. Field. Boston: Kluwer-Nijhoff, pp. 313–348.

Wright, Gavin (2006). "Productivity Growth and the American Labor Market: The 1990s in Historical Perspective." In *The Global Economy in the 1990s: A Long-Run Perspective*, edited by Paul W. Rhode and Gianni Toniolo. Cambridge: Cambridge University Press, pp. 139–160.

CHAPTER 16

America's First Culinary Revolution, or How a Girl from Gopher Prairie Came to Dine on Eggs Fooyung

SUSAN B. CARTER

ACCORDING TO culinary scholars, American food retained a strongly British character through most of its history.[1] This American food was "a cuisine with no mysteries: simple, spiceless, nutritious food. No tricks: the carrot is the honest carrot, the potato is not ashamed of being a potato, and the steak is a bloody giant" (Paz 1972, p. 74). Millions of immigrants from around the globe could not bring ethnic food to the American table. Writing in the 1970s, at the beginning of America's food revolution, Waverly Root and Richard de Rochemont concluded: "For good or for ill, the United States was perhaps a political melting pot, perhaps a cultural melting pot, perhaps an ethnical melting pot, but it is not a culinary melting pot. Its capacity for digesting esoteric gastronomic contributions is narrowly limited" (Root and de Rochemont 1976, p. 276). Americans' embrace of a varied, international cuisine is a relatively recent phenomenon (Hess and Hess 1972; Root and de Rochemont 1976; Pillsbury 1998; Kamp 2006; Kiple 2007).

Chinese food was the exception. Beginning in the early twentieth century, Chinese restaurants began appearing outside Chinatowns and the cuisine entered the cultural mainstream (Light 1974; Comer 2000; Barbas 2003; Coe 2009; Liu 2009).[2] As early as 1900 the *New York Times* declared the city "'chop suey' mad" ("Heard about Town," 1900). Twenty years later Americans struggled to recall a time when Chinese food was *not* a part of their experience. Asked, "Do you remember way back when?" a *Chicago Daily Tribune* reader responded: "Chop suey first appeared and we lamped it with suspicion and then tried to eat it with a set of chopsticks" ("In the Wake of the News," 1920). "It was considered slumming to

419

visit a Chinese restaurant" ("In the Wake of the News," 1921) was a winning entry in 1921.

The popularity of Chinese food, especially chop suey, inspired artists working in a variety of media. Samantha Barbas (2003) provides some examples: the popular tune "Who'll Chop Your Suey (When I'm Gone)" (1925)[3] and Carol Kennicott's escape from Gopher Prairie to a Minneapolis Chinese restaurant in Sinclair Lewis's *Main Street* (1998 [1920]). There are many others. Chop suey restaurants formed the backdrop for countless O. Henry short stories. Louis Armstrong named his first composition "Cornet Chop Suey" (1925). Ashcan artist John Sloan (1871–1951) painted "Chinese Restaurant" in 1909 as part of his effort to portray *typical* New York scenes earlier artists had ignored. Abstract artist Max Weber (1881–1961) juxtaposed images, including frenetically rushing waiters, in his "Chinese Restaurant" (1915) to express the jarring effect of this popular meeting place on American culture. Edward Hopper (1882–1967), perhaps America's best-known realist painter, completed "Chop Suey" (1929) in the same year as his iconic "The Lighthouse at Two Lights."[4]

To be sure, the food served in these restaurants was not traditional Chinese (Yu 1987; Coe 2009). But to dismiss it because it was "inauthentic" misses the point.[5] The absence of bread and dairy products, tea served at every meal and drunk out of handleless cups without cream or sugar, unusual ingredients, and the use of meat as a flavoring rather than as the focus of the meal are just some of the ways in which Chinese food offered Americans an undeniably exotic experience.[6]

In the nineteenth century, Chinese Americans' food patterns mirrored those of other ethnic immigrant groups. As Donna Gabaccia (1998) demonstrates, Italians, Jews, Germans, Mexicans, and Chinese all sought to maintain their traditional cuisines after their arrival in the United States. They did so, in part, by importing, growing, and processing specialty ingredients and by supporting local chefs who knew, or who were willing to learn, old world recipes. But, initially at least, outsiders had to travel to ethnic enclaves in order to experience the food. Over time, ethnic importers, wholesalers, retailers, and restaurateurs sought to expand their businesses by locating outside their traditional neighborhoods and offering their foods to the general public. In Gabaccia's telling the process was similar for all ethnic groups, but clearly the Chinese were different. In 1900, on the eve of America's chop suey craze, eating and drinking establishments employed a mere 0.4 percent of the Chinese labor force, an even smaller share than that for the labor force as a whole (0.8 percent).[7] But in the decades that followed this number grew rapidly so that at its peak in 1950 over a third of Chinese workers were employed in the industry. Greek immigrants also became restaurateurs, but they operated diners serving chops, mashed potatoes, boiled carrots, and other "American" fare (Miller 1909; Saloutos 1964; Gabaccia 1998). Prior to the late 1940s, and excepting eateries located in ethnic enclaves, only the Chinese were offering non-coethnics a culinary alternative.

The Chinese entry onto the American culinary scene could hardly be more surprising. It occurred during the Chinese Exclusion Era, the period between 1882 and 1943 when stringent laws limited Chinese immigration to the United States and restricted the options of Chinese residents. Fewer than 106,000 Chinese were living in the United States at the time the first law was passed. Over time their numbers fell so that by 1920 there were fewer than 62,000 Chinese in a U.S. population of more than 105 million.[8]

Here I tell the story of how the Chinese accomplished America's first culinary revolution. It focuses on the labor market, in particular on an *institutional regime* shift within the labor market prompted by the passage of the Chinese Exclusion Act in 1882. The approach is inspired by the work of Gavin Wright, for whom the institutional regime is central to understanding labor-market outcomes. By institutional regime Wright means the set of institutions within which workers and firms operate and the assumptions and behaviors of the economic actors that structure their relationships and narrow the range of possible labor-market outcomes.

Rosenbloom and Sundstrom (this volume) argue that the salient characteristics of these institutional regimes are their coherence and persistence. "Coherence" means that "important institutional elements are complementary and mutually reinforcing and therefore tend to occur together as a set." As Wright had earlier noted:

Economic institutions arise in response to the pressures and conditions of a particular era, some of which may be eternal, but many of which are fleeting. Once in place, institutions change relatively slowly and incrementally as new pressures develop. . . . But in the meantime many kinds of behavior, by employers and workers, will have adapted to the institution rather than vice versa: workers adapt their skills, their effort level, their leisure-time activities to the job definitions and promotion system; employers adapt hiring standards, supervision, and technological strategies to the same systems. (Wright 1987a, pp. 318–319)

"Persistence" means that "Once established, institutional regimes are sticky, with periods of relative institutional stability punctuated by crisis periods of relatively rapid change" (Rosenbloom and Sundstrom, this volume). Thus the abolition of slavery and the North's victory in the Civil War prompted the reorganization of southern agriculture away from large plantations worked by gang labor and toward the cultivation of small plots worked by tenant farm families. As former slaves and lacking governmental assistance, blacks entered this new institutional regime without capital or political power. This left them with few resources for overcoming their poverty and for fighting racist laws and racist practices in education, employment, and the administration of justice. Once in place, this institutional regime persisted for more than half a century, ending only after another set of crises forced its abandonment.

In a similar way the Chinese Exclusion Act brought an end to one institutional regime and prompted the creation of another. Prior to the act, during America's era of open borders, Chinese immigrants to the United States behaved much like those from other countries. Young men arrived anticipating a brief stay. They worked in low-skilled jobs, lived frugally, and saved their money. Many returned home with savings they used to pay off debt and to purchase assets. While in the United States they worked in industries and regions where labor demand was growing, wages were high, and employment easy to find. New immigrant communities were formed where jobs were to be had. For family and friends back home, these communities helped fund travel and provided housing and employment assistance once in the United States. Between 1850 and 1880 the number of Chinese living in the United States grew from several hundred to over

105,000. Almost all were young males living in California and other western states working in mines, on farms, and in construction.

The Exclusion Act brought this regime to an abrupt end. The act took aim at the key elements of the regime by thwarting the entry of laborers and condoning employment discrimination. The act performed exactly as intended: it disrupted the flow of Chinese immigrants and encouraged the early return of many Chinese residents. The flow of Chinese immigrants into the United States, which had been averaging several thousand per year, dropped to a trickle. Over the following 40 years the Chinese population fell by more than 40 percent.

Exclusion fundamentally transformed the earlier labor-market institutional regime. Under the new law, Chinese entry was largely limited to merchants and to the Chinese-born children of American-born Chinese men. The Chinese responded by developing elaborate strategies that made them appear to qualify as members of an authorized group and to overcome the daunting hurdles to their entry imposed by the U.S. Immigration Service. These new strategies required lots of money, far more than what was required for immigration under the earlier regime.

To overcome employment discrimination once in the United States, the Chinese shifted into the retail and service sectors and opened their own businesses. These competitive sectors required some capital, but not too much. They provided an attractive alternative to wage work with racist white employers. As long as the Chinese were willing to expand into new locations, their small numbers relative to the total population meant that their enterprises could increase almost indefinitely without depressing prices or profits. In effect, the demand for their product was perfectly elastic. For entrepreneurial Chinese with the requisite capital, only labor posed a potential limit to their indefinite expansion. But as an unintended consequence, the Chinese Exclusion Act created the preconditions for the requisite large, disciplined, and inexpensive labor pool. The Exclusion Act put U.S. entry and employment out of reach of the majority of would-be Chinese immigrants unless they had the support of a wealthy merchant. The new institutions that emerged from the crisis broke traditional family bonds and replaced them with individual relationships in the guise of "paper families." These new institutions were more profit-oriented and better funded than earlier ones. Merchants could count on the cooperation of the immigrants they sponsored. They could train immigrants in the provision of a standardized product, deploy them to remote communities, work them long hours, and relocate them whenever business considerations advised. This labor supply gave the merchants an unparalleled degree of control over the character, quality, and distribution of their business operations. When Americans expressed interest in exotic ethnic food, the Chinese were poised to respond.

THE CHINESE EXCLUSION ACT OF 1882

The Chinese Exclusion Act was the first American law to specify race as a criterion for immigration. It was passed only a third of a century after the Chinese began arriving in the United States in large numbers. These immigrants came from an eight-county region on the western edge of the Pearl River Delta to the south and west of Canton (Guangzhou) with an estimated 45 percent coming from the single county of Taishan.[9] Located in close proximity to the commercial centers of Canton, Macao, and Hong Kong, the region was one of the wealthier areas in China during the early nineteenth century, with a long history of involvement in both internal and international trade (Kwong and Miscevic 2005, p. 20). However, the Opium Wars (1839–1842 and 1856–1860) devastated the region's economy, prompting many young men to accept employment as coolies in Peru, Cuba, and the Sandwich Islands. The discovery of gold in California and then Australia in the mid-nineteenth century brought foreign labor recruiters to the region looking for low-wage laborers to work the new mining claims, build infrastructure, and provide local services (Kwong and Miscevic 2005, pp. 36–38; Clay, this volume).

Migrants' transportation and related costs were funded by relatives or extended familial networks. Successful migrants were expected to not only repay the loans but also sponsor others. These reciprocal arrangements reinforced and reproduced the strong geographic concentration in emigrants' origins (Watson 1975). As the number of migrants grew, Chinese merchants stepped in to supplement family organizations by offering, on credit, tickets for the transpacific passage as well as food, shelter, clothing, and job placement services until the first paychecks arrived

(Kwong and Miscevic 2005, pp. 76–79). In some cases these merchants were also employed as subcontractors to American employers, managing their Chinese employees and provisioning them with familiar food, clothing, and cultural goods (Kwong and Miscevic 2005, p. 79). Robert Spier (1958) showed that as early as the mid-1850s, and even in remote locations such as construction sites for the transcontinental railroad, the Chinese were able to eat their customary foods prepared with customary implements and served in their customary manner. Madeline Hsu documented the activities of many of these Chinese merchants, demonstrating that some made vast fortunes for themselves and, by stimulating demand for their ethnic goods in America, increased employment in China's export sector (Hsu 2000, pp. 31–40).

Shortly after the arrival of the Chinese, and in response to public uprisings, California and other western states passed laws limiting the ability of the Chinese to make mining claims and own land (Boswell 1986; Brown and Philips 1986; Tsai 1986, pp. 13–14). These laws channeled Chinese employment into laborers' positions in mining, construction, personal services, agriculture, and manufacturing.

In the 1870s the economic prospects for Chinese in the American West deteriorated significantly. By then many of the early mining claims had been extinguished, a severe economic depression increased the unemployment rate across the nation, and the completion of the transcontinental railroad in 1869 intensified industrial competition from eastern manufacturers. As unemployment rose, racial violence intensified (Brown and Philips 1986; Kwong and Miscevic 2005, pp. 60–73). Western politicians eager for reelection were joined by southern politicians who favored immigration restriction as a way of maintaining their political influence in Congress. Tight presidential races in 1876 and 1880 persuaded even Republicans who had championed the cause of racial equality for blacks to join the call for exclusion. They felt they needed the western vote (Coolidge 1909; Sandmeyer 1973 [1939]; Saxton 1971; Gyory 1998; McKeown 2008). In 1882 Congress passed the Chinese Exclusion Act, a law that severely limited the number and characteristics of Chinese who were allowed to enter the United States and which put substantial restrictions on the activities of Chinese already in the country.

Other countries around the Pacific Rim soon followed suit (Lee 2003). These restrictions, and the response they provoked, changed the institutional regime within which the Chinese American labor market operated.

SOME CONSEQUENCES OF THE CHINESE EXCLUSION ACT

Under the Chinese Exclusion Act only "treaty merchants" and their families, religious figures, scholars, and the foreign-born children of American-born Chinese *men* were allowed to enter the country. Chinese were barred from naturalization and required to carry identification papers. Many Chinese business activities were penalized (Hsu 2000, p. 55). The law specifically prohibited the entry of the skilled and unskilled laborers who accounted for the largest share of Chinese immigrants prior to its passage. Chinese in the United States at the time of its passage were barred from reentry should they return to China. Enforcement was tough and even persons with proper credentials faced harsh interrogation upon their entry (Barde 2008).

One immediate effect of the law was to drastically reduce the inflow of immigrants. In 1882 39,579 Chinese immigrants were granted admission. The average annual number admitted over the previous five years had been a little over 15,000. In the five years following the implementation of the act, annual entries averaged fewer than 1,700. Because there were few Chinese women, because most men planned to return to their families in China, and because many states passed anti-miscegenation laws, the Chinese population displayed virtually no natural increase. The average age of Chinese in America rose and their numbers fell. In 1880 the Chinese population numbered 105,465 with an average age of 31.2 years. At its trough in 1920, the population had shrunk to roughly half this level while the average age had climbed to 37.7 years.

In spite of its sizable impacts on the population stocks and flows, the Exclusion Act did little to reduce the expressions of racism directed toward the Chinese. Pfaelzer (2007) describes continuing episodes of mob action that resulted in murder, the seizure of Chinese property, and the forced abandonment of their businesses and homes. White workers actively opposed Chinese employment (Saxton 1971; Light 1972; Brown and Philips 1986; Daniels 1988; Kwong and Miscevic 2005, pp. 106–115). Professional organizations refused to admit them. Occupational licensing laws in most states prohibited them from practicing law, accounting, and medicine. Many states excluded the Chinese from practicing barbering and working at race tracks (Konvitz 1946, pp. 190–200). Disparaging attitudes toward the Chinese were so pervasive that some were expressed even in scholarly journals. Wright observes: "It is chilling to go back to [John R.] Commons' 1909 article and find him railing against the 'competitive menace' of the 'Chinaman' and the 'foreign immigrant' as stridently as he does against 'prison labor, child labor, and long hours of labor' " (Wright 1987a, p. 333). As late as 1927, almost 50 years after the passage of the Exclusion Act, a survey of Americans found "only 27.0 percent who said they would accept Chinese as fellow workers, 15.9 percent as neighbors, and 11.8 percent as friends" (Tsai 1986, p. xi).

Still, because markets for final products and for unskilled labor were well integrated, competitive pressures led to employment opportunities even for those facing the most extreme manifestations of racial discrimination. Thus, as Wright and Warren Whatley have shown, black workers operating within the racist institutions in the American South enjoyed wages equivalent to those of southern white workers in similar jobs. Although the southern labor market operated separately from that of the rest of the country, it coordinated wages within the region and presented profit opportunities to employers who put aside their racist views when making hiring and pay decisions (Wright 1987b; Whatley 1985).

Much the same appears to have been true for the Chinese. Martin Brown and Peter Philips demonstrate that, despite the heated objections of white workers, California employers in competitive industries such as boots and shoes and cigars hired Chinese workers. They could not afford not to. High transportation costs made many raw materials expensive. In order to compete in national and international product markets, following the completion of the transcontinental railroad in 1869, California manufacturers felt special pressure to lower labor costs. Brown and Philips argue: "The employment of cheap Chinese labor was seen as the key to opening up the national market to California [products]" (Brown and Philips 1986, p. 72). Thus, even during the racially turbulent decade of the 1870s, Chinese employment in many competitive California industries such as boots and shoes and cigars grew (Brown and Philips 1986, p. 67).

The problem for the Chinese was the same as that facing blacks: how to gain access to the better-paying sectors where competitive forces worked less well. As Wright notes: "The problem for blacks was not maneuvering *within* the labor market, it was overcoming the barriers to getting *out* of the labor market, such as the capital requirements for moving up the farm ladder, or the racial restrictions on skilled or supervisor jobs in industry" (Wright 1987a, p. 322). In this respect, however, the Chinese had an advantage. Even during the period of open borders, their strong transnational community offered them access to capital markets. Because the Chinese Exclusion Act limited entry to those with the strongest ties to merchants, it served to improve capital access for the population able to enter or to remain in the country.

HUIGUANS

The Chinese benefited from their *huiguans*, transnational Chinese mutual aid societies built around similarity of dialect and surname. The first American huiguan was organized in San Francisco in 1851. By 1862, when there were six, they joined together in a federal association with the English name Chinese Consolidated Benevolent Association. As the Chinese moved into new cities they brought their huiguans with them, establishing local branches that operated with some autonomy while retaining strong ties to similar organizations in other cities. San Francisco's Chinese Benevolent Association remained the most prominent branch and was known to Americans as the Chinese Six Companies (Hoy 1942; Lai 1987; Tsai 1986; Brown 1995; McGlinn 1995; Hsu 2000; Yee 2003).

The huiguans provided a wide variety of services to Chinese Americans. Tsai notes that they were the first contacts incoming Chinese made upon their arrival in America and the last before their departure (Tsai 1986, p. 48). The huiguans also helped their members find employment and obtain credit and insurance. They provided public goods such as fire safety, garbage collection, and even police protection that were often denied the Chinese by hostile white communities. They made provisions for their members' observance of religious rituals, adjudicated disputes, and provided legal services. In collaboration with merchants, they organized trade between China and the United States, including the importation of Chinese specialty foods such as rice, soy products, sauces, dried seafood, and ethnic fruits and vegetables that were otherwise unavailable in the United States at the time.

Access to credit provided the Chinese with an alternative to wage work. In industries such as cigar making and in services such as laundries, the Chinese could simply go into business for themselves, perhaps hiring other Chinese as wage laborers, and compete against white businesses in the product market. The Chinese had begun to adopt this strategy even before the Chinese Exclusion Act. This can be seen in Table 16.1, which displays the industrial distribution of the Chinese labor force by region from 1870 through 1940. As early as 1870, 11 percent of the Chinese were employed in laundries, many of which were owned and operated by the Chinese themselves. Others owned or worked in Chinese-owned manufacturing operations or in retail establishments. But an unintended consequence of the Exclusion Act made self-employment even more attractive and more possible than it had been before the act's passage.

CHINESE RESPONSES TO THE EXCLUSION ACT

The Chinese Exclusion Act imposed considerable hardship on the Chinese in the United States and on their suppliers and home communities in China. The Chinese response was noncompliance. Despite the stringent entry restrictions, recent scholarship shows that a surprisingly large number of Chinese were able to enter the United States. Using the Integrated Public Use Microdata Series (IPUMS) samples from the manuscript censuses, Chew and Liu (2004) show that although the number of Chinese at each census is consistent with a "no migration" model, there was in fact quite a lot of in- and outmigration of Chinese. Their conclusions derive from their discovery of many more individuals in the young-adult age groups than would be predicted by the number of those ten years younger in the previous census. They write, "No plausible combination

TABLE 16.1 *Industrial Distribution of Chinese Employment by Region,*
1870–1930

	Total	Northeast	Midwest	South	West
1870					
Restaurants	0.2	—	—	—	0.2
Laundries	11.0	—	—	—	11.0
Food stores	1.3	—	—	—	1.3
All else	87.5	—	—	—	87.5
1880					
Restaurants	0.4	0	0	0	0.4
Laundries	13.9	100	100	0	11.9
Food stores	1.6	0	0	0	1.6
All else	84.1	0	0	100	86.1
1900					
Restaurants	0.5	0	0	0	0.6
Laundries	34.1	81.6	100	85.7	16.9
Food stores	3.4	0	0	7.1	4.2
All else	62.0	18.4	0	7.3	78.3
1910					
Restaurants	7.4	9.2	11.1	8.5	5.6
Laundries	20.9	60.2	66.7	31.9	7.4
Food stores	6.2	0	0	31.9	12.7
All else	65.5	30.6	22.2	27.7	74.3
1920					
Restaurants	17.3	32.8	47.8	22.2	12.2
Laundries	22.1	55.5	39.1	44.4	11.5
Food stores	7.4	5.5	0	7.4	7.0
All else	53.2	6.2	13.1	26.0	69.3
1930					
Restaurants	27.7	42.0	32.4	34.4	15.6
Laundries	24.7	42.0	50.0	21.9	6.6
Food stores	8.8	0.6	0	28.1	13.2
All else	38.8	15.4	17.6	15.6	64.6

Notes: "Chinese" identified using the race variable. Industry identified using the "IND1950" variable. Percentage distribution across industry includes only those identified with an industry. "Restaurants" are IND1950 code 679, "Eating and drinking places." "Laundries" are IND1950 code 846, "Laundering, cleaning and dyeing." "Food stores" are IND1950 code 636, "Food stores except dairy." Columns for each year total to 100. In 1870 there were too few Chinese outside the west for the computation of meaningful distributional statistics from the IPUMS sample.

Source: Ruggles et al. (2008).

of vital rates accounts for the observed population structures" (Chew and Liu 2004, p. 65). Erika Lee's investigation of the reports of the commissioner-general of immigration for the period 1910 through 1924 suggests that these later migrants were quite different from the laborers who predominated prior to exclusion. She finds that a large proportion of the men were new or returning merchants or sons of merchants and that the women were merchants' wives and daughters (E. Lee 2006, pp. 8, 11). She is also impressed by the volume of the flow, concluding: "Considering the immense barriers that the Chinese exclusion laws posed to new immigrants, returning residents, and citizens alike, the fact that over 300,000 Chinese successfully defied exclusion is testament to their persistence and motivation" (E. Lee 2006, p. 21). As the total Chinese American population in the United States in 1920 was less than 62,000, those 300,000 entries imply a comparably large number of departures and a substantial churning of the resident population.

Some insight into how the character of the Chinese community was affected by migration is provided by Table 16.2, which compares attributes of the Chinese who had migrated to the United States during the ten years prior to the census with the rest of the Chinese American population. Given the stringency of the restrictions and of border enforcement, it is surprising to see that recent migrants accounted for a substantial share of the Chinese American population throughout the Exclusion Era. In the year with the lowest value, 1910, their share is 11.3 percent. In 1900 it is almost a third. Between 1910 and 1930, even as immigration law was becoming more restrictive and the native-born Chinese population was beginning to grow through natural increase, the proportional representation of recent arrivals grew. In 1910 the recent arrival share was 20.4 percent.[10]

The growing share of recent arrivals is important, in part, because their personal characteristics differed from those of American-born Chinese and from those who arrived earlier. Recent arrivals were younger, less likely to settle in the western states, and more likely to be engaged in the growth sectors of their era. The English-language fluency of these new arrivals was comparable to that of their peers who had been in the country much longer. In 1910 42 percent of Chinese recent arrivals could

TABLE 16.2 *Recent Chinese Immigrants as Compared with All Other Chinese,*
Continental United States, 1900–1930

Characteristic	Recent Arrivals				All Other Chinese			
	1900	1910	1920	1930	1900	1910	1920	1930
Percent of total	31.3	11.3	15.2	20.4	68.7	88.7	84.8	79.6
Percent male	98.7	92.4	90.8	83.0	97.7	93.5	86.7	77.1
Average age	29.9	29.4	28.1	27.5	41.9	42.8	41.4	32.4
Percent who speak English	11.3	42.3	76.1	71.6	50.7	53.1	78.2	75.2
Percent living in the West	9.9	62.6	55.1	41.5	66.2	56.3	63.8	60.1
Percent restaurant workers	0.2	3.3	15.6	28.5	0.2	7.7	17.5	23.9
Percent laundry workers	6.4	19.0	30.5	21.2	20.5	20.7	24.1	22.4
Percent head of household (if male)	4.8	14.4	12.2	23.4	22.0	24.7	34.3	41.3
Percent nonrelative (if male)	92.7	81.7	78.1	68.6	75.6	69.2	57.7	47.5
Percent spouse of household head (if female)	66.7	30.0	87.5	84.0	45.5	46.2	47.5	42.1
Percent nonrelative (if female)	33.3	50.0	12.5	8.0	40.9	26.9	15.0	6.6

Notes: "Recent arrivals" are defined here as foreign-born Chinese who immigrated to the United States during the 10 years prior to the census date. "Percent restaurant workers" and "Percent laundry workers" refer to the male population 14 years of age and older. The "Percent who speak English" and the relationship to household head measures refer to the population 14 years of age and older.

Source: Ruggles et al. (2008).

speak English; in 1920 the share was 76 percent. The living arrangements of recent migrants demonstrate the pervasiveness of the transnational networks that were essential to migration during the Exclusion Era. Recent migrants were much more likely than the others to be living in households as a nonrelative. Some of the "households" were boarding houses, but many were headed by coethics and included only one or two nonrelatives.

Under the new law there were only two potentially large classes of persons born in China who could legally enter—merchants and their immediate families and the China-born children of American-born men.[11] To qualify as a merchant one had to show proof of ownership of a trading company or similar business organization. This requirement could be satisfied by having one's name listed as a partner in an American business organization. In response to the new law a transpacific market for such listings developed. Chinese Americans, operating through their huiguans, sold "partnerships" to Chinese wishing to enter the United States. Emma Woo Louie describes some evidence:

During the Chinese exclusion period, a Chinese store may have had many more owners than was expected of a small business because being a merchant was a viable way of making a living in this country and to being able to bring a wife from China. For example, in 1906, the Man Jan Company in San Francisco listed 29 partners and the Peking Bazaar listed 18 partners in 1916. No doubt some were laborers who were partners in name only because this was the only way they could bring their families to this country. (Louie 1998, p. 101)

To enter as the China-born child of an American-born male required that the American first establish his citizenship with immigration authorities, usually by showing an American birth certificate. He then had to spend time in China. Upon his return he could either bring his China-born child with him or, as was more common, bring evidence of a child or children born to him while he was abroad. These claims of children born in China created "slots" that could later be used to facilitate the immigration of the child or children but also of persons who would otherwise be denied entry. There was strong demand for these "slots." Evidence suggests that transnational Chinese organizations bought and sold them and that they provided coaching to potential immigrants on strategies for getting through U.S. border control. Unrelated persons making use of these slots are referred to as "paper sons" (because almost all of those making use of the slots were males) or more generally, "paper families" (Lau 2007).

Though the Chinese had strong family, business, and fraternal ties prior to the Exclusion Act, scholars now argue that U.S. immigration law and the Chinese response to it transformed and strengthened those ties. Lau writes:

Adoption of these techniques was not without long-term consequences for the Chinese—they were forced to change their names, adopt fictitious family histories, and maintain these deceptions over time until these fictions themselves became inescapable elements of the stories the Chinese told about themselves. . . . The need for the paper slot to roughly match the individual seeking to enter created a market that extended beyond immediate kinship. And the need to learn and create a plausible family in the eyes of immigration inspectors required a substantial level of coordination within the Chinese community in the United States and China. As the network of paper kin developed and was maintained over time, the Chinese became mutually interdependent, liable, and obligated to each other. (Lau 2007, p. 7)

Hsu concludes, "Economic and legal discrimination did not discourage Chinese from coming; it only made those who managed to immigrate less inclined to settle permanently and much more dependent on other Chinese" (Hsu 2000, pp. 56–57). McKeown characterizes the transformation as a shift from identity based on family and kinship to identity as an individual, albeit one clothed in the language of family ties (McKeown 2008). Kwong and Miscevic emphasize the appearance of "smaller profit-based groups whose most impressive feature was their ability to acquire and disseminate the information needed to outsmart American immigration authorities" (Kwong and Miscevic 2005, p. 141).

IMPACTS OF THE CHINESE EXCLUSION ACT ON THE INDUSTRIAL AND GEOGRAPHIC DISTRIBUTION OF THE CHINESE

These strong networks allowed the Chinese to move more decisively into self-employment and to better insulate themselves from the racial prejudice of white employers and employees. Self-employment, in turn, created economic incentives to sponsor the migration of other Chinese eager to come to the United States. In a laundry, restaurant, or grocery store, a new arrival could be put to useful work, supporting himself and even enhancing the profitability of the owner.[12] Given the tiny number of Chinese resident in the United States and the large extent of the potential market, possibilities for these kinds of immigrant-subsidized small-business initiatives must have seemed endless.

The industrial distribution of Chinese employment by region, both before and after the Exclusion Act, is displayed in Table 16.1. It illustrates the wholesale refocusing of Chinese economic strategy effected by the law. Prior to the Exclusion Act, the Chinese resided in the West and were employed as laborers in mines, on railroads, and in agriculture. The only hint of what was to come is the large (11 percent in 1870) and growing presence (13.9 percent in 1880) of the Chinese in the laundry business. Following the Exclusion Act, the Chinese moved into the East, Midwest, and South where they provided services, either as self-employed entrepreneurs or as employees of coethnics. Overall Chinese employment in laundries more than doubled between 1880 and 1900 as a direct result of their movement out of the West and into new regions where they worked almost exclusively as launderers. Employment in these laundries involved long hours of work, often in isolation from other Chinese (Siu 1987). But as Wright points out, what are unattractive conditions to some may be precisely suited to the objectives of others.

Many labor historians write as though the long struggle for a shorter work week were a simple matter of good versus evil. But most of the time, implicitly or explicitly, there is a trade-off between hours and take-home pay. For immigrant workers, living away from home for the purpose of making money, and planning to return as soon as they have reached their target, long hours may be exactly what they want. (Wright 1987a, p. 333)

It is difficult to imagine a group for whom long hours were better suited.

Personal services, by their nature, must be supplied in close proximity to the customer. To reach their clientele the Chinese had to move out of Chinatowns and into the communities and neighborhoods where these customers lived. Even as the total number of Chinese in the country fell, small towns across America witnessed the arrival of an often solitary Chinese laundryman.

One measure of the timing and extent of this Chinese American diaspora can be constructed with published census data and summarized using the Duncan index of dissimilarity in state of residence. The index indicates the percentage of some group that would have to change their state of residence in order for their proportionate distribution to be the same as that of the comparison group. The results of comparing the proportionate distribution of the Chinese and non-Chinese populations across states and over time as shown in the published censuses is presented in the first column of Table 16.3. The index plummets from 97.3 in 1870 to only

TABLE 16.3 *Duncan Indexes of Dissimilarity in Residence by State Chinese versus Non-Chinese and Blacks versus Non-Blacks, 1870–1930*

	Chinese versus Non-Chinese	Blacks versus Non-Blacks
1870	97.3	66.6
1880	93.6	66.6
1890	85.4	—
1900	70.0	66.2
1910	65.7	67.7
1920	55.6	49.1
1930	57.4	54.5

Note: To compute the Duncan Index of Dissimilarity, first calculate the percentage distribution of the population of two groups across states. Then take the absolute value of the differences. Sum the absolute value of the differences and divide by two. The resulting index should be interpreted as the percentage of one group (or the other) that would have to move across state boundaries in order to make the proportionate distribution of the two groups equal. Data used to calculate indexes comparing blacks and non-blacks were unavailable for 1890.

Sources: Data used to calculate indexes comparing Chinese and non-Chinese are from the published census reports. Those used to calculate indexes comparing blacks and non-blacks are from the IPUMS.

55.6 by 1920. To provide some perspective, column 2 displays the same index for the black versus the nonblack population. It shows that the impact of the fabled "Great Migration" was to reduce the Duncan index from 67.7 to 49.1 between 1910 and 1920, after which it rose to 54.5 in 1930. Measured in these terms, the diaspora of the Chinese was even more impressive.

Similar calculations using county-level data for 1920 are useful in placing the geographic dispersion of the Chinese population in an even broader context. Using this metric the index for Chinese is 64.0, substantially lower than that for the numerically similar Japanese (87.5) and (foreign-born) Portuguese (91.1). At this county level of aggregation it is even lower than that of the black population, which numbered almost 10.5 million and had already begun its Great Migration to the North. While the Italians were more geographically dispersed than even the Chinese, they were also more than 25 times as numerous.[13]

For such a tiny population to achieve such a high degree of geographic dispersion, individuals had to move into communities where there were very few persons like themselves. If the 61,639 Chinese resident in the 48 states in 1920 were distributed equally across the 3,063 counties at the time, each county would be home to approximately 20 Chinese (average county *total* population was almost 34,363). The actual distribution of Chinese was not so far from this average figure. While 61.2 percent of all counties had no Chinese residents at all, that percentage falls by half, to 30.7 percent, when we restrict the sample to counties with a population of 25,000 or more. Fully 10.4 percent of all counties and 14.4 percent of counties with populations of 25,000 or more had exactly one Chinese resident. Another 20.3 percent of counties had from two to 20 Chinese persons, 36.9 percent if we limit the sample to the more populous counties. Every county with a population of 250,000 or more—and such counties were home to approximately a third of the total population—had at least one Chinese resident. To maintain communications over so vast a geographic area required strong networks indeed.

FROM CHINESE LAUNDRIES TO CHINESE RESTAURANTS

Chinese began entering the restaurant industry in large numbers during the first decade of the twentieth century. It was a time of growth in demand for restaurant services generally. In 1900 restaurants were not the only, or indeed even the most important, venue for procuring meals outside the home. Hotels, boarding houses, and even saloons and taverns outnumbered restaurants and surely sold more food (Pillsbury 1990). Before the widespread availability of electricity, single men and women working away from their parents' homes lived in boarding houses and hotels without access to their own personal cooking facilities. These establishments typically offered the "American Plan," in which meals were included in the price of lodging. Saloons competed for the lucrative alcohol trade by offering free or heavily subsidized meals to accompany the drinks.

Growth in per capita income, urbanization, and the advent of trolley service (most restaurants were located in the city center) further expanded the market for restaurant services. Employment for women, especially white-collar employment, created a new clientele. The Volstead Act ("Prohibition") outlawed a major competitor. Electricity and the residential building boom of the 1920s generated alternatives to the boarding house. The automobile stimulated travel, leading to a restaurant boom at vacation spots such as Newport, Niagara Falls, Atlantic City, and Miami. The share of total employment in eating and drinking establishments rose from 0.84 percent in 1900 to 1.55 percent in 1930 (calculated from Ruggles et al. 2006).

Interest in Chinese food in the American popular culture dates from about 1900. Adventuresome Caucasians visited Chinatowns in San Francisco, New York, and other large cities as early as the 1870s, but these excursions were not a part of the cultural mainstream. Gabaccia described the visitors as "culinary tourists in search of inexpensive exoticism" (Gabaccia 1998, p. 102). Barbas reported white journalists' names for them: "gawkers," "slummers," "curiosity seekers," "up to no good" (Barbas 2003, p. 671). Opium, gambling, and prostitution appear to have been the primary quest of at least some diners.

Despite (or perhaps because of) the opprobrium, big-city newspapers regularly reported on these culinary adventurers. A three-column story in the 1889 *Boston Globe* led with the headline "Lizard's Eyes and Bird's Nest Soup by Pig-Tailed Chefs; How Almond-Eyed Celestials Serve Up Boston Baked Beans" ("Chinese Restaurants," 1889). When a *Washington Post* correspondent learned he was being invited to dinner in New York's Chinatown, his initial response was "Thanks, awfully. But my palette is not educated up to rats and dogs yet." By the end of the evening, however, he declared the meal "not only novel, but it was good, and to cap the climax the bill was only 63 cents!" ("New York's China-Town," 1886). Yet the American public remained suspicious. An 1885 *Boston Globe* article began: "The average American when he first approaches the Chinese table does so in fear and trembling. Vague presentiments of ragout of rats, mayonnaise of mice, and similar luxuries float through his mind" ("Chinese Cooking," 1885). Yu (1987) attributes the turning point in the public perception of Chinese food to the 1896 visit of Li Hongzhang, a prominent Chinese general and statesman. His stay in New

York generated tremendous media attention and an interest by the general public in all things Chinese. Yu argues that the Chinese community in New York used the favorable media attention to build patronage for their restaurants. It was shortly after his visit that the first New York Chinese restaurant outside Chinatown opened its doors (see also Coe 2009 and Liu 2009).

As was the practice in those days, New York City newspaper coverage of Li's visit was picked up by newspapers in smaller cities and towns, generating interest in Chinese food all across the country. Initially the food was available only in big cities, and this gave it an aura of sophistication. Sinclair Lewis reflects this aura when he writes of Carol and Will Kennicott's temporary escape from Gopher Prairie and excursion to Minneapolis:

They had all the experiences of provincials in a metropolis. . . . They were tired by three in the afternoon, and dozed at the motion-pictures and said they wished they were back in Gopher Prairie—and by eleven in the evening they were again so lively that they went to a Chinese restaurant that was frequented by clerks and their sweethearts on paydays. They sat at a teak and marble table eating Eggs Fooyung, and listened to a brassy automatic piano, and were altogether cosmopolitan. (Lewis 1998 [1920], p. 231)

Soon, however, Chinese restaurants began appearing in smaller cities and even little towns. Elsewhere, using restaurant listings in the Business Classified section of city directories, I show that in 1900, Providence, home to about one-third of Rhode Island's residents, accounted for seven out of 10 of its ethnic restaurants. Consistent with Gabaccia's model, the ethnic restaurants primarily served coethnics. The Chinese restaurants were located in the downtown, part of the 4th ward that was home to 42 percent of Providence's Chinese. Over time the number of Chinese restaurants increased and more of them located outside their ethnic enclave. By 1910 there were 12 Chinese restaurants in the state, six new ones in Providence and one new one each in Pawtucket and Woonsocket. A decade later the number of Chinese restaurants more than doubled for a total of 26, with new locations in Newport, Westerly, and three small towns. Within Providence, Chinese restaurants sprouted outside the downtown. By 1930 half the cities and towns in the state could claim a Chinese restaurant. Gopher Prairie, Minnesota, may not have had a Chinese restaurant in 1920, but Warren, Rhode Island, (population 7,841) did (Carter 2009).

CONCLUSION

The Chinese Exclusion Act of 1882 forced the transnational Chinese community to devise new institutions to continue its migrations and maintain connections between those in the United States and their families back home. Paradoxically, the new institutions that emerged from the crisis *broke* traditional family bonds and replaced them with individual relationships in the guise of "paper families." These new institutions were smaller, more profit oriented, and better funded than earlier ones. They allowed the Chinese to move out of the low-skilled wage work that had been their primary employment and into self-employment. The first industry they chose was laundry, a competitive industry with low capital requirements that effectively offered a subsistence wage to a seemingly unlimited number of people (viewed from the perspective of Chinese immigrant flows) who were willing to work long hours in remote locations. When Americans became interested in exotic food, the Chinese were perfectly situated to respond. No other ethnic group had developed the same kinds of transnational, business-oriented institutions that allowed them to funnel exotic ingredients and young, eager, hardworking, and loyal workers to America and oversee their deployment across communities around the country. Their singular history provided the Chinese with both the motivation and the capacity to carry out America's first culinary revolution.

NOTES

Many people have listened to this talk and offered me their excellent advice and generous encouragement. Many thanks go to participants in the Smith College Faculty Seminar; the University of California, Riverside Economics Colloquium; the Conference in Honor of Gavin Wright; the 2008 meetings of the Social Science History Association; the Cliometrics Society session at the 2009 Allied Social Sciences Association meetings; the 2009 Asia-Pacific Economic and Business History Meeting; the Von Gremp Group in Economic History Seminar at UCLA; and the 2009 Cliometrics Conference. Special thanks go to Bob Barde and to the editors of this volume, who read and commented on an early draft. Richard Sutch was there at the beginning of this project and has been a constant and inspiring source of support and suggestions throughout. Thank you, Richard!

1. A large strand of the literature on American cuisine focuses on the impacts of technological and organizational changes in production and marketing on its quality. The primary cultural interest in this literature is in the public's response to advertising and in governmental and professional efforts to "improve" the American diet. See Cummings (1940); Levenstein (1988, 2003); Pollan (2006). Culinary style is little mentioned.

2. Scholars who document and analyze the popularity of Chinese food in post–World War II America include Lovegren (1995); Brenner (1999); Inness (2006); Hsu (2008); Lee (2008); and Liu and Lin (2009).

3. Sidney Bechet, composer. First recorded January 8, 1925, by the Clarence Williams Publishing Company.

4. For other examples of the influence of Chinese food on the American culture of the early twentieth century see Coe (2009).

5. Root and de Rochemont (1976, p. 277) and Hess and Hess (1972, p. 236) dismiss Chinese restaurants in precisely these terms.

6. For others who emphasize the exotic character of Chinese food in early twentieth-century America, see "Secrets of the Chinese Viands" (1903); Barbas (2003); Coe (2009); Liu (2009).

7. These and subsequent figures were calculated from the IPUMS samples from the various census years. Employment in eating and drinking establishments is identified by the variable "Ind1950," code 679. Chinese is identified by the variable "Race," code 4.

8. Calculated from the decennial censuses.

9. The 45 percent figure is for the year 1876. After passage of the Chinese Exclusion Act in 1882, the proportion of Chinese hailing from Taishan is estimated to have grown to over 50 percent. See Zo (1971) as cited by Kwong and Miscevic (2005), p. 19.

10. There is an important new institutional literature documenting the impact of the Chinese migration on the institutional development of U.S. border control and immigration policies. See Ngai (2004); McKeown (2008).

11. Altogether there were 10 classes of Chinese exempt from exclusion but only the merchants and China-born children of American-born Chinese men were numerically important. See Tsai (1986).

12. Yee (2003) provides a detailed example of these institutions in his story of Lee Gim, whom he calls "The Father of Chinese American Supermarkets."

13. The IPUMS sample for 1920 does not permit a more detailed study of the geographic dispersion of the Chinese. Except for California and Hawai'i, no state has more than 71 individuals included in IPUMS.

REFERENCES

Barbas, Samantha (2003). "'I'll Take Chop Suey': Restaurants as Agents of Culinary and Cultural Change." *Journal of Popular Culture* 36: 669–686.

Barde, Robert Eric (2008). *Immigration at the Golden Gate: Passenger Ships, Exclusion, and Angel Island*. Westport, CT: Praeger.

Boswell, Terry E. (1986). "A Split Labor Market Analysis of Discrimination against Chinese Immigrants, 1850–1882." *American Sociological Review* 51: 352–371.

Brenner, Leslie (1999). *American Appetite: The Coming of Age of a Cuisine.* New York: Avon Books.

Brown, Martin, and Peter Philips (1986). "Competition, Racism, and Hiring Practices among California Manufacturers, 1860–1890." *Industrial and Labor Relations Review* 40: 61–74.

Brown, Rajeswary Ampalavanar (1995). "Introduction: Chinese Business in an Institutional and Historical Perspective." In *Chinese Business Enterprise in Asia,* edited by Rajeswary Ampalavanar Brown. London: Routledge, pp. 1–26.

Carter, Susan B. (2009). "Celestial Suppers: The Political Economy of America's Chop Suey Craze, 1900–1930." Unpublished manuscript, Riverside, CA.

Chew, Kenneth S. Y., and John M. Liu (2004). "Hidden in Plain Sight: Global Labor Force Exchange in the Chinese American Population, 1880–1940." *Population and Development Review* 30: 57–78.

"Chinese Cooking" (1885). *Boston Daily Globe,* July 19. ProQuest Historical Newspapers Boston Globe, p. 9.

"Chinese Restaurants" (1889). *Boston Daily Globe,* June 23. ProQuest Historical Newspapers Boston Globe, p. 23.

Coe, Andrew (2009). *Chop Suey: A Cultural History of Chinese Food in the United States.* New York: Oxford University Press.

Comer, James (2000). "North America from 1492 to the Present." In *The Cambridge World History of Food,* vol. 2, edited by Kenneth F. Kiple and Kriemhild C. Ornelas. New York: Cambridge University Press, pp. 1304–1323.

Coolidge, Mary Roberts (1909). *Chinese Immigration.* New York: H. Holt and Company.

Cummings, Richard Osborn (1940). *The American and His Food: A History of Food Habits in the United States.* Chicago: University of Chicago Press.

Daniels, Roger (1988). *Asian America: Chinese and Japanese in the United States since 1850.* Seattle: University of Washington Press.

Gabaccia, Donna R. (1998). *We Are What We Eat: Ethnic Food and the Making of Americans.* Cambridge, MA: Harvard University Press.

Gyory, Andrew (1998). *Closing the Gate: Race, Politics, and the Chinese Exclusion Act.* Chapel Hill: University of North Carolina Press.

"Heard about Town" (1900). *New York Times,* January 29, ProQuest Historical Newspapers The New York Times, p. 7.

Hess, John L., and Karen Hess (1972). *The Taste of America.* Urbana: University of Illinois Press.

Hoy, William (1942). *The Chinese Six Companies.* San Francisco: Chinese Consolidated Benevolent Association.

Hsu, Madeline (2000). *Dreaming of Gold, Dreaming of Home: Transnationalism and Migration between the United States and South China, 1882–1943.* Stanford, CA: Stanford University Press.

Hsu, Madeline Y. (2008). "From Chop Suey to Mandarin Cuisine: Fine Dining and the Refashioning of Chinese Ethnicity during the Cold War Era." In *Chinese Americans and the Politics of Race and Culture,* edited by Sucheng Chan and Madeline Y. Hsu. Philadelphia: Temple University Press, pp. 173–194.

Inness, Sherrie A. (2006). *Secret Ingredients: Race, Gender, and Class at the Dinner Table.* New York: Palgrave Macmillan.

"In the Wake of the News" (1920). *Chicago Daily Tribune*, June 21; ProQuest Historical Newspapers Chicago Tribune, p. 19.

"In the Wake of the News" (1921). *Chicago Daily Tribune*, April 4; ProQuest Historical Newspapers Chicago Tribune, p. 23.

Kamp, David (2006). *The United States of Arugula: How We Became a Gourmet Nation*. New York: Broadway Books.

Kiple, Kenneth F. (2007). *A Movable Feast: Ten Millennia of Food Globalization*. New York: Cambridge University Press.

Konvitz, Milton R. (1946). *The Alien and the Asiatic in American Law*. Ithaca, NY: Cornell University Press.

Kwong, Peter, and Dusanka Miscevic (2005). *Chinese America: The Untold Story of America's Oldest New Community*. New York: The New Press.

Lai, Him Mark (1987). "Historical Development of the Chinese Consolidated Benevolent Association/Huiguan System." *Chinese American: History and Perspectives* 1: 13–51.

Lau, Estelle T. (2007). *Paper Families: Identity, Immigration Administration, and Chinese Exclusion*. Chapel Hill, NC: Duke University Press.

Lee, Erika (2003). *At America's Gates: Chinese Immigration during the Exclusion Era, 1882–1943*. Chapel Hill: University of North Carolina Press.

Lee, Erika (2006). "Defying Exclusion: Chinese Immigrants and Their Strategies during the Exclusion Era." In *Chinese American Transnationalism: The Flow of People, Resources, and Ideas between China and America during the Exclusion Era*, edited by Sucheng Chan. Philadelphia: Temple University Press, pp. 1–21.

Lee, Jennifer 8. (2008). *The Fortune Cookie Chronicles: Adventures in the World of Chinese Food*. New York: Hachette Book Group.

Levenstein, Harvey A. (1988). *Revolution at the Table: The Transformation of the American Diet*. New York: Oxford University Press.

Levenstein, Harvey A. (2003). *Paradox of Plenty: A Social History of Eating in Modern America*. Berkeley: University of California Press.

Lewis, Sinclair (1998 [1920]). *Main Street*. New York: Signet Classics.

Light, Ivan H. (1972). *Ethnic Enterprise in America: Business and Welfare among Chinese, Japanese, and Blacks*. Berkeley: University of California Press.

Light, Ivan H. (1974). "From Vice District to Tourist Attraction: The Moral Career of American Chinatowns, 1880–1940." *Pacific Historical Review* 43: 367–394.

Liu, Haiming (2009). "Chop Suey as Imagined Authentic Chinese Food: The Culinary Identity of Chinese Restaurants in the United States." *Journal of Transnational American Studies* 1. Available at http://escholarship.org/uc/item/2bc4k55r.

Liu, Haiming, and Lianlian Lin (2009). "Food, Culinary Identity, and Transnational Culture: Chinese Restaurant Business in Southern California." *Journal of Asian American Studies* 12(2): 135–162.

"Local Merchants to Welcome Frog Visitors" (1931). *The Pittsburgh Courier*, August 1; ProQuest Historical Newspapers Pittsburgh Courier, p. A7.

Louie, Emma Woo (1998). *Chinese American Names: Tradition and Transition*. Jefferson, NC: McFarland.

Lovegren, Sylvia (1995). *Fashionable Food: Seven Decades of Food Fads*. Chicago: University of Chicago Press.

Mark, Diane Mei Lin, and Ginger Chin (1982). *A Place Called Chinese America*. Dubuque, IA: Kendall Hunt.

McGlinn, Lawrence (1995). "Power Networks and Early Chinese Immigrants in Pennsylvania." *Journal of Historical Geography* 21: 430–445.

McKeown, Adam M. (2001). *Chinese Migrant Networks and Cultural Change: Peru, Chicago, Hawaii, 1900–1936.* Chicago: University of Chicago Press.

McKeown, Adam M. (2008). *Melancholy Order: Asian Migration and the Globalization of Borders.* New York: Columbia University Press.

Miller, Herman (1909). "Greeks Invade Cheap Restaurant Field." *Chicago Daily Tribune,* May 2; ProQuest Historical Newspapers Chicago Tribune, p. D3.

"New York's China-Town" (1886). Special Correspondence of THE POST.ALLAN FORMAN. *Washington Post,* July 25; ProQuest Historical Newspapers The Washington Post, p. 5.

Ngai, Mae (2004). *Impossible Subjects: Illegal Aliens and the Making of Modern America.* Princeton, NJ: Princeton University Press.

Paz, Octavio (1972). "Eroticism and Gastrosophy." *Daedalus* 101: 67–85.

Pfaelzer, Jean (2007). *Driven Out: Roundups and Resistance of the Chinese in Rural California.* New York: Random House.

Pillsbury, Richard (1990). *From Boarding House to Bistro: American Restaurants Then and Now.* Cambridge, MA: Unwin Hyman.

Pillsbury, Richard (1998). *No Foreign Food: The American Diet in Time and Place.* Boulder, CO: Westview Press.

Pollan, Michael (2006). *The Omnivore's Dilemma: A Natural History of Four Meals.* New York: The Penguin Press.

Root, Waverley, and Richard de Rochemont (1976). *Eating in America: A History.* New York: William Morrow and Company.

Ruggles, Steven, Matthew Sobek, Trent Alexander, Catherine A. Fitch, Ronald Goeken, Patricia Kelly Hall, Miriam King, and Chad Ronnander (2008). *Integrated Public Use Microdata Series*: Version 4.0 (online database). Minneapolis: Minnesota Population Center. Available at: http://usa.ipums.org/usa/.

Saloutos, Theodore (1964). *Greeks in the United States.* Cambridge, MA: Harvard University Press.

Sandmeyer, Elmer (1973 [1939]). *The Anti-Chinese Movement in California.* Urbana: University of Illinois Press. [Originally issued as the author's PhD dissertation.]

Saxton, Alexander (1971). *Indispensible Enemy: Labor and the Anti-Chinese Movement in California.* Berkeley: University of California Press.

"Secrets of the Chinese Viands" (1903). *Chicago Daily Tribune,* September 6; ProQuest Historical Newspapers Chicago Tribune, p. 36A.

Siu, Paul C. (1987). *The Chinese Laundryman: A Study in Social Isolation.* New York: New York University Press.

Spier, Robert F. G. (1958). "Food Habits of Nineteenth Century California Chinese." *California Historical Society Quarterly* 27: 79–84, 129–135.

Tsai, Shih-Shan Henry (1986). *The Chinese Experience in America.* Bloomington: Indiana University Press.

Watson, James L. (1975). *Emigration and the Chinese Lineage: The Mans in Hong Kong and London.* Berkeley: University of California Press.

Whatley, Warren (1985). "A History of Mechanization in the Cotton South: The Institutional Hypothesis." *Quarterly Journal of Economics* 100: 1191–1215.

Wright, Gavin (1987a). "Labor History and Labor Economics." In *The Future of Economic History*, edited by Alexander J. Field. Boston: Kluwer-Nijhoff, pp. 313–348.

Wright, Gavin (1987b). "Postbellum Southern Labor Markets." In *Quantity and Quiddity: Essays in U.S. Economic History*, edited by Peter Kilby. Middletown, CT: Wesleyan University Press, pp. 98–134.

Yee, Alfred (2003). *Shopping at Giant Foods: Chinese American Supermarkets in Northern California*. Seattle: University of Washington Press.

Yu, Renqui (1987). "Chop Suey: From Chinese Food to Chinese American Food." *Chinese America: History and Perspectives* 1: 87–99.

Zelin, Madeleine (2005). *The Merchants of Zigong: Industrial Entrepreneurship in Early Modern China*. New York: Columbia University Press.

Zo, Kil Young (1971). "Chinese Emigration into the United States, 1850–1880." PhD diss., Columbia University.

Selected Publications of Gavin Wright

BOOKS

Reckoning with Slavery: A Critical Study in the Quantitative History of American Negro Slavery (with Paul David, Herbert G. Gutman, Richard Sutch, and Peter Temin). New York: Oxford University Press, 1976.

The Political Economy of the Cotton South: Households, Markets, and Wealth in the Nineteenth Century. New York: Norton, 1978.

Technique, Spirit, and Form in the Making of the Modern Economies: Essays in Honor of William N. Parker (coedited with Gary R. Saxonhouse). Greenwich, CT: JAI Press, 1984.

Old South, New South: Revolutions in the Southern Economy since the Civil War. New York: Basic Books, 1986. (Awarded the Owsley Prize by the Southern Historical Association.)

Historical Statistics of the United States, Earliest Times to the Present: Millennial Edition (with Susan B. Carter, Scott S. Gardner, Michael R. Haines, Alan L. Olmstead, and Richard Sutch). New York: Cambridge University Press, 2006.

Slavery and American Economic Development. Baton Rouge: Louisiana State University Press, 2006.

BOOK CHAPTERS AND ARTICLES

"Econometric Studies of History." In *Frontiers of Quantitative Economics*, edited by Michael Intriligator. Amsterdam: North-Holland, 1971, pp. 412–458.

"The Political Economy of New Deal Spending: An Econometric Analysis." *Review of Economics and Statistics* 56 (1974): 30–38.

"Prosperity, Progress, and American Slavery." In *Reckoning with Slavery: A Critical Study in the Quantitative History of American Negro Slavery*, by Paul A. David, Herbert G. Gutman, Richard Sutch, Peter Temin, and Gavin Wright. New York: Oxford University Press, 1976, pp. 302–336.

"Cheap Labor and Southern Textiles before 1880." *Journal of Economic History* 39 (1979): 655–680.

"The Efficiency of Slavery: Another Interpretation." *American Economic Review* 69 (1979): 219–226.

"Cheap Labor and Southern Textiles, 1880–1930." *Quarterly Journal of Economics* 96 (1981): 605–629.

"The Strange Career of the New Southern Economic History." *Reviews in American History* 10 (1982): 164–180.

"Night Work as a Labor Market Phenomenon: Southern Textiles during the Interwar Period" (with Martha Shiells). *Explorations in Economic History* 20 (1983): 331–350.

"New Evidence on the Stubborn English Mule and the Cotton Industry" (with Gary Saxonhouse). *Economic History Review* 37 (1984): 507–519.

"Two Forms of Cheap Labor in Textile History" (with Gary Saxonhouse). In *Technique, Spirit, and Form in the Making of the Modern Economies: Essays in Honor of William N. Parker*, edited by Gavin Wright and Gary Saxonhouse. Greenwich, CT: JAI Press, 1984, pp. 3–32.

"History and the Future of Economics." In *Economic History and the Modern Economist*, edited by William N. Parker. Oxford: Basil Blackwell, 1986, pp. 77–82.

"Labor History and Labor Economics." In *The Future of Economic History*, edited by Alexander J. Field. Boston: Kluwer-Nijhoff, 1987, pp. 313–348.

"Postbellum Southern Labor Markets." In *Quantity and Quiddity: Essays in U.S. Economic History*, edited by Peter Kilby. Middletown, CT: Wesleyan University Press, 1987, pp. 98–134.

"American Agriculture and the Labor Market: What Happened to Proletarianization?" *Agricultural History* 62 (1988): 182–209.

"Black Labor in the American Economy since Emancipation: What Are the Lessons of History?" (with Warren Whatley). In *The Wealth of Races*, edited by R. F. America. Westport, CT: Greenwood Press, 1990, pp. 67–90.

"The Origins of American Industrial Success, 1879–1940." *American Economic Review* 80 (1990): 651–668.

"Economic Consequences of the Southern Protest Movement." In *New Directions in Civil Rights Studies*, edited by Armstead L. Robinson and Patricia Sullivan. Charlottesville: University of Virginia Press, 1991, pp. 175–183.

"The Rise and Fall of American Technological Leadership: The Postwar Era in Historical Perspective" (with Richard R. Nelson). *Journal of Economic Literature* 30 (1992): 1931–1964.

"Increasing Returns and the Genesis of American Resource Abundance" (with Paul A. David). *Industrial and Corporate Change* 6 (1997): 203–245.

"Towards a More Historical Approach to Technological Change." *Economic Journal* 107 (1997): 1560–1566.

"How and Why I Work in Economic History." In *Passion and Craft: How Economists Work*, edited by Michael Szenberg. Ann Arbor: University of Michigan Press, 1998, pp. 283–304.

"Can a Nation Learn? American Technology as a Network Phenomenon." In *Learning by Doing in Markets, Firms, and Countries*, edited by Naomi Lamoreaux, Daniel Raff, and Peter Temin. Chicago: University of Chicago Press, 1999, pp. 295–326.

"The Civil Rights Revolution as Economic History." *Journal of Economic History* 59 (1999): 267–289.

"Economic History as a Cure for Economics." In *Schools of Thought: Twenty-Five Years of Interpretive Social Science*, edited by Joan W. Scott and Debra Keates. Princeton, NJ: Princeton University Press, 2001, pp. 41–51.

"Arbitraging a Discriminatory Labor Market: Black Workers and the Ford Motor Company, 1918–1947" (with C. L. Foote and W. Whatley). *Journal of Labor Economics* 21 (2003): 493–532.

"General Purpose Technologies and Surges in Productivity: Historical Reflections on the Future of the ICT Revolution" (with Paul A. David). In *The Economic Future in Historical Perspective*, edited by Paul A. David and Mark Thomas. Oxford: Oxford University Press, 2003, pp. 135–166.

"Order without Law? Property Rights during the California Gold Rush" (with Karen Clay). *Explorations in Economic History* 42 (2005): 155–183.

"Productivity Growth and the American Labor Market: The 1990s in Historical Perspective." In *The Global Economy in the 1990s: A Long-Run Perspective*, edited by Paul W. Rhode and Gianni Toniolo. Cambridge: Cambridge University Press, 2006, pp. 139–160.

"Resource-Based Growth Past and Present" (with Jesse Czelusta). In *Natural Resources: Neither Curse Nor Destiny*, edited by Daniel Lederman and William Maloney. Stanford, CA and Washington, DC: Stanford University Press and the World Bank, 2006, pp. 183–211.

"The Economics of the Civil Rights Revolution." In *Toward the Meeting of the Waters: The Civil Rights Movement in South Carolina*, edited by Winfred O. Moore Jr. and Orville Vernon Burton. Columbia: University of South Carolina Press, 2008, pp. 383–401.

Index